遺址、墓葬分佈圖　Distribution of major Neolithic to Warring-states sites and burials in Guangdong

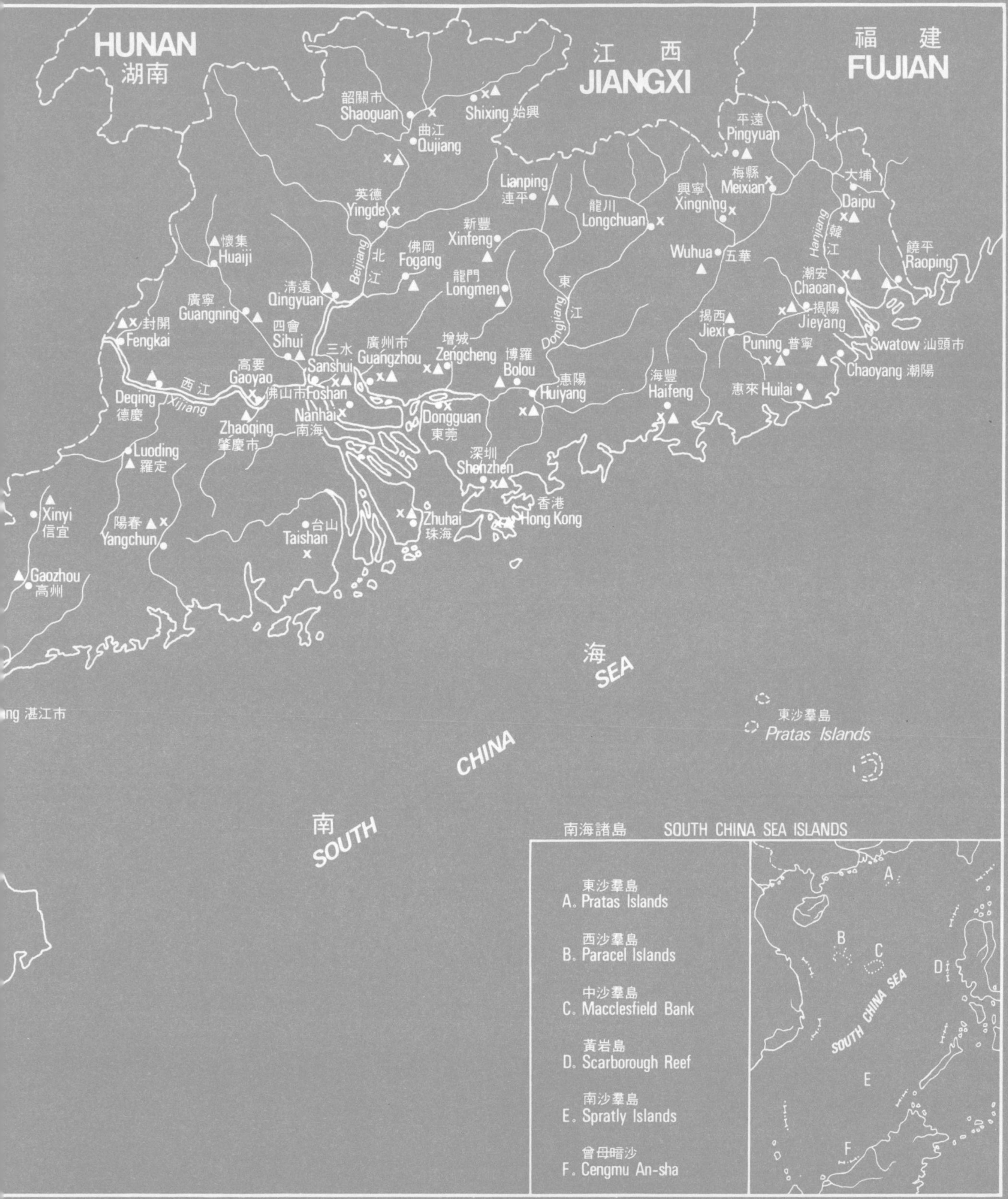

▲ 青銅時代遺址或墓葬　Bronze age sites or burials

廣東出土先秦文物
Archaeological Finds from Pre-Qin Sites in Guangdong

廣東省博物館・香港中文大學文物館合辦
Jointly presented by the Guangdong Provincial Museum
& the Art Gallery, the Chinese University of Hong Kong

香港中文大學文物館
一九八四年九月二十二日至十一月四日

22nd Sept to 4th Nov 1984
Art Gallery, the Chinese University of Hong Kong

鳴謝：
本圖錄承　文物館館友協會贈資出版印行，謹此致謝。

Acknowledgement

The publication of this catalogue was made possible by a grant from the Friends of the Art Gallery.

粵方展品說明：邱立誠、于非素、古運泉
港方展品說明：林業強
設計：麥耀翔
翻譯：黎淑儀、李婉華、黃莎莉
攝影、繪圖：葉立中、陳國強、關子鴻
編輯：林業強

Original Entries (Guangdong): Qiu Licheng,
　　Yu Feisu, Gu Yunquan
Original Entries (Hong Kong): Peter Y.K. Lam
Design: Philip Y.C. Mak
Translation: Lai Suk Yee, Lee Yuan Wah,
　　Wong Sar Li
Photography & illustrations: Sidney L.C. Yip,
　　Bruce K.K. Chan, Kwan Tze Hung
Editor: Peter Y.K. Lam

目錄：

1. 前言   7
2. 廣東新石器時代考古若干問題的探討   13
3. 廣東青銅器時代概論   45
4. 廣東東周時期青銅器墓葬制芻議   87
5. 年表   100
6. 展品目次   103
7. 彩版   106
8. 展品說明及圖版   116
9. 主要參考書目   296

Contents

1. Forewords   8
2. Several Problems Related to the Archaeology of Neolithic Guangdong   30
3. A General Discussion on the Bronze Age of Guangdong   64
4. A Preliminary Discussion on the Bronze Burial Systems in E. Zhou Guangdong   93
5. Chronological tables   101
6. List of exhibits   104
7. Colour plates   106
8. Entries and plates   116
9. Selected Bibliography   297

前　言

廣東北依南嶺，南臨大海，山川秀麗，土地肥美，氣候宜人，物產豐富。早在十萬年前的舊石器時代，我們的祖先已在這塊土地上勞動、生息、繁衍。其後的新石器時代，祖輩們活動區域更加廣泛，在東起潮汕平原，西至北部灣沿海，北起南嶺，南至海南島的土地上，發現了四百多處新石器時代遺址。一九七三年在曲江縣馬壩鎮石峽，發現了大型的新石器時代晚期的遺址和墓葬羣，被確認爲"石峽文化"，爲廣東新石器時代考古開創了新的領域。在近幾年開展的文物普查中，曲江縣境內又發現了"石峽文化"類型的遺址數十處。一九七八年佛山市郊河宕遺址發掘以來，在南海縣境內亦發現類似的貝丘遺址三十九處，其中有幾處面積近萬平方米。從廣東新石器時代遺址和墓葬出土的遺物觀察，各種類型的文化遺存之間有很多相似之處，也有一定的差異，同屬於幾何印紋陶文化系統，與長江中下游的新石器時代文化有不同程度的聯繫。這些文物清楚地告訴人們，新石器時代由於磨製石器的出現和使用，人們的生產、生活方式較之舊石器時代有了很大的進步。馬壩等地出土的碳化稻谷表明，我們的祖先已逐漸從以採集經濟和漁獵經濟爲主，向以栽培水稻爲主的原始農業經濟發展。增城金蘭寺新石器時代晚期遺址出土的陶祖，說明原始的母系氏族社會組織已經解體，取而代之的是父系氏族社會組織。但由於這一時期的生產水平仍較落後，人類抵禦自然災害的能力較差，致使祖輩們所經歷的新石器時代是如此漫長。可以看出，他們在從野蠻時代向文明時代進軍的路上是那樣的步履艱難。廣東青銅器的發現可以追溯到三十年代，先是在香港，繼之又在海豐採集到了青銅器，開始給史學界提出了如何認識廣東青銅文化的問題。新中國成立後，發現青銅文化的遺址三百多處。六十年代，在清遠縣發現了以青銅器爲主要陪葬品的兩座墓葬，七十年代以後，又在四會、肇慶、廣寧、德慶、羅定、博羅、始興、揭陽、廉江、饒平等市、縣發現青銅器時代的墓葬六十多座。這些青銅文化的遺址和墓葬的發現證明，廣東從周代已進入青銅器時代。春秋以後的青銅器數量迅速增加，鑄造工藝達到了相當高的水平。戰國後期還出現了鐵器。廣東青銅器時代的文化，既有明顯的地方特點，也有楚文化和中原文化的影響。

幾年來，省港之間多次聯合舉辦文物、書畫展覽，增進了相互之間日益密切的文化交流，推動和加強了雙方對廣東古代歷史文化的認識和研究。這次廣東省博物館與香港中文大學文物館聯合舉辦的《廣東出土先秦文物展覽》，是省港之間文化學術交流的又一新成果，展覽共展出文物一百件，其中廣東省博物館提供展品八十件，香港中文大學文物館提供展品二十件。

香港中文大學文物館館長高美慶女士，副館長林業強先生及各位人士，爲籌辦這次展覽，付出了大量辛勤的勞動；並蒙熱愛家鄉的各界人士鼎力支持，在此我們謹表示衷心的感謝！希望這次展覽的舉辦，能爲進一步繁榮省港之間的文化學術交流作出積極、有益的貢獻。

廣東省博物館　古運泉

FOREWORD

The province of Guangdong is bound by the Nanling Mountains in the north and the sea in the south. Its landscape is beautiful, soil fertile, climate equable and produce abundant. As early as ten millennia ago in the Palaeolithic period, our ancestors toiled and multiplied on this land. Later, during the Neolithic period their activities expanded and covered a much wider area. More than four hundred Neolithic sites have been discovered across the plains of Chaozhou and Swatow in the east, extending to the coast of Beibuwan in the west and from the Nanling in the north to the Hainan Island in the south. In 1973 at Shixia, Maba, Qujiang county, a large scale late Neolithic dwelling and burial site was discovered. The subsequent excavations led to the identification of a "Shixia Culture" and opened up new horizons in the study of Neolithic archaeology in Guangdong. In recent years as a result of archaeological surveys in Qujiang county dozens of "Shixia type" sites have been located. Following the 1978 excavation of the Hedang site in the suburb of Foshan, thirty-nine similar shell mound sites were discovered. Several of these sites occupy an area of nearly ten thousand square metres. The study of the Neolithic sites and finds from the burials revealed that all of the cultural types in Guangdong exhibit many similarities as well as a certain degree of disparities. They all belong to the geometric pottery cultural complex and relate to the Neolithic cultures at the middle and lower Yangzi River.

The finds from these areas clearly indicate that the appearance and the use of polished stone implements greatly improved the productivity and the ways of life of the people as compared to that of the Palaeolithic period. Remains of carbonized cereals unearthed at Maba and other sites show that our ancestors gradually moved from the economy based mainly on food-gathering, fishing and hunting towards a primitive agrarian economy of growing paddy cereals. A pottery fertility model from the late Neolithic site at Jinlansi, Zengcheng, indicates that the matriarchal society had been disintegrated and replaced by the patriarchal form of society. However owing to the relatively low productivity level of this period and the inability of the people to withstand natural calamities, it took our ancestors a long time to pass the Neolithic period. It is understandable that they must have endured much hardship in their journey to a civilized age.

The discovery of bronzes in Guangdong can be traced back to the thirties of the present century. They were discovered first in Hong Kong and then in Haifeng. This initiated the study of Bronze Age culture in Guangdong among historians. After the establishment of New China, more than three hundred Bronze Age sites have been discovered. In the sixties, two tombs were found in Qingyuan county, where the major finds were bronzes. Again, after the seventies, more than sixty tombs of the Bronze Age were discovered in the following cities and districts: Sihui, Zhaoqing, Guangning, Deqing, Luoding, Boluo, Shixing, Jieyang, Lianjiang and Raoping. These discoveries testify that a bronze culture was already flourishing in Guangdong during the Zhou dynasty. After the Spring and Autumn period, the quantity of bronzes increased rapidly and the skill in casting had reached a high standard. The later period of the Warring-States also saw the appearance of iron tools. The bronze culture of Guangdong exhibited not only regional characteristics but also reflected the influence from the Chu State as well as from central China.

For the past few years, the museums in Guangdong have actively been collaborating with the Art Gallery of the Chinese University of Hong Kong in joint exhibitions on calligraphy, painting and archaeological finds. This increasingly intimate cultural exchange has promoted and enriched the knowledge in the study of ancient history and culture in Guangdong. The present joint exhibition, "*Archaeological Finds from Pre-Qin Sites in Guangdong*" is another renewed collaboration between Guangzhou and Hong Kong. Of the hundred exhibits on display, eighty come from the Guangdong Provincial Museum and the remaining twenty pieces are from Hong Kong collections.

We wish to extend our heartfelt thanks to Dr. Mayching Kao, Curator and Mr. Peter Lam, Assistant Curator and the staff of the Art Gallery for their hard work in the preparation of this exhibition and also to members of the public for their enthusiastic support. We also hope that this joint exhibition will promote further cultural and academic exchange between Guangzhou and Hong Kong bringing forth constructive and profitable contributions.

Gu Yunquan
Guangdong Provincial Museum

前　　　言

《廣東出土先秦文物展覽》，由廣東省博物館及香港中文大學文物館聯合舉辦，是近年來本館與廣東的博物館第四度合作。展覽的重點在通過考古發現的實物資料，探討廣東地區在新石器時代至戰國的歷史文化的發展。穗方的展品，全屬近三十年來考古工作的收獲，較重要的遺址及墓葬均已包括在內。尤其是被稱為開創廣東新石器時代考古新領域的曲江縣馬壩鎮石峽出土文物，便有展品十八項之多。至於港方展品，則以本港所出土者為主，並輔以麥兆良神父於三、四十年代在粵東採集的陶器及青銅器。從總數達一百項深具代表性的展品，當可呈示先秦時代廣東人民的生活情況及物質文明的水平，並可藉此研究華南文化的特色，及與中原文化的關係。

香港的史前考古工作，有近六十年的歷史，發展的經過已有多位學者發表專文詳述，香港博物館亦曾於一九七五年舉辦《香港考古學五十年》的回顧展覽，因此不必在此贅述。比較值得一提的有下列幾點：首先是廣東青銅器早在三十年代已在香港發現，發現者芬戴禮神父，更提出了青銅器文化的概念，其特徵即共出的夔紋（芬神父稱之為雙"F"紋）的硬陶器。這些理論在日後廣東省大量出土的青銅器時代文物中亦得到了印證。

其次，在七十年代於南丫島深灣進行的考古發掘，為香港考古學樹立了里程碑。這遺址的重要性，在於其深厚的文化層堆積，有些地方深達三·三米。在長達六千年的聚居期中，呈現了連續不斷、時代次序井然的文化層，配合其他考古遺址如舂坎灣、龍鼓洲和大嶼山萬角咀的發現，為香港史前史的研究，奠下穩固的基礎。

香港位屬廣東，從本港的出土文物可以看到自新石器時代開始，已經與華南文化有著緊密的血緣。隨著三十年來廣東文物的大量出土，和國內學者的精密研究，對於廣東史前文化，建立了相當清晰的系統。這些研究成果，為香港史前考古學提供了足資借鑒的楷模。而香港所發現的文物亦有助於使廣東史前文化的研究更為充實。

今次的《廣東出土先秦文物展覽》，乃承接去年穗港聯合舉辦《穗港漢墓出土文物》的成功基礎上展開。通過這兩個展覽，除了能夠藉着學術上的交流切磋，將香港考古發現納入廣東考古、以至華南考古的大範疇，另一方面，更期望能引起廣大市民對古代研究的興趣，及對保存歷史文物的關心。朝著這些目標，在展覽期間將舉辦有關廣東先秦考古的專題研討會，聚集穗港學者專家於一堂，交流研究心得。又出版展覽專刊，詳細序錄展品及刊登研究專文，又將安排專人講解，使參觀者較易掌握展品的特點，發揮文化教育的意義。

是次展覽的籌備工作，仍是由兩館共同負擔。展覽專刊的出版，荷蒙廣東省文化廳徐恒彬副廳長、廣東省博物館朱非素女士及邱立誠先生分別就廣東省先秦考古諸問題惠撰專文。本館同寅則負責展品攝影及本刊的編印與英譯工作。

是次展覽得以順利舉行，尚賴廣東省文化廳和廣東省博物館的鼎力支持，新華社香港分社的協助，與及本校中國文化研究所鄭德坤所長的指導；又蒙市政局香港博物館惠借珍藏，在此謹致深切的謝意。而本校文物館館友協會除慨贈展覽專刊全部印刷經費之外，更在英譯方面惠予協助，在此謹致衷心的感謝。

高美慶
香港中文大學文物館

FOREWORD

The "*Exhibition of Archaeological Finds from Pre-Qin Sites in Guangdong*", jointly organized by the Guangdong Provincial Museum and the Art Gallery of the Chinese University of Hong Kong, represents our fourth co-operative project with museums in Guangdong in recent years. The present exhibition hopes to study the historical and cultural developments of the Guangdong region from Neolithic to the Warring States periods, based on artifacts and data collected from archaeological excavations.

The exhibits contributed by the Guangdong Provincial Museum to the present exhibition are all drawn from archaeological finds in the last thirty years. Most of the major dwelling and burial sites have been included, especially the site at Shixia of Maba town, Qujiang county, said to have heralded a new era in Neolithic archaeology in Guangdong, is represented by no least than eighteen items. The exhibits from Hong Kong are primarily selected from local excavations, supplemented by a few examples of pottery and bronze collected by Fr. Raphael Maglioni in eastern Guangdong. Together these one hundred exhibits should be able to demonstrate the life of the Guangdong people and the level of their material culture in pre-Qin times. They can also serve as basis for the study of the cultural characteristics of South China and their relationship to developments in Central China.

Prehistoric archaeology began in Hong Kong some sixty years ago. Its history has been documented by a number of articles and monographs, in addition to a major retrospective exhibition, "*50 Year of Hong Kong Archaeology*", at the Hong Kong Museum of History in 1975. While there is no need to recount its development here, a few important achievements do merit our attention. One is the discovery of bronze artifacts in Hong Kong as early as the thirties by Fr. Daniel J. Finn. Fr. Finn also proposed the concept of Bronze Age Culture in Hong Kong with a kind of pottery decorated with what he called "double-F" design, excavated from the same sites, as one of its characteristics. These discoveries were subsequently confirmed by large quantities of cultural relics from Bronze Age sites in Guangdong.

In addition, the excavations undertaken at Shenwan (Shum Wan), Lamma Island in the seventies can best be described as a landmark in Hong Kong archaeology. The importance of this site lies in its extensive cultural deposits, reaching a depth of 3.3 metres in some areas. The sequence of layers at this site spans 6,000 years, including all the phases of prehistory in Hong Kong. Together with discoveries in other archaeological sites such as Zhongkanwan (Chung Hom Wan), Longguzhou (Lung Kwu Chau) and Wanjiaozui (Man Kok Tsui), Shenwan furnishes a solid foundation for the study of Hong Kong pre-history.

The present exhibition follows the highly successful "*Exhibition of Archaeological Finds from Han Tombs at Guangzhou and Hong Kong*" held last year. It is hoped that these two exhibitions, in promoting cultural and academic exchanges between Guangdong and Hong Kong, would contribute to bring local archaeology into the larger context of Guangdong archaeology, or even South China archaeology. We also hope that the exhibitions would stimulate in the general public an interest in the study of Hong Kong's past and the concern for the preservation of cultural and historical relics. With these objectives in mind, relevant activities are being planned in conjunction with the present exhibition. The first is a seminar organized in association with the Centre for Chinese Archaeology and Art of this University, on pre-Qin archaeology in Guangdong, which would bring together scholars from Guangdong and locally. Conducted tours are to be arranged for schools and community groups for educational purposes. The publication of this monograph featuring scholarly essays and detailed entries on the exhibits also helps to achieve our goals.

The present exhibition is again a joint effort of two museums, its planning and organisation shared by the staff of the Guangdong Provincial Museum and the Art Gallery. The Art Gallery staff assumes the responsibility for photography and publication of this monograph, with articles contributed by Mr. Xu Hengbin, Deputy Director of the Department of Culture of Guangdong Province, Ms. Zhu Feisu and Mr. Qiu Licheng, both of the Guangdong Provincial Museum.

We are deeply grateful to the Department of Culture of Guangdong Province, the Guangdong Provincial Museum and the Xinhua New Agency (Hong Kong Branch) for their support and assistance. We are also indebted to Professor Cheng Tek'un, Director of the Institute of Chinese Studies as well as Centre for Chinese Archaeology and

Art, for his personal guidance. To Hong Kong Museum of History of the Urban Council, we acknowledge our most sincere gratitude for the loan of the majority of Hong Kong exhibits. The Friends of the Art Gallery of the Chinese University not only provide us with a generous grant for the printing of this monograph, they also render valuable editorial assistance in our English translations. For their continued support we offer our heartfelt appreciation.

Mayching Kao
The Art Gallery
The Chinese University of Hong Kong

廣東新石器時代考古若干問題的探討

朱非素
廣東省博物館

廣東地處偉大祖國的南疆,自古以來是我國歷史文化的一個組成部份。廣東秦漢以前的歷史,古文獻記載寥寥無幾。近幾十年來,經過考古調查和發掘,獲得了豐富的實物資料。廣東的考古學者們通過對具體材料的研究,使我們對秦漢以前的這段歷史,有了初步的了解和認識。本文就近年來田野考古新收獲為基礎,以大陸發現的遺址為主,對廣東新石器時代考古學文化中的若干問題,談談個人的粗淺認識。

廣東有優越的自然地理環境。夏長冬暖,雨量充沛,作物生長季長。粵北山勢高峻,山間有眾多的小盆地,粵中丘陵起伏,沿海山丘錯落。珠江水系和韓江水系大小支流流經山間盆地、谷地,到下游形成大片冲積平原。優越的自然條件,為古代居民獲取生活資料提供了許多方便。在大小河流附近的石灰岩洞穴、山崗、台地和南海海濱,迄今已發現了四百多處距今一萬年至三千五百年前新石器時代人類居住和活動過的遺址及遺物地點。

一、廣東早期遺存的發現

早期遺存共發現十多處,主要分佈在粵北和粵西石灰岩發育地區。一類遺址未見陶器共存,有大量打製礫石石器和少量刃部磨光石器及穿孔石器。另一類遺址是大量打製的礫石石器、部份刃部磨光石器和夾砂粗陶器共存。

(一) 無陶器共存的遺存

經過發掘的洞穴遺址,以陽春春灣獨石仔和封開漁澇黃岩洞為代表。

陽春春灣獨石仔遺址[①]:洞穴在山的東麓,洞口高出當地河面10米,洞高15米,寬2－8米,深40米。洞內文化層堆積分上下兩層,年代分早晚兩期,堆積厚達2.8米。為灰褐色砂土和灰黑色砂粘土膠結層,包含大量螺殼、灰燼、炭屑、燒骨、石器、獸骨、智人牙齒等遺物。石器用河礫石作原料,用單面打製而成,器體大型。器類有砍砸器、刮削器、石錘、石砧、石片、穿孔石器等。上文化層和下文化層遺存的特點基本一致,不同點是上文化層打製石器比下文化層要規整,加工修整較細,並出現少量刃部經磨製的石器。穿孔石器用鑿打穿孔的方法穿孔,再在孔痕上加磨,使之光滑。下文化層不見刃部經磨製的石器,穿孔石器的孔痕未經加磨。骨器多出於下層,有骨鏃、骨錐等(圖一,1,2,3,4)。堆積中的獸骨、燒骨經鑑定,有犀、貘、獼猴、豪豬、熊、豹、野豬、水鹿、麂、水牛等,其中犀和貘為現代絕滅種,其他是現生種動物化石。上層螺殼經14C測定(ZK 714)為公元前12950±300年。

封開黃岩洞洞穴遺址[②]:洞穴位於石灰岩孤峯西南山麓,洞口高出當地河面15米,洞口寬5米,高6米。洞內有三處含遺物的灰褐色或淺灰色砂質粘土膠結層。出土大量用單面打製和少量交互打製法製作的砍砸器、刮削器,還有石核、石錘等,刃部加磨和穿孔石器少見(圖一,5、6、7、8、9)。膠結層中有炭屑、灰燼、燒土和燒骨,古代居民食用後廢棄的大量螺、蜆、蚌的殼及豪豬、野豬、鹿、麂等動物遺骨化石。值得注意的是堆積中發現了兩個個體的晚期智人顱骨和肢骨,與現代人體質特徵一致,一個是中年男性,一個是兒童,骨骼均已輕度石化,發現時,骨架凌亂,無明顯葬坑和葬式。螺蚌殼經14C測定有兩個數據(ZK 676,677)為公元前9980±200年、9000±300年。

上述兩處洞穴遺址文化面貌的共同特點:
(1)打製石器佔90%以上,用河礫石作石器原料,多石核石器,石片石器少見。
(2)穿孔石器的鑽孔方法都用雙面鑿打。
(3)未曾發現陶器。
(4)共生動物羣絕大多數為現生種。
(5)人們選擇石灰岩洞穴作棲息之所。經濟生活主要從事漁獵和採集生產活動。
(6)洞穴堆積是以砂粘土為主要成份的灰色、灰褐色或灰黑色膠結層。這些特點說明了遺址的年代較早,同屬於一種考古學文化。

(二) 有陶器共存的遺存

包括洞穴和貝坵遺址。洞穴遺址分佈在始興、仁化、英德、曲江、連南、羅定、懷集等地石灰岩溶洞中,統稱青塘類型洞穴遺址[③]。石器取河礫石為原料,打製石器佔90%以上。堆積為灰褐色砂土膠結層,含大量圓田螺屬的殼和現生動物遺骨化石,還有燒骨、炭屑、紅燒土、人的肢骨等。這些特點同黃岩洞、獨石仔洞穴遺存相近。不同之處是絕大部份打製石器用交互打製法；少數叉部磨光的石器，已初具石斧、石錛的雛型（圖二，1、2、4）；堆積中有陶片共存，器類單一，僅見圓底罐（釜）。陶質為夾砂紅陶，手製，胎壁厚薄不勻，器表素面或飾繩紋。陶器燒製方法，可能用平地堆燒，火候低，經上海硅酸鹽研究所測定，燒成溫度為680°C。

潮安石尾山和陳橋村兩處貝坵遺址[4]，是目前廣東境內年代較早的貝坵遺址。其文化特徵：

(1)以打製石器為主，用河礫石做石料，使用交互打製法成形。器形有採蠔用的"蠔蠣啄"、手斧狀器、砍砸器和磨製石錛。而石尾山遺址沒有發現磨製石器（圖二，3、5）。

(2)陶器全是夾砂粗陶，不見泥質陶。灰胎較多，其次有紅、黑胎。火候低，手製、器類單一，僅見敞口和斂口圓底罐（釜）。器表素面磨光或拍印籃紋，多數在頸、肩部壓印蚶齒紋和刻劃紋。部份夾砂陶罐的頸部、肩部繪一周寬帶狀赭紅彩，這類彩繪陶是廣東至今發現的年代較早的彩陶，其特點反映了自身的原始性（圖二，9、10）。

(3)陳橋村發現的骨器，製作水平比前期提高，已經掌握了選料、切割、磨光等加工技術，文化層中發現有很多切割過的骨料。骨器種類亦增加，有錛、刀、錐、鏃、針、笄等，與江西省萬年仙人洞遺址出土的骨器，在製作技術水平方面不相上下（圖二，6、7、8）。

(4)埋葬習俗與前期一樣，無明顯墓坑。陳橋村遺址發現了代表10個個體的人骨，男女老幼都有，在貝坵堆積層中出土，葬式不明。

青塘類型洞穴遺址和潮安石尾山、陳橋村貝坵遺址，都出土了不少哺乳類動物，包括牛、豬、鹿等的牙齒和肢骨，還有魚骨、龜殼。近海的貝坵遺址有大量海貝和牡蠣、蜆、蛤、蚶和淡水的蜆、蚌等，洞穴遺址堆積的貝殼都是淡水螺、蚌等。據此分析，上述遺址的古代居民是過着以採集、漁獵為主的經濟生活。

（三）遺址的年代

年代最早的遺址是陽春獨石仔和封開黃岩洞。文化面貌比華南地區有名的早期洞穴遺址——廣西桂林甑皮岩和江西萬年仙人洞要原始。獨石仔和黃岩洞的打製石器佔90%以上，不見陶器共存，葬式不明；甑皮岩和仙人洞打製石器佔50%—60%，出土了數量可觀的夾砂繩紋陶片、磨光石器和骨器。甑皮岩遺址已形成了特殊的埋葬習俗——蹲葬式。陽春獨石仔和封開黃岩洞的年代，距今約八千年至一萬年以上。其次是青塘類型洞穴遺址，仍以打製石器為主，開始有陶器，但數量少，製作和燒造陶器水平低，僅見器表磨光或繩紋的夾砂陶，年代距今約七千年。潮安陳橋村和石尾山屬廣東早期新石器時代的晚一階段，有成型的半磨製石錛和大量骨器、骨料出土，陶器數量增加，出現了圖案簡樸的彩繪陶，年代距今約六千多年。

二、廣東中期文化遺存

同早期相比，遺址的數量增加，範圍擴大了，發現文化遺存的地方，有江河兩岸河谷台地或河流經過的山間盆地附近的低崗，下游冲積平原或附近零星山崗，還有臨海港灣沙丘，沙丘的位置一般距海平面6—10米，有一條發源於附近丘陵的淡水河流經沙丘入海。這些地方有豐富的海產或淡水貝類、魚類，附近有茂密的森林，可供捕撈和狩獵。

經過調查、發掘的較重要的貝坵遺址有增城金蘭寺下層、東莞萬福庵下層、新會羅山嘴[5]、南海西樵區的百東、聯新、崇南、河崗等地。海邊沙丘遺址有台山廣海莆草山塘、遂溪江洪鯉魚地、海豐沙坑、深圳大小梅沙。山崗遺址有著名的南海西樵山中期遺存和東麓細石器遺存[6]，曲江馬壩石峽遺址下層早期文化層。中期遺存的文化特徵：

(1)保留早期特點最明顯的是仍以打製石器為主，原料亦多數採用河礫石。石器邊緣和尖端用交互打製法，部份叉部磨光。

(2)磨製石器比早期增加，器體和邊緣仍遺留有打製痕跡。雙肩石錛開始出現（圖三，6、7、11）。

(3)貝坵遺址出土較多的骨、角、蚌器，器類有斧、錛、刀、錐、鏃、針等。沙丘和山崗遺址中的骨角器、蚌器因不易保存，至今未見出土。

(4)陶器的數量增加。繩紋夾砂陶是這時期陶器的共同特徵，有夾砂紅陶和黑陶，還有少量泥質陶。例如增城金蘭寺下層，夾砂陶佔82.5%，磨光紅陶佔13.6%，彩陶佔3.9%，未見幾何印紋陶[7]。陶器用手製，器壁厚，火候低，易碎裂。常見的器類有圓底罐（釜）陶器座和圈足盤、豆等，罐口沿為敞口，窄沿外折，圓肩，鼓腹，圓底。還有晚期遺存少見的夾砂陶盤和豆。陶器紋飾以繩紋為主，有粗有細，其次是籃紋（或稱條紋）、刻劃紋和素面磨光。刻劃紋多飾在陶器口沿、頸、肩部，或加劃在繩紋上，刻劃紋樣有多種，如直線紋、波浪紋、斜方格紋、曲尺紋等（圖三，8、12—16）。

(5)彩繪陶器的出現是這個時期的特點之一。大量夾砂陶與少量彩陶共存。出彩陶的遺址僅見於東莞萬福庵下層、增城金蘭寺下層、深圳小梅沙、海豐沙坑。其中深圳小梅沙和海豐沙坑出土的彩陶圈足盤較為完整。彩繪圖案用弧線、條紋、圓點組成。這類風格的彩陶可能受仰韶文化的影响，但地方特點更濃厚一些，如不用仰韶文化常見的黑色彩，而用赭紅色彩,彩陶的畫面不見於其他同期遺存。繪上彩的圈足盤是廣東中期遺存的典型器(圖三,9、10)。

(6)埋葬習俗:該期發現的墓葬材料甚少,僅見一次葬和二次甕棺葬墓各一座。一次葬墓坑不明顯,如遂溪江洪鯉魚地貝坵遺址一號墓,屍骨在貝殼堆積層中發現,葬式為頭東腳西的仰身直肢葬,西邊出土了部份小孩屍骨,可能是一起埋葬的,因骨架保存甚差,無法鑑定性別和年齡。隨葬品有小石斧一件,蠔殼刀一件,裝飾品為四件穿孔的蚶殼,還有作為祭食隨葬的四十多個海蚶。新會羅山嘴貝坵遺址發現的甕棺葬,是把揀拾屍骨置於夾砂大陶甕中的二次葬。中期墓葬隨葬品少,多數只用貝殼、穿孔龜甲、魚脊椎骨、獸骨製成的佩飾、串飾和小件石器隨葬。

(7)經濟生活主要是捕撈、採集和狩獵。當時人們居住和活動的地域,多在江河沖積台地和下游沖積平原或海灣附近高坎的沙丘;遺址出土的石器以打製石器為主,有些河礫石雖不曾打製但經人工使用過,留下了敲砸後的疤痕,這時的磨製石器僅有小型器;陶器器形簡單,器類少;部份遺址有大量貝殼、獸骨堆積。由以上特點分析,人們賴以生存的經濟生活,主要是捕撈和到附近森林去採集和狩獵。廣東目前發現的中期遺存,遺址範圍較小,文化層不太厚,說明人們定居的時間短,一方面符合漁獵、採集生產活動要經常流動的特點,另一方面表明廣東這時人類活動的羣體與黃河、長江流域同期諸文化相比,要小得多。

(8)年代:根據文化層疊壓關係和文化內涵推斷遺址的年代。增城金蘭寺和東莞萬福庵貝坵遺址有疊壓關係,下層都是中期遺存,而金蘭寺中層和萬福庵上層為晚期遺存。中期遺存中南海西樵山遺址較重要⑧,根據以往採集和試掘出土的遺物分析,它是新石器時代人們採石和製作石器的重要遺址,出土了大量數以萬計的打製石器、石核、石片和半成品,尚未發現古代居民聚居的地方和遺跡堆積,所以陶片數量很少。遺址裡的文化遺存可分三類,第一類是細石器遺存,細石器用燧石、半透明瑪瑙石製成,不見磨光石器和陶器。細石器在東麓旋風崗、太監崗出土。第二類是打製石器與繩紋夾砂陶共存(圖三,1—5)。第三類是打製石器與曲尺紋、葉脈紋泥質陶圜罐、夾砂陶釜共存。後兩類遺存的石器多數採用西樵山盛產的霏細岩製成,同時有少量磨光石斧、石錛的半成品、殘次品出土。以上三類遺存之間未發現有地層疊壓關係。上文提及的西樵山中期遺存即第一類和第二類遺存。同時期的遺存在西樵山附近的百東、河崗、聯新、崇南等地魚塘底、水涌和水田底亦發現。上述中期遺存的年代,距今約六千年。

此外,台山廣海莆草山塘沙丘遺址和遂溪江洪鯉魚地貝坵遺址,與上述中期遺存有所區別。其文化特徵是遺址的夾砂陶佔95%以上,陶色以夾砂粗黑陶為主,夾砂紅陶少見,紋飾以粗籃紋為主,其次才是細繩紋、刻劃紋。器類單一,鯉魚地僅見夾砂直口圜底陶罐,莆草山塘有夾砂圜底罐和夾砂紅陶圈足盤,形制與小梅沙出土的彩陶盤相似,但沒有發現彩陶。夾砂陶器的表和裡經過仔細打磨,顯得平滑、細密,而陶胎中間夾雜許多粗砂粒。手製,火候低。石器有少量經磨製的小型有肩石錛和梯形錛。更多的是當時人們取貝肉用的礫石石錘或砍砸器,形狀都不規則,無明顯加工製作的痕跡,唯石錘兩面或雙側有使用後留下的凹痕。從遺址所處的地理位置和出土少量小型石器及貝坵遺址出土大量動物遺骨、海產蚌殼分析,人們亦過着漁獵、採集的經濟生活。年代距今約五千多年。

三、廣東晚期文化遺存的類型與分區

晚期文化遺存的地點,數量比中期增加,遺址範圍擴大,文化層堆積厚,遺物豐富。根據現有考古調查和發掘資料,分析考古學文化的類型及其之間的差別,初步把分佈地域分為四區:粵北區;粵東區;珠江三角洲區及沿海港灣;雷州半島和海南島地區。

(一)粵北區

山崗遺址較多見,北江的大小支流經遺址附近。山崗相對高度約15—30米,附近的河谷、盆地、緩坡地為原始農業生產活動提供了肥沃的土地。

粵北區的曲江馬壩石峽、東華圍,曲江周田鯰魚轉、馬蹄坪,曲江龍歸葡勺山,始興新村、澄陂,韶關走馬崗等遺址較重要。可分為兩種文化類型:以石峽文化和鯰魚轉類型為代表。

1. 石峽文化⑨⑩

1972年在曲江縣馬壩墟獅子岩山之間的山崗發現。文化層分上、中、下三疊層。"石峽文化"即指遺址的下文化層。其文化特徵:

①陶器以圈足器、三足器、圜底器為主。三足器特別發達、極少平底器,不見凹底器。子口、帶蓋、圈足鏤孔是石峽文化器形的特點之一。器類比廣東境內同期文化遺存出土的陶器器類要多得多,炊煮器有盤形鼎、盆形鼎、釜形鼎、鬶、甗、圜底釜;飲食器有三足盤、圈足盤、豆、壺、白陶鼎、罐、觶形器等。其中鼎、釜、盤、豆、壺、罐等是常見的典型陶器(圖四,1—15)。陶器以素面為主,約佔70%以上,少數器表飾繩紋、籃紋、刻劃紋、附加堆紋、幾何印紋、鏤孔裝飾較常見。幾何印紋

紋樣不如河宕類型和鯰魚轉類型的發達。僅見方格紋、曲尺紋、旋渦紋、重圈紋、印痕淺且顯得錯亂。陶器用輪製成形爲主，輔以模製和手製，燒成溫度爲900°－1000°C。夾砂陶佔40％，泥質陶佔60％。陶色繁雜，有灰陶、灰褐陶、黑陶、紅陶、土黃陶、橙黃陶等，白陶僅一件。

(2)出土大量磨製精緻，種類繁多的石器，是石峽文化的另一特點。器類包括鑊、鏟、錛、鑿、鏃、鉞、錐等。其中石鏟，長身石錛、石鑊是常見的石器，器體大型，裝上短木柄後，可用於鋤地、翻土、鬆木、砍伐樹木、挖掘墓坑。石鑊的形製較爲獨特，爲厚體狹長條形，斷面梯形或近方形，器身中部或靠上段特厚，正面平直或內凹，背面拱起，側視呈弓形，又稱"弓背錛"，單面下斜叉，形狀猶如現代的鐵鎬，其他類型的遺存至今尚未發現過（圖五，1－8）。

(3)埋葬習俗：有氏族公共墓地，墓坑爲東西向長方形豎穴土坑墓，無葬具。多數墓坑用火燒烤成紅燒墓壁。流行單人二次遷葬，屍骨集攏成堆置墓底的東南隅。一次葬普遍流行頭東腳西仰身直肢葬。二次葬墓中有兩套隨葬品：一套完整的爲二次葬時放置，另一套隨葬品是隨同屍骨從一次葬墓坑裡遷來的。堆放在填土中或墓底，多數已殘缺不全，這種葬俗較少見。部份二次葬屍骨堆上或附近撒有鮮紅的硃砂。隨葬品質量和數量已有優劣、多寡的差別，集中地反映在隨葬石製生產工具的數量、質量以及裝飾品種類和精美方面。

(4)裝飾品種類多，製作十分精美，是石峽文化又一獨特之處。有石臂環、石玦、石璜、石笄、石珠、石管、石瑗、石璧、各種佩飾和廣東罕見的石琮。人們把製作石器時最先進的技術，如切割、磨製、鑽孔等方法運用在製作裝飾品的工藝上，可以切割硬度達六度的水晶石和綠松石，器表通體磨光，光潔度很高。裝飾品的形製和組合與江蘇、浙江新石器時代晚期的良渚文化相似，工藝製作水平亦不相上下。

(5)從出土的大型石器，如鑊、鏟、長身石錛和加工穀物用的石磨棒（圓柱形河礫石）、石磨盤（橢圓扁體河礫石）及墓裡、灶坑中出土的炭化稻米、稻穀[11]等遺物分析，原始農業是石峽文化的基本經濟部門。用於狩獵的武器——石鏃，佔出土石器總數的一半以上，說明狩獵在日常生產活動中，仍佔重要的地位。

(6)年代：依據墓葬與地層及墓葬之間疊壓和打破關係，石峽遺址上、中、下三疊層代表着三個不同時期。石峽文化又可分爲三期。經14C測定有三個數據：壹期79號墓（BK76024）爲公元前2270±110年（樹輪校正：2730±155年），貳期43號墓（BK75046）爲公元前2380±90年（樹輪校正：2865±185年），叁期26號墓（BK75050）爲公元前2070±100年（樹輪校正：2480±150年）。79號墓14C測定數據同墓葬分期略有出入，但從另一個側面說明石峽文化一期至三期墓葬延續時間不很長，各期之間的間隔不大。

石峽文化遺址，主要分佈在粵北地區偏北，近年來在始興縣城南墨江南岸新村、曲江縣烏石床板嶺、馬壩坭嶺等遺址，出土了釜形鼎、三足盤、豆、子口圈足罐、石琮等石峽文化的陶器和裝飾品。珠江三角洲地區和沿海沙坵遺址，至今尚未發現石峽文化的遺物。粵北北部鄰接江西、湖南兩省，江西清江筑衛城下層和清江三橋樊城堆遺址下層出土了子口罐、三足盤、盤形鼎、陶豆、袋足鬹等陶器，形製與石峽文化同類器物相似，但陶質和陶器器類組合又有差異，江西新石器時代晚期遺址，都是以夾砂紅陶爲主要特徵，磨製石器的種類和數量不及石峽文化的多。因此，石峽文化的"來龍去脈"，還有待今後考古的新發現才能進一步解決。

2.鯰魚轉類型文化遺存[12]

鯰魚轉遺址於1959年發現，位置在曲江縣西北周田墟，爲一處山崗遺址，滇江（北江支流）流經遺址附近。馬蹄坪遺址在它的東面，相距10公里。

與鯰魚轉、馬蹄坪遺址同類型的文化遺址，還有石峽遺址中文化層，曲江龍歸葡勺山、韶關走馬崗和始興城南澄陂遺址。鯰魚轉、馬蹄坪遺址代表了該類型早期階段，其文化特徵：

(1)打製石器佔石器總數的一半，有砍伐器、敲砸器和打製石刀，均用河礫石製成。磨製石器中部份爲半磨製，不少是通體磨光，器類有斧、有段錛、梯形錛、鑿、鏃、矛、石磨盤和磨棒（河礫石製成）。

(2)陶器中夾砂陶佔88％，陶色以灰色最多，其次是紅陶。火候低，均手製。陶器紋飾有繩紋、籃紋，幾何印紋已初具幾何圖案形，包括曲尺紋、方格紋、旋渦紋，但印痕較淺，有交叉疊印，顯得錯亂，夾砂陶器有短頸敞口圜底罐（釜），泥質陶器除罐以外，還有圈足盤（圖六，1）。

石峽遺址中文化層、曲江龍歸葡勺山、韶關走馬崗和始興城南澄陂遺址的年代比較鯰魚轉遺址要晚。文化特徵：

(1)陶器器形以圜底罐、圈足器、凹底器較多見，不見平底器，三足器極少。敞口、高領、折肩或廣肩是器形的特點之一。典型陶器有罐、尊、細把豆、圈足盤、陶器座等（圖六，13－21）。夾砂陶約佔20％－30％，泥質陶以灰陶爲主，其次是橙紅陶（區別於磚紅色的紅陶）。泥質陶器表拍印幾何紋的達65％以上，幾何印紋比石峽下層和鯰魚轉遺址發達得多，除曲尺紋、方格紋、重圈紋外，還有複線長方格紋、雙線方格紋、雙線方格凸點紋、雲雷紋、葉脈紋及曲尺雲雷組合紋、曲尺和複線長方格組合紋。拍印花紋技術比前期嫻熟，紋樣纖細、工整,印痕深且整齊清晰。陶製技術已採用慢輪修整口沿和圈足（圖六，2－12）。

(2)石器磨製技術精良，有大小不等的長身錛、梯形錛、有段錛、有肩錛、三稜形鏃。同時有少量穿孔石戈、石矛出土。而不見石峽文化典型的磨製石器。

(3)埋葬習俗：有氏族公共墓地，僅在石峽中層發現了三十二座墓，其中十三座無隨葬品，三座墓的塡土和死者周圍堆放大小石塊，其餘僅見少量隨葬品。墓坑爲東西向長方形淺穴土坑墓，流行單人一次葬，無葬具，無燒烤墓坑習俗，未發現二次遷葬。隨葬品除少數是日常實用陶器外，多數是器形小，器壁薄的明器。

(4)有居住遺迹和窰址發現，是一種方形或圓形的居址，只見排列不規則的柱洞，未發現明顯的居住面，面積約8－10平方米。陶窰平面爲圓形或橢圓形的窰坑。

(5)從出土石器數量、種類較多和遺址所處的地理環境分析，上述遺址的居民主要從事原始農業，其次是採集和狩獵活動。

(6)年代：鯰魚轉、馬蹄坪遺址的年代與石峽文化（石峽下層）相當或稍早。龍歸葡勺山，韶關走馬崗、始興澄陂和石峽中層等遺址的年代距今約三千五百年——四千年。

石峽中層和石峽下層之間有地層叠壓和墓葬打破關係，時間有先後是無疑的。但文化特徵卻明顯的不同，石峽文化流行的子口三足器，富有特色的大型石器，如鑵、鏟、長身錛、鉞及裝飾品中的寬帶臂環、璧、琮、瑗等，石峽中層不曾發現。中層陶器流行敞口、高領、折肩或廣肩、圈足罐和尊，歛口深盤矮喇叭足盤，弦紋細把豆和夾砂陶器座。石峽文化流行的紅燒壁墓坑、單人二次遷葬的葬俗，在石峽中層蕩然無存。兩層之間這樣明顯的差別，看不到一脉相承的發展序列。究其原因，時間有先後此其一，另一點更主要的因素是石峽中層和下層分屬於兩個不同類型的文化遺存。石峽中層與鯰魚轉類型文化特徵更爲一致，而且陶器器形和幾何印紋同廣東省境內其他地區新石器時代晚期文化有更多相同之處。

（二）粵東區

包括韓江中游和韓江三角洲冲積平原和沿海低地區。韓江的中游和支流流經的地區，以山崗遺址爲多，山崗的相對高度約20－70米，少數遺址在高達280－350米的山坡或山頂發現。韓江三角洲及沿海地勢較低，多數是貝坵和沙坵遺址。經過發掘和試掘的遺址有揭陽地都蜈蚣山、埔田寶山崠、曲溪五堆、普寧廣太虎頭埔、池尾北山，潮陽左宣恭山、赤牛山、象山、牛頭坪、九斗尾、九嶺、糞箕坑等遺址。以典型陶器和紋飾爲依據，把粵東新石器時代晚期遺存，初步分爲三類，代表着三個發展階段。

(1)潮陽左宣恭山遺址爲代表[13]，還有赤牛山遺址。文化特徵是夾砂陶與磨製石錛、鏃共存，幾何印紋陶不發達。夾砂陶佔70%－80%，以夾砂黑陶爲主，素面爲多，籃紋次之。幾何印紋佔10%，以方格紋爲多，其次是曲尺紋，印痕不太規整，罐身飾附加堆紋。器類有釜和罐。

(2)揭陽地都蜈蚣山遺址爲代表，稍晚的遺址還有揭陽埔田寶山崠、牛寮角和普寧廣太虎頭埔窰址。蜈蚣山遺址文化特徵是夾砂陶、幾何印紋陶與磨光石器共存。夾砂陶佔50%－60%，表裡橙紅色，胎灰黑色，飾繩紋和籃紋較多。泥質陶器上拍印幾何紋增多，除方格紋、曲尺紋以外，還有長方格紋，複線長方格紋，間斷籃紋，方格凸塊紋，雙線方格紋等。器類增加，有夾砂釜、圈足罐、豆、器座。釜、罐形制爲敞口、斜領、圓肩、圈足或圜底。手製，泥質陶的火候較高。埔田寶山崠遺址，與蜈蚣山不同的特點是寶山崠除夾砂陶釜、罐、器座之外，還出土了夾砂釜鼎、子口折腹鼎和泥質鏤孔圈足盤。鼎足形狀各異，有扁圓條形、楔形、瓦形和一件丁字形鼎足。瓦形鼎足、楔形足、子口折腹鼎及鏤孔高圈足盤與石峽文化同類器形相近，丁字形足即正面呈瓦形，斷面爲丁字形，是江西省新石器時代晚期最流行的鼎足[14]。由此證明，距今四千年前，寶山崠的古代居民同粵北石峽文化和贛江流域的原始部落早已有了文化交往。

發達的幾何印紋陶是這時期粵東地區古文化的特點之一。1982年在普寧縣廣太虎頭埔發現了一處燒造幾何印紋陶器的窰羣，共十一座。窰址建在崗頂南坡，順山坡挖成半地穴式。一種是平面呈葫蘆形的橫穴窰，火膛在前，窰室在後，前低後高，中間由火道相連，窰室中部有一紅燒土台，是放置陶器的地方，高出窰室底部20－40厘米，土台周圍是火道。窰室結構同河南陝縣三里橋龍山文化晚期的陶窰相似，不同的是三里橋窰室底部爲四條平行的溝狀火道，而虎頭埔是環形火道，富有地方特色。另一種窰是平面呈圓角方形或長方形的窰坑，無火膛、火道、燒製陶器時，可能把燃料堆放於坑底，其上置陶器，陶器上面用植物的莖桿塗泥封頂，留幾個火眼，與現代雲南傣族燒陶窰相似。由於長時間用於燒製陶器，窰壁紅燒土層厚達2－4厘米，窰裡出土的陶器僅陶罐一類，有高領敞口和折沿敞口，多數圓肩，部份爲折肩，圓鼓腹，凹底或矮圈足。陶器上拍印的花紋，多達十多種，集粵東地區新石器時代晚期幾何印紋紋樣之大成，包括複線長方格紋、斜方格紋、籃紋、編織紋、蓆紋、葉脈紋、曲尺紋、重圈紋及上述花紋的各種變體紋。泥質陶罐的肩、腹部飾3－6周帶條狀附加堆紋，這是廣東境內其他地區少見的裝飾。罐的圈足較矮，猶如一圈泥條粘接在罐底，泥質豆爲素面深盤矮喇叭形足（圖七：1－13）。

(3)普寧池尾後山遺址爲代表，以雞形壺（尊）、方格紋陶罐與磨光石器共存爲特徵。形製獨特的雞形壺，器身橫截面爲橢圓形，尖唇，高領，用手捏合罐口沿中部而成壺口，一端口大，一端口小，頭尾之間附寬帶狀把手，器底內凹，除口沿外，通體拍印方格紋。目前這種雞形壺只限於粤東地區有出土。與之共存的陶器器類以方格紋罐最常見，形制爲敞口，高領，束頸，沿稍外折，折肩或折腹，凹底或平底，除口沿外，通體拍印方格紋，這種方格紋罐上述兩類遺存中不見。其他陶器還有直口缽、小盂、小杯、豆、大甕等（圖八，1－13）。相同的遺存在揭陽曲溪五堆、埔田嶺後崬亦發現。三類遺存發現的石製生產工具，多數爲中小型石器，包括長身錛、有段錛、有肩錛、有段有肩錛、梯形錛等，其中梯形錛最常見，有肩錛的雙肩多數下削呈鈍角，其他石器還有鑿、鏃、刀、錐等。

遺址年代：上述三類遺存之間，未發現有地層叠壓或墓葬打破關係。從文化特徵分析，時間有先有後。第一類夾砂陶比例大，幾何印紋數量少，爲粤東新石器時代晚期的前一段，距今約五千年。第二類幾何印紋發達，已出現專門燒造幾何印紋陶罐的陶窰和專職從事製陶的氏族成員，同時發現了子口折腹鼎及各類鼎足和丁字形鼎足，年代應與石峽文化相當。第三類幾何印紋陶花紋紋樣銳減，而方格紋發達，與雞形壺共存的方格紋陶罐，其形制特徵同粤東青銅時代早期的饒平浮濱類型文化出土的方格紋陶罐有相似之處，粤東地區到了早期青銅時代，幾何印紋亦不發達。這類遺址裡未發現浮濱類型文化遺存中較多見的大石戈、大口尊和釉陶尊等。由此把第三類遺存暫定爲粤東新石器時代末期或進入早期青銅時代過渡類型的文化遺存，年代距今約三千五百年。假如這是可以成立的，那麼粤東地區新石器時代中期至青銅時代早期的文化序列，已有了一個粗略的輪廓。

（三）珠江三角洲地區——河宕類型文化遺存

這裡因山地海岸下沉所形成的海灣，成了廣大的三角洲沖積平原。貝坵、沙坵、山崗遺址零星散佈在三角洲附近的低崗、土墩，海邊的沙丘上。較重要的貝坵遺址有佛山河宕[15]，南海大同灶崗[16]、螺崗，西樵百西魷魚崗，丹灶通心崗，東莞龍江村，高要金利茅崗[17]，增城金蘭寺中層。山崗遺址有深圳鶴地山，西樵山遺址晚期遺存（第三類遺存）。沙坵遺址有深圳南頭赤灣村。

河宕遺址是1977年冬在佛山市郊瀾石河宕舊墟發現的，發掘面積750平方米。發現了十分豐富的遺物、遺跡和墓葬。是珠江三角洲地區新石器時代晚期具有代表性的遺址，爲此把這一地區的同期文化遺存，暫時定名爲"河宕類型文化遺存"。

河宕類型文化的內涵和特徵：

(1)遺物中以陶器最豐富，特徵明顯，有典型性。陶器形制流行圜底器、圈足器、凹底器，不見平底器和罕見三足器。陶質分夾砂陶和泥質陶，兩類陶質的比例，不同遺址之間有差別。（見附表）

陶器胎質比較表

地點 \ 名稱 百份比	夾砂陶 %	泥質陶 %	備註
深圳赤灣村	88.4	11.6	
深圳鶴地山	81	19	
增城金蘭寺中Ⓐ層	58.3	41.7	中層的上層
增城金蘭寺中Ⓑ層	91	9	中層的下層
河宕灰土層	21.1	79.9	(2)層
河宕貝殼層	25.8	74.2	(3)層
南海灶崗	29	71	

高要茅崗遺址夾砂陶的比例比河宕遺址還要小。本區陶器的陶色較繁雜，有灰陶、黑陶、紅陶、橙紅陶等，不同地點，陶色亦有差別。高要茅崗遺址以黑陶爲主，其次是灰陶。河宕、灶崗、螺崗、魷魚崗、通心崗等遺址的陶器以橙紅陶、橙黃陶和淺黃陶最常見，灰陶少見。

珠江三角洲地區新石器時代晚期是廣東境內幾何印紋陶最發達的地區。中期陶器上常見的繩紋、籃紋已減少，刻劃紋罕見或不見。幾何印紋紋樣有曲尺紋、大小方格紋和變體方格紋、複線交叉方格凸點紋、葉脈紋、編織紋、雲雷紋、雙線方格紋、凸點紋等三十多種。罐、尊、釜的頸或肩部以下拍印1－3周雲雷紋，緊接着拍印曲尺紋，是本區組合花紋的特點之一（圖九，4－6）。同時有少量彩陶，用赭紅色在罐盤口沿、肩部繪條彩和寬帶彩，這類彩陶僅見於河宕、螺崗遺址。陶器多數用手製，口沿和圈足經慢輪修整後，遺留下明顯的凹凸弦紋和有意製成的凸棱、勾沿，這是河宕類型陶器形制上的顯著特徵。燒成溫度達1000°C以上。陶器器類不及石峽文化的陶器種類多，夾砂陶器有夾砂釜和陶器座，深圳赤灣村還出土了燒烤食物用的長方形有孔夾砂陶算，不見鼎類炊煮器。形制特徵爲敞口，寬口沿外折，束頸，圓肩，圜底，扁球腹的夾砂陶釜，是河宕類型文化的典型器。泥質陶器有凹底罐、圈足罐（尊）、歛口淺盤矮喇叭形足圈足盤、弦紋高喇叭形足陶豆。罐的肩部有折肩或廣肩，

部份肩部素面，罐腹和底部拍印幾何紋（圖九，1－3；7－17，圖十，1－3，14－17，19）。河宕、茅崗遺址陶器上發現了不少刻劃符號，這是粵北、粵東地區所少見的。刻劃符號有"｜"、"‖"、"‖|"、"十"、"⻊"、"↑"、"×"、"]["、"⌒"、"⩵"等。

(2)石器多通體磨光，製作精緻，以中小型石器為主，有雙肩錛、有肩有段錛和長身錛、梯形錛等較多見，有肩錛有雙肩明顯呈直角和雙肩呈鈍角的兩種。斧、鑿少見，大型錛類極罕見。部份遺址少數石器的石料、形製特點與西樵山遺址出土的石器相同，進一步證明西樵山遺址直至新石器時代晚期仍是周圍原始部落集中到這裡採石，製作石器的場所。（圖十，7－10，18）

(3)貝坵遺址中同石器共存的骨器，是用動物的骨和角製成的，有骨錐、角錐、魚鏢、骨梭、笄、鑿、針等。

(4)埋葬習俗：從河宕遺址七十七座、金蘭寺中層四座墓、灶崗六座墓的材料分析，墓葬為東西向淺穴土坑墓，部份墓坑挖在貝殼層中，因此墓坑的範圍、墓口不太明顯。灶崗遺址六座墓，無明顯墓坑，骨架上的貝殼和泥土相當堅硬，很可能經過夯打。貝坵遺址發現的墓葬，人骨已輕度石化，因此骨架保存尚好。流行單人仰身直肢葬，個別有二次葬，這種二次葬不同於石峽文化把屍骨集攏成堆置墓底東西隅，而是把人骨架按仰身直肢葬重新放置。河宕遺址墓葬中，成年男性的頭部一律向西，女性的則相反，頭部均向東。灶崗遺址墓葬死者的頭向為東南。多數墓中無隨葬品，或有也僅1－3件，男性墓多隨葬石錛一件或其他器物，女性墓多隨葬陶紡輪。發現墓主人生前有人工拔牙的習俗[18]，拔除雙側或單側的上第二門齒。以河宕為例，拔牙個體的出現率達82.6%。這種人工拔牙的風俗，在我國山東、江蘇、福建、湖北等省新石器時代晚期墓葬中亦發現。從體質特徵分析，具有南亞蒙古人種的特徵，有關專家認為，"河宕頭骨的許多特徵可以和赤道人種相比較的程度大於他們和典型的北方蒙古人種相比的程度，但他們還應該屬於蒙古人種的南邊緣類型"。男性平均身高約166厘米，女性約154厘米。

(5)裝飾品除石臂環、石塊、石管外，還有用象牙製的大臂環和製作精美，薄如蛋殼，光潔潤滑的亞腰形象牙筒。

(6)河宕類型貝坵遺址堆積裡，出土數量相當多的哺乳動物和水生動物的遺骸，很少有大型石器出土，說明採集、漁獵是當時人們的主要生產活動。熱帶和亞熱帶潤濕的氣候和江河、淺海沙灘，附近的茂密森林，為原始部落提供了豐富的物質來源，因此原始農業的產生和發展可能比粵北區要遲一些。

(7)居住遺址：一種是"干欄式"的水上木構建築，一種是紅燒土面或硬土居住面的"窩棚式"建築。水上木構建築在高要金利茅崗石角村前的魚塘中發現。清理了三組建築遺存，平面佈局均為長方形，前後總長14.7米，兩排木柱之間相距1.64－1.7米。建築遺存尚保留有木柱、木樁、樹皮板、木楔、木板塊等。木柱是支撐建築物的主體，絕大部份鑿有長方、正方或扁圓形的榫孔，柱頂鑿凹槽，木柱頂端同魚塘的積泥平齊，下面便是厚達4.50－5米的貝坵文化層堆積（圖十，11－13）。這是廣東境內的首次發現。後一種"窩棚式"居住遺跡在河宕和灶崗遺址發現，硬土居住面和紅燒土面的中間或一邊有火塘或火燒土堆，居住面的直徑約1.5－3米，附近發現排列不規則的柱洞。

(8)年代：經14C測定：增城金蘭寺中層用貝殼測定（ZK103）為公元前2085±95年（樹輪校正：2495±145年）；高要茅崗用木頭測定有三個數據（ZK710、708、707）為公元前2340－2120年（樹輪校正：2815－2540年）；佛山河宕③層用貝殼測定有四個數據（ZK526、527、528、546）為公元前3070－2955年（樹輪校正：3550－2680年）、河宕②層有三個數據，兩個用人骨測定（ZK548、547）為公元前1890－1655年（樹輪校正：2250－1960年），一個用木炭測定（ZK647）為公元前2150±80年（樹輪校正：2580±135年）；南海灶崗用貝殼測定（ZK545）為公元前3455±120（樹輪校正：4100±140年）。綜觀上述14C測定的數據，用貝殼測定的數據偏早一些。若把珠江三角洲地區屬於河宕類型的文化遺存年代定為距今五千年至三千九百年是合適的。其中深圳赤灣村沙丘遺址、鶴地山遺址、增城金蘭寺中⑧層代表着河宕類型文化遺存的早期階段。

（四）雷州半島和海南島地區[19]

因該區的原始文化遺存，未進行過大規模的考古發掘，只能根據五十年代有限的調查時探集和試掘出土的資料作粗略的分析。以海南島的原始文化遺存為例，其文化特徵：

(1)遺址的分佈：河流兩岸有山崗遺址，海邊港灣有少數沙坵和貝坵遺址。部份山崗遺址，常見地表散佈米字紋、水波紋和方格紋帶戳印的漢代陶片，地層出土了磨光石器與夾砂粗紅陶共存的遺物。

(2)陶器：陶質有夾砂粗紅陶和泥質紅陶。流行紅陶，這是海南島原始文化遺存特點之一。陶器火候高，手製，表面抹平。花紋簡單，只有籃紋、劃紋和方格紋，部份陶器口沿飾紅色陶衣。器類少，多為大型圓底罐，還有泥質紅陶豆。而標誌着大陸地區新石器時代晚期特點的幾種幾何印紋，如曲尺紋、複線長方格紋、雙線方格紋、雲雷紋等，在海南島至今尚未發現。

(3)石器多數為通體磨光，有錛和斧，斧的數量比大陸同期文化遺存出土的要多。以長身、梯形、雙肩錛、斧較多見。
(4)年代的探討。同一時期不同地域之間文化的差異和雷同，往往要借助於器物形態學。在各類器物中，無疑的，唯有陶器這類日用器皿最能明顯地說明問題的關鍵所在。關於海南島原始文化遺存的來源，一種說法，它是土生土長的，但缺乏早期的考古材料可以佐證。另一種說法，認為這類器表飾籃紋、划紋的夾砂粗紅陶罐，泥質紅陶豆和雙肩石錛同珠江三角洲中期新石器時代文化有相似之處，推測大約距今五六千年前，居住在大陸的部份居民沿着南海海濱，從東到西，橫渡瓊洲海峽，到達海南島定居。這種以夾砂紅陶、泥質紅陶和通體磨光的有肩、長身錛、斧共存的文化遺存，在海南島一直延續到秦漢時期，才接受了大陸先進的鐵器時代文化。或者這類文化遺存是代表五六千年前的海南島原始文化，而三四千年前的晚期文化，還未被我們發現和認識。這種推論是否正確，有待今後考古的新發現，才能解決。

西江兩岸地區和東江流域地區的文化遺存，未經大規模考古發掘，材料不足，很難說明問題。以往考古學者把粵東平行嶺谷區（相當於梅縣和惠陽部份地區）新石器時代文化作為單獨的"地域性的不同羣體"敘述。實際上東江下游已進入珠江三角洲或接近三角洲平原，文化類型與佛山河宕貝坵類型文化大同小異。東江上游的龍川、河源縣晚期文化與石峽文化和石峽中層近似。梅縣地區包括梅江流域的晚期文化與粵東韓江三角洲同期文化相同。

四、餘論

廣東新石器時代考古學文化是豐富多彩的，根據近十幾年來的考古發現和研究，對於廣東境內新石器時代的文化面貌、分佈情況、年代序列及發展規律，有了初步的認識。
(1)石器製作和形制的變化：早期遺存出土打製礫石石器，多數用單面打製法製成，極少數石器刃部加磨。在有早期夾砂陶共存的遺址裡，石器用交互打製法，刃部磨光的梯形石錛已出現；中期遺存仍以用交互打製法製成的礫石石器為主，刃部磨光石器數量增加，富有地方特色的雙肩石錛已出現；晚期石器大都份通體磨光，製作精緻，器類繁多。選料、切割、鑽孔、磨光等製作技術日臻完善。常見石器有長身錛、有肩錛、有段錛、有段有肩錛、梯形錛和少量的斧和鑿、鏃等。粵北區的石峽文化有另外一套石製生產工具的組合，表明了自身的特色。
(2)居住地點的選擇和經濟生活的關係：早期居民多數選擇石灰岩洞穴作為棲身之所，過着採集和漁獵的生活；中期的古代居民，不少聚居在靠河邊的山崗、台地和海邊的高坎沙丘，這些地方，有取之不盡的食物來源，人們過着捕撈水生動物、蚧殼及採集為主的經濟生活，同時亦進行集體狩獵。各遺址出土了陶紡輪，說明新石器時代中期的人們，已學會了紡織；到了晚期，視地理環境、自然條件和獲取生活資料的來源不同，經濟生活類型亦不同。聚居地附近有盆地或緩坡，適宜於原始農業生產活動，經濟生活類型則多數以從事原始農業生產為主，出土較多大型的石鏟、錛、钁等工具。聚居在三角洲主河道及其支流附近、海灣附近山崗或沙丘的原始部落，則以捕撈河裡或淺海、沙灘上豐富的魚類、貝類作為食物的主要來源，遺址中缺少大型石製生產工具，說明原始農業還不太發達。
(3)富有特色的陶器和幾何印紋：早期部份遺址不見陶器，有陶器共存的，只有夾砂陶，不見泥質陶，器形單一，僅見夾砂圜底罐（釜），花紋只有繩紋或素面無紋。手製，火候低；中期仍以夾砂陶佔多數，開始有泥質陶。器形除夾砂圜底罐以外，還有夾砂和泥質矮圈足盤和豆。花紋除繩紋外，還有籃紋、划紋、刺點紋。幾何印紋極少見。手製，火候低，粵東、珠江三角洲地區文化遺址出現了彩陶，其他地區尚未發現；晚期陶器最主要特色是幾何印紋陶十分發達，器表拍印幾何紋達50%－80%以上，紋樣有曲尺紋、方格紋、葉脈紋、雲雷紋、"梯子形"格紋、編織紋、複線長方格紋、重圈紋等。然而，每組花紋紋樣的大小，線條的纖細或粗獷，印痕的深淺，因地域不同又有許多差異。陶器上拍印幾何印紋以珠江三角洲地區的河宕類型文化遺存最為發達，不僅種類多，而且花紋線條粗獷、印痕深、夾砂陶器上亦拍印幾何紋。其次是粵北區。粵東區的幾何印紋花紋的線條纖細，清晰而流暢，泥質陶罐上常見有兩周到六周帶條狀或繩索狀附加堆紋。河宕類型流行罐頸或折肩下先拍印一至三圈雲雷紋，緊接着拍印曲尺紋，這種組合紋粵北很少見，粵東則至今未曾發現。

陶器器形與前期相比，在數量增加的同時，還出現泥質陶罐、弦紋細把豆和折肩罐等新的器類，夾砂陶器座也較多見。河宕類型陶罐流行敞口、高領、折肩或廣肩，高圈足或凹底，平底器和三足器極罕見。粵東流行小侈口，圓肩，大鼓腹，矮圈足或凹底，有少量三足器和平底器。子口帶蓋的三足器為粵北晚期石峽文化的典型器。陶器燒成溫度相當高，一般在900°－1000°C之間。製陶時使用輪製或器物的口沿和圈足用慢輪修整，輔以手製和模製，因而陶器外形比較規整。
(4)裝飾品從無到有：早期遺址不見裝飾品；中期貝坵、沙坵遺址出土用動物肢骨；魚脊椎骨，貝殼穿孔磨製成的各類裝飾品；晚期裝飾品增多且製作十分精美，有象牙環、象牙筒形器、石環、玦、璜、珠、管、水晶玦、綠松石片。石峽文化還出土了原始宗教祭祀用的禮器——琮、璧等。

(5)埋葬習俗：早期的葬俗不清楚；中期為淺穴土坑墓的單人一次葬和單人二次甕棺葬；晚期粵北石峽文化流行單人二次遷葬，墓坑用火燒烤過，河宕類型墓葬則流行單人仰身直肢葬，生前有人工拔牙風俗。晚期都有氏族公共墓地。

關於廣東新石器時代考古學文化的區、系、類型問題的探討，是擺在我們面前的新課題。本文就現有考古資料所作的探索，僅是個人的粗淺認識。深入準確地概括廣東新石器時代考古學文化的全貌，還有待今後考古的新發現，深入研究和探討。

註　釋

①邱立誠等：《廣東陽春獨石仔新石器時代洞穴遺址發掘》，《考古》1982年5期。

②宋方義等：《廣東封開黃岩洞洞穴遺址》，《考古》1983年1期。

③廣東省博物館：《廣東翁源縣青塘新石器時代遺址》，《考古》1961年11期。

④廣東省文物管理委員會：《廣東潮安的貝丘遺址》，《考古》1961年11期。

⑤廣東省博物館：《廣東中部低地新石器時代遺存》，《考古學報》1960年2期。

⑥曾騏：《西樵山東麓的細石器》，《考古與文物》1981年4期。

⑦莫稚：《廣東考古調查發掘的新收獲》，《考古》1961年12期。

⑧廣東省博物館：《廣東南海西樵山出土的石器》，《考古學報》1959年4期。

⑨廣東省博物館等：《廣東曲江石峽墓葬發掘簡報》，《文物》1978年7期。

⑩朱非素等：《談談馬壩石峽遺址的幾何印紋陶》，《文物集刊》3期。

⑪楊式挺：《談談石峽發現的栽培稻遺跡》，《文物》1978年7期。

⑫廣東省文物管理委員會等：《廣東曲江鯰魚轉、馬蹄坪和韶關走馬崗遺址》，《考古》1964年7期。

⑬廣東省博物館：《廣東東部地區新石器時代遺存》，《考古》1961年12期。

⑭江西省博物館等：《清江築衛城遺址發掘簡報》，《考古》1976年6期。

⑮楊式挺等：《談談佛山河宕遺址的重要發現》，《文物集刊》3期。

⑯廣東省博物館：《廣東南海縣灶崗貝丘遺址發掘簡報》，《考古》1984年3期。

⑰楊豪等：《廣東高要縣茅崗水上木構建築遺址》，《文物》1983年12期。

⑱韓康信、潘其風：《廣東佛山河宕新石器時代晚期墓葬人骨》，《人類學學報》第一卷第1期。

⑲廣東省博物館：《廣東海南島原始文化遺址》，《考古學報》1960年2期。

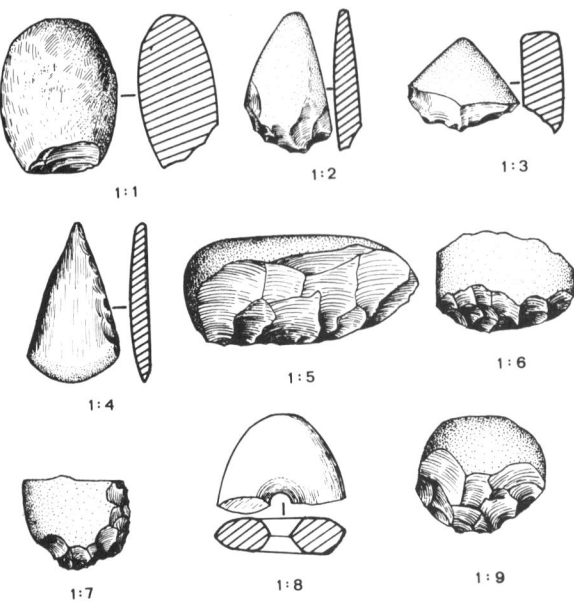

圖一 陽春獨石仔，封開黃岩洞出土石器

1.石錘（陽春獨石仔） 2,3,5,6,9.砍砸器（獨石仔，黃岩洞） 4.切割器（獨石仔） 7.刮削器（黃岩洞） 8.穿孔石器（黃岩洞）

圖二 翁源青塘，潮安陳橋村出土石器、骨器、陶片

1,2.砍砸器（翁源青塘） 3.手斧狀器（潮安陳橋村） 4.石錛（翁源青塘） 5.石錛（潮安陳橋村） 6.骨斧（潮安陳橋村） 7,8.骨笄（潮安陳橋村） 9.蚶齒紋夾砂陶片（陳橋村） 10.籃紋（石尾山）

Fig. I: Stone Implements Unearthed from Dushizai, Yangchun and Huangyandong, Fengkai

1. Stone hammer (Dushizai, Yangchun) 2,3,5,6,9. Choppers (Dushizai and Huangyandong) 4. Cutter (Dushizai) 7. Scraper (Huangyandong) 8. Perforated tool (Huangyandong)

Fig. II: Stone Implements, Bone Objects and Pottery Sherds Unearthed from Qingtang at Wengyuan and Chenqiaocun at Chao'an

1,2. Choppers (Qingtang, Wengyuan) 3. Handaxe shaped tool (Chenqiaocun, Chao'an) 4. Adze (Qingtang, Wengyuan) 5. Adze (Chenqiaocun, Chao'an) 6. Bone axe (Chenqiaocun, Chao'an) 7,8. Hairpins (Chenqiaocun, Chao'an) 9. Gritty pottery sherd with zig-zag pattern (Chenqiaocun) 10. Basket pattern (Shiweishan)

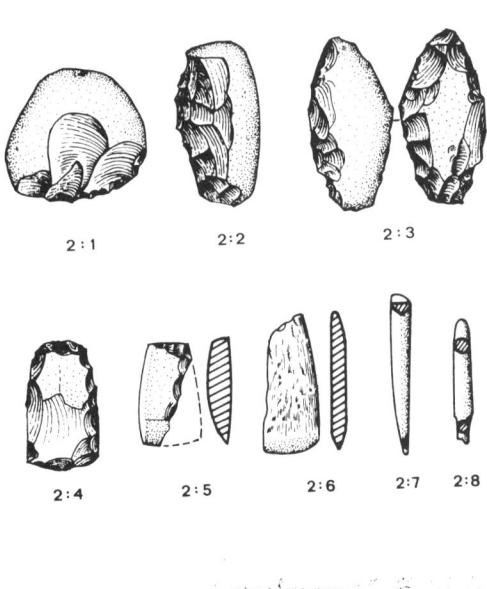

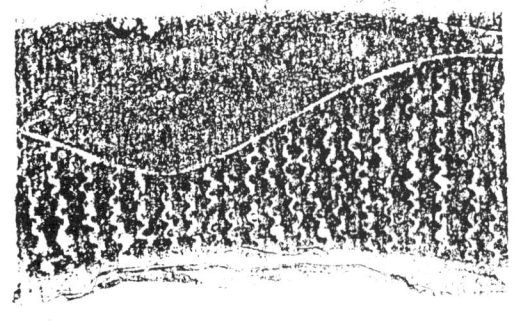

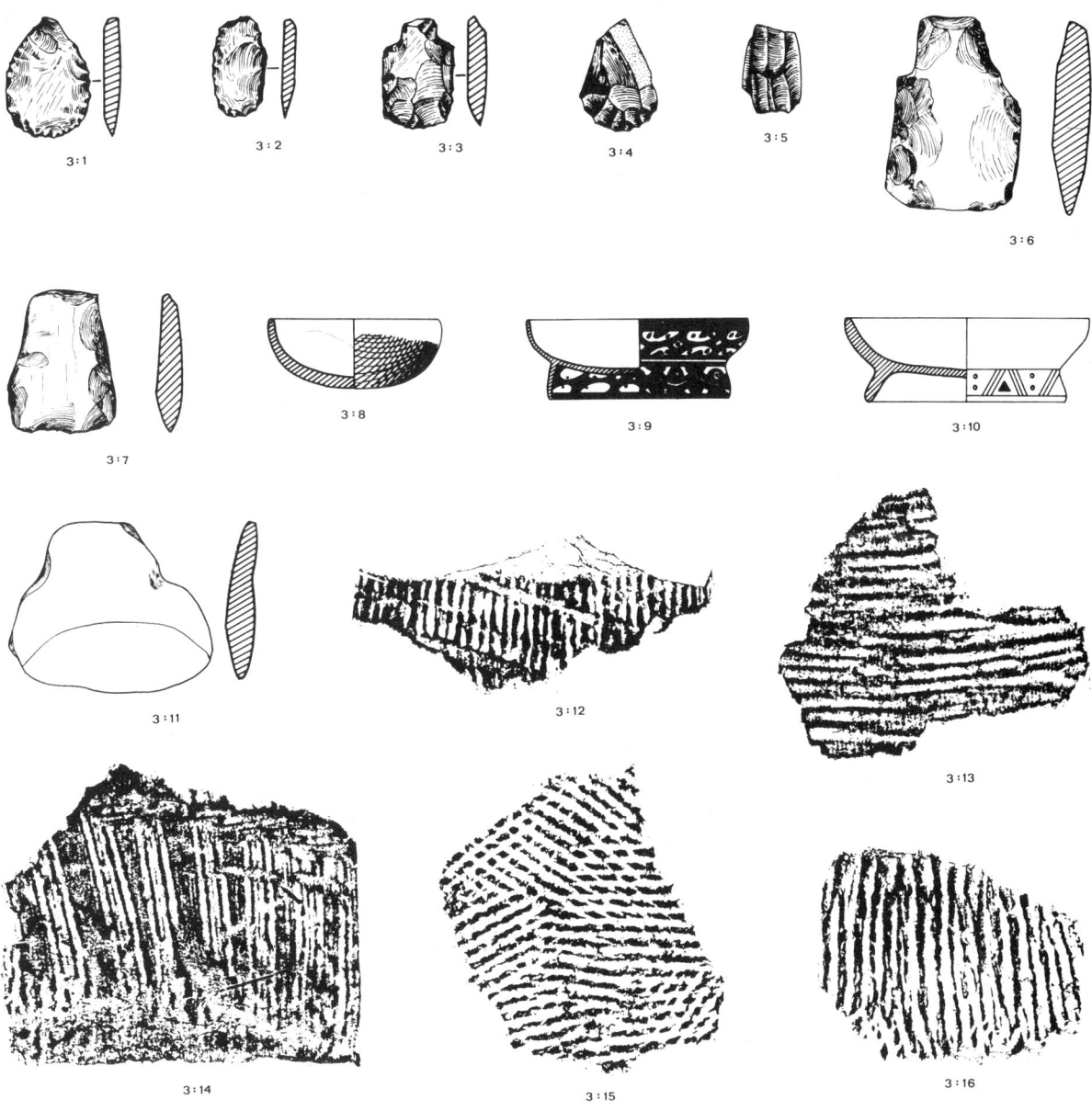

图三 石器、陶器、花纹拓片

1-3. 打制石器（南海西樵山）
4-5. 细石器（南海西樵山）
6. 有肩石锛（新会罗山咀）
7. 梯形石锛（东莞万福庵）
8. 夹砂陶钵（金兰寺下层）
9. 彩陶盘（深圳小梅沙）
10. 彩陶盘（海丰沙坑）
11. 有肩石斧（台山广海山塘）
12. 间断篮纹（金兰寺下层）
13. 篮纹（遂溪，鲤鱼地）
14. 划纹（南海）
15, 16. 绳纹、篮纹（新会罗山咀）

Fig. III: Stone Implements, Pottery and Rubbings of Patterns

1-3. Chipped stone tools (Xigiaoshan, Nanhai)
4-5. Microliths (Xigiaoshan, Nanhai)
6. Shouldered adze (Luoshanzui, Xinhui)
7. Trapezoid adze (Wanfu'an, Dongguan)
8. Gritty pottery bowl (lower layer of Jinlansi)
9. Painted pottery basin (Xiaomeisha, Shenzhen)
10. Painted pottery basin (Shakeng, Haifeng)
11. Shouldered adze (Shantang, Guanghai, Taishan)
12. "Broken" basket pattern (lower layer of Jinlansi)
13. Basket pattern (Liyudi, Suiqi)
14. Incised pattern (Nanhai)
15-16. Corded pattern and basket pattern (Luoshanzui, Xinhui)

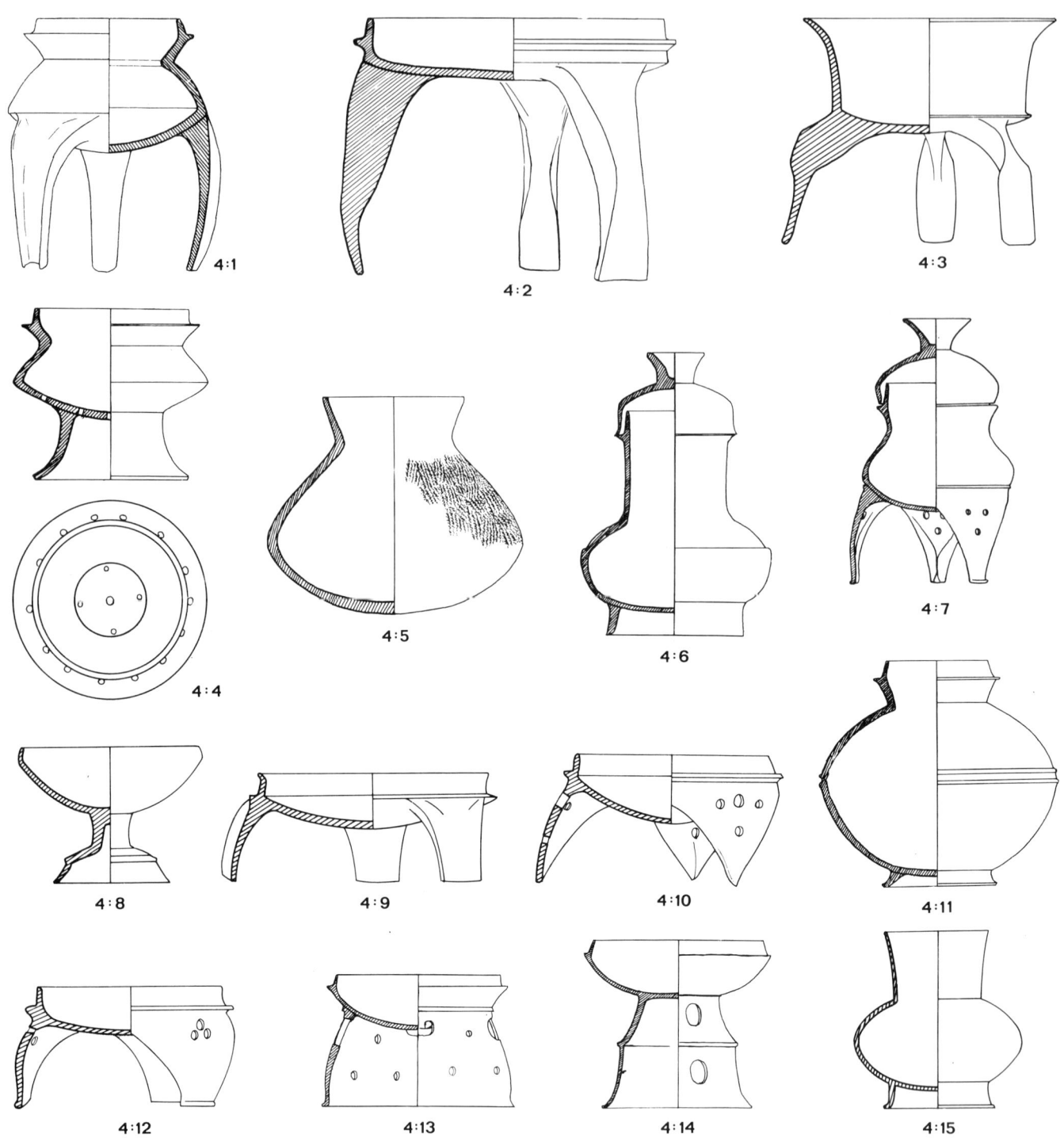

圖四　石峽文化墓葬出土陶器

1. 子口折腹釜形鼎　2. 盤形鼎　3. 盆形鼎　4. 子口圈足甑　5. 釜　6. 子口帶蓋圈足罐　7. 白陶鼎　8. 豆　9, 10, 12. 三足盤　11. 子口圈足壺　13, 14. 圈足盤　15. 壺

Fig. IV: Pottery from Burials of Shixia Culture

1. Fu-tripod with stepped mouth and angular body 2. Dish-tripod 3. Basin-tripod 4. *Zeng* with stepped mouth and footring 5. Cauldron 6. Jar with stepped mouth and cover 7. White pottery tripod 8. Stem-cup 9. 10. 12. Tripodic basins 11. Vase with stepped mouth and footring 13. 14. Basins with footring 15. Vase

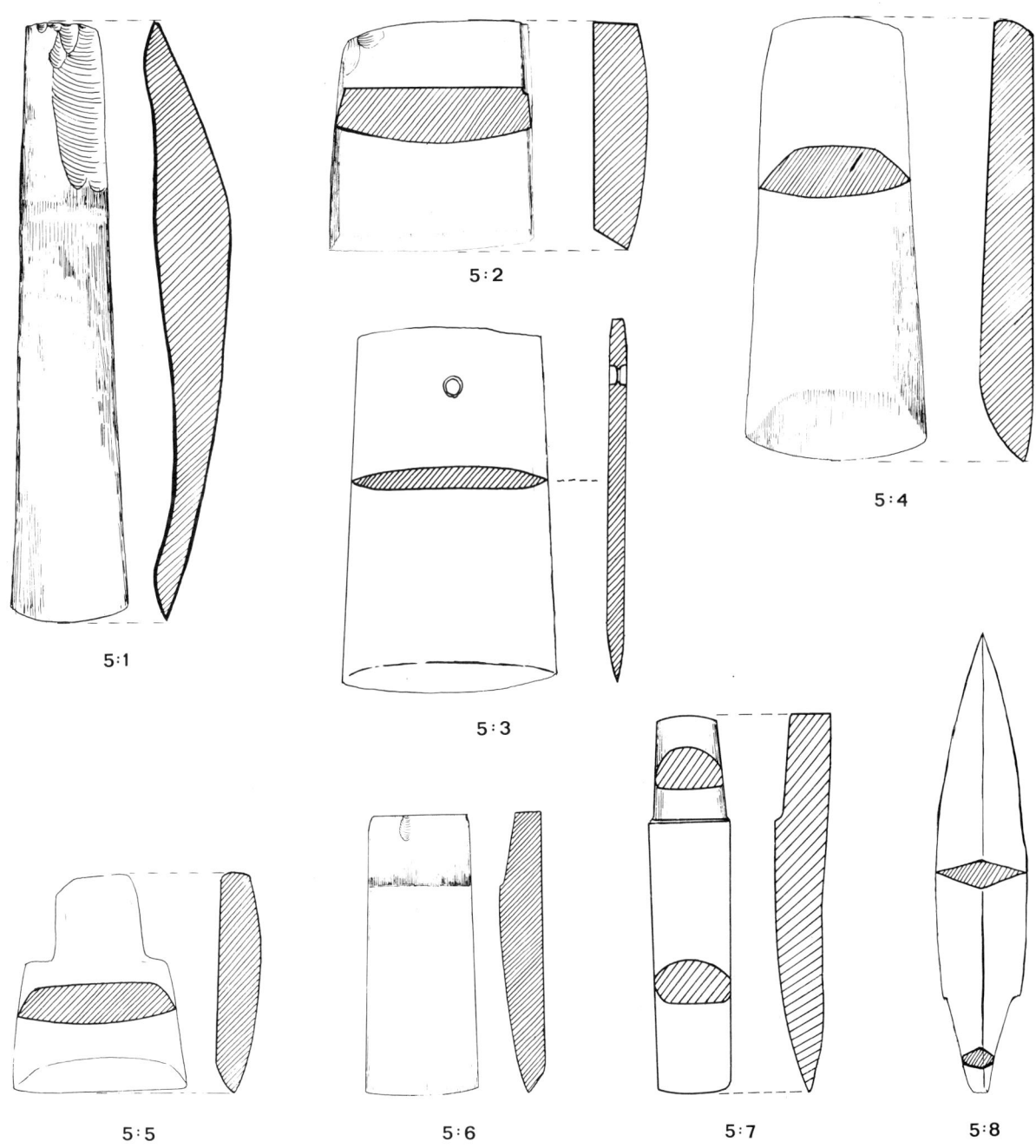

圖五　石峽文化墓葬出土石器
1. 石钁
2. 梯形石錛
3. 石鏟
4. 長身石錛
5. 有肩石錛
6. 有段石錛
7. 有段石鑿
8. 石鏃

Fig. V: Stone Implements from Burials of Shixia Culture
1. Pickaxe
2. Trapezoid adze
3. Shovel
4. Long adze
5. Shouldered adze
6. Stepped adze
7. Stepped chisel
8. Arrowhead

图六 陶器和鲶鱼转类型几何印纹拓片

1.曲尺纹（鲶鱼转） 2,3.叶脉纹、斜方格纹（澄陂） 4.篮纹 5.方格纹 6.曲尺纹 7.复线方格凸方块纹 8.曲尺、长方格组合纹 9.云雷纹 10,12.复线长方格纹 11.双线方格纹（4-12.石峡遗址中层） 13.陶尊 14.陶罐 15.凹底罐 16.方格纹罐 17.复线长方格纹罐 18.圈足盘 19.弦纹细把豆 20.陶器座 21.有流带把陶壶（15-17,21.石峡中层墓葬出土，余均中层出土）

Fig. VI: Pottery and Rubbings of Geometric Designs of Nianyuzhuan Type

1. Angular pattern (Nianyuzhuan) 2. 3. Herring-bones, rhomboids (Chengbo) 4. Basket 5. Square 6. Angular pattern 7. Multi-lined squares with lattices 8. Angular and rectangles 9. Spirals 10. 12. Multi-lined rectangles 11. Double-lined squares (4-12. middle layer of Shixia site) 13. Pottery vase 14. Pottery jar 15. Jar with indented bottom 16. Jar with square pattern 17. Jar with multi-lined rectangles 18. Basin with footring 19. Small stemcup with groove bands 20. Pottery stand 21. Pottery vase with spout and handle (15-17. 21. from tombs at middle layer of Shixia, rest from middle layer)

圖七 幾何印紋陶紋樣拓片

1. 長方格紋 2. 曲尺紋 3. 間斷籃紋 4. 菱格凸塊紋 5. 籃紋、細繩紋（揭陽寶山岽） 6. 曲尺紋 7. 重圈、繩紋組合紋（揭陽蜈蚣山） 8. 重圈、曲尺組合紋 9. 間斷籃紋 10. 籃紋、重圈組合紋 11. 席紋 12. 長方格紋 13. 葉脈紋（普寧虎頭埔）

Fig. VII: Rubbings of Geometric Designs

1. Rectangles 2. Angular pattern 3. Broken basket pattern 4. Rhomboids with lattices 5. Basket pattern, fine cord pattern (Baoshandong, Jieyang) 6. Angular pattern 7. Concentric circles on corded ground (Wugongshan, Jieyang) 8. Concentric circles on angular ground 9. Broken basket pattern 10. Basket and concentric circles 11. Mat pattern 12. Rectangles 13. Herring-bones (Futoupu, Puning)

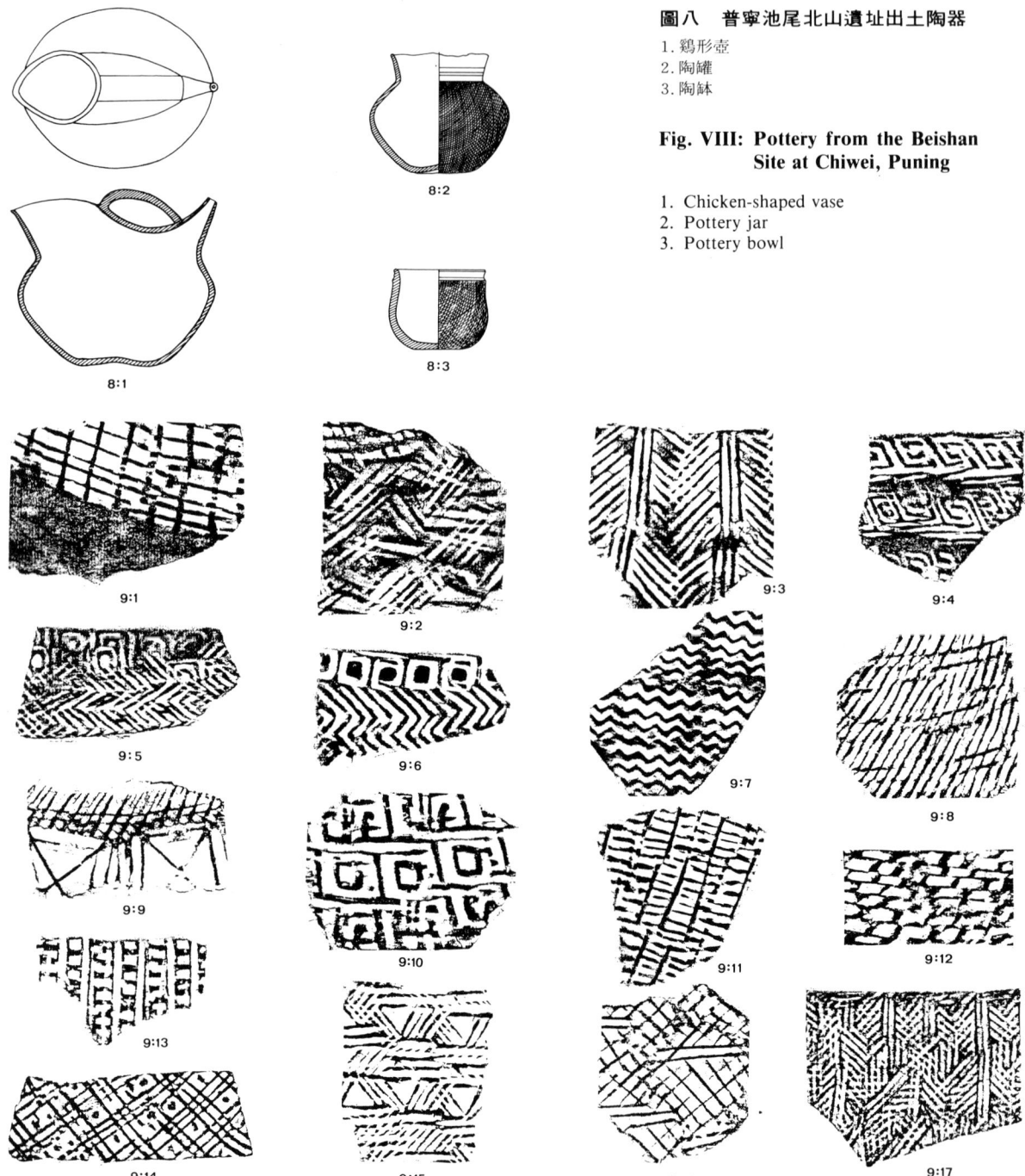

圖八 普寧池尾北山遺址出土陶器
1. 鷄形壺
2. 陶罐
3. 陶缽

Fig. VIII: Pottery from the Beishan Site at Chiwei, Puning

1. Chicken-shaped vase
2. Pottery jar
3. Pottery bowl

圖九 河宕類型幾何印紋拓片

1,2,3. 方格紋、複線三角紋、葉脈紋（灶崗） 4-6. 雲雷曲尺組合紋 7. 曲尺紋 8. 複線長方格紋 9. 大方格交叉紋 10. 雲雷紋 11. 梯子格紋 12. 斜長方格 13. 梯子格紋 14. 複線方格凸點紋 15. 複線三角紋 16. 方格紋 17. 葉脈紋 （4-10. 河宕 11-17. 茅崗）

Fig. IX: Rubbings of Geometric Pattern of Hedang Type

1. 2. 3. Squares, multi-lined triangles, herring-bones (Zaogang) 4-6. Angular and spirals 7. Angular pattern 8. Multi-lined rectangles 9. Large squares with crossed-diagonals 10. Spirals 11. Trapezoids 12. Oblique rectangles 13. Trapezoids 14. Multi-lined squares with lattices 15. Multi-lines triangles 16. Squares 17. Herring-bones (4-10. Hedang; 11-17. Maogang)

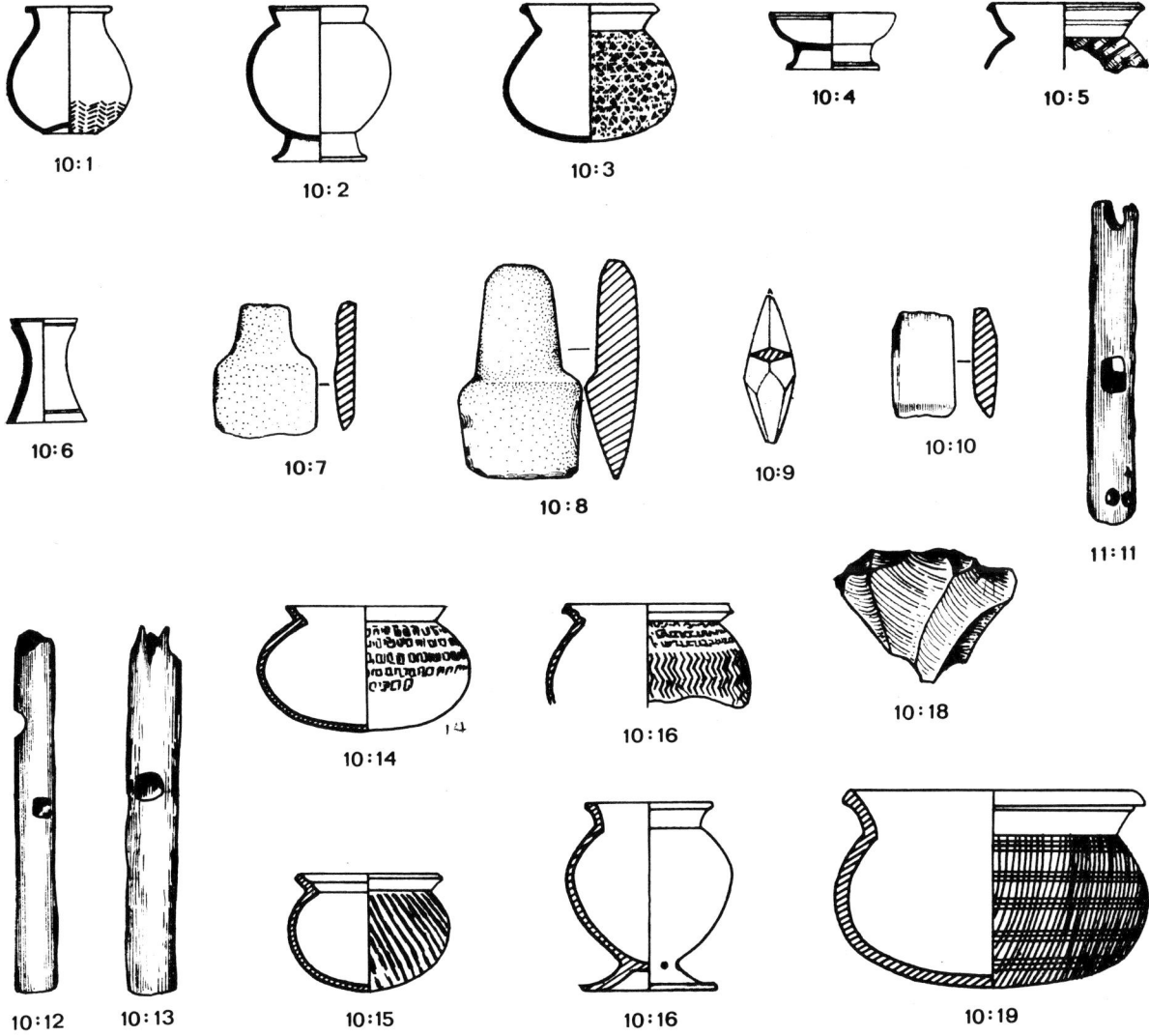

圖十 陶器、石器、木構件

1. 凹底罐
2. 圈足罐
3、5. 夾砂釜
4. 圈足盤
6. 器座
7. 有肩石錛
8. 有肩有段石錛
9. 石鏃
10. 梯形石錛
11-13. 木柱
（1-13. 茅崗出土）
14.-16. 夾砂釜
17. 圈足罐（河宕出土）
18. 細石器（灶崗出土的西樵山橦形石核）
19. 夾砂釜（金蘭寺中層M4）

Fig. X: Pottery, Stone Implements and Wooden Implements

1. Jar with indented bottom 2. Jar with footring 3. 5. Gritty pottery cauldron 4. Basin with footring 6. Pottery stand 7. Shouldered adze 8. Shouldered and stepped adze 9. Arrowhead 10. Trapezoid adze 11-13. Wooden pillars (1-13 from Maogang) 14-16. Gritty pottery cauldron 17. Jar with footring (from Hedang) 18. Microlith (pyramidal stone core of Xiqiaoshan type, from Zaogang) 19. Gritty pottery cauldron (from M4, middle layer, Jinlansi)

Several Problems Related to the Archaeology of Neolithic Guangdong

Zhu Feisu
Guangdong Provincial Museum

Guangdong, situated at the southern border of China, has all along been an integral part of Chinese culture and history. However historical records of Guangdong before the Qin and Han periods are scarce. It is only in the recent decades, as a result of extensive archaeological investigations and excavations that we can have a slight understanding of pre-Qin and Han Guangdong. Based on these recent archaeological finds mainly from sites in China Mainland, I would like to give my personal view on some issues in archaeology and culture of Neolithic Guangdong.

Guangdong has many advantages both in natural resources and geographical environment such as long summers, warm winters, and abundant rain fall, and a long season for agriculture. To the north of the province there are many small basins among high and steep mountains, while in the middle region and along the coast are undulating hills and valleys. The Zhujiang and Hanjiang pass across these basins and valleys to form large areas of alluvial plain in their lower reaches. These favourable conditions provide a most suitable environment for the ancient people. About four hundred sites of Neolithic period have been found along rivers and coastal regions in limestone caves, hillocks and plateaus, dating from 10,000 to 3,500 B.P.

I. Early Sites:

More than ten early sites have been discovered in limestone developing area in northern and western Guangdong. There are two types of sites: the first has no pottery but with a large quantity of chipped gravel tools, and a few stone implements either with polished blades or perforated. The second type has a great many chipped gravel tools, a few stone tools with polished blades as well as coarse tempered pottery.

(A) Sites without pottery:

Represented by the two excavated sites of Dushizai, Chunwan, Yangchun county and Huangyandong, Yulao, Fengkai county.

The Dushizai site, Chunwan, Yangchun county[1]: This cave is situated at the eastern slope of a mountain, with its opening 10 metres above river level. The cave is 15 m. high, 2-8 m. wide and 40 m. deep. The two layers of cultural deposit are 2.8 m. in depth and are mixtures of greyish brown and greyish black sandy clay, containing large amount of snail shells, ashes, charcoal, burned bones, stone implements, animal bones and teeth of *Homo sapiens sapiens*, etc. Stone implements are made from river gravels, unifacially chipped and of large size. The shapes include choppers, scrapers, hammers, drills, flakes and perforated tools. The characteristics of the upper and lower layers are basically the same but in the upper layer, chipped stone implements are more regularly shaped and finely retouched. A few of them are with polished blades. Perforations are usually made by the stricking method and polished smooth. In the lower layer no stone tools with polished blades has been found and perforations are never polished smooth. Moreover most bone implements, such as arrowheads, awls are from the lower layer (Fig. 1:1-4). Animal bones and burnt bones from the deposit have been identified and include rhinoceros, tapir, monkeys, pigs, bears, leopards, boars, water deer, muntjac, buffalo, etc. Among these, rhinoceros and tapir are extinct species, the rest are preserved animal fossils. A shell specimen from the upper layer (ZK714) has been radiocarbon dated to 12950 ± 300 B.C.

The Huangyandong cave site in Fengkai[2]: This cave is situated at southwestern slope of a limestone peak. The cave is 5 m. wide, 6 m. high and with its opening 15 m. above river level. Three cultural deposits of greyish brown or light greyish sandy clay were found inside the cave. A lot of stone choppers and scrapers were unearthed. Most of them are unifacially chipped with only a few alternately chipped. There are also stone cores, stone hammers, and a few stone tools with polished blades or perforations (Fig. 1:5-9). Besides which there are charcoal slack, ashes, burnt clay, burnt bones, shells of snails and clams, fossils of pig, boar, deer and muntjac. It should be noticed that there are skull and limb bones of two *Homo sapiens sapiens* of late phase, one of a male adult of middle age, and the other of a child. The bones are slightly fossilized and they have identical features of modern man. At the excavation, the bones were so scattered that neither the tomb pit nor the burial orientation was discernable. Two specimens of shells of snails and clam (ZK676, 677) have been radiocarbon dated to B.C. 9980±200, and B.C. 9000±300.

Common cultural features of the above two cave sites are:

1. More than 90% of stone tools are chipped from river gravels, mostly from cores and only a few from flakes.

2. Perforations are hammered from both sides.

3. No pottery.

4. Co-existing animals are mainly of preserved species.

5. Limestone caves were chosen for dwelling places. Fishing, hunting and food gathering were the main productive activities.

6. Deposits layers are of sandy clay in grey, greyish brown or greyish black colour, indicating an early date belonging to a common archaeological culture.

(B) Sites with potteries:

These include cave sites and shell mound sites. Cave sites are distributed in limestone caves in Shixing, Renhua, Yingde, Qujiang, Liannan, Luoding, Huaiji, etc., and are collectively known as Qingtang type cave sites[3]. These sites share similarities with those of Huangyandong and Dushizaidong sites in following aspects: stone implements are made from river gravels and with over 90% are chipped. The deposits are of greyish brown sandy clay, containing a great many of shells of round snails, fossils of preserved animals, burnt bones, charcoal, red burnt earth, and human limb bones, etc. There are also dissimilarities: chipped stone tools are mostly chipped alternately; some stone tools with polished blades approaching prototypes of stone axes and adzes (Fig. II:1, 2, 4); pottery sherds of round bottomed jars have been found from the deposits, they are red gritty tempered pottery, handbuilt, with uneven walls and plain or corded surfaces. These jars were probably open-fired. The firing temperature has been examined by the Shanghai Institute of Ceramics to be around 680°C.

Two shell mound sites of an early phase have been discovered in Shiweishan and Chenqiaocun in Chao'an. The cultural characteristics are:

1. The majority stone tools are made from river gravels and are chipped alternately, the common shapes are "oyster picks", handaxe-shape tools, choppers and polished adzes. No polished stone tools has been found from the Shiweishan site. (Fig. II: 3,5).

2. All potteries found are coarse tempered, fine earthenware is absent. Mostly grey coloured, occasionally in red or black, these potteries are low fired, hand built and in limited forms of round bottomed jars with flared or inturned mouth. These jars have their surfaces either polished and undecorated or impressed with simple basket pattern. Many jars are impressed with "blood clam border" pattern or incised or carved around their necks and shoulders, a few others are painted with ochre coloured broad bands. This type of painted pottery is the earliest and most primitive type so far discovered in Guangdong (Fig. II:9, 10).

3. Bone artefacts found from Chenqiaocun are made in a more advanced technique in the choosing of raw material, cutting and polishing. Many pieces of artificially cut bones have been found in the cultural layer. There is an increased variety of bone implements such as: adzes, knives, awls, arrowheads, needles, and hairpins. The technical standard is comparable to that of the bone specimens from Xianrendong in Wannian, Jiangxi (Fig. II: 6, 7, 8).

4. Burial custom is the same as in the former phase, there is no evidence of tomb pits. Human bones of ten individuals of male and female, old and young have been found from shell mound sites in Chenqiaocun, but all are without clear burial configuration.

Qingtang type cave sites and shell mound sites in Shiweishan and Chenqiaocun in Chao'an yield a great many teeth and limb bones of mammals such as ox, pig, and deer, and also fish bones and tortoise shell. The coastal shell mounds contain many sea shells of oyster, "razor clam", clam, "blood clam" and freshwater clams, but shells from cave sites are all of freshwater snails and clams. This indicates that the inhabitants of these sites led a simple life of fishing, hunting and food gathering.

(C) Dates of the sites:

Dushizai in Yangchun and Huangyandong in Kaifeng are the earliest sites. Their cultural characteristics are even more primitive than the well known cave sites in southern China — Zengpiyan in Guilin, Guangxi and Xianrendong in Wannian, Jiangxi. For instance, at Dushizai and

Huangyandong, chipped stone tools are over 90% of all stone implements, and there are no pottery nor apparent burial configurations, while at Zengpiyan and Xianrendong, chipped stone tools and bones have been found. At Zengpiyan, squatting burial was also practised. The date of Dushizai and Huangyandong is 8,000 to 10,000 B.P. or earlier. Then come the Qingtong type cave sites. In these sites chipped stone tools constitute the majority of the relics. Pottery begins to appear in small amount, but both the making and firing technique are primitive, and only coarse tempered pottery with polished or corded surfaces has been found. The date of these sites is 7,000 B.P. Chenqiaocun and Shiweishan in Chao'an belong to the late stage of early Neolithic period in Guangdong. There are partly polished stone adzes and many bone artefacts as well as raw bones. Pottery increases in quantity and simple painted pottery appears. The date is about 6,000 B.P.

II. Sites of Middle Phase:

Comparing to the early phase, sites of this period are more in number and widely distributed. Sites have been found over plateaus, hillocks and basins along rivers; hillocks and alluvial plains in lower river regions and coastal sand mounds of 6 to 10 metres above sea level. The last type of sites are normally cut through by a river from nearby hills. These sites with plentiful supply of shells and fish from sea or freshwater, and animals from nearby forest were ideal places for hunting and fishing.

The major shell mound sites which have been investigated or excavated include the lower layer of Jinlansi, Zengcheng; lower layer of Wanfu'an, Dongguan; Luoshanzui, Xinhui[5]; and also Baidong, Lianxin, Chongnan and Hegang in Xiqiao, Nanhai. Coastal sand mound sites include Pucaoshan at Guanhai, Taishan; Liyudi at Jianghong, Suiqi; Shakeng at Haifeng; Dameisha and Xiaomeisha at Shenzhen. Hillock sites include the well known middle phase sites and microlith sites[6] at Xiqiaoshan, Nanhai, and the lower layer of the Shixia site at Maba, Qujiang.

The cultural characteristics of the middle phase are:

1. The majority of the finds are chipped stone tools mostly made from river gravels. This is obviously a feature carried over from the early phase. However there are also stone tools with their edges and points chipped alternately, and some have polished blades.

2. Polished stone tools are greater in number than in the early phase, though still with chipped marks all over and along edges. Double shouldered adzes make their first appearnace (Fig. III: 6, 7, 11).

3. Shell mound sites yield a great number of bone, horn and shell objects, including axes, adzes, knives, awls, arrowheads and needles. Such objects are not preserved in sand mounds or hillock sites.

4. The amount of pottery found increases. Tempered pottery in black or red colour with corded pattern is most representative of this period. There are also a few fine earthenware. For instance, in the lower layer of Jinlansi of Zengcheng, the distribution of pottery types is: tempered pottery: 82.5%, polished red pottery: 13.6%, painted pottery: 3.9%, geometric pottery: absent[7]. The pottery is hand built, thick walled, low fired and fragile. The common shapes are jars with rounded bottoms, pottery stands, basins with footrings, and stem-bowls. Jars are with flared mouth, out-turned narrow rim, round shoulder, robust body and round bottom. Basins and stem-bowls are rare in late phase sites. The main decoration is fine or coarse corded pattern, together with basket pattern (or striated pattern) or incised pattern. Some are polished but undecorated. Incised patterns including striated, wave, rhomboid and angular designs are done on rims, necks and shoulders, or over corded patterns (Fig. III: 8, 12-16).

5. Another characteristic is the appearance of painted pottery, though in small amount alongside coarse tempered pottery. Sites yielding painted wares include the lower layer of Wanfu'an, Dongguan; lower layer of Jinlansi, Zengcheng; Xiaomeisha, Shenzhen and Shakeng, Haifeng. Nearly complete painted basins with footrings have been found in Xiaomeisha and Shakeng. The painted patterns consist of arcs, straight lines and dots. There seems to be a very remote influence from the Yangshao culture, but the colour pigments used is ochre, not the usual black as in Yangshao, and the design is not seen in contemporaneous sites of other regions. A strong local feature is discernable. Among the painted wares, basins with footrings are most representative in middle phase sites in Guangdong (Fig. III: 9, 10).

6. Burial custom: Well preserved tombs of this phase are few. Only a primary burial and a secondary (i.e. the dead was buried twice) urn burial have been found. The primary burial tomb pit located at tomb No. 1 at the shell mound site, Liyudi, Jianghong, Suiqi is not obvious. Found in the shell deposit layer was a skeleton in a upface extended posture and lying in a east-west direction. Part of a child's skeleton was unearthed from its western side. The poor condition of the latter gives no indication of its sex and age. Burial

objects include one small stone axe, one oyster shell knife, four perforated "blood clams", and about 40 sea "blood clams". The burial urn was found at a shell mound site at Luoshanzui, Xinhui. It was a secondary burial and the bones were collected and placed in a large tempered pottery urn. Burial ojects of the middle phase are few, and mostly are pendent or stringed ornaments made from shells, perforated tortoise shells, fish vertebrae and bones, and tiny stone objects.

7. The economy was mainly maintained by fishing, food gathering and hunting. The dwelling sites are alluvial plateaus alongside rivers, alluvial plain in lower river regions, and upraised sand mounds on bays. Stone implements unearthed from these sites are mostly chipped. There are also river gravels without chipping but with signs of being used as hammering tools. The only polished stone implements are of small size. Pottery shapes are simple and limited. Some sites have rich deposits of many shells and animal bones. Middle phase sites found in Guangdong are of small scale with thin cultural layers, indicating that the dwelling period at each site was rather short and group activities in Guangdong were in much smaller scale than those of the Huanghe and Changjiang regions.

8. Date: The dates of these sites can be determined by relative stratigraphy and cultural contents of the deposits. Shell mound sites at Jinlansi of Zengcheng and Wanfu'an of Guangdong are with clear stratified layers. The lower layer belongs to the middle phase while the middle layer of Jinlansi and the upper layer of Wanfu'an are of the late phase. Among middle phase sites, Xiqiaoshan is a comparatively significant one[8]. According to surface finds and excavated relics, it is an important quarry and stone workshop site. Over 10,000 pieces of chipped stone tools, cores, flakes, and some unfinished products have been found but as no dwelling sites or deposits has been located, pottery sherds are few. There are three types of cultural contents. The first type is represented by microlithes made from chert and semi-illuminative agate. Neither polished stone tools nor pottery ware have been found. These microlithes were unearthed from Xuanfenggang and Taijianggang in the eastern slope. In the second type, chipped stone tools co-exist with corded tempered pottery (Fig. III: 1-5). In the third type, chipped stone tools co-exist with earthenware jars with footrings and tempered pottery cauldrons decorated with angular meander and herring bone patterns. Stone implements from the latter two types are mostly made from felsite of Xiqiaoshan. There is also a small number of polished stone axes and adzes which are half-finished or of inferior quality. No relative stratigraphy data is available for these three types of sites, but the Xiqiaoshan sites of the middle phase mentioned above include the first and second types. Contemporary remains have also been found in fish ponds, streams or rice fields in Baidong, Hegang, Lianxin and Chongnan near Xiqiaoshan. The date for middle phase sites is about 6,000 B.P.

Moreover the sand mound site at Pucaoshantang in Guanghai, Taishan and the shell mound site at Liyudi in Jianghong, Suiqi have different characteristics from the above remains of the middle phase. The main cultural characteristic is that over 95% of the pottery is tempered and mostly in black with only a few in red. The main pottery decoration is coarse basket pattern, the others are fine cord pattern and incised pattern. Shapes are simple; from Liyudi the only shape found are jars with straight mouth and round bottom, whereas from Pucaoshantang there are jars with round bottom and basins with footring. The basin is similar in shape to the painted basin from Xiaomeisha discussed above, but no painted pottery was found. The tempered pottery was hand built, low fired, and with both inside and outside highly polished until smooth and compact, though there is coarse sand in the clay body. The majority of stone tools are hammers and choppers made of gravel. Intended for picking shells, they are irregularly shaped and have not been worked on except a few grooves from wear and tear. In addition there are a few polished small shouldered adzes and trapezoidal adzes. Considering the geographic location of the sites, the negligible amount of small stone tools excavated, and vast quantities of animal bones and sea shells found in the shell mound sites, would indicate that the chief economic activities of the ancient people were fishing, hunting and food gathering. The date for these sites is about 5,000 B.P.

III. Types and Regional Distribution of Late Sites:

In comparison with the middle phase, sites of the late phase are greater in number and more extended in area. In addition, the cultural layers are thicker, yielding more relics. Based on available archaeological materials, late sites can be divided into the following four regions: (i) northern Guangdong, (ii) eastern Guangdong, (iii) Zhujiang delta and coastal area, and (iv) Leizhou Peninsula and Hainan Island.

(i) Northern Guangdong

Sites are mostly found in hillocks with relative height of 15 to 30 metres. The tributaries of

Beijiang flow nearby and the river valleys, basins and slopes provide a very fertile soil for primitive agriculture.

The more important sites in the northern Guangdong region are Shixia and Donghuawei at Maba, Qujiang; Nianyuzhuan and Matiping at Zhoutian, Qujiang; Pushaoshan at Longgui, Qujiang; Xincun and Chengbo in Shixing; and Zoumagang in Shaoguan. Two cultural types can be differentiated, represented by Shixia culture and Nianyuzhuan culture.

(A) Shixia culture[9, 10]:

Shixia culture was discovered in 1972 among hillocks of Shiziyan, Mabaxu in Qujiang county. Cultural deposits are in three stratified layers, of which the lowest layer represents Shixia culture with the following characteristics:

1. Of the pottery excavated, tripods are the most common, the others are round-bottomed or with footring. Very few flat-bottomed vessels were found and none with indented base. A characteristic shape of Shixia pottery is stepped-mouthed with cover and perforated footring. Apart from this, the pottery shapes are more varied than those from contemporary sites in Guangdong. For example, for cooking vessels there are several types of tripods in addition to pitchers, steamers and round-bottomed pots (*fu*). As for drinking and food vessels there are basins with three legs or footrings, stem-bowls, vases, tripods, jars, goblets, etc. Of all the shapes, tripods, *fu*, dish, stem-bowl, vase and jar are the most common shapes (Fig. IV: 1-15). Over 70% of the pottery is undecorated, the rest is ornamented with corded and basket marks or impressed geometric designs. Other decorative techniques include incising, applying and openwork. The impressed geometric pattern, mostly square, angular, spiral designs and concentric circles are less developed than those of Hedang or Nianyuzhuan types. Also the impressions are usually shallow and irregular. The pottery is mainly produced by the wheel, though some are hand built. The firing temperature is around 900° to 1000°C. Tempered pottery makes up 49%, the rest being earthenware. Their colours are quite complex, ranging from grey, brown, black, red to yellow, with even one piece in white.

2. Another characteristic of Shixia culture is represented by stone implements which are abundant in quantity, highly polished and varied in shape. The shapes include pickaxe, shovel, adze, chisel, arrowhead, broad-axe, awl, etc. Among these, shovels, long adzes and pick-axes are the most common. Large in size, these can be hafted with short handles, and would be most useful in digging and loosening soil, chopping wood or digging grave pits. The pickaxe is quite unique in shape and has not been found elsewhere. It has a long thick body that is even thicker in the middle or upper part, with trapezoidal or nearly square cross-sections. Its front is either straight or concave but its back side is always convex, presenting a bow-shaped lateral view. Therefore it has been called "adze with bow-shaped back". The bevelled blade is unifacial, very similar to the modern iron pickaxe (Fig. V:1-8). This is a unique shape and has not been found in sites of other cultural types.

3. Burial custom: A tribal burial ground with rectangular tomb pits in an east-west orientation has been discovered. No tombs furnishings was used. Most of the tomb pits have red burnt walls. Individual and secondary burials were in common practice with bones gathered in a pile and placed in the south-eastern corner at the bottom of the tomb pit. As for primary burial the body was usually placed in an extended position, with the ventral side facing upward and the head pointing to the east. Two sets of burial objects have been found in secondary burials. With one complete set placed at the time of the second burial, the other set, moved together with the bones from the first burial, was often incomplete and damaged. It is found at the floor of the pit or in the earth filling. Such a burial custom is not commonly seen. In some secondary burials, bright red vermilion has been found scattered over the bones or nearby. The quantity and quality of the burial objects can be differentiated, mainly through the number and the craftsmanship of the stone implements and ornaments.

4. Another characteristic of Shixia culture is the stone ornaments. There are many finely executed types such as bracelets, slit-rings, *huang*, hairpins, beads, tubes, disc rings, pendants and even *cong*, which is extremely rare in Guangdong. The most advanced techniques for stone, such as cutting, polishing and drilling have all been applied to these ornaments. Even crystals and turquoise with hardness of six degree could be cut and the entire surfaces polished to a high shine. These ornaments are similar in shapes and combinations to those of the Liangzhu culture of the late Neolithic period in Jiangsu and Zhejiang (Fig. VI), with comparable level of craftsmanship.

5. In view of the discovery of such large stone implements as pickaxes, shovels, long-adzes, as well as motar and pestle for grain processing, and also carbonized rice and grains from tomb pits and stove pits[11], the basic economy for the Shixia

people was primitive agriculture. However, stone arrowheads, which is the weapon for hunting, made up more than half of the total number of stone artifacts excavated, indicating that hunting was still a major activity for livelihood at that time.

6. Date: The dates of the sites can be derived from the study of relative stratigraphy of the burials. There are three cultural layers at the Shixia site representing three different phases. Three radiocarbon dates are available: Tomb No. 79, Phase I (BK76024): 2270 ±110 B.C., (dendrochronologic calibrated: 2730 ±155 B.C.); Tomb No. 43, Phase III (BK75046): 2380 ±90 B.C. (dendrochronologic calibrated: 2865 ±185 B.C.); Tomb No. 26, Phase III (BK75050): 2070 ±100 B.C. (dendrochronologic calibrated: 2480 ±150 B.C.) Even though the radiocrabon date of Tomb No. 79 does not conform entirely to the periodization of the tombs, it indicates that Phase I develops into Phases II and III in a short time, with only brief intervals between the phases.

Sites of Shixia culture are mainly distributed in the northern part of northern Guangdong. In recent years pottery and ornaments of Shixia culture such as tripod-*fu*, tripod-basins, stem-bowls, jars with stepped mouth and footring as well as stone *cong* have been unearthed from Xincun of Shixing, Chuangbanling at Wushi of Qujiang and Liling at Maba of Qujiang. In the region of Zhujiang delta and coastal sand mounds, no remains of Shixia culture has been discovered. Since northern Guangdong is adjacent to Jiangxi and Hunan provinces, the Shixia pottery ware can be compared to those excavated from the lower layers of the sites at Zhuweicheng and Fancheng, both located in Qingjiang of Jiangxi. There are similarities in pottery shapes, but differ in quality and combination. The late Neolithic sites in Jiangxi yielded tempered red pottery which is their distinct characteristic. Polished stone implements are also less in quantity and variety than those of Shixia culture. Therefore, the origin and development of Shixia culture await further archaeological discoveries.

(B) Cultural remains of the Nianyuzhuan type[12]:

The Nianyuzhuan site was found in 1959 at Zhoutianxu, north-west of Qujiang county. It is a hillock site with the Zhengjiang, a tributary of Beijiang, flowing nearby. The Matiping site is 10 m. to its east.

Other sites belonging to the same type include the middle layer of the Shixia site, Pushaoshan at Longgui of Qujiang, Zoumagang at Shaoguan and Chengbo at south Shixing city. The Nianyuzhuan and Matiping sites represent the early phase of this culture with the following characteristics:

1. Of all the stone implements found, about half are chipped from river gravels into cutters, choppers and knives. The polished stone tools are half finished, though some are completely polished. The shapes include axe, stepped adze, trapezoidal adze, chisel, arrowhead, spearhead, saddle-quern and roller (made from river gravels).

2. Tempered pottery makes up 88% of the pottery finds. Mostly grey ware with some in red, they are low fired and hand built. The surface is decorated with cord and basket marks, and geometric impressed designs with angular, square and spiral patterns made their appearance, however, the shallow and irregular impressions show the primitive stage. Tempered pottery is represented by jars with short neck, flared mouth and round bottom, whereas earthenware includes jars and basins with footring (Fig. VI:1).

The middle layer of the Shixia site as well as sites at Pushaoshan, Zoumagang and Chengbo are of later date than the Nianyuzhuan site. Their cultural characteristics are:

1. The more common pottery shapes are vessels with round bottom, indented base or footring. Tripodic shapes are rarely seen and none with flat base. In addition, the shapes are characteristized by flared mouth, high neck, angular or broad shoulder. Typical wares include jars, bowls with small stem, footed basins, pottery stands, etc. (Fig. VI: 13-21). Tempered pottery takes up about 20 to 30%, as for the earthenware, it is mostly grey, with some in orange red. More than 65% of the earthenware is decorated with geometric impressed patterns, apparently much more developed than at lower Shixia and Nianyuzhuan sites. Apart from angular and square designs and concentric circles mentioned before, there are spiral and herring bone motifs, variations of the square pattern, some even embellished with lattices, and combinations of the above. With more sophisticated technique, the patterns formed are refined and regular, the impressions deep and clear. The turn-table was also used for trimming mouth rims and foot rings (Fig. VI: 2-12).

2. The polishing technique for stone tools have become quite advanced, the shapes include long adzes in various sizes, trapezoidal adzes, stepped adzes, shouldered adzes and three-bladed arrowheads. A few perforated stone halberds and stone spearheads have been unearthed, but polished ones like those in Shixia culture were absent.

3. Burial custom: A tribal burial ground with 32 tombs has been excavated in the middle layer of the Shixia site. No burial objects have been found in 13 of them; in 3 of them piles of stones were placed around the dead or in the earth filling, the rest were buried with funerary objects. The tomb pits, dug in an east-west orientation are rectangular and shallow. The walls of the pits were not burnt and were not equipped with tomb furnishings. Single primary burial was the prevalent custom and no secondary burial has been found. Except for a few pieces that were for daily use, the pottery excavated is small and thin-walled, apparently for burial.

4. Dwelling as well as kiln sites have been found. Remains of dwellings, each occupying an area of 8 to 10 square metres, are either square or round. Yet only irregularly arranged post holes have been discovered, no obvious living areas has been identified. The pottery kilns found have either round or oval chambers.

5. An analysis of the geographic environment of the sites and the greater number and types of stone implements indicate that the people mainly lived on primitive agriculture, supplemented by food gathering and hunting.

6. Date: Nianyuzhuan and Matiping sites are contemporaneous with Shixia culture (the lower layer) or slightly earlier. The dates for the other four sites of Nianyuzhuan culture are about 3,500 to 4,000 B.P.

The middle and lower layers of the Shixia site follow a temperal sequence, as testified by the presence of stratified layers and tombs breaking through them. However, these two stratified layers have obvious different cultural characteristics. The stepped-mouth tripodic pottery vessels popular in Shixia culture, or its characteristic large size stone tools such as pickaxe, shovel, long adze, broad-axe and ornaments such as bracelet, disc-ring, and *cong*, are all absent from the middle layer. On the other hand, pottery excavated from the middle layer has flared mouth, tall neck, angular or broad shoulder. Besides, the common shapes are jars with or without footrings, deep basins with contracted mouth and splayed foot, stem-bowls with incised bands and tempered pottery stands. The burial custom is also different; the baked wall pits and single secondary burial, prevalent in Shixia culture have totally disappeared in the middle layer. Such obvious differences indicate a non sequential relationship between these two layers. Though this can be explained by differences in time, a better explanation would be that they belong to separate cultures. The middle layer of Shixia can be identified with the Nianyuzhuan type, especially since the shapes and geometric impressed decorations of its pottery show greater affinity to the finds in other sites of late Neolithic culture in Guangdong.

(ii) **Eastern Guangdong**

This region includes the middle reaches of Hanjiang, the alluvial plain of Hanjiang delta and the lowland along the coast.

The area along the middle reaches of Hanjiang and its tributaries has mainly hillock sites, the relative height is 20 to 70 metres, though some sites may be located as high as 280 to 350 metres. In the Hanjiang delta and coastal lowland, shell mound and sand mound sites are generally found. Excavations and trial borings have been conducted at Wugongshan at Didu, Baoshandong at Butian, Wudui at Ququi, all from Jieyang. In Puning discoveries were made at Futoubu at Guangtai, Beishan at Chiwei, and in Chaoyang, there were sites at Zuoxuangongshan, Chiniushan, Xiangshan, Niutuiping, Jiudouwei, Jiuling, Fengjikeng, etc.

Based on representative pottery types and decorations, late Neolithic sites in eastern Guangdong can be classified into the following three types, representing three stages of development:

(A) The first type is represented by Zuoxuangongshan[13] and Chiniushan sites in Chaoyang. Its special features are the co-existence of tempered pottery with polished stone adzes and arrowheads, and the limited amount of geometric impressed pottery. Tempered pottery, mainly grey ware, amounts to 70 to 80 percent of the pottery finds. The surface is mostly plain, except for some decorated with the basket pattern. The proportion of geometric impressed pottery is 10%, most of them have the square pattern, with a few ornamented by the angular pattern. The impressed units are not regularly arranged and some jars have applied decorations. The pottery shapes include pots and jars.

(B) The second type is represented by the Wugongshan site at Didu of Jieyang, also included are sites of slightly later date at Baoshandong and Niuliaojiao in Jieyang and the Futoubu kiln site in Puning.

The cultural characteristic of the Wugongshan site is the co-existence of tempered pottery, geometric impressed pottery and polished stone implements. The proportion of tempered pottery is 50 to 60%.

The exterior and interior of the vessels are baked to an orange red colour, but the body is greyish black. Many are decorated with corded and basket patterns. There is an increased number of earthenware impressed with geometric designs. In addition to square and angular patterns, there are variations of square and rectangular designs as well as basket designs. Shapes have also increased, including pots, jars with footring, stem-bowls and pottery stands. The pot and the jar usually have flared mouth, slant neck, round shoulder; they either have footring or round bottom. All are hand built, with higher firing temperature for the earthenware.

The Baoshandong site in Butian differs from the Wugongshan site in that it yielded also tempered pottery *fu*-tripod, tripod with stepped mouth and angular body, and earthenware basin with perforated footring, in addition to tempered pottery *fu*, jars and stand. Shapes for the tripod legs vary, including flattened round shape, cuneiform shape, curve shape and one piece which has T-shaped legs (curved in the front and T-shaped in cross-section). The curve-shaped tripod legs, cuneiform shaped legs, tripods with stepped mouth and angular body, and basin with high perforated footring are similar to Shixia wares. The T-shaped leg was the most popular tripod leg shape in late Neolithic period in Jiangxi province[14]. This may indicate a cultural relationship between Baoshandong, Shixia in northern Guangdong and Ganjiang valley in Jiangxi some 4,000 years ago.

The flourish of geometric impressed pottery is one of the cultural characteristics of this ancient period in eastern Guangdong. A group of 11 kilns for firing geometric impressed pottery was found at Futoubu, Guangtai, Puning county in 1982. The kilns are half underground pits dug along the southern slope of a hill. One type is gourd shaped horizontal draught kiln with the firing box in the front and the kiln chamber at the back, connected by a heat channel. Inside the kiln chamber is a raised platform of burnt earth on which the pottery pieces were placed. It slopes towards the front and is 20-40 cm. above the floor and surrounded by a radial heat channel. This kind of kiln structure is quite similar to that of the late Longshan period in Sanliqiao in Shaanxian, Henan. The only difference is that the Sanliqiao kiln has four parallel heat channels at the floor of the chamber while the one at Futoubu has a radial one, which is rich in local colour. Another type of kiln designs has either a rectangular chamber or a square one with rounded corners. There is no firing box or flues. During the firing, fuel was probably piled up at the floor of the pit and the pottery wares were placed directly above. Then a mixture of plant stems and clay would seal up the pottery, leaving some holes as smoke vents. In a way this design is similar to modern "open-fire" kilns used by the Tai people in Yunnan. Due to a long period of use, these kiln walls have accumulated layers of baked earth as thick as 2 to 4 cm. Only pottery jars have been found from these kilns. They have a tall neck, flared or angular flared mouth. Many have round shoulders though some are angular. The body is round and robust, the bottom indented or footed. Almost all geometric patterns of late Neolithic period can be found in eastern Guangdong. These include square, rectangular, rhomboid, basket, weaving, mat, herring-bone, concentric circle designs as well as variants of some of the above. Three to six clay strips are applied to the shoulder and body of earthenware jars. This decorative technique is rarely seen in other regions in Guangdong. The footring of jars is so low that it must have been formed by a circular clay strip attached to the bottom. Earthenware stem-bowls are shaped with plain deep dishes raised on low splayed foot (Fig. VII: 1-13).

(C) The third type is represented by Houshan site at Chiwei, Puning, identified by the co-existence of chicken-shaped pitchers, pottery jars decorated with square pattern and polished stone implements. The chicken-shaped pitchers are quite unique in shape. The body is oval in cross-section. The upper part has sharp mouth rim, tall neck. The mouth rim has been pressed inwards in the centre; to form two spouts, one large and one small, and a flat handle is attached to the side. The base is indented. Except for the mouth rim, the body is impressed with square patterns. Chicken-shaped pitchers so far limited to the eastern Guangdong area are often found alongside jars with square patterns. The jar is with flared mouth, with slightly out-turned rim, tall neck, contracted neck, angular shoulder or angular belly, depressed or flat bottom. This kind of jar is not found from the two types mentioned earlier. Other pottery vessels include basin with straight mouth, small basin, small cup, stem-bowl and large urn (Fig. VIII: 1-3). Similar pottery wares have been found at Wudui, Quqi of Jieyang, and Linghoudong of Butian.

Stone tools found from the above three types are mostly of small to medium sizes. There are long adzes, stepped adzes, shouldered adzes, stepped and shouldered adzes, trapezoidal adzes, etc. with the last item most commonly seen. In addition there are chisels, arrowheads, knives and awls.

Date of the sites: There does not seem to have any distinct stratified layers in these three types. However, they have been dated to different periods of time due to their different cultural content. The first type, with a large proportion of tempered pottery and only a small amount of geometric impressed pottery, is dated to the early phase of the late Neolithic period of Guangdong, about 5,000 B.P. The second type, with more developed geometric pottery, pottery kilns, geometric impressed jars and professional potters, is contemporaneous to Shixia culture, especially because of the discovery of tripods with stepped mouth and angular body, various shapes of tripod legs, particularly the T-shaped ones. For the third type, geometric designs for pottery declined abruptly with the exception of square pattern. The pottery jars with square pattern, found alongside chicken-shape pitchers, have certain affinity to those unearthed from Fubin-type culture of Raoping of early Bronze Age in eastern Guangdong. However, geometric impressed pottery was no longer popular in the early Bronze Age in eastern Guangdong. Moreover, large stone halberds, vase with wide mouth and glazed pottery, which are commonly found from the sites of Fubin-type culture, are not seen at this type of sites. Therefore, this type may be considered to be a transitional phase in the development from late Neolithic period to early Bronze Age in eastern Guangdong with a date of about 2,500 B.P. If this point can be established, we then have a rough idea about the cultural sequence in eastern Guangdong for this period.

(iii) Hedang type cultural sites in the Zhujiang delta

Shell mound, sand mound and hillock sites are distributed in the Zhujiang delta where a vast alluvial plain is formed by the lowering shore line.

The more important shell mound sites are Hedang at Foshan[15], Zaogang and Luogang at Datong of Nanhai[16], Youyugang at Baixi of Xiqiao, Tongxingang at Danzao, Longjiangcun in Dongguan, Maogang at Jinli of Gaoyao, and the middle layer of Jinlansi in Zengcheng. Hillock sites include Heideshan in Shenzhen and late phase sites in Xiqiaoshan. Sand mound sites have been located at Chiwancun in Nantou of Shenzhen.

The Hedang site was found in the winter of 1977 in the old market of Hedang, Lanshi, suburb of Foshan city. From the excavated area of 750 square metres, abundant artifacts from both dwelling and burial sites have been discovered. This is a representative site of the late Neolithic period in the Zhujiang delta region, so that contemporary sites from this region have been tentatively called "Hedang-type culture".

The characteristics of the Hedang-type culture are:

1. Pottery finds are the most abundant and show distinct characteristics. Common shapes are with footring, round or indented bottom. Flat bottom wares are absent and tripodic wares are rarely seen. Both tempered pottery and earthenware have been found in different proportions in different sites, tabulated as follows:

Percentage of tempered pottery and earthenware in Hedang-type sites

Type Percentage Location	Tempered Pottery %	Earthenware %	Remarks
Chiwancun, Shenzhen	88.4	11.6	
Hedishan, Shenzhen	81	19	
Middle layer A, Jinlansi, Zengcheng	58.3	41.7	upper middle layer
Middle layer B, Jinlansi, Zengcheng	91	9	lower middle layer
Grey earth layer, Hedang	21.1	79.9	second layer
Shell layer, Hedang	25.8	74.2	third layer
Zaogang, Nanhai	29	71	

The percentage of tempered pottery in Maogang, Gaoyao is even smaller than in Hedang sites. The pottery has many colours, varying from site to site. In Maogang, Gaoyao black ware is predominant, followed by grey ware. In Hedang, Zaogang, Luogang, Youyugang and Tongxingang, wares in orange red, orange yellow and light yellow are more commonly seen, whereas grey ware is hardly noted.

Zhujiang delta is the area where geometric impressed pottery was best developed in late Neolithic Guangdong. Corded and basket patterns common in the middle Neolithic period declined in use while striations have almost disappeared. On the other hand, there are thirty varieties of geometric impressed designs, including angular, square, herring bone, basket and spiral patterns and variations of some of them. One to three bands of spiral pattern stamped on the neck or shoulder of jars and pots in combination of angular pattern is a special feature of pottery decoration in this region (Fig. IX: 4-6). A few painted pottery has also been found but limited to Hedang and Luogang sites. They are jars or basins decorated with ochre lines or bands around the mouth rim or shoulder. The pottery is mostly hand made, but the turn-table has been used to trim the rim and footring, so that obvious grooved bands and raised ridges or curved rims are left behind. Such formal characteristics are peculiar to

Hedang-type. The firing temperature is above 1000°C. Pottery types are fewer than in Shixia culture. For tempered pottery, there are pot and stand; and from Chiwancun, Shenzhen a rectangular grate for cooking food has been unearthed. No tripodic cooking vessels have been found. Features of typical shapes are flared mouth, out-turned broad rim, contracted neck, round shoulder and round bottom. Tempered pot with squat globular body is a typical vessel of the Hedang type. For earthenware there are jar with indent bottom, jar with footring, shallow dish with contracted mouth, dish with low splayed footring, stem-bowl with ribbed and high splayed foot. The jars are usually with angular or broad shoulders, with the body bottom and part of shoulder stamped with geometric patterns (Fig. IX: 1-3, 7-17, X: 1-3, 14-17, 19).

Engraved marks such as "I", "II", "III", "+", "X", "↑", "X", ")(", "⌣" and "出" have been found on Hedang and Maogang pottery yet these are seldom seen on wares in northern and eastern Guangdong regions.

(2) Most of the stone implements are polished all over, finely made. They are mainly small to medium pieces, double shouldered adzes, shouldered and stepped adzes, long adzes and trapezoidal adzes are the most common shapes. Shoulders of the shouldered adzes are either straight angled or blunt angled. Axes and arrowheads are rare and big shovels are extremely so. In some sites, the materials and shapes of some stone implements are close to those of Xiqiaoshan site, providing further proof that Xiqiaoshan was still a stone workshop for nearby primitive tribes right down to the late Neolithic period (Fig. X: 7-10, 18).

(3) Bone tools have been found alongside stone implements in shell mounds. They were made from animal bones and horns, including bone and horn awls, fish spear, bone shuttle, hairpin, chisel, needle, etc.

(4) Burial custom: Based on the analysis of seventy-seven tombs in Hedang, four tombs in the middle layer of Jinlansi and six tombs in Zaogang, tomb pits are shallow and in an east-west orientation. Some of the tomb pits were dug in shell layers so that their size and edges are not well defined. There are no obvious tomb pits for the six tombs at the Zaogang site. A layer of shells and earth on the skeleton is so hardened that it could have been rammed. Bones found from shell mound tombs are slightly fossilised and therefore quite well preserved. Single, upfaced and extended burial is popular. Even though some instance of secondary burial have been discovered, they differ from Shixia culture which piled up the bones in the southeastern corner of the tomb pit. Instead, the skeleton is arranged in the original extended posture. In Hedang tombs, the head of male adults always faces the west and females in the opposite direction, except for Zaogang site, the head of the buried faces southeast. Most of the tombs do not have burial objects, some with only one to three pieces, including a stone adze for males and pottery spindle whorls for females. Tooth-pulling custom is observed from the buried dead, with the removal of the second incisor on one side or both sides. For instance, in Hedang the percentage for tooth-pulling is as high as 82.6%. Such a custom has been found in many late Neolithic sites in Shangdong, Jiangsu, Fujian and Hubei. The physical features of the bones show characteristics similar to the Southasian Mongoloid. Some specialists are of the opinion that the similarities between the skulls of Hedang man and equator man are greater than those between Hedang man and the northern Mongoloid. However, the Hedang man still belongs to the southern marginal type of Mongoloids. The average height is 166 cm. for male and 154 for female.

(5) In addition to bracelets, slit-rings and tubes made of stone, other ornaments include large bracelets and tubes made of ivory. The latter has very thin walls highly polished, showing a sophistication in technique.

(6) From the deposits of Hedang-type shell mound sites many bones of mammals and aquatic animals have been discovered. The scantly large stone implements recovered further indicates that food gathering and fishing were the main productive activities. The wet sub-tropical weather, rivers, sandy bays, and dense forest provided the primitive people with abundant material sources, so that primitive agriculture developed slower than in northern Guangdong.

(7) Dwelling: There are two types, one is "pile-structure" type in wood built above water and the other is the shed type built on burnt or hardened earth. Remains of the former have been found in fish ponds in front of Shijiaocun, Maogang, Jinli of Gaoyao. From the three groups unearthed, the ground plan is rectangular, measuring 14.7 cm. from the front to the back. The distance between two pillars varies from 1.64 to 1.7 m. Remains include pillars, piles, wedges and boards made of wood and bark. Wooden pillars form the main structural support, most of them have rectangular, square or elliptical mortises. The top end of the pillars is grooved and on the same level

with the soil of the fish pond, underneath is found the shell mound cultural layer as deep as 4.5 to 5 m. (Fig. X: 11-13). This is the first discovery made in Guangdong. The shed type architecture have been found in Hedang and Zaogang sites. At the middle or along one side of the hardened or burnt earth surface are located burnt pits or earth mounds. The dwelling area is about 1.5 — 3 m. in diameter and surrounded by irregularly arranged post holes.

(8) Date: Several radiocarbon dates are available: Shell specimen from middle layer of Jinlansi site in Zengcheng (ZK103): 2085±95 B.C. (dendrochronologic calibrated: 2495±145 B.C.); three wooden specimens from Maogang site of Gaoyao (ZK710, 708, 707). 2340 to 2120 B.C. (dendrochronologic calibrated: 2815-2540 B.C.); four specimens from the third layer of Hedang site in Foshan (ZH526, 527, 528, 546): 3070-2955 B.C. (dendrochronologic calibrated: 3550-2680 B.C.); two human bones from second layer of Hedang site (ZK548, 547): 1890-1655 B.C. (dendrochronologic calibrated: 2250-1960 B.C., another date with test on charcoal (ZK647): 2150±80 B.C. (dendrochronologic calibrated: 2580±135 B.C.); shell specimen from Zaogang in Nanhai (ZK545): 3455±120 B.C. (dendrochronologic calibrated: 4100±140 B.C.). A review of the above dates shows that those from shell specimens are generally earlier than the other objects. It would be appropriate to put the date for Hedang-type culture in Zhujiang delta at 5,000 to 3,900 B.P., with Hedishan and Chiwancun sites in Shenzhen and the lower middle layer of Jinlansi in Zengcheng representing its early phase.

(iv) Leizhou Peninsula and Hainan Island[19]

In the absence of large-scale archaeological excavations conducted in this region, our study can only base on limited material gathered from surface finds and trial excavations from the 1950's. Taking the Hainan Island as an example the characteristics are as follows:

(1) **Distribution of sites**: There are hillock sites along the river banks, and a few sand or shell mound sites located off coastal bays. From some hillock sites, Han pottery sherds with stamped basket, net and wave patterns are found scattered on the surface. Polished stone implements and red coarse tempered pottery are unearthed from the deposits.

(2) **Pottery**: There are red coarse tempered pottery and red earthenware. The presence of red ware is characteristic of the primitive sites of Hainan Island. They are high fired, hand made and with smooth surface. The decorative patterns are quite simple including basket, square and striated pattern. Some are decorated with red slip at the mouth rims. The shapes are also few, mostly large jars with round bottom and red earthenware stem-bowls. Geometric patterns characteristic of late Neolithic period on the mainland have not been found on Hainan Island.

(3) **Stone implements**: Most of them are polished all over, including long, trapezoidal, and double shouldered adzes and axes. Axes are more abundant than in contemporary sites in the mainland.

(4) **Possible date**: Typology of vessels can usually help to demonstrate similarities and differences of contemporary cultures in different regions. Among all vessels, pottery for daily use is the most illustrative. The origin of primitive cultural remains on Hainan Island has been a subject of dispute. Some consider them indigenious, yet not supported by early archaeological evidence. Others say that because of similarities to the middle Neolithic culture of Zhujiang delta in some of the excavated materials such as red coarse tempered jars with basket or striated designs, red earthenware stem-bowls, and double shouldered adzes, it is possible that about 5,000 to 6,000 ago ancient people from the mainland crossed the Qiongzhou Strait and settled down in Hainan Island. This type of culture, characterized by red tempered pottery and earthenware, polished shouldered, long adzes and axes, continued in Hainan Island until Qin and Han periods, when it was replaced by the iron culture from the mainland. Therefore, these artifacts may represent the primitive culture on Hainan Island some 5,000-6,000 B.P. As for its late phase in 3,000 to 4,000 B.P., no evidence has been found. The accuracy of this estimation still depends an evidence from new archaeological discoveries.

Sites along the banks of Xijiang area and Dongjiang valley have not been extensively excavated so that there is not sufficient material to give a clear picture. In the past, archaeologists considered the Neolithic culture of Pingxinglinggu area (i.e. Meixian and part of Huiyang) in eastern Guangdong an independant "regional group". Actually, the lower reaches of Dongjiang close to its alluvial plain if not already entered the Zhujiang delta, its cultural content is similar to that of shell mound type culture at Hedang, Foshan. The late Neolithic culture in Longchuan and Heyuan in the upper reaches of Dongjiang resembles Shixia culture, especially the middle layer of Shixia. Moreover, the late Neolithic culture in Meijiang valley of Meixian area is similar to the contemporary culture in Hanjiang delta in eastern Guangdong.

IV. Conclusion

With archaeological discoveries and research carried out during recent decades, we have arrived at a preliminary understanding of the Neolithic culture in Guangdong with respect to cultural content, distribution, dates and development. This can be summarized as follows:

(1) The evolution of the production and shapes of stone implements: Most of the stone implements found in early phase sites are made from gravels and unifacially chipped. Only a few have polished blades. From sites with both stone and tempered pottery finds, stone implements are chipped alternately and trapezoidal adzes with polished blades have already appeared. Very few middle phase sites have been excavated, with mainly gravel stone implements alternately chipped. The amount of implements with polished blades have increased, and double shouldered adzes with strong local features also made their appearance. Stone implements of the late phase are mostly wholly polished, and variously shaped. Great technical advancement has been made, with regard to choosing the material as well as cutting, drilling, and polishing techniques. There are long adzes, shouldered adzes, stepped adzes, trapezoidal adzes, and a few axes, chisels and arrowheads. Shixia culture has its own combination of stone implements.

(2) Relationship between choice of dwelling places and livelihood: Guangdong people in the early phase often chose to dwell in limestone caves and lived on food gathering and fishing. In the middle phase they gathered in hillocks and plateaus along river banks or coastal sand mounds where there were an inexhaustible supply of food. They lived on aquatic animals, shell-food as well as food gathering, supplemented by group hunting. Pottery spindle whorls have been unearthed from many sites indicating that the people by this time have learned weaving. In the late phase, different modes of economic living have developed for people in regions with different physical environments and natural conditions. In dwelling places with basins or slopes the ancient people lived on primitive agriculture. Therefore, from these sites were excavated large stone shovels, adzes, and pickaxes. For the primitive tribes living in deltas along streams or the tributaries, coastal hillocks or sand mounds, fish and shell food from water were the main food sources. In these sites, large stone implements are lacking, indicating that primitive agriculture was not well developed.

(3) Characteristic pottery and geometric patterns: Sites of early phase are either with pottery or with only tempered pottery. No earthenware has been found. The only shapes found is round bottom jars (*fu*), which are hand built, low fired, undecorated or with corded pattern. In the middle phase, earthenware began to appearance even though tempered pottery still dominated. Other than the round bottom jar of tempered pottery, there are also basin with low footring and stem-bowl in both tempered pottery and earthenware. The surface is decorated by corded, basket and striated patterns, geometric impressed patterns are extremely rare. The pottery is hand built and low fired. Painted pottery have been found but only in sites in eastern Guangdong and Zhujiang delta. Highly developed geometric impressed pottery marks the late phase making up 50 to 80% of the pottery finds. There are angular, square, herringbone, spiral, ladder shaped, basket, repeat-lined rectangular, concentric patterns, etc. However, there are variations in the size of pattern units, width of lines, depth of impressions, etc. in different regions. Yet the highest development is no doubt reached by the sites of Hedang-type culture in Zhujiang delta. The geometric patterns have great variety, the lines are thick and deeply stamped, and found even on tempered pottery. Northern Guangdong comes second. The patterns of eastern Guangdong have fine and fluent lines, and two to six clay strips or braid bands are usually applied to earthenware jars.

In Hedang-type culture, jars are usually decorated with one to three bands of spiral patterns and then angular patterns below the neck or angular shoulder. This kind of combination is rarely found in northern Guangdong and never in eastern Guangdong.

In comparison with earlier phases there is an increase in the amount of pottery and in shapes. There are earthenware jars, stem-bowls with grooved bands and small stems, jars with angular shoulder and tempered pottery stands. Pottery jars of the Hedang type have flared mouth, tall neck, angular or broad shoulder, high footring or indented bottom. Vessels with flat bottom or three legs are rare. In eastern Guangdong slightly flared mouth, round shoulder, robust body, low footring or indented bottom are popular pottery shapes. There are also some tripodic or flat bottom vessels. Vessels with stepped mouth, cover and three legs are the most typical for late Shixia culture in northern Guangdong. The firing temperature is as high as 900°C to 1000°C. The pottery shapes have become more regular because they are either wheel turned or with the footring or mouth rim trimmed on the turn-table. Yet some are still hand made.

(4) Ornaments: No ornaments has been found in early phase sites. In the middle phase, finely made ornaments of polished and perforated animal bones, fish vertebrae and shells were unearthed from shell mound or sand mound sites. Ornaments increase in number and improve in craftsmanship in the late phase. There are ring and tube made of ivory, ring, slit-ring, bead and tube of stone, in addition to crystal slit-ring and turqoise flakes. Primitive ritual vessels for religious ceremony such as *cong* and disc rings were unearthed from sites of Shixia culture.

(5) Burial custom: Burial custom in the early phase is not clear. In the middle phase, there are shallow earth tomb pits for single and primary burial and urn-burial for single and secondary burial. in the late phase, single and secondary burial with burnt tomb pits is in common practice in Shixia culture in northern Guangdong, while single upfaced extended burial is popular in Hedang-type culture, where there is also artificial tooth-pulling custom. Public tribal graveyard appeared in the late phase.

The study of Neolithic culture in Guangdong with respect to regions and types is a new subject. This essay is only a preliminary investigation based on archaeological evidence. In order to grasp a more complete and accurate understanding of Neolithic culture in Guangdong, we await further archaeological discoveries and more profound studies.

Footnotes:

1. Qiu Licheng, et al, "Excavation of the Neolithic Cave Site at Dushizai, Yangchun County, Guangdong", *Kaogu*, 1982:5.
2. Song Fangyi, et al, "Cave Site at Huangyandong, Fengkai, Guangdong", *Kaogu*, 1983:1.
3. Guangdong Provincial Museum, "Neolithic Site at Qingtang, Wengyuan County, Guangdong", *Kaogu*, 1961:11.
4. CPAM, Guangdong Province, "Shell Mound Sites at Chao'an Guangdong", *Kaogu*, 1961:11.
5. Guangdong Provincial Museum, "Neolithic Sites in Lowland Region of Middle Guangdong", *Kaogu xuebao*, 1960:2.
6. Zeng Qi, "Microlithes from Eastern Slope of Xiqiaoshan", *Kaogu yu wenwu*, 1981:4.
7. Mo Zhi, "New Archaeological Finds in Guangdong", *Kaogu*, 1961:12.
8. Guangdong Provincial Museum, "Stone Implements Unearthed at Xiqiaoshan, Nanhai County, Guangdong", *Kaogu xuebao* 1959:4.
9. Guangdong Provincial Museum, et al, "Brief Excavation Report of Neolithic Burials at Shixia, Qujiang County, Guangdong", *Wenwu*, 1978:7.
10. Zhu Feisu, et al, "On Geometric Pottery from Shixia, Maba", *Wenwu jikan*, 1981, Vol. III.
11. Yang Xiting, "On the Remains of Rice Cultivating at Shixia", *Wenwu*, 1978:7.
12. CPAM, Guangdong Province, et al, "Sites of Nianyuzhuan, Matiping at Qujiang, and Zoumagang at Shaoguan in Guangdong", *Kaogu*, 1964:7.
13. Guangdong Provincial Museum, "Neolithic Sites in Eastern Guangdong", *Kaogu*, 1961:12.
14. Jiangxi Provincial Museum, et al, "Brief Excavation Report of the Zhuweicheng Site in Qingjiang", *Kaogu*, 1976:6.
15. Yang Xiting, et al, "On the Important Discoveries at Hedang Site, Foshan", *Wenwu jikan*, 1981, Vol. III.
16. Guangdong Provincial Museum, "Brief Excavation Report on Shell Mound Site at Zaogang, Nanhai County, Guangdong", *Kaogu*, 1984:3.
17. Yang Hao, et al, "Remains of Wooden Structure above Water at Maogang, Gaoyao County, Guangdong", *Wenwu*, 1983:12.
18. Han Kanxin and Pan Qifeng," Human Bones from Late Neolithic Burials at Hedang, Foshan, Guangdong", *Renleixue xuebao*, Vol. I, No. 1.
19. Guangdong Provincial Museum, "Sites of Primitive Culture in Hainan Island, Guangdong", *Kaogu xuebao*, 1960:2.

廣東青銅器時代概論

徐恒彬

公元前214年秦統一嶺南之前，廣東的社會文化發展到何等程度？這是研究嶺南考古和歷史的學者長期探索的重要課題。隨着考古工作的拓展和深入，發現越來越多的實物資料，證明秦以前廣東經歷過青銅器時代，社會文明達到相當的高度。本文試圖依據考古發現的實物資料，對廣東青銅器時代的歷史文化，進行初步的研討，以求達到拋磚引玉，繁榮學術，增進省港交流的目的。

一、青銅器時代文化發現概述

廣東青銅器時代文化的發現歷史，可以分為開始期和發展期兩個階段：

（一）開始期

從1932年起，到1949年止，這個時期的工作有兩個明顯的特點，一是香港和粵東發現較多，二是從事考古和研究工作的外國傳教士不少，中國學者不多。這一時期，雖然不可避免的帶有那個時代的局限和不足，但對於所取得的科學成果，後人不能不給予應有的重視。

早期發現和研究青銅器時代文化的學者，當首推芬戴禮（Fr. D. Finn, 1886－1936年）。芬氏在1932年於香港仔神學院附近海邊的沙堆中，偶爾發現了青銅器殘片，進而又在南丫島的考古發掘中，發現匕首等青銅器與夔紋（亦稱雙"F"紋）硬陶器共存。在其後發表的研究報告中，芬氏最早定出"青銅器文化"這一概念，論述這一文化的特徵是帶種類繁多的盤曲紋，即所謂雙"F"紋或夔紋的硬陶器。同時很有見地的指出：中原文化和所謂南蠻文化並沒有一個整齊劃一的界限，而南蠻或是華南沿岸的先民在未完全接受中原青銅器文化影響之前，已經不斷模仿北方的文化特徵。

戈斐侶氏（W. Schofield, 1888－1968年）1937年在香港大嶼山石壁遺址發掘出土的青銅斧鑄範，具有重要的意義。這一發現有力的證明廣東地區已經能夠鑄造青銅器。同時發現了地層叠壓關係，首次揭示了新石器時代文化層早於青銅器時代文化層的相對年代關係。

意大利傳教士麥兆良（Fr. R. Maglioni, 1891-1953年）於1936－1939年間，在粵東地區收集到的青銅戈、斧、鈴等器物和銅斧、銅鈴鑄範，擴大了當時青銅器的發現地區和器類。

中國學者從1938年起越來越多地為青銅器時代考古和研究做出貢獻。陳公哲先生在香港東灣、大灣和沙崗背發現青銅斧、鏃、篦刀（銅銳）及鑄造銅斧、魚鈎的鑄範等遺物。陳先生還繼《新安縣志》後，首次在石壁沙崗背發現了"迴紋"石刻，開闊了青銅器文化的探究領域。顧鐵符和饒宗頤先生在粵東地區做了調查研究，記載了今揭西縣河婆鎮南八里建學校掘出銅刀頭、矢鏃、陶碗等文物，同時指出還發現了"鑄造空首銅斧之石模"。饒先生在研究韓江流域史前文化時認為："自吳越至江西、福建、廣東，流衍於台灣，均流行於幾何印紋陶……是為南方型之越族文化"，探討了廣東青銅器文化的族屬問題。

（二）發展期

從1949年10月到現在。其顯著特點為：1.以廣東大陸為中心地區，地域廣闊，遍及全省；2.以中國學者為多，從事田野考古和研究的人員劇增；3.具有廣泛的羣衆性和普及性，多數新發現都是從事工農業生產的羣衆首先發現，然後經由專業人員進行清理或發掘，資料的可靠性和科學性顯著提高；4.作為專題開展研究，擴大了深度和廣度，成果比較顯著。

新中國成立後，極為重視文物考古工作。廣東在1953年就成立了文物管理委員會，1956年2月成立省文物工作隊，同年開始第一次全省文物普查工作，繼而又展開了配合工農業生產建設的廣泛考古調查發掘。從1982年起，又開展第二次文物普查，這次普查的深度和廣度遠遠超過五十年代，今年可以基本完成。

經過三十多年羣衆性和專業性相結合的廣泛深入的工作，在青銅器時代考古方面取得的主要收獲是：

1. 擴大了青銅器的發現範圍

出土青銅器的地區，從過去的香港和粵東地區，擴展到粵中、粵北和粵西地區，目前除海南島沒有發現以外，其它地區均有所發現。出土有信宜龍紋銅盉、惠陽竊曲紋鼎、博羅銅鐘、連平甬鐘和虎鈕錞于等精美和大型的青銅器。

2. 發現越來越多的青銅器時代的墓葬

對青銅器時代的墓葬，六十年代前一直沒有認識，1962年春清遠縣三坑馬頭崗集中出土了二十五件青銅器、完整的勾連雷紋方格紋陶罐和礪石等文物後，才逐步認識這是青銅器時代的墓葬。真正發掘並弄清墓室結構，應該從1972年發現德慶縣馬墟落雁山戰國墓開始，此後逐步揭開了廣東青銅器時代墓葬之謎。初步統計總數達六十座以上，其中多數以青銅器為主要隨葬品，最大的肇慶松山戰國墓隨葬青銅器達百件以上。出土青銅器總數超過七百五十件，由開始期僅發現少量工具和兵器，到現在可依器形和用途分成炊器、容器、樂器、雜器、兵器和工具六大類，不僅大的品類增加，而且工具和兵器本身的種類也顯著增加。

3. 基本弄清了青銅器時代的文化類型和相對年代

開始期發現的夔紋陶遺存，發現越來越多，已達二百處以上。通過發掘和探討，認識到夔紋陶類型的文化，是繼新石器時代的曲尺紋類型的文化之後而出現的青銅器時代文化。夔紋陶類型的文化之後，又出現米字紋類型的文化，目前已發現遺址一百二十處以上。米字紋類型的文化是廣東青銅器時代的晚期文化，除繼續使用和隨葬大量青銅器外，還發現兩件鐵器。夔紋陶類型的文化，上限相當於西周，下限到戰國早期。米字紋陶類型的文化，上限在戰國中期，下限可延續到秦。

除上兩類型的文化之外，還發現了地方性的饒平浮濱類型文化，以原始青瓷和釉陶為特徵，共存有青銅器，分佈地區在粵東一帶，進一步豐富了廣東青銅器時代文化的內涵。這一類型文化的時代大體與夔紋陶類型文化同時。

二、青銅器時代文化類型

歷經半個世紀多的探索、調查、採集和發掘積累了相當豐富的青銅器時代實物資料，使我們對廣東青銅器時代文化的內涵越來越明晰。從現有材料分析，廣東的青銅器時代文化可分為三種類型，即夔紋陶類型、米字紋陶類型和浮濱類型。

（一）夔紋陶類型

夔紋陶器亦稱F紋、雙F紋陶器，由於在共存器物中出土有青銅器，早在五十多年前就被芬戴禮氏定為青銅器時代文化，並認為這類陶器的花紋"和殷周青銅器上的夔紋有很相似的地方"。新中國成立後，經過廣泛的調查和發掘，對夔紋陶類型的青銅文化認識更加深入。（展品69，70，72）

1. 這一類型文化遺存，除海南島和雷州半島尚未發現外，其餘地區均發現有這類遺存，總數已達二百處以上。北部延伸到湖南、江西界境，東部及於福建南部，西北部直達廣西東北部地區。從分佈情況看，這一文化類型的中心當在珠江三角洲及其周圍地區。

2. 夔紋陶類型文化的出現和發展，不僅是"模仿北方的文化特徵"，經過深入調查和發掘，探討了這一類型文化產生和演變的內在聯繫。廣東的幾何印紋陶文化經歷了漫長的發生、發展、鼎盛和衰落過程，跨越了新石器時代、青銅器時代，進入了鐵器時代。青銅器時代的夔紋陶類型文化，是由新石器時代的曲尺紋陶類型的幾何印紋陶文化發展進化而來，是廣東幾何印紋陶的鼎盛時期，印紋水平達到最高峰。

分佈關係和地層關係說明，曲尺紋陶、夔紋陶和米字紋陶往往在同一遺址出現。三者在同一遺址出土的有紫金縣在光頂、曲江縣東華圍等八處；前兩者在同一地區出土的有潮陽縣赤牛山、博羅縣宿崗嶺、曲江縣石峽等二十四處遺址；後兩者在同一遺址出現的有連平縣矮山寨、佛崗縣倉邊嶺等八處；前者和後者同地發現的有龍川縣坑仔里、東莞縣上麥村等十五處遺址。這種現象的存在說明三者之間的連續性和發展關係。其中最具說服力的是在曲江縣石峽遺址發掘的地層堆積關係，夔紋陶類型的文化層土灰黑，土質細鬆，疊壓在曲尺紋陶類型文化層上面，出土夔紋陶片、釉陶片、原始瓷器、少量磨光石器和鉞、矛、匕首、鏃、錐、篾刀等16件青銅器。証實夔紋陶類型的文化是在曲尺紋陶類型文化的基礎上發展而來，在發展過程中，吸收了來自北方的青銅器文化的影響、達到廣東幾何印紋陶文化的鼎盛階段。

這一類型文化的陶器品種增多，造型美觀，流行圜平底器、大型器較多，圈足器較少，常見器類有缶、罐、尊、豆、盂、缽、盤、碗、杯等。陶器的火候雖然一般較高，硬度較大，但也有不少質地鬆軟的器物和夾砂陶器。花紋的變化更為顯著。多是以陽紋為主、陰紋為輔的紋飾，印模雕刻精緻，構圖嚴整，拍印技術高超，花紋清晰、整齊、美觀，給人以浮雕感。夔紋有重鉤、雙頭、圓頭、鉤形、鉤形直身等多種形式，多數拍印規整，少數重疊錯亂。方格紋不論大或小，都均勻整齊劃一。雙線、複線加點方格紋不見了，代之以回字紋、菱形紋。雲雷紋有的方方正正近似回字紋，有的相勾連，有的彎轉流暢。此外，還有籃紋、圓圈紋、重圈紋、旋渦紋、網結紋、繩紋、篦點紋、劃紋和弦紋等延續使用的紋飾。單一花紋極少見，普遍使用組合花紋，是這一類型文化陶器紋飾特點之一。（圖一、1—14）

3. 在清遠、羅定、四會和懷集發現了夔紋陶類型文化的墓葬六座，都是長方形土坑豎穴墓，只有四會烏旦山墓可看出分前後室，前室低於後室15厘米，並在正中挖一長方形底坑埋葬一個大陶罐，墓殘長5.7（前室長1.2、後室殘長4.5）、寬3.5，殘深0.6米。其餘為單室墓，最大的羅定南門垌1號墓，長4、寬2、挖深1.7米，隨葬青銅器百件以上。清遠二號墓底部鋪砂岩碎石。共出土青銅器266件，礪石9件，陶器6件。銅器上的花紋有些與同期陶器上的花紋一致。如清遠縣馬頭崗春秋墓銅甬鐘上的勾連雲雷紋，四會縣大旺農場鳥旦山戰國墓出土銅鐸上的勾連雲雷紋、銅盂上的S紋、羅定縣太平公社南門垌1號戰國墓出土銅矛上的S紋、銅鼎上的雲雷紋等，都能在夔紋陶類型的陶器花紋上找到。與青銅器一起隨葬的還有夔紋陶類型文化的陶器缶和罐，拍印雲雷紋、變體夔紋、蓆紋等。

4. 夔紋陶類型文化遺址中還發現了釉陶和原始青瓷器，粵東和粵北地區發現的較多。筆者在揭陽調查親身採集到夔紋原始青瓷片，胎質灰白厚重，上印夔紋、釉色青灰。曲江馬壩石峽遺址上文化層出土釉陶和原始瓷已佔陶器總數的1.53%。原始瓷器胎質灰白，施青綠或黃綠色釉，有缽、豆、缸等器型，有的為厚胎，先刻劃雲雷紋，然後施釉；有的印方格紋；還有的飾篦點紋、弦紋，雖然已是原始瓷器，但仍然保持同期印紋陶器上的一些花紋裝飾。這時的釉陶和原始瓷儘管數量較少，却代表着新的發展方向，是廣東當時的新技術和新產品。

5. 夔紋陶類型文化的時代，根據墓葬出土青銅器斷代，下限到戰國前期，上限目前仍不甚確切，從新石器時代晚期的河宕遺址出土陶器花紋已向夔紋陶類型陶器花紋過渡這一特點分析，上限可能達到西周初期。

（二）米字紋陶類型

米字紋的準確稱呼應為方格米字紋或方格對角線十字紋，包括方格米字紋、方格十字紋、方格對角線紋、方格十字加點紋、重方格十字紋、雙線方格十字紋等多種形式。米字紋陶器興起後，完全代替了夔紋陶器。米字紋陶類型文化遺址發現有一百二十處以上，不但有青銅器共存，而且在粵北地區發現了兩件鐵器，表明已進入鐵器時代。

1. 米字紋陶類型的文化遺址和墓葬分佈地域比夔紋陶類型文化分佈更廣，雷州半島和海南島地區亦有米字紋陶器出土，墓葬不僅粵西地區發現較多，粵東地區發現也不少。（展品99，100）

2. 米字紋類型的陶器是廣東幾何印紋陶的衰落時期，雖然胎質硬、火候高、扣之有鏗鏘聲與夔紋類型的陶器相同，但製法、紋飾和形制已發生了很大的變化。製法從模製拍印為主，發展為輪製為主，模製拍印為輔。製法的演進不僅引起了幾何印紋的衰退和劃紋的興起，而且使器物的形制也隨之變化。平底器代替了圜底器，甕、罐、缶等大型陶器仍然使用模製法加工和拍印米字、方格等紋飾，盂、碗、盒、杯等小型陶器則多為輪製，飾劃紋和刺點紋。增城縣西瓜嶺窰址出土器物中，印紋仍佔89.89％，劃紋佔10.13％，兩者的組合紋佔0.02％。印紋中最多的是米字紋，達54％，其次是方格紋，佔28.99％，雲雷紋、蓆紋及其組合紋極少。劃紋中絕大多數是水波紋，還有篦紋、條紋及組合紋。釉陶也是一個重要組成部份，有黃褐、灰黑兩種釉色，多為蘸釉，厚而不勻，露胎多，釉淚多。始興縣白石坪山窰址出土的陶器多為輪製，有甕、罐、罍、盂、盆、碗、碟、缽、杯、盒、鼎等器型，印紋降為66.75％，釉陶的數量顯著增加，達到5.7％。印紋中最多的是米字紋，達42.2％，方格紋佔40.9％，雲雷紋僅佔0.73％，米字方格、雲雷方格組合紋分別佔3.23％和0.27％。

3. 米字紋陶類型文化的墓葬發現較多，據不完全的統計在40座以上。分佈於肇慶、羅定、廣寧、揭陽、佛山、四會、龍門、龍川、深圳、湛江等地。隨葬青銅器近五百件、礪石29件、陶器101件、金玉、琉璃等其它器物10件。大件陶器多飾米字紋。墓葬形制有兩種：一為長方形土坑豎穴墓，分單室和雙室兩種。雙室僅德慶落雁山墓，前室長1.15、後室長3.6、寬1.5米，前室低於後室20厘米，正中挖一底坑埋大陶匏壺。廣寧的單室墓底鋪河卵石；一為土坑豎穴木槨墓，無墓道，僅肇慶松山大墓一座。長8、寬4.7、深6米，墓底中間有小腰坑，以棺室為中心分前後室和左右室。

4. 米字紋陶類型文化的時代上限與夔紋陶類型文化相接，下限與秦漢文化相聯，屬於廣東戰國中、晚期文化，時間比較明確。

（三）浮濱類型

是1974年冬新發現的一種青銅器時代文化類型，分佈於粵東地區。同類的釉陶器過去在惠陽、普寧、潮安等地零星發現，難於辨識文化類別。自從在饒平縣浮濱公社橋頭大隊塔仔金山和聯饒公社深塗大隊頂大埔山發現二十一座土坑墓後，才逐漸得到認識。墓的結構分為二類：一類有二層台，一類無二層台，都是長方形土坑墓。最大的長2.6、寬1.08、深1米，最小的長1.2、寬0.6米。墓內的隨葬器物有不同大小的大口長頸圓底小圈足尊、圈足盤、圓底罐、豆、壺、盂、缽等釉陶器、原始青瓷器和陶器。原始青瓷器的胎質灰白，火候較高。釉色多棕褐，釉下印有平行細密的長條紋、方格紋和細繩紋。器物口沿和肩部往往刻劃各種符號，有"王"、"十"、"×"、"‖"、"‖"等字。還隨葬有石錛、石鑿、石戈、石矛、石環、石玦、石璜等石器，磨製均精緻光滑，其中戈、矛的形製已明顯仿銅製兵器。青銅器僅發現一件銅戈，無胡無闌，援部平直微彎，內短，援和內的後部各有一穿，鑄工粗糙，可能屬地方土造。（展品46-52）

對於這類文化的時代認識分歧很大，有的以銅戈和大口尊類為依據定為商代，有的以出土原始青瓷器較多定爲周代，還有的認爲屬於春秋時期。筆者以爲斷定浮濱類型文化的時代，首先要依據它本身的特點，然後還要從它在廣東幾何印紋陶文化發展序列中的地位來考慮，才能比較確切的斷定時代。離開了這些基本點，單從個別器型比較相似與否，不可能把握問題的實質，得出符合歷史實際的結論。從上述觀點出發，有理由認爲浮濱類型的文化應該是廣東青銅器時代的一種地方性文化，中心在饒平周圍地區，文化的特點也主要是地方性的，所以不可能爲商代。它的時代當與夔紋陶類型文化相同，故在遺址中有所交叉。夔紋陶類型的文化遺址中已有較多的釉陶和原始青瓷器，這一情況也可與浮濱類型文化釉陶和原始青瓷器多而相互映。

三、青銅器的特徵

廣東出土青銅器初略統計達八百件以上，其中十分之九以上出自墓葬。根據出土情況和特點，可分爲兩個時期：

第一期從西周起，到戰國早期，即夔紋陶類型文化時期。這一期又分爲前後兩期，前期到春秋中期，後期爲春秋晚期到戰國早期。

前期發現的青銅器不多，僅有三十多件，除饒平縣浮濱一件青銅戈是在墓區採集外，其餘都是在遺址或窖藏中出土，出土最多的是馬壩石峽遺址上層，共發現十六件銅器。

龍紋鎏耳盉 1974年10月在信宜縣松香廠出土，時代屬西周，是目前廣東發現的最早、最精、最重要的青銅器。通高26.2、口徑14.2厘米。造型新穎，形體厚重，花紋繁縟，鑄造精細。盉身似鬲，口沿外侈，流較長，三足分襠。頸中部飾一周帶狀夔紋。肩上有一條斜角雷紋。腹部以襠爲界，每足都由雷紋構成一組饕餮紋，兩組之間各有一條夔龍。蓋和流上飾龍紋，龍頭是立體的。造型和花紋與上海博物館藏龍紋盉相似，所不同的是上博爲半環耳，信宜盉爲鎏耳。鎏耳構造巧妙，由兩個鏤空的夔龍相合而成，兩龍之間以小圓柱相連，上部的小圓柱剛好被盉身特鑄的一條小龍口咬住，體現了匠人的聰明才智，利用了重力原理。（輔助照片五）

雲雷紋甬鐘 1979年7月在惠來縣華湖公社出土。甬長10、身長25、口寬20、壁厚5厘米。鐘體厚重，正反面各有18枚，枚不長。正面上部和鼓部飾三條帶狀折線紋，鉦部、鼓部正中爲四個"王"形雲雷紋，兩側篆部和鼓上均飾雲雷紋。甬不高，上有一環紋。此鐘紋飾獨特，具有濃重的越南地方色彩。時代應不晚於春秋。（圖二）

鐵場甬鐘 博羅縣鐵場公社梅村出土，共三個，鐘體厚重，舞部飾勾連雲雷紋，鑄工粗糙，有不少氣孔，其一通高40、甬高13、口寬22.8厘米。

忠信甬鐘 出土於連平縣忠信公社彭山。甬長13.5、身長36、口寬25.5厘米。甬下端有干，鐘的背面無紋，無鉦篆之間的界線，只有十八個枚，正面鉦篆之間以突起的雙線紋和排列整齊的尖狀小乳釘爲界，亦有十八個枚，鼓中飾三個扁平微突成品字形的乳釘。（展品59）

忠信錞于 與鐘同出。高52.3厘米。形狀上大下小，橫斷面爲橢圓形。頂上原有虎形鈕，出土後散失。頂部鈕座飾斜格雷紋，肩部飾一周勾連雷紋，下飾三角形紋。兩側鼓部飾虺紋，由八條大小不等的虺盤繞成一組花紋。虺頭睜雙眼，身披鱗片，形像生動。口部飾三角紋、勾連雷紋、繩紋。（展品60）

竊曲紋鼎 惠陽縣出土。侈口束頸，腹扁圓，三足似獸蹄狀。腹部飾竊曲紋和三角紋，足上部飾饕餮紋。

兵器和工具等小件青銅發現較多，以石峽上層出土爲主，其特徵爲：

矛 形制大體相近。身作柳葉形，尖鋒部扁平實心，中脊起棱，扁圓，無鼻鈕，有一穿，長11.3厘米。

匕首 器身單薄，形制與香港出土相近，鋒刃薄，中間微起，格部不明顯，把部有一孔。

戈 發現於饒平、海豐等地。海豐戈形制類似商周銅戈，微胡，有欄，直身稍彎，內上有一穿，飾人像紋和勾連雲雷紋。

鉞 叉部爲扇形，斜肩，銎爲長方形，有一周凸棱，銎口裏邊有的留朽木痕跡，兩側正中有明顯的鑄縫，長8.5厘米。

篾刀 形似柳葉，扁薄呈弧形，前端呈三角形尖鋒，尾平，中起脊棱，長8.5厘米。

錐 斷面爲方形，一端漸細成尖，長7.3厘米。

鏃 有圓鋌和扁條形鋌，凸脊，兩葉較窄，斷面呈菱形，鋒銳。另有一獨特形制，中間靠前鋒部份爲凸脊，脊後有血漕直通鋌端，殘長6厘米。

後期由於發現了六座墓葬，而且都是以隨葬青銅器爲主，其中最大的羅定一號墓出土銅器百件以上，比較大的清遠一號墓出土25件，二號墓出土39件，六座墓共計出土青銅器達266件，礪石、陶器等隨葬品僅有十六件。依據形制和用途的不同，可以分爲炊器、容器、樂器、兵器、工具和雜器六大類，以件數而論兵器和工具數量最多。各類器物特點如下：

炊器 主要是鼎，有二種形制，一式體扁圓，下部稍寬，底圜平，壁薄，多數無紋，實足長，足端外撇，斷面呈半圓。二式，斂口，深腹，圜底，三足作馬蹄形，附耳，有蓋。花紋鑄造精美，口下飾二周雲紋組成的帶狀花紋，中間隔一周綯紋，蓋上花紋與鼎身相同，足上飾蟠螭紋。通高20.6、口徑23厘米。

容器 包括水器、酒器、存儲器等。器形有罍、缶、盉、鑒等。

罍　出土於清遠一、二號墓。其一卷平口，圓腹，環耳，小圈足，身飾繁縟的羽狀雲紋、絢紋。高33.6、口徑22.8、腹徑37.6、底徑17.6厘米。其二折沿平口，短頸、鼓腹，矮圈足，肩腹部有對稱的半環耳。器身蟠虺紋和三角紋，腹上部飾四個羽狀紋組成的圓餅紋。高28.2、口徑18.8、腹徑35.6、底徑20厘米。

缶　直口，口下一周凸棱，圓腹，四環耳，圈足，素面無紋。高45、口徑19.2、腹徑38、底徑22厘米。

盉　以羅定一號墓出土爲精，直口、圓肩、圓腹，圜底，鋬耳，半環形把，三馬蹄足，肩腹飾細緻的S紋、絢紋、三角紋，平蓋亦飾S紋，紐上有鏈與把相連。把作龍形，前有雙角和蟠螭紋構成的頭面，中有雙脊，後有捲尾。盉咀爲獸頭形，張口豎耳。咀上飾細雷紋，把上飾S形雲紋。鋬耳由蟠蛇組成。三足上部飾蟠螭紋。通高29、口徑12、通寬29.8厘米。

鑒　直口平沿，腹微鼓，平底，三足脱落，僅留三個乳釘狀接頭，飾細密的蟠虺紋。口徑36.6、底徑21、高14.2厘米。

樂器　主要爲甬鐘，鉦、鐸較少。

鐘　清遠一、二號墓分別出土五、七個。羅定出六個，形制、花紋一致，大小順序基本符合規律，通高分別爲37.5、32.5、27.5、25.9、23.1、19.5厘米。清遠墓則花紋、大小和形制不甚規則，顯係湊合組成。均爲甬鐘。羅定鐘瘦身、長枚，飾勾連雲雷紋，與湖北曾侯乙墓編鐘之一組相同。清遠銅鐘，二號墓出土多與羅定鐘相同，一號墓出土之鐘，器身寬，枚短，較厚重，顯然不同於前二者。（圖九、2）

鉦　清遠墓瘦高，羅定墓矮粗，均厚重，應爲實用器。尺寸分別爲通長35.7、27.2、口徑13.3、14.8厘米。

鐸　長方形短甬，體扁圓而寬短，上飾雷紋和繩索紋。

兵器　有劍、矛、匕首、戈、鏃、戚、鐓等。

劍　分爲長短兩種，一式：劍身短，扁薄，脊較突起，上飾盾形花紋，把的尾端有孔，後附橢圓形玉首。二式：圓首，把上有箍，格呈菱形，鍔刃微收，中脊高起，鋒尖。（圖十、1）

矛　形制和大小變化較大。清遠墓矛尖鋒，凸脊，圓銎。羅定一號墓矛分爲六式，突出的爲一式大矛，長身、寬葉、脊棱突出，方形紐，圓銎，脊兩邊各有一組由斜角雷紋組成的圖案。顏色青綠，上有一層藍色痕跡。通長24.6、葉寬5.1厘米。四式、五式矛上鑄有符號。（圖十、3、4）

匕首　有的與香港、曲江出土形制相似，有的似錐鑿，短刺，刃圓平，把上有環首，中爲方孔，一件上立一象，一件上立一人。（圖十三、4）

戈　發現較少。廣州暹崗出土一件，直援較短，寬胡，欄部四穿，飾雲雷紋。

戚　器身扁長，空鏊作扁圓形，正面飾獸面紋。長11.5、寬6.8厘米。

鏃　薄翼，脊較高，鋌作四棱形，尾尖細。長7、寬1.1厘米。

鐓　圓形，實足。

工具類　主要爲斧、鉞、篾刀等器。

斧　細長，窄刃，兩邊略呈弧形，圓刃，銎爲長方形。清遠二號墓斧長8.8、刃寬3.1厘米。四會墓斧上有"王"字形符號。

鉞　形制與前期相同，銎部有的飾勾連雲雷紋圖案。大者長9.4、小者長8.3厘米。（圖九、1）

篾刀　同於前期，羅定一號墓出土飾"王"字形符號。

雜器類　僅有人首柱形器一種，清遠一號墓和羅定一號墓均有出土，每墓隨葬四件，構造稍異。清遠柱形器，上寬下窄，作長條方形，中空，末端有對穿的榫孔，上端呈胸形，斜肩，頸較高，上爲人首。圓臉，平目合口，鼻寬微扁，額上鯀草葉紋，頭圓突，頂起脊爲髻，圓耳貫孔。高42.5、寬3.6、厚3.2厘米。從柱部中空可看出應裝在木柱上，通過榫來固定。羅定柱形器爲實心，長方形，下部漸收小，有鍥形孔，孔內有插梢。無胸無頸，方頭方面，鼻樑突起，眼、口凹陷，無耳。通長24、頭寬3.5、柱寬2.2厘米。這種結構不同於上一種，用法顯然有區別，是插入孔中起到拴住和裝飾作用的。（圖十三、3、5，展品81，82）

第二期　爲戰國中、晚期，屬於米字紋陶類型文化時期。遺址出土青銅器甚少，主要是墓葬中出土。發現墓葬四十多座，青銅器五百件以上，其中肇慶松山大墓，隨葬青銅器108件，陶器21件，金玉、石、琉璃器10件。大類與第一期後期相同，一些器類增加了新的品種，產生了新的工藝，形制亦有新的變化，現摘要介紹如下：

炊器　除鼎之外，出現銅鍋，見於肇慶大墓。直身，口部有折沿，沿上有一對繩索形半環耳。口徑48、高30厘米。鍋上佈滿黑烟，應爲實用器。鼎的形制也有變化，小型鼎增多，器壁變薄，有馬蹄足、三角形足，蓋上花紋繁縟，飾絢紋和蟠虺紋。其中一件僅高6.9、口徑14.5厘米。（圖三）

容器　增加錯銀銅罍、提梁壺、三足盤、附耳筩等新器形。

錯銀銅罍　口平，沿寬厚，頸稍高，肩緩平，腹圓，平底加圈足，肩部有雙耳，鋪首作鴉頭形。有蓋，上有紐和環。蓋上、口沿、頸部、肩部、腹部和圈足上都有錯銀花紋，花紋由相勾連的鳥紋和雲氣紋組成，輕快流暢，生動活潑，變化多樣。細線爲錯銀，粗線填朱漆色，出土時顏色紅艷。身高22、

口徑14.9、腹徑24、底徑14.8厘米。（圖五，輔助照片七）

提梁壺 肩部有兩個獸頭鋪首耳，上銜鍊和提梁，蓋上有雙環，鍊從環中出。造型美觀，比例勻稱。蓋中飾竊曲紋，提梁上飾羽狀紋，肩上一周蟬形紋，腹部六周蟠虺紋，圈足上有一周絢紋。通高30、口徑7、腹徑19、底徑11厘米。（圖六，展品84）

三足盤 直口直身，有一對獸面鋪首環耳，三足作獸蹄形。器身花紋細緻，以上下相對的勾形羽狀紋為主體組成圖案，羽狀紋內有纖細的S形圓渦紋和三角形渦紋。口徑57、通高10厘米。（圖七，展品85）

附耳筩 形如圓柱式桶，口稍向裏收，底比口和器身稍小。上部附對稱的兩個半圓形耳，附耳中還有貫耳。飾三組帶狀花紋，上中二組由相連的勾連雷紋、S形圓渦紋和柵紋組成，下一組由兩條柵紋組成。耳上飾S形圓渦紋和羽狀紋。口徑42、高46厘米。（圖八，展品86）

樂器 有鐘和鐸。鐘的形制與第一期後期之羅定鐘相同，肇慶大墓之甬鐘，由六個組成，最大的通高56.5、口長25厘米。（圖十一、十二）

兵器 亦是劍、七首、矛、鏃等器形。劍中突出的是肇慶大墓出土的插心劍，圓首，莖作圓柱形，莖上有二道箍，有格，中脊呈褐色，刃部鋒利，顏色較黑，通長71、身長59.5厘米。格上刻鏤花紋，鑲嵌玉石，莖上圓箍也有精細的雷紋。肇慶大墓之鏃形體特殊，出土時聚集在一起，用絲麻類線纏裹，有的鋌部還有連接筒的漆皮。鏃身大，雙翼，中有脊，前鋒尖，翼端銳，有三角形和條形血槽。殘長14、最寬處2.8厘米。矛的形制更加規整，更相似於北方戰國矛的形制，不少矛上有"王"字形符號，有的飾盾形花紋。（圖十，3）

工具 發現了鋤、鎒、靴形鉞、鑷形器等，斧、鉞、篾刀、鑿、削刀等仍然流行。鋤、鎒僅廣寧墓出土，鋤呈瓦狀，鎒為凹字形，應是農業用具。靴形鉞發現於德慶、廣寧等地，形似靴子，有銎。篾刀種類更多，前鋒三角形，後端平，斷面呈"人"字形，一般長5-10厘米。廣寧墓出土幾件前鋒向上翹起成鈎，後半截有繩索捆綁痕跡，應裝木、竹柄。有的後半部飾"王"字形符號。鑷形器僅見於肇慶，出土十二把，正面圓，背面平，器身彎曲，上寬下收成尖刃，銎半圓形，長7.8、寬3.4厘米。雙肩銅錛，作長方形，折肩，寬刃，有弧刃和直刃兩種。弧刃適作錛，直刃既作錛，又可劈削。

雜器 人首柱形器仍然使用，發現難於定名的圓形器和方印形器，出土於四會高地園墓、廣寧墓和肇慶大墓。圓形器頂有紐，內穿圓環；方印形器上部如覆斗狀，有紐和環，下為方柱形。器心都灌鑄鉛塊，保持一定重量。方印形器長寬均為6厘米。以形制和加鉛保持重量而論，疑屬權類。

從以上器形和紋飾分析，廣東出土的青銅器有四種值得注意的情況：

1. 與中原地區出土的同類器物完全相同，如清遠墓的兩件銅罍，羅定墓出土的銅盉等。

2. 與長江流域地區出土的同類器物相似，如鼎，分為折沿直口、盤口半環耳、斂口附耳等式，三實足細長外撇，耳飾雲雷紋、絢紋和繩紋，壁甚薄。這類鼎在江蘇、江西、湖南等地均有出土。各式劍與嶺北流行的式樣一致。

特別值得注意的是廣東出土青銅器與楚國的青銅器關係尤為密切。肇慶墓出土的錯銀銅罍、銅提梁壺、三足盤，四會墓的銅盉，羅定墓的銅鑒、銅鼎、銅缶，以及連平出土的錞于等，形制、花紋和製法都與楚地出土的青銅器一樣。如肇慶錯銀銅罍，花紋由相勾連的鳥紋和雲氣紋組成，生動流暢，工藝精緻，是楚國的典型作品；同墓出土的大銅鼎、銅劍與長沙楚墓出土的完全一樣。廣東喜用鐘，大中型墓葬內均有鐘隨葬，羅定、肇慶等墓出土的銅鐘，甬高、身瘦、枚長，形制和花紋都與湖北隨縣曾侯乙墓的編鐘一致，而與其它地區不同，雖然其中不少是本地鑄造，但明顯是仿楚式鐘。

3. 與廣西、雲南、貴州等西南地區有一定聯繫。青銅器中的靴形鉞和戚二種，楚地少見，多見於滇、桂、黔。還有肇慶墓的附耳筩，直筒、雙附耳，飾上中下三組帶狀花紋，中上二組由相勾連的雷紋、S形圓渦紋和柵紋組成，下一組由兩條柵紋組成。這是廣西等地的典型器物，與銅鼓文化有着共存關係。

4. 地方特色明顯的青銅器也不少，其中比較突出的器形有人首柱形器、雙肩銅錛、人形把七首、扇形鉞、圓形、方形器等。

此外還有盤口鼎、篾刀、大型矛、大型鏃等器型，均有明顯地方特點，不一一贅述。

廣東青銅器的重要特點之一，是以王字形紋為標記。以王字形紋為標記的青銅器，主要有矛、篾刀和斧。矛的形制與戰國流行的矛形制相似，但在圓銎部份鑄一雙線王字形紋飾記號。篾刀，前端尖翹，兩側有刃，背面隆起，後端平直，多數起脊，橫剖面呈人字形，其中一部份尖翹成鈎，廣寧出土不少留有麻匹綁扎的痕跡，後部應綁有竹木柄，顯然是編織使用的工具，多在背上或裏面鑄雙線王字形紋記號。斧，一般是長身斧上飾王字形符號，扇形鉞上多飾變形雲雷紋圖案花紋。王字形紋青銅器除在廣東德慶、肇慶、四會、廣寧、羅定等出土外，在廣西、湖南、江西、江蘇等省亦有發現。

與王字形紋同出的青銅器上還有工字形紋飾記號，亦屬於廣東使用的標記之一，不過數量少，只見於矛上，疑為王字形紋的簡略。

從湖南長沙出土之"越王"銅矛和邵陽出土的"王"字形矛可以看出，這類"王"字形標記應起源於越國,由鳥篆簡化而來,越國被楚滅亡後仍然流行於廣東地區。

四、青銅器冶鑄技術

為了進一步了解廣東地區的青銅文化,探討廣東地區先秦時期的青銅冶鑄生產,在合金成份和加工工藝上有那些特點,由廣東省博物館、中國科學院自然科學史研究所華覺明、哈爾濱科技大學黃渭馨、王秀蘭合作,選取春秋戰國時期的青銅器共38件,進行冶鑄技術的檢測研究。在所選標本中計有金屬錠1件、工具類14件、兵器類14件、容器類4件、樂器類3件、人首柱形器2件,除博羅縣出土銅甬鐘為春秋時期外,其餘均屬戰國時期。根據多種手段的分析測定,使我們確知廣東青銅器的冶鑄技術已達到相當的水平。

(一)青銅器的鑄造工藝
廣東境內目前尚未發現青銅時代的鑄銅遺址,但海豐縣和香港曾出有早期的石範和陶質魚鈎範與斧範。依據器物形制、鑄造遺痕並和其他地區所出同類器物及鑄範等冶鑄遺存相比較,可以判斷各類器件的鑄造工藝。大體分為以下幾種型式:

1.單面範(有芯)
如鏵出自四會鳥旦山,釜部厚度約1.6毫米,中空部份由泥芯形成。鑄範應是用實物或泥質模具翻出的,然後經陰乾和焙燒,再糊以草楷泥,待乾,即可供澆注。泥芯可即用鑄範翻製,經修削,開設澆口,和鑄範相配。兩扇鑄範中的一扇為平板範,另一扇有範腔,形成器形及紋飾。分型面上設有榫卯,使範配合嚴密。

2.雙面範(無芯)
如鏃範,廣寧銅鼓崗所出銅鏃,鋌部側面中線處有鑄縫,係用雙面範鑄成。羅定等地出銅鏃多件,形制相似又能採取一範多鑄的鏃範鑄造。
又如劍範,內澆口是開設在劍把側面,斷茬呈扁圓狀,長約1厘米,寬0.4厘米,合範處鑄縫也很明顯。在劍首頂端還開設有出氣口,澆注時,型腔內氣體得由此逸出。採用頂澆,目的在於保證劍鋒澆鑄完整。

3.雙面範(無芯,不平分型面)
篾刀的形制較為特殊,形似柳葉,前端為三角形銳鋒,尾平,中有脊棱。鑄範依據刀的形狀,採用不平分型面。

4.雙面範(有芯)
如鉞,兩扇鑄範均開設型腔,鑄後於合範處有明顯鑄縫,如羅定所出銅鉞兩側鑄縫均未磨去,清晰可見,花紋是一起鑄出的。為保證銅液能順利澆入和提高壓頭,這類鑄範在澆注時都應加設澆口範,其它如斧、鋤、矛等帶銎叉器都採取這種鑄法。
又如人首柱形器,側面有鑄縫並略有錯位,梢孔是由型芯形成的。

5.複合範(渾鑄法)
如博羅所出春秋時期的甬鐘,通高39厘米,甬高12.8厘米,銑長26.8厘米,銑間22.6厘米,鼓間17.2厘米,壁厚0.7-1.1厘米,鉦部以小乳釘排列成界劃,枚較尖長,舞部有勾連雲雷紋。甬短,中空,和鐘腔相通,表現出一定的原始性。它的鑄型應從甬端側面中線處至兩欒有連續的鑄縫,表明鑄型是由兩片鐘範和兩件泥芯(鐘體泥芯直通甬端,甬部鐘鈎另設泥芯)組成,枚和乳丁則是在範面上加工而成。這是中原地區早期甬鐘的通行做法,鐘的鼓部和底緣頗多氣孔和縮孔,銅水顯然是由鐘的底緣澆入的(倒澆)。這也是中原地區早期甬鐘的通行做法。就鐘的主要尺度比值來說,銑間與銑長之比為0.84,鼓間與銑長之比為0.64,和《考工記》所載鐘制:"十分其銑,去二以為鉦,以其鉦為銑間,去二分以為之鼓間"(即二種比值分別為0.8和0.6)基本一致,干的弧度較平,和河南淅川下寺春秋晚期楚墓所出編鐘略近。
羅定出土的戰國早期編鐘(甬鐘)共6件,其中1、2、4鐘各36個枚,3、5、6鐘各24個枚,看來原先不屬於同一組。但各鐘的尺度遞變率大體符合規範,其通高依次為37.5、32.5、27.5、25.9、23.1、19.5厘米,相鄰鐘的遞變率為1.15、1.18、1.06、1.12、1.18。鐘體一面有鉦部界劃和鼓部勾連雷紋,另一面只有枚而無界劃和紋飾,舞部和甬部均素面,於鉦部上緣和舞部有透空的窄縫,壁內相應部位為凹入的槽孔。鐘的形體窄長,例如1號鐘銑長為25.8,銑間為15.8,鼓間為11厘米,銑間與銑長的比值為0.6,鼓間與銑長之比為0.4,和《考工記》所載鐘制有較大的差別。鐘下緣壁厚均勻(約4毫米),無音脣結構,有些鐘內的泥芯尚未去除。據此可知,鐘應是明器,鑄作較為簡率,鑄造工藝和通常做法大體相同,但為便於裝配泥芯,採用了自帶泥質芯撐,鑄後在鉦部、舞部形成透空窄縫(不是原先認為的調音孔),這種工藝措施一般都用於紐鐘,在甬鐘上施用是第一次發現,具有地區特點。
肇慶所出戰國晚期的一組六枚甬鐘,舞部、鉦部也有透空窄縫,鼓部也有一面有粗率花紋,鐘體下緣壁厚均勻(4毫米),無音脣結構,甬中空,鐘腔相通,但因泥芯有裂縫,銅水滲入,鑄後並未全部清除。這些情況和羅定編鐘類似,看來也是作為明器使用的。(展品83)

6.複合範(分鑄法——鑄接)
如廣寧所出戰國晚期銅鼎(M13:1),斂口,侈腹，三實足較長而外撇，鼎腹有兩條鑄縫，其中一條與一足對應自口沿延至足端，另一條在另二足間與鼎底圓形鑄縫相交，鼎體厚約2毫米，附耳厚僅1毫米，內有泥芯。據此可知，鼎的鑄型由腹範兩塊，頂範一塊和鼎體泥芯與底範組成。附耳先鑄，去除部份泥芯放入腹範內，在澆注鼎體時鑄接成一體，故耳的周圍有銅水包覆的痕跡並能搖動。（展品87）又如羅定所出戰國早期銅鼎（M1：1），斂口，深腹，馬蹄形足，有蓋，分飾雲紋，絢紋和蟠螭紋。出土時已殘，器底中心有圓形鑄縫，中有長75毫米，寬2毫米的澆口殘茬，器腹有等分的三條鑄縫相接，鼎足內有泥芯，外表面有對開的兩條鑄縫，鼎足和鼎腹相接處可見有從外包覆的銅水痕跡，鼎體和耳、足都是分別鑄造的。鼎體鑄型由腹範三塊、頂範（帶澆口）一塊、泥芯與底座組成。鼎足和鼎耳均先鑄，再在澆注鼎體時與之鑄接。

羅定出土的銅盉（M1：7）是戰國青銅器中的精品，盉體和獸形流口、龍形提梁、鋬耳及盉蓋滿飾精細的三角紋、雲紋、絢紋、龍紋、雷紋和蟠螭紋。盉體渾鑄，盉足，流口，提梁，鋬耳和蓋均分鑄再鑄接。其中如提梁包括龍尾均中空，內腔由泥芯形成，由龍角等處鑄縫殘跡可知鑄型用三件鑄範組成。流口花紋精美，有明顯的刻鏤痕跡，鑄後曾經過細緻的加工。鋬耳也是鑄接的，在盉內壁相應部位有凸棱以保證該處有較大壁厚，使接鑄較為牢靠。盉蓋上的鏈，質輕、似由鉛錫合金製作，一端伸入提梁內使之連接。盉足底部有圓孔，是鑄造時用來支撐泥芯的，足與盉體相接處也有銅水由外包覆的痕跡。足的上端正面飾以蟠螭紋，兩側有鑄縫，可見紋飾單用一塊分範形成。

7. 複合範（分鑄法——焊接）
如羅定所出銅鑒，上口直徑約35厘米，自口沿至器底約高13厘米，腹部有兩條對應的鑄縫，在鑄縫中段有縱向排列的兩個凸榫，鑒底也鑄出三個榫。據此可見，鑒腹是用對開的鑄型澆注的，兩附耳和三鑒足均分鑄，然後分別用鉛錫合金焊於預鑄的凸榫部位。由於年代久遠，焊接合金氧化銹蝕，導致耳、足脫落。（展品88）

（二）青銅器的合金成份
根據試樣的不同情況，採用化學定量，光譜，原子吸收光譜和微能分析等方法，測定了34件青銅器的化學成份，對所有試樣都作了金相檢驗，其中32件測定了硬度或顯微硬度。

1. 合金分類
從所測結果可看出，這些青銅器除了含有多種雜質外，主要成分是銅、錫和鉛。另外，在若干件青銅器中發現了磷和砷。據此，分為三類：

錫青銅：合金中僅含少量的鉛，如性能要求較高的劍即屬於此類。

銅錫鉛三元合金：合金中除銅、錫兩種主要元素外，還含有數量甚多的鉛，如小鑒含鉛量高達19%。鉛在合金中呈條、塊或網狀。

含有特殊元素的銅錫鉛合金：在若干青銅器中含有一定量的磷，有的還發現有大量的鉍和砷。

2. 合金成份的配比
各類青銅器按其功能在成份配比上有其特點，按鐘、鼎、武器、生活用具、工具和其它分作五類，各類青銅器合金配比是合理的，其趨向大體是：

鐘鼎類，含錫量及含鉛量均較高，錫一般在13—16%之間。選用這種成份能使鐘色澤悅目，紋飾清晰。

武器類，包括劍、鏃、鈹、矛等，在性能上不僅要求鋒利，而且要堅韌，含錫量為12—22%左右，含鉛甚少，基本上在2%以內。

由此可知，各類青銅器是按照使用及工藝的要求而有適宜的錫、鉛配比範圍，從而在性能上表現了一定的規律性。隨着含錫量增加，硬度增高，而鉛之加入量愈多，則硬度相應降低。

有些青銅器的硬度值與相近成分的其它器件差別甚大，我們對此進行了金相組織觀察及其它測試，得知除部分器件含有較高的錫外，其它青銅器硬度偏高的原因是由於金相組織與一般狀態不同，或者含有一般青銅器所沒有的元素如磷、砷等。

（三）鑄後加工及熱處理工藝
金相檢測表明，38件青銅器均為鑄件，除一般鑄態枝晶組織外，還發現其它組織形態，顯然鑄後還經過加工，以滿足成形及性能之需要。如鈹的鑄後加工硬化、斧的退火處理、表面處理及激冷處理等。

1. 加工硬化
羅定太平公社一號墓出土的青銅鈹，成分為Sn 13.9%，Pb 5.2%，Zn 0.1%，但與同樣含錫量的其它兵器相比，硬度高出許多，化學分析未見特殊元素存在，金相顯微組織存在明顯的方向性，鑄端枝晶細小，有明顯的扭轉變形與扭斷現象，與通常見到的鑄態枝晶顯然不同。說明銅鈹表面黑色及藍色加熱痕跡，是鑄造成形後經過加工、硬化形成的。

2. 熱處理、退火工藝
斧的成份（Sn 14.4%，10.96%）與鼎含錫量相近（15.2%），但金相觀察表明其組織不同。從試樣外觀有明顯的經過加熱的色澤，可以判斷，該斧在鑄後經過反覆加熱鍛打，從而獲得充分退火的條件，所以形成∝單相組織。

3. 表面處理

戰國的劍、鈹、矛和鏃等，它們的表面出現一層深綠色的保護層，光亮而不銹蝕。經檢測劍的表層硬度值比深層高。對羅定太平公社出土的青銅鏃作了金相、能譜與硬度分析，從金相圖上可見其表面與心部有明顯交界面，能譜分析說明表面被覆層含有較高的鉻，而心部則不含鉻。

4. 篾刀的激冷處理

篾刀含錫量為19.5%，但與其組織和成分相近的鏃（Sn 18%）完全不同。篾刀有明顯的針狀析出物，具有激冷處理的特徵。

從以上對春秋戰國時期青銅器鑄造工藝的分析來看，壁形簡單的生產工具、兵器等多用單面範和雙面範，具有複雜形狀的容器和樂器用複合範。除尚未發現失蠟鑄件外，幾乎所有該時期的鑄造方法，如渾鑄、分鑄法中的鑄接和焊接都已使用，雖然有些器物形制、紋飾有地區特點，工藝方法都是和中原地區一致的。用以盛水的鑒，一般不需經受很高溫度，足分鑄焊接。鼎用於炊事，常需加溫，如採用焊接的足，在較高溫度下，低熔點合金將熔化，導致足脫落，因而採用鑄接的足或實足。前述羅定、廣寧所出銅鼎是用鑄接的鼎足，廣寧第16號墓出的一件鼎則用實足，鼎底有烟炱，顯係實用器，它的底部厚度僅1毫米，口沿也只2毫米厚，顯示了相當高的冶鑄技術水平。

巴納（N. Barnard）曾對南丫島深灣C層所出小型青銅器作了金相分析，發現於鑄態組織中有帶孿晶的純銅晶粒。同樣的現象也發現於殷墟銅器。這表明本地區所出某些早期青銅器年代雖較殷商為晚，在熔煉技術上却和殷商時期有類似之處，表現出一定的原始性。

合金成份的配製也和中原地區一樣，對錫、鉛成份與器件性能的關係已有明確的認識。這在銅劍的製作上表現得更為突出。值得注意的是複合範的使用，肇慶插心劍的劍脊和劍刃用不同含錫量的青銅分別鑄造（先鑄劍脊再接鑄劍刃），劍脊含錫量低，色黃，刃部含錫量較高，發白，利用合金成分不同從而機械性能也不同的這一特性，使劍刃堅利，易於磨銳，劍脊柔靱，能耐碰擊，達到剛柔兼備的性能要求，就是《荀子》所說的：“白者所以為堅也，黃者所以為靱也，黃白相雜則堅則靱，良劍也。”這種劍過去多出於中原地區（如著名的少虞劍）和江西等地，在嶺南地區還是首次發現。

銅錫鉛三元合金的多量使用也是衡量青銅冶鑄技術發展的一個重要標誌。銅、錫、鉛三元合金在小屯時期已經少量出現，到春秋戰國時期成為銅器合金配製的主流。從廣東出土戰國青銅器的合金成分看，屬於三元合金的有7件，約佔檢測總數的25%，可見在合金配製技術上同樣已早脫離初始的發展階段而和中原地區相接近了。

在鑄後加工方面，關於青銅刃具鍛造、熱處理工藝的鑒定與確認具有重要的意義。曾經有一種意見認為中國在先秦時期只懂得鑄造，鍛造技術很不發達，甚至有認為中國到漢代才有退火工藝的。實際的情況是，先秦青銅器的製作雖以鑄造成型為主，但對於工具、兵器等刃具來說，為了提高其硬度常需進行冷作，在使用了一段時間後，鋒刃變鈍，又需鍛打修整，在這過程中為消除加工硬化現象以利再鍛，就得進行退火處理。唐蘭、郭寶鈞等徵引《詩經》所說：“鍛乃戈矛”、“取厲取鍛”等，早就明確提出了這一點。但過去所作實物檢驗較少，有時僅憑對戈戟表面觀察，科學根據似覺不夠充分。而在這次廣東出土青銅器的檢驗中，發現多件刃具經過鍛打、退火以至激冷處理。這就確鑿地證明，先秦時期對刃具的鑄後加工和熱處理是一種普遍實行的工藝措施並具有多種工藝型式，從而提高了工具和兵器的使用效能，促進了生產發展。特別是青銅篾刀，主要用來修削竹篾，要求堅硬銳利，採用高錫青銅鑄造。但很高的含錫量又使鋒刃十分脆硬，極易崩刃甚至折斷，經過激冷處理，可以提高靱性，有利於改善使用性能。這種組織在先秦青銅器中目前尚為首次發現，是值得引起重視的。關於青銅刃具的表面鉻化處理，北京鋼鐵學院和成都科技大學田長滸曾先後發現箭鏃表層有鉻，這次在廣東青銅器中又一次發現了這類實例，說明這類器件並非偶然出現，應是有意識予以處理而形成的，其形成機理及功能目的則尚得進一步探討。

廣東省具有良好的發展青銅冶鑄的自然條件，粵西、粵北和粵東地區都有豐富的銅礦和錫礦資源。陽春縣崗美公社有錠和戰國青銅鉞同出。它的全長約20.6厘米，寬6.2厘米，呈不規則的長方型，兩端略圓，一面的表層有許多氣孔，較平，另一面略成弧形，截面最厚處約為15毫米，未見澆口遺跡，說明是從煉爐中排出，在砂床中凝固成形的。人首柱形器在春秋時期已經出現，可以認為廣東地區在該時期以前已有自己的青銅鑄造生產。銅錠出土地點距石綠銅礦不遠，該礦區至今仍在開採。據此認為，銅錠在本地所產，和戰國銅斧屬於同一時期，如果這個判斷是正確的話，那麼，本地區至遲在戰國晚期已能自行採銅和煉銅了。冶銅技術和製陶有密切的關係，廣東地區在新石器時代盛行幾何印紋陶，商周時期燒製的印紋硬陶，硬度高，燒成溫度達1000°C以上，這就為青銅冶鑄業的發展提供了必需的高溫技術以及造型材料製備和陶範製作的技術。早期石範和陶範已在香港和海豐發現，而盤口鼎的製作說明複合陶範也已使用。可見青銅器除少數來自北方外，大部分應是本地鑄造的。（展品91）

嶺南地區自古以來就和中原地區相通。從以上有關青銅器形制及冶鑄技術的研究來看，它的青銅冶鑄業是直接在中原地區特別是楚文化的影响下建立起來的，同時又和西南少數民族地區存在一定的聯繫。某些器物的形制、花紋以至工藝處理雖然有地區特色，其技術路線和工藝形式則和中原地區和楚文化相一致，作爲商周青銅文化之一分支，其統一性是高於地區性的。

五、青銅器時代廣東社會狀況

對於青銅器時代廣東的社會情況我們知道的還不多，僅據考古資料和稀少的文獻記載了解其部分風貌。

（一）廣東人的形像和習俗

1. 人物形像

社會是由人組成的，青銅器時代廣東人是什麼樣子？這是頗爲令人感興趣的問題。從已發現的實物資料中，可看到以下四種人物面貌：

（1）海豐人

見於《廣東考古發現》第95頁銅戈照片上。戈的援部微彎，內部近直，中下一圓孔，上部飾人物圖像。人是正面形像，頭圓身瘦，手和脚分向兩邊，突出的特點是頭頂上豎立兩支長羽毛，羽毛分向兩邊。（圖十三、1，展品53）

（2）香港和曲江人

飾於銅匕首上的兩個人頭圖像，雖然分別發現於香港石壁和曲江縣石峽兩地，但人物頭像完全相同。圓臉，大眼，小鼻，開口，頭頂飾分向左右的兩個雲雷紋式的髮髻。從海豐銅戈人物頭飾的長羽毛，可以證明"雲雷紋式的髮髻"是從羽毛演變而來。（圖十三、2，展品61）

（3）清遠人

一爲人首銅柱上的人，一爲銅匕首上的人。

銅柱上的人圓臉，深目，寬鼻，閉口，大耳貫孔，額上綴草葉狀紋，頭頂凸脊，既表示髮髻，也可爲鑄孔。（圖十三、3）

匕首上的人像爲一裸體人，臉圓，可看出眼、鼻、口，雙手叉腰，雙足分立，從胸腹部構造觀察似女像。（圖十三、4）

（4）羅定、四會、廣寧人

均爲人首柱上面的頭像。羅定人頭近方，臉扁圓，眼和口均較寬，鼻垂直，沒飾髮式。四會和廣寧人頭圓，猴面，尖嘴，深目，矮鼻。（圖十三、5）

在這四種人中，海豐人最早，以戈的形制斷代當爲西周，其次爲香港和曲江人，出土於春秋遺址，時代最遲的是羅定、四會和廣寧人，屬於戰國時期。關於這些人的族屬問題，依《漢書·地理志》記載："自交趾以至會稽，七八千里，百越雜處，各有種姓"，秦漢之前，廣東人屬於"百越"的一支，習稱南越，故廣東人當時的族屬爲南越族。

2. 生活習俗

依據文獻和考古資料，大致能看出居住在廣東的南越人有以下一些風俗習慣：

（1）斷髮紋身

《墨子》、《韓非子》、《戰國策》等戰國時的文獻多統稱越人"劗髮紋身"、"斷髮紋身"，漢代的《史記》等書也有同類記載。其中主要談廣東的是《淮南子》一書，其《原道訓》云："九疑之南，陸事寡而水事衆，於是人民被髮紋身，以像鱗蟲，短綣不絝，以便涉游，短袂攘卷，以便刺舟，因之也。"九疑山在湖南蘭山縣西南，靠近南嶺，"九疑之南"無疑是指廣東及其以南地區，這些地區也有"被髮紋身"習俗。漢高誘在注中指出："被翦也，紋身，刻畫其體內，點其中，爲蛟龍之狀，以入水，蛟龍不傷也。"翦與剪通，"被髮"即是"斷髮"。"紋身"是一種圖騰祖先崇拜，有的刻畫呈"蛟龍之狀"，有的是其它紋祥，視不同部落而定，並非各處都一樣。海南島黎族紋身，是爲了死後能被祖先認出，使自己能回到祖先的懷抱，同高誘所注基本一致。

（2）契臂

《淮南子·齊俗訓》曰："故胡人彈骨，越人契臂，中國歃血，所由各異，其於信一也。"契，高誘注爲"刻臂出血"，係刻臂而表示信約或盟誓的風俗，流行於廣東等越地。

（3）喜食魚蛇蛤蚌螺

最早見於《逸周書·王會解》，越人喜"海蛤"、"蟬蛇"、"文蜃"、"玄貝"等。《淮南子·精神訓》說："越人得髯蛇以爲上肴，中國得而棄之，無用"。《鹽鐵論·論菑篇》云："蓋越人美蠃蚌"。廣東人嗜食蚌、蛤、螺、蛇之風實可追溯到新石器時代，嶺南發現大批貝丘遺址，蛤、蚌、蜆、螺、龜、鱉殼甲和魚骨堆積成丘，此風一直延續至今，本地人仍然喜歡吃這些東西，並譽爲美味佳肴。正如張華在《博物志》中所說："東南之人食水產……食水產者，龜、蛤、螺、蚌以爲珍味，不覺其腥臊也。"因爲北方人視吃蛇、蛤、蜆等爲奇聞，故多見於文字記載，而對廣東的南越人嗜魚較他處爲盛，則較少記載。

（4）多住"干欄式"房屋

張華《博物志》云："南越巢居，北溯穴居，避寒暑也"，沈懷遠《南越志》說南越"栅居"都是"干欄式"房屋，即建在樹木或立柱上的房屋，上邊住人，下邊養牲畜。這種房子到漢以後依然通行，出土的陶屋模型中經常見到的是這種"干欄式"房屋。考古發現材料證明，粵北崗丘遺址有建在地面上的房子，珠江三角洲地區的貝丘遺址也有地面燒過的普通房屋，不全是"干欄式"房屋。"干欄式"木構建築遺址在高要縣茅岡發現，用較粗的木頭爲柱，柱之間有榫孔以橫木聯結，上面建房屋，房下臨水，屬於水上建築遺址。這些房屋遺跡均屬新石器時代晚期或稍遲一些，距今約四千年左右。

(5) 信鬼雞卜

《史記‧孝武本紀、封禪書》和《漢書‧郊祀志》中，均有南越族人"俗信鬼"、"而以雞卜"的記載。南越人祠鬼和雞卜皆由越巫掌管，巫師在南越社會中佔有相當重要的地位，雞卜沿用的時間相當長，黎族一直到解放前還完整地保留着。

(6) "以孔雀珥門戶"

僅見於《鹽鐵論》一書，似在門戶上飾孔雀式珥，為南越風俗特點之一。

3. 神秘的石刻藝術

廣東青銅器時代常見的是青銅器、陶器和玉石器等類的工藝美術品，脫離工藝品的藝術品目前僅見浮雕石刻一種。這些青銅器時代的石刻藝術品集中發現於香港地區，據云珠海市的島嶼上也有發現。

最早記載石刻的文獻是1819年的《新安縣志》。繼1939年陳公哲先生在石壁沙崗背發現"迴文石刻"之後，發現越來越多。僅據秦維廉著《香港古石刻》一書的記載，就有石壁、蒲台、東龍、大浪灣、長洲、大廟灣、滘西洲等處。

香港古代石刻充滿了神秘色彩，十分令人費解。經過香港學者的長期調查和研究，取得了重要成果，其中基本一致的看法是：

(1) 石刻的時代應屬於青銅器時代。
(2) 石刻花紋多數與廣東青銅器時代陶器上的花紋、特別是青銅器上的花紋一致。
(3) 石刻的起源和形成，顯然與當時的風俗習慣有關，包含着今天我們難於理解的意義。

從已見到的資料看，石刻都是浮雕刻成，花紋與陶器、青銅器上的紋飾一致，都是圖案性的花紋，不是寫實性的圖畫。花紋分為三種：一為動物形的花紋，數量較少，其中明顯的有東龍的鳥紋、蒲台和長洲的蛇紋等；一為單純的圖案花紋，數量較多，在青銅器上多數都可以找到同樣的紋飾。如：下石壁石刻屬於典型的雲雷紋，上石壁石刻則是標準的方格米字紋，蒲台的圖案花紋與銅矛、銅鐘上的花紋一致，滘西洲石刻與銅矛上的部分符號花紋一致。還有一種是動物形花紋與單純的圖案花紋相結合的花紋，如大浪灣石刻，有的似蛇頭、有的是雲雷紋，有的難於識別。以筆者所見，上述三種花紋除東龍的鳥紋之外，均見於廣東出土的青銅器或陶器。大浪灣石刻中間的蛇頭，與惠來縣出土的銅鐘上的雲雷紋、"王"字形紋相似，其實質應與雲雷紋有密切關係。東龍鳥紋的出現並非偶然，從海豐銅戈人圖象上的羽毛和香港、曲江匕首人頭像上的雲雷紋羽毛可以得到啟示，雲雷紋的起源有可能來自鳥的羽毛，人頭上插羽毛是當時流行的風俗。為什麼要插羽毛？一可能是表示對鳥的崇拜，屬於圖騰制度的一種遺俗，一可能是一種成人禮儀的遺俗，標誌着人的成丁或成年。由此可見，鳥紋、蛇紋、雲雷紋和羽毛頭飾之間存在着深刻的聯繫，需要我們進一步探索。

(二) 廣東的階級關係

商周青銅器達到兩廣，進而傳來青銅鑄造技術，至遲在春秋時期嶺南地區已能鑄造青銅器。青銅器的鑄造和使用，大大提高了生產力水平，推動南越的社會發展，產生了奴隸制度。有關廣東存在奴隸制的最早材料，是清遠縣馬頭崗發現的春秋末至戰國初期的兩座墓葬。這兩座墓葬的規模比較大，可惜遭到破壞，形制已無法了解。隨葬器物計有罍、編鐘、鉦、矛、斧、鉞、匕首、鏃、鑿、人首柱形器、篾刀等青銅器64件，還有夔紋方格紋和方格紋篦紋陶罐及礪石等。鑄造精美的銅罍、成套的銅編鐘、較多的兵器及銅鉦等器物，表明墓主人絕非普通人，而是奴隸主貴族。奴隸制的存在，從該墓隨葬的人首銅柱形器上得到進一步證明。人首的雙耳穿孔可貫，額中鯨刻↓形記號，顯然塑造了奴隸的形象。《左傳》載：楚子將圍宋，使子玉復治兵，"終日而畢，鞭七人，貫三人耳。"《史記‧孫子吳起列傳》載：魏龐涓"恐孫臏賢於己，疾之，則以法刑斷其兩足而鯨之。"貫耳和鯨首是戰國時的刑法，說明南越的奴隸制度已比家長奴隸制進了一大步，管理奴隸和罪人已有一定的刑法和制度。《淮南子‧齊俗訓》指出："胡人便於馬，越人便於舟"，因此這種人首柱形器為車飾的可能性不大，同雲南石寨山的杖頭飾用法也不同。 應用奴隸形象為人首柱形器，只有掌握一定權威的奴隸主才能享用，因而說明這些墓的主人身份應是奴隸主貴族。其它墓出的人首柱形器雖無鯨首貫耳，但形象醜陋，也是奴隸制思想意識的反映。

奴隸的來源主要來自掠奪戰爭。《漢書‧高帝紀》說："越人之俗，好相攻擊"，南越內部及其與西甌、駱越、閩越之間，經常進行械鬥和戰爭。春秋之後，楚國"鎮爾南方夷越之亂"，"南平百越"，與南越多次發生戰爭。戰國時的南越墓葬，極其重視隨葬銅兵器，多數墓內都有銅劍，一般是兩把，楚越式大劍和短劍，還有矛、鏃等成套搭配隨葬。廣寧以隨葬銅劍為中心的小型墓葬羣，埋葬集中，兵器配置有規律，很可能是駐軍的葬地。不少墓中還有銅工具葬，說明軍隊並沒有完全脫離生產。《漢書‧地理志》云："吳越之君皆好勇，故其民至今好劍，輕死易發"戰國時廣東的南越也是這種情況。喜歡用劍，故死後普遍隨葬。《淮南子‧說山訓》記載了一個諷刺越人不曉射箭的笑話，說越人射遠反向天上發矢，結果只能落在五步之內。《漢書‧嚴助傳》淮南王上武帝書也說：越人"不能陸戰，又無車騎弓弩之用"。考古發現的材料證明，廣東的南越族使用弓箭是極為普遍的，遠在新石器時代就大量製造和使用石箭鏃，春秋戰國時期，舉凡隨葬銅兵器的墓葬，幾乎都有銅鏃伴隨出土。《史記·越王勾踐世家》說：楚威王大破越，"而越以此散，諸族子爭立，或為王，或為君，濱於江南海上，服朝於楚。"並不是說"江南海上"原來沒有人，越散之後才有越人。由於閩越、南越、西甌、駱越等地原來的土著，已經發展了較高的文化，所以"諸族子"，即越國貴族，才有基礎散於各處"為王"、"為君"。南越等地在戰國時已經建立小的王國或君國，故賈誼在《過秦論》中談到秦統一嶺南時指出："百越之君俛首係頸"。《淮南子·人間訓》記載，西甌有君名譯吁宋，被秦軍殺死後，西甌人又"相置桀駿為將"。當時南越的情況與西甌的情況應是差不多的，也會有君、將等類的體制。清遠、肇慶、羅定發現的大墓，"鐘鳴鼎食"的墓主人，有可能是南越君、將之類貴族的墳墓。

（三）廣東的經濟情況

1. 手工業有重要發展

(1)青銅鑄造業是南越冶金業的主要部門。

廣東青銅器冶鑄技術前文已經專題論述，此處不再贅覆。在認識冶鑄銅錫的同時，廣東人對鉛亦有所認識。肇慶大墓內的方形器中心注一塊鉛心，利用鉛較重的特點起加重墜壓的作用，能區別鉛和錫的不同性能，分別加以利用，在冶金術上也是一項進步。同墓還出土金柄玉環，金是鑄在玉環上的，類似的器物在其它地區尚未發現，為研究廣東製造金器提供了線索。

(2)製陶業空前興盛和發展

製造幾何印紋陶是廣東的重要手工業部門，需要量大，使用範圍廣，是人民生活不可缺少的日用品。春秋戰國時，廣東製陶技術有重大發展，主要反映在以下三個方面：

a. 幾何印紋陶在春秋時期達到鼎盛階段，花紋整齊精美，以陽紋為主，陰紋為輔，風格製法仿青銅器花紋，器形也仿青銅器，造型與印紋和諧美觀，達到空前高的水平，多數陶質硬，火候高，燒窰技術明顯提高。

b. 輪製技術日趨普遍，戰國時期逐步淘汰幾何印紋陶器。幾何印紋陶適宜於用陶拍模製陶器技術，無法適應輪製技術的需要。隨着社會的發展，人口的增多，人們對陶器的需要量越來越大，生產效率低的模製技術逐漸被輪製技術代替，輪製不需要拍打，拍印花紋無法適應大量的輪製陶器，出現了與輪製相適應的劃紋技術，在戰國晚期與西漢初期基本代替了幾何印紋陶器，成為最流行的紋飾，幾何印紋只剩方格紋和少量米字紋。輪製代替模製是製陶業的一大飛躍，進一步促進了手工業與農業的分工，使製陶業走向專業化、商品化，模製陶器適合家庭手工業生產，輪製則適合專業作坊生產。作為商品大量生產的輪製陶器，刻劃標記符號和文字極為盛行，多數器物上都有。隨着製陶的專業化和大量生產，窰爐結構也起了變化，由原來的豎穴式窰，發展為長條形窰，火候高、裝燒數量多。增城西瓜嶺戰國窰長達9.8米、寬達2米，可說是龍窰的早期雛形。

c. 產生和發展了青瓷器和釉陶器

春秋遺址中已經有較多青瓷和釉陶器。曲江石峽遺址夔紋陶文化層中，出土胎質灰白、表面施青綠或黃綠色釉的青瓷器，器形有缽、豆、缸等。釉陶與青瓷佔出土陶器總數的1.53%。青瓷和釉陶在粵東地區發現較多，粵北、粵西都有。這種新產品、新技術代表着新的發展方向，經過戰國時期，到漢以後成為主要的陶瓷品種。

(3)其它手工業部門也有發展

玉石器在新石器時代晚期磨光石器的基礎上，仿照青銅兵器，製造出精琢細磨的石刀、石劍、石戈、石矛等兵器。

肇慶戰國墓中隨葬漆器，惜已腐爛，僅見到黑、紅色的小塊漆片。有的漆器上還貼飾小塊金箔。

紡織品僅在陶器和銅器上遺留麻布和絲絹痕跡。《漢書·地理志》云海南島"男子耕農種禾稻苧麻，女子桑蠶織績"。廣東絲麻紡織在漢代之前亦應比較發展，漢以來葛布（苧麻布）是重要貢品，這種麻織品是廣東人的一項重要發明和創造。

青銅篾刀為最流行的一種青銅工具，有尖，兩面刃，還有尖為勾形的，適合刮削竹篾、編織竹器使用。在廣寧的銅盤器底部見到竹器編織痕跡，說明竹編的盛行。

2. 農業生產明顯進步

"五羊銜谷，萃於楚庭"雖是神話傳說，但透過神話可以看到廣東農業生產發展的一些情況。原始社會晚期，珠江三角洲地區以貝丘遺址為主，屬於捕撈魚獵經濟類型，農業生產落後。周時，有一些以羊為圖騰的農業部落的人，來到珠江三角洲的番禺一帶，帶來"一莖六出"的優良稻種，傳播了種植水稻的耕種技術，使這一地區的部落從以捕撈和漁獵為生活的主要來源，發展為以栽培水稻從事農業為主要生活來源，"飯稻羹魚"，生活安定，人畜興旺，不再有飢荒之苦。種植水稻從北部丘陵地區擴展到珠江三角洲和南部沿海地區，這是農業生產的一個重大發展，對廣東的社會進步和經濟發展有着深刻影響。《淮南子·說山訓》云："稻生於水而不能生於湍瀨之流"，漢初之前，南方不僅已種植水稻，而且對水稻所需的水量已有所掌握，栽培技術得到提高。《漢書·地理志》說，海南島不僅種植水稻，還種苧麻和採桑養蠶。此外廣東還是著名的熱帶、亞熱帶果品產地。

春秋戰國時，廣東的農業生產技術比原始鋤耕農業有了很大進步，但仍然處於"火耕水耨"的階段。火耕，首先要砍倒樹木，因此青銅工具的使用，較之磨光石器效率高得多。無論遺址還是墓葬，都有大量斧、鉞、鑿、錛等青銅工具出土，廣寧戰國墓還有銅鋤、銅䥽等耕種工具隨葬，證明農業生產力確有顯著提高。到戰國晚期，始興白石坪遺址發現鐵斧、鐵䥽。鐵器的使用意義重大，爲農業生產提供了可以普遍使用的銳利武器，對開墾荒野、提高耕種效率和推動農業生產的發展，具有重要作用，使廣東的農業生產進入了一個嶄新的階段。

3.出現了都市，商業和交通顯著發展

廣東最早的都市是番禺，秦漢爲南海郡治所，三國吳時改爲廣州。關於番禺的城市起源問題，一向爭論較大。起源於"楚庭"之說，出自晉裴淵《廣州記》"昔高固爲楚相，五羊銜谷，萃於楚庭"的記載。《羊城古鈔·古蹟》記載："周時，南海有五仙人，衣五色衣，騎五色羊，來集楚庭，各以谷穗一莖六出留與州人，且祝曰：願此闤闠永無飢荒。言畢，騰空而去，羊化爲石。"廣州遂因此神話傳說而有五羊城、羊城、仙城、穗城之稱。城市和都會的出現，是階級社會的產物，是政治、經濟、交通發展的產物。西周時廣東進入青銅器時代早期，生產力提高不大，築城條件尚未形成。屈大均在《廣東新語·宮語》中認爲"越宮室始於楚庭"，春秋時，周惠王胙命楚成王後，"南海臣服於楚，作楚庭"，"地爲楚有，故築庭以朝楚。"無論從時間或從資料上看，屈大均的觀點都頗有道理，有宮室亦應有城。起源於越相公師隅築"南武城"之說，也有不少道理。根據《古本竹書紀年》的記載，公師隅確有其人，越王曾使其"獻乘舟始罔及舟三百、箭五百萬、犀角、象齒"等與魏通好，牽制楚國。《廣東通志·列傳》云："越王無疆爲楚所敗，其子孫遯處於南海上，周赧王時有自立爲王者。隅以無疆初避楚居東武，有怪山浮來鎮壓其地，因名東武山。乃往相度南海，將依山築南武城，以擬之，而越王不果遷。"中山大學廣東通志館主任兼專修溫廷敬在案語中指出："今廣東有南武城磚及越王宮磚出土，是城爲已築。"是時廣東應有"南武城"。

儘管戰國時南越築城問題尚有爭論，然而番禺作爲一個著名都會是確鑿無疑的。《淮南子·人間訓》記載秦始皇發五路大軍統一嶺南，其中"一軍塞鐔城之嶺"，鐔城在廣西興安縣以北，"一軍處番禺之都"，秦以前確有"番禺之都"，故秦時才得以爲南海郡治所。此外，《史記》和《漢書》中關於番禺爲珠璣、象齒、犀革、果、布等珍貴特產的重要貿易都會的記載，並非僅限於秦漢，秦以前已經存在，秦以後有很大發展。

廣東的社會面貌在春秋戰國時有很大發展和變化，與中原地區交通聯繫進一步加強，文化越來越接近。故春秋末年至戰國時期有不少人稱著於中原，見於文獻的有周敬王三十八年（公元前482年）南海人勇獲爲吳王夫差將，參與黃池會盟；南海人高固爲楚威王相，公師隅爲越王相等，如果沒有社會經濟和文化的發展，這種情況是不可能出現的。

以上所論仍然存在不少問題，懇請各位學者，特別是香港地區的學者給予指正，希望粵港學者加強交流和研討，使廣東地區的青銅器時代考古和研究取得更大的成果。

一九八四年四月

參考文獻

葉祖康：《近五十年香港考古工作概況》《香港考古學會雜誌》1975年第6卷

秦維廉：《香港考古》香港考古學會

麥兆良：《粵東考古發現》香港考古學會

陳公哲：《香港考古發掘》《考古學報》1957年第4期

饒宗頤：《韓江流域史前遺址及其文化》

秦維廉：《香港古石刻》香港基督教中國宗教文化研究社

施戈斐侶：《大嶼山石壁遺址考古勘探》香港考古學會

秦維廉：《南丫島深灣考古遺址調查報告》香港考古學會

何紀生：《略論廣東周時期的青銅文化及其與幾何印紋陶的關係》《文物集刊》3 文物出版社 1981年

徐恒彬：《試論楚文化對廣東歷史發展的重要作用》《中國考古學會第二屆年會論文集》文物出版社 1982年

周世榮：《湖南楚墓出土古文字叢考》《湖南考古輯刊》第一集 1982年

廣東省文管會：《廣東清遠發現周代青銅器》《考古》1963年第2期 《廣東清遠的東周墓葬》《考古》1964年第3期

廣東省博物館：《廣東廣寧縣銅鼓崗戰國墓》《考古學集刊》1981年 《廣東四會鳥旦山戰國墓》《考古》1975年第2期 《廣東羅定出土一批戰國青銅器》《考古》1983年第1期 《廣東肇慶市北嶺松山古墓發掘簡報》《文物》1974年第11期

華覺明、黃渭馨、王秀蘭、徐恒彬：《廣東省出土青銅器冶鑄技術的研究》第一屆全國古代技術史學術會議論文 1983年

李仲達、華覺明、張宏禮：《商周青銅器的合金成份——兼論"鐘鼎之齊的形成"》1982年第二屆化學史學術會議論文

徐恒彬：《"斷髮紋身"考》《民族研究》1982年第四期

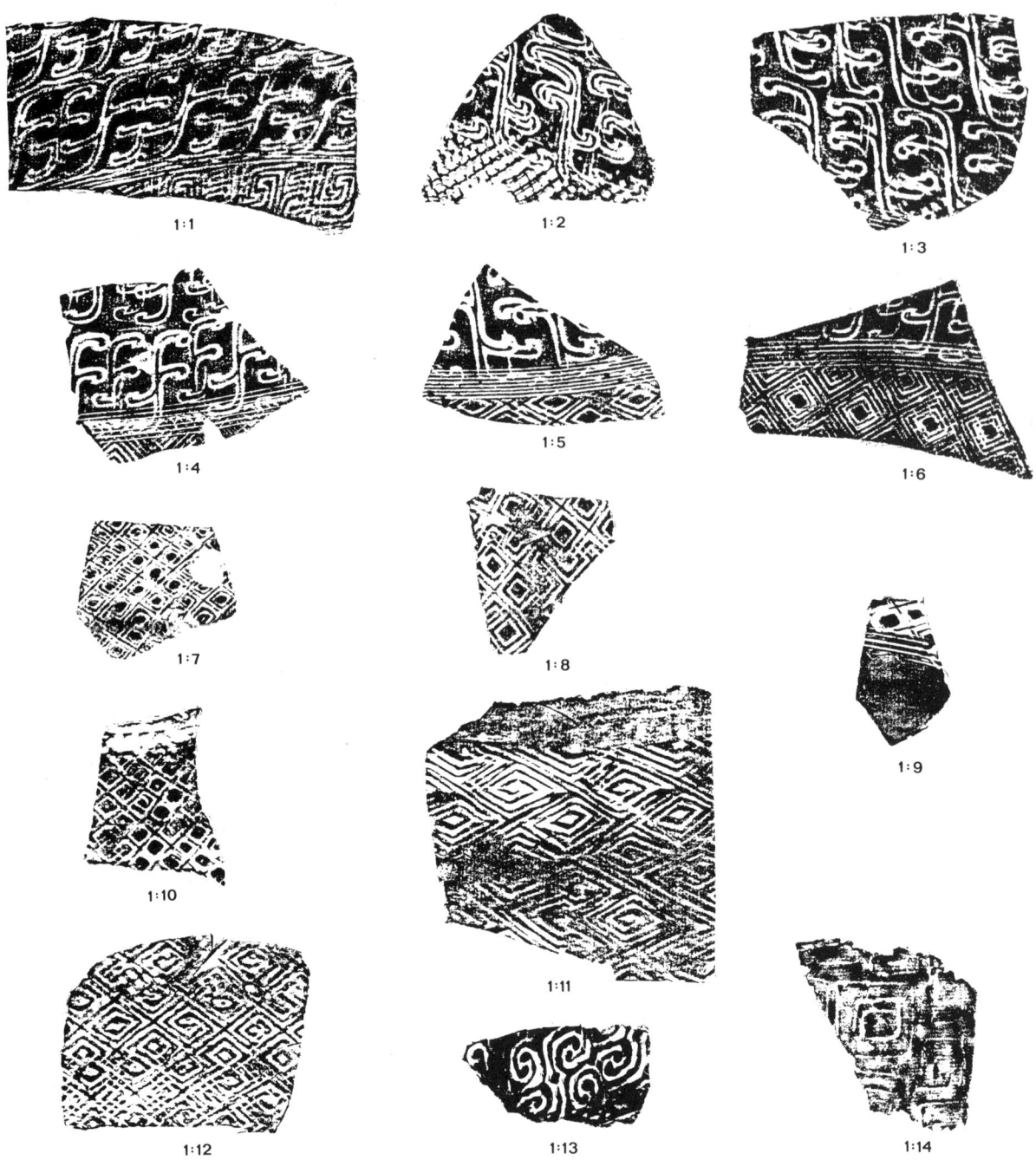

圖一 夔紋陶類型陶器花紋

1. 夔紋和勾連雲雷紋 2. 夔紋和方格紋 3. 夔紋 4. 夔紋和雲雷紋 5. 夔紋和菱形紋 6. 夔紋和雲雷紋 7. 回字紋 8. 回字紋 9. 回字紋 10. 回字紋 11. 雲雷紋 12. 雲雷紋 13. 勾連雲雷紋 14. 原始瓷片上的雲雷紋

Fig. I: Decorative designs of "Double-F" pottery:

1. Double-F and interlocking spirals 2. Double-F and net pattern 3. Double-F 4. Double-F and spiral pattern 5. Double-F and rhomboid pattern 6. Double-F and spiral pattern 7. Lozenge 8. Lozenge 9. Lozenge 10. Lozenge 11. Spiral pattern 12. Spiral pattern 13. Interlocking spirals 14. Spiral pattern on proto-porcelain sherd

圖二　惠來雲雷紋鐘

圖三　肇慶松山大墓出土鍋和鼎

圖五　肇慶松山大墓錯銀銅罍

Fig. II: Bell with Spiral Pattern from Huilai

Fig. III: Pan and Tripod Unearthed from the Big Tombs at Songshan, Zhaoqing

Fig. V: Bronze Jar with Silver Inlaid from the Big Tomb at Songshan, Zhaoqing

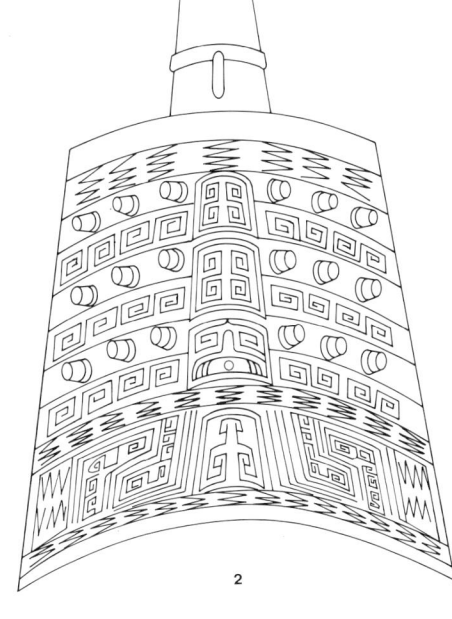

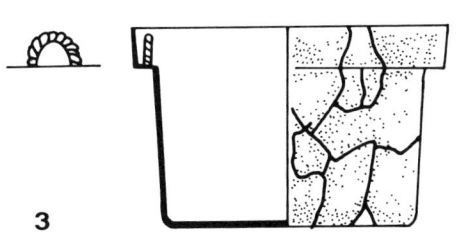

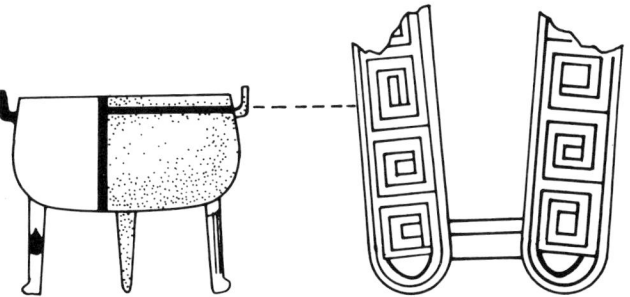

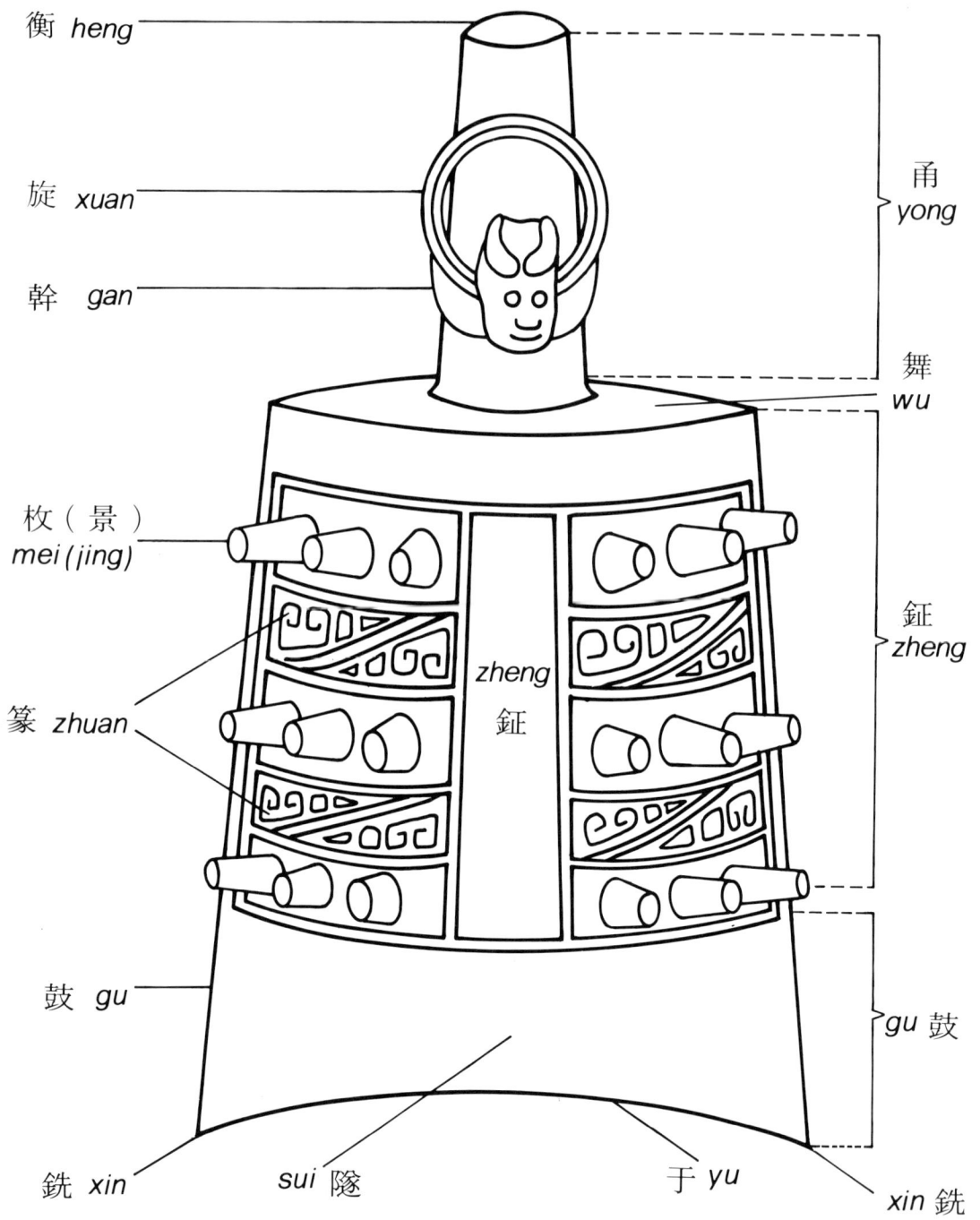

圖四　鐘的各部份名稱

Fig. IV: Various Parts of a Bronze Bell

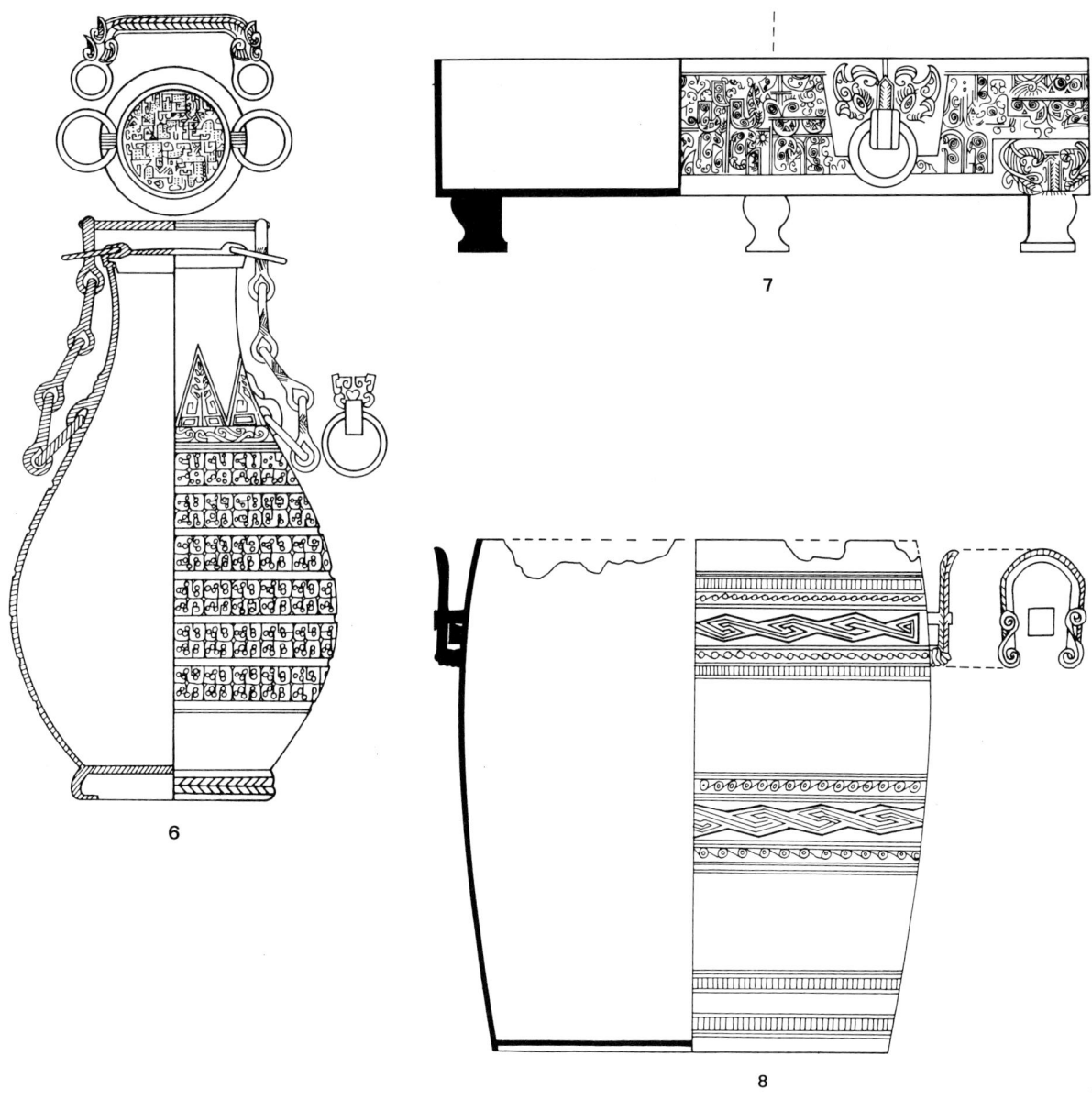

圖六　肇慶松山大墓提梁壺

圖七　肇慶松山大墓三足盤

圖八　肇慶松山大墓銅筲

Fig. VI: Bottle with Chain-handle from the Big Tomb at Songshan, Zhaoqing

Fig. VII: Tripod Basin from the Big Tomb at Songshan, Zhaoqing

Fig. VIII: Bronze Bucket from the Big Tomb at Songshan, Zhaoqing

9:1

9:2

10:1
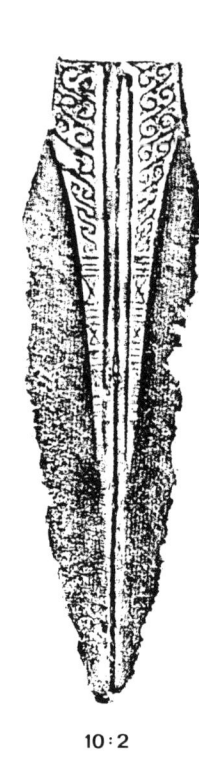
10:2

10:3
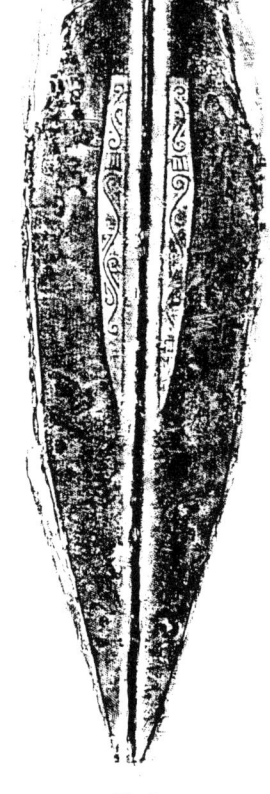
10:4

圖九　羅定太平一號墓銅鉞和銅鐘鼓部花紋

1.鉞　2.鐘

圖十　羅定太平出土銅器

1.劍　2.矛　3.矛上"王"字形符號　4.大銅矛

Fig. IX: Rubbing of Bronze Designs from Tomb No. 1 at Taiping, Luoding

1. Axe   2. Bell

Fig. X: Bronzes from Taiping, Luoding

1. Sword   2. Spearhead   3. "*Wang*"-marks on spearheads   4. Large bronze spearhead

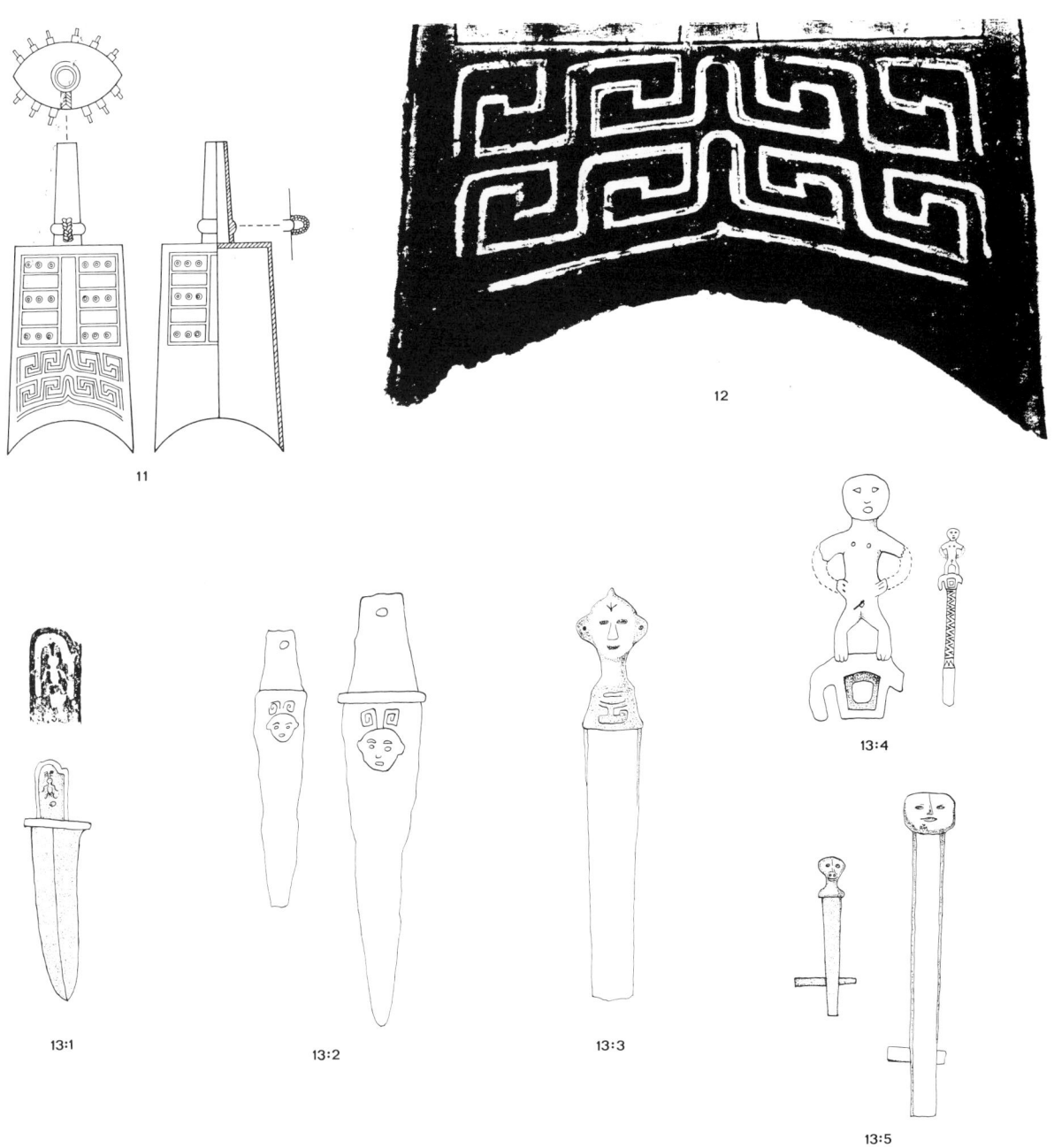

圖十一　肇慶松山大墓銅鐘

圖十二　肇慶松山大墓銅鐘鼓部花紋

圖十三
1. 海豐銅戈人像　2. 香港和曲江銅匕首人頭像　3. 清遠人首柱形器人頭像

Fig. XI: Bronze Bell from the Big Tomb at Songshan, Zhaoqing

Fig. XII: Rubbing of Design on the Bronze Bell from the Big Tomb at Songshan, Zhaoqing

Fig. XIII:
1. Bronze halberd from Haifeng
2. Bronze daggers from Hong Kong and Qujiang
3. Human-headed shaft from Qingyuan

A General Discussion on the Bronze Age of Guangdong

Xu Hengbin

For a long time students of Lingnan archaeology and history have endeavoured to trace the social and cultural development in Guangdong before and after the Qin unification in 214 B.C. As a result of increasing archaeological evidence from excavations, it is now confirmed that there was a Bronze Age in Guangdong before the Qin and there existed a rather sophisticated well-developed civilization. This paper is a preliminary attempt to discuss with archaeological evidence the historical culture of the Bronze Age in Guangdong. It is hoped that this will stimulate further research on this topic and accomplish the aim of cultural exchange between Guangzhou and Hong Kong.

I. The Discovery of Bronze Age Cultures:

The history of the discovery of Bronze Age cultures in Guangdong can be divided into two periods:

A. Initial period:

Spaning from 1932 to 1949 this period has two obvious characteristics. The first is that the discoveries were centred in Hong Kong and eastern Guangdong. The second is that the scholars involved were mainly foreign missionaries with few Chinese scholars. Evidently it was unavoidable that the results were much limited by both their age and circumstances, nevertheless their scientific approach and achievements should not be overlooked.

Fr. D. Finn (1886-1936) was one of these pioneer figures. In 1932 he discovered accidently some bronze fragments in a sand-heap near the Regional Seminary of Aberdeen, Hong Kong. Further excavations in Nanyadao (Lamma Island) led to the discovery of bronze daggers and other bronze artifacts in association with hard geometric pottery impressed with "Double-F" pattern. In subsequently published research papers, Fr. Finn was the earliest to use the term "Bronze Age culture". He also singled out the hard pottery with many variants of "Double-F" patterns as the main feature of this bronze culture and at the same time pointed out with keen insight that there was no clear cut distinction between the culture of Central China and that of the "Southern Barbarians". The "Southern Barbarians" or the people of the South China coastal area had already been emulating the cultural characteristics of the north before they were completely under the shield of influence of the Bronze Age culture of Central China.

The discovery of moulds for casting bronze axes in Shibi (Shek Pik), Lantao Island, Hong Kong by W. Scholfield (1888-1968) had an important significance. This discovery proves that bronzes were locally cast in Guangdong. Stratigraphy at the same site also reveals for the first time the relative chronology of the Neolithic cultural layer and the Bronze Age layer.

An Italian priest, Fr. R. Maglioni (1891-1953) in 1936-1939 collected bronze halberds, axes, and bells and also moulds for axes and bells in E. Guangdong. This expands both the area of discovery and the type-forms of bronzes in Guangdong.

From 1938 onwards more and more Chinese scholars contributed to the research and field work on the Bronze Age of Guangdong. Mr. Chen Gongzhe discovered bronze artifacts and moulds in Dongwan (Tung Wan), Dawan (Tai Wan) and Shagangbei (Sha Kang Pei) in Hong Kong. He also discovered the rock carving in Shagangbei at Shibi. This was a new discovery since the publication of the *"Gazetter of the Xin'an County"* and widened the scope for the study of Bronze Age culture. Investigations and researches were also made by Messrs. Gu Tiefu and Rao Zongyi in the eastern Guangdong area. Their published papers narrate the discoveries of bronze knives, arrowheads and pottery bowls at a school building site eight kilometres south of Hepozhen, Jiexi county. At the same site a stone mould for casting bronze socketed axes was also found. In his study of pre-historic culture in the Hanjiang area Mr. Rao says, "Geometric pottery, popular in Wu Yue, Jiangxi, Fujian, Guangdong and even in Taiwan ... is a southern version of the Yue tribal culture". This provides a preliminary survey on the problem of native tribes of Guangdong Bronze Age.

B. Development period:

Starting from October, 1949 to the present, this period has the following characteristics: (i) China mainland became the main region under investigation. The area is much wider and sites are found all over the province. (ii) Chinese scholars form the majority and there is a sharp increase in number in both field archaeologists and indoor researchers. (iii) There is a wide mass participation and popularization. Most of these new discoveries were first reported by the mass who took part in industrial or agricultural production and were excavated or "cleared up" by professionals. This increases substantially the reliability and scientific value of the finds. (iv) Special topics of research are underway. This both deepens and widens the scope and achieves a much better result.

Since the establishment of New China, special emphasis has been given to archaeological and cultural work. A committee for the protection of Archaeological Material was set up in 1953 in Guangdong and in February 1956 a provincial archaeological team was formed. In the same year the first general archaeological survey over the whole province began and was followed by extensive surveys and excavations to coincide with construction, industrial and agricultural projects. As from 1982 a second general archaeological survey has been launched. The size and scope of this present survey far supersedes the previous one and is expected to be completed by the end of this year.

After three decades of thorough and extensive work with mass participation and professional support, the major archaeological finds in Bronze Age Guangdong include:

1. The area of discoveries much expanded:

In the past, bronzes were only found in Hong Kong and eastern Guangdong, but now Bronze Age sites have been discoveried in central, northern and western Guangdong. To date apart from Hainan Island, Bronze Age sites scattered all over the province. Important finds include a ewer from Xinyi, a tripod from Huiyang, bells from Boluo, a drum and bells from Lianping. These are all exquisite and finely cast vessels of monumental size.

2. The discovery of Bronze Age burials:

Prior to the sixties nothing was known of Bronze Age burials in Guangdong. It was only in the spring of 1962, following the discoveries in Matougang, Sankeng, Qingyuan county of 25 pieces of bronze objects, a pottery pot with lozenge pattern, polishing stone and other objects that the first Bronze Age burial site was reckoned. This was succeeded by the discoveries of a group of Warring-States tombs at Loyanshan, Maxu, Deqing county, in which the tomb construction was excavated. From then onwards the veil of Bronze Age burials in Guangdong was unfolded. According to a preliminary count up there are more than sixty burials. Most of these have bronzes as their main funerary accessories. The largest of these is a Warring-States tomb at Songshan, Zhaoqing, in which more than one hundred bronzes were found. The total number of bronzes discovered so far amounts to more than 750 pieces. In the past there were only chance finds of bronze tools and weapons. Now the type forms are much varied, they can be classified into six categories of cooking vessels, containers, musical instruments, miscellaneous objects, weapons and tools. Not only the forms increase but there are also numerous variations within the last two categories.

3. Bronze Age cultural types identified and their relative dates determined:

Following the discovery of more than 200 "Double-F" sites, we have now a clearer picture of the cultural content of this "Double-F" pottery culture and we know that it developed out of the "Angular meander pottery culture" of the Neolithic period. The "Double-F" pottery culture was succeeded by the "Basket-pottery" culture, sites of which now amount to more than 120. This is a late Bronze Age culture in Guangdong. Bronzes were still in use and put into tombs, but two iron objects have also been discovered. As to the dates of the "Double-F" culture, its upper limit corresponds to that of W. Zhou with a lower limit extending to the Warring-States period, whereas the dates of the "Basket-pottery" culture roughly spans from mid. Warring-States to Qin.

Apart from the two types mentioned above, there is a Raoping Fubin culture which has a strong regional feature. It is characterized by proto-porcellaneous greenware and glazed pottery coexisting with bronzes. Its sites scattered around eastern Guangdong. The identification of this culture further enriches the cultural content of the Bronze Age in Guangdong. The date of this culture is roughly contemporaneous with the "Double-F" type.

II. Types of Bronze Age Cultures:

After more than half a century of research, investigations and excavations, there has accumulated an abundant amount of archaeological finds of the Bronze Age, and we can now have a better and clearer understanding of the

Bronze Age cultures of Guangdong as a whole. From an analysis of available material, the Bronze Age culture in Guangdong can be classified into three types: "Double-F" pottery" type, "Basket-pottery" type and "Fubin type" as mentined earlier.

(A) "Double-F" pottery type:

More than fifty years ago this type was identified by D. Finn as a Bronze Age culture as bronze objects were found in association with geometric pottery impressed with "F", "Double-F" designs (or *kuei*-pattern). He also reckoned that the impressed designs on the pottery "shares similarities with the *kuei*-dragon motif found on bronzes of the Shang and Zhou period". After 1949 there have been extensive investigations and excavations, and we have a much clearer understanding of this "Double-F" Bronze Age culture.

(1) With the exception of Hainan Island and Leizhou peninsula more than 200 sites of this culture have been discovered all over the province. With the Zhujiang Delta and the surrounding area as its centre, this culture spreads northwards to Hunan and southern Jiangxi, eastwards to southern Fujian and north-westwards to the north-eastern part of Guangxi.

(2) The appearance and development of the "Double-F" culture did not come out merely from "emulating the cultural characteristic of the north". After thorough investigation and field work, it is evident that the geometric pottery culture in Guangdong underwent a long process of inception, development, flourishment and decline, it also spanned from the Neolithic, through the Bronze to the Iron Age. We know that the "Double-F" culture of Bronze Age derived out of the "Angular-meander" pottery type of the geometric pottery culture and was the climax of Guangdong geometric pottery culture both in quality and technical skill.

As can be testified by the distribution and stratigraphy of excavated sites, angular meander pottery, "Duble-F" pottery and "Basket" pottery frequently occur in the same site. All three types were discovered at eight sites in Zaiguangding, Zijin county and Donghuawei, Qujiang county etc. The first and the second types were found at twenty-four sites including Chiniushan, Chaoyang county, Sugangling, Bolo county and in Shixia, Qujiang county. The second with the third types were found at eight sites in Aishanzhai, Lianping county, Sugangling, Boluo county and in Shixia, first and the third types were both unearthed at fifteen sites in Kengzaili, Longchuan county and Shangmaicun, Dongguan county. Their co-existence in the same site provides evidence to support the theory of a continuity and relationship between these three pottery types. Among the sites, the most convincing one is the excavation at Shixia, Qujiang county. The soil of the "Double-F" pottery layer at this site is fine and soft, dark grey in colour and is found overlying the 'angular meander culture' layer. Within this layer fragments of "Double-F" pottery, glazed sherds, proto-porcellaneous greenware, small amount of polished stone together with sixteen bronze objects of axes, spears, knives, arrowheads, awls and small knives were excavated. This discovery shows that the "Double-F" pottery culture developed out of the 'angular meander culture' and at the same time received influence from the Bronze Age cultures in the north, resulting in a most flourished local geometric pottery culture.

The pottery shapes in this culture are very varied. Vessels are normally with flat bases, ring-feet are rare. The forms are refine, elegant and of large sizes. Common types include urns, jars, vases, stem-cups, basins, dishes, bowls and cups. Most of them are high fired and are very compact but occasionally vessels of soft material and coarsely tempered ware are also produced. The decoration is frequently in raised relief supplemented by intaglio designs and impressed from a finely carved mould that produces clear and neat impressions. The "Double-F" pattern with numerous variations:— double-hooked, double-headed, round-headed, hook-shaped or straight body with hooked heads — are stamped neatly and seldom overlapped. The net pattern, whether large or small is always very regular. The "double-lined net" and "the net with lattice" patterns are now replaced by the meander pattern and lozenge design. Some varieties of square spiral ("cloud-thunder") pattern are very similar to spiral meanders, sometimes interlocked or with round corners. Besides all these, basket, circles, double-circles, whorls, net, cord, dotted combings, incised and grooved patterns continued to be in vogue. Designs are usually arranged in bands. This is one of the characteristics of this culture (Pl. 1:1-14).

(3) Six rectangular shaft earth pit tombs of "Double-F" pottery culture were excavated in Qingyuan, Luoding, Sihui and Huaiji, but only the tomb found in Niaodanshan, Sihui county was differentiated into front and rear chambers. The front chamber was 15 cm. lower than the rear. There was a rectangular pit hollowed out in the centre of the front chamber, inside which a large pottery urn was buried. The remaining portion of this tomb

was 5.7 metres long (1.2 metres in the front chamber, 4.5 in the back), 3.5 metres wide and 0.6 metres deep. The other tombs were all of single chamber type. The largest of all these was tomb No. 1 in Nanmengdong, Luoding county, which measured 4 metres in length, 2 metres in width and 1.7 metres in depth, and buried with more than 100 bronze accessories. Tomb No. 2 of Qingyuan, with crushed sandy stones lying on the floor, yielded 266 bronzes, 9 polished stones and 9 pottery items. Some of the bronze decorations of the "Double-F" culture are identical to those found on contemporary pottery wares. Examples can be seen in the interlocking square spirals on a bronze bell from the Spring and Autumn Tomb at Matougang, Qingyuan county, the interlocking square spirals on a bell and the S-shaped patterns on a ewer from the Warring-States Tomb at Niaodanshan, Dawang Farm, Sihui county, the S-shaped pattern on a bronze spearhead and the square spirals on a bronze tripod from the Warring-States Tomb No. 1 at Nanmengdong, Taiping Assembly Hall, Luoding county. Parallels of all these designs mentioned above can be found on "Double-F" pottery wares. Pottery urns and pots with stamped square spirals, stylised 'kuei-dragon' designs, mat patterns were also buried together with bronze items in the "Double-F" pottery culture layer.

(4) Glazed pottery and proto-porcellaneous greenware were also found at the sites of this culture, especially in northern and eastern Guangdong. In an investigation in Jieyang, the present writer has collected fragments of proto-porcellaneous greenware impressed with "Double-F" pattern. The greyish white body is heavy, thick and covered with a greyish green glaze. Glazed pottery and proto-porcellaneous greenware constitute 1.53% of the total finds from the upper cultural layer at the Shixia site, Maba, Qujiang county. The proto-porcellaneous ware consists of pots, stem-cups and jars with a greyish white body and a blue green or olive green glaze. Some of them are thick and heavy with square spiral pattern incised under the glaze. Still others are impressed with net pattern or dot-combed and grooved. They still preserve some of the designs of the contemporary geometric pottery. The glazed ware and the proto-porcellaneous greenware though in small amount represent an innovation and a new direction in technical development in pottery production in Guangdong.

(5) Judging from the bronzes excavated from burials, the lower limit date of the "Double-F" pottery culture corresponds to the first half of the Warring-States period. Its upper time-limit is still open. However pottery decorations found from a late Neolithic site at Hedang exhibit transitional features akin to patterns of "Double-F" pottery. This indicates that the upper limit may extend to early Western Zhou.

(B) Basket pottery type:

The "basket pattern" should be more accurately defined as a "Union Jack" design within a square, i.e. a cross with two diagonals enclosed by a square. There are many variations such as "Union Jack" in square, cross in square, crossed diagonals in square, cross in square plus lattice, cross in double squares, cross in double-lined squares, etc. (Exhibits 99,100). After the emergence of basket pottery, "Double-F" ware was completely replaced. More than 120 basket pottery culture sites have been discovered so far. Pottery wares were found in assocaition not only with bronze items but two iron tools were found in the northern Guangdong region. This shows that Guangdong had entered into Iron Age.

(1) The distribution of both dwelling and burial sites of basket pottery culture is much wider than that of the "Double-F" pottery. Even in Leizhou peninsula, Hainan Island, basket pottery ware has been found. Burials are most abundant in western, as well as in eastern Guangdong.

(2) Basket pottery represents the decline of Guangdong geometric pottery. Although the hard paste, high firing and compact body are similar to "Double-F" pottery, its manufacturing process, decoration and shape change a great deal. They were mainly turned on the potter's wheel rather than coiled and padded with a stamp and anvil. This innovation not only induced the decline of impressed geometric decoration, but also stimulated the technique of incision as well as more varieties of vessel shapes. Flat bottomed ware substituted those with round bases. Large vessels such as urns, pots, and cauldrons were still hand modelled and padded with basket or net pattern. However, small objects like bowls, boxes, and cups were often wheel made and decorated with incised bands and combed dots. Among the finds from the kiln site at Xigualing, Zengcheng county stamped pattern makes up 89.89%, incised pattern comprises 10.13% and 0.02% is with the two types combined. Of the impressed decoration

the majority is basket design (54%), then comes net pattern (28.99%). There are very few examples decorated in square spirals, mat pattern or a combination of the two. Most of the incised decorations are of waves, combings, striations or their combinations. Glazed pottery in either yellowish brown or dark grey also constitutes one of the important components of the finds. The glaze was usually thickly and unevenly applied, leaving many drippings and a large part of the body unglazed. Pottery wares from the kiln site at Baishipingshan, Shixing county are mostly wheel made. Shapes include ewers, pots, large containers, jars, basins, bowls, plates, cups, boxes and tripods. Incised design drops to 66.75%, but the quantity of the glazed ware increases sharply to 5.7%. The basket pattern is the most common type amongst the impressed decorations, up to 42.2%, whereas the net pattern comprises 40.9%, square spirals, 0.73%; basket with squares, 3.23% and square spirals with squares, 0.27%.

(3) According to a rough estimate, more than 40 burials of the basket pottery culture have been discovered in Zhaoqing, Luoding, Guangning, Jieyang, Fushan, Sihui, Longmeng, Longchuan, Shenzhen, Zhanjiang, etc. About 500 bronzes, 29 polishing stones, 101 pottery wares and 10 pieces of miscellaneous objects of jade, glass, etc. were excavated. Large vessels are always impressed with the basket pattern. There are two types of tombs. One is the rectangular shaft earth pit type with either single or double chambers. The only tomb with double chambers was at Luoyanshan, Deqing county. Its front chamber was 1.15 metres long and the rear chamber was 3.6 metres long and 1.5 metres wide. The front chamber which was 20 cm. lower than the rear had a large gourd-shaped urn buried in a pit in the centre. The single chambered tomb in Guangning was laid with pebbles on the floor. Another rectangular shaft earth pit tomb in Songshan, Zhaoqing with a wooden chamber but no access ramp was 8 metres long, 4.7 metres wide and 6 metres deep. There was a small "waist-pit" in the centre and four chambers were attached to the central one where the coffin was placed.

(4) The date of the basket pottery culture is very definite. The upper limit links up with the "Double-F" culture, and the lower limit was succeeded by the Qin and Han dynasties corresponding to the middle or late Warring-States culture of Guangdong.

(C) Fubin type:

This is a new Bronze Age cultural type first discovered in the winter of 1974 and is now known to be scattering all over eastern Guangdong. Sporadic finds of glazed pottery of similar types were unearthed in Huiyang, Puning and Chao'an This makes the identification of the cultural type difficult. It was only after the discovery of twenty-one rectangular earth pit tombs at Fubin and Lianrao, Raoping that we gradually have a better recognition of this cultural type. The tombs are all rectangular shaft earth pit tombs, with two different types of structure. One is stepped while the other is not. The largest one is 2.6 metres long, 1.08 metres wide and 1 metre deep; the smallest one 1.2 metres long, 0.6 metres wide. The burial accessories include glazed ware, proto-porcellaneous greenware and earthenware such as flared-mouth jars with long neck, round bottom and small foot-ring, basin with foot-ring, pots with round bottom, stem-cups, vases and different types of bowls. The greenware was fired in relatively high temperature with a greyish white body and impressed with long, fine striations, net patterns and fine cord pattern under a dark brown glaze. A variety of marks such as "Wang", "+", "||", and "|||" were incised on the rims and the shoulders. The stone burial objects include adzes, chisels, axes, spearheads, rings, split-rings, and arch-shaped pendants, all are finely polished. The spearheads and axes are obviously in imitation of bronze prototypes. Only one bronze halberd was discovered. It is of very simple shape without blade projections. There is only one hole in the tang and blade respectively for hafting. It was roughly cast and probably made locally (Exhibits 46-52).

There is a great divergence of views on the dates of this culture. It has been identified as of the Shang period on the basis of the appearance of bronze halberds and flared-mouth jars. It has also been dated to the Zhou because of the large quantities of proto-porcellaneous greenwares. There is a third opinion to put it within the Spring and Autumn period. From the present writer's view, without first considering the characteristics of the culture and the role it played in Guangdong geometric pottery culture as a whole, to propose a date merely by comparison of individual vessel forms is not reliable nor realistic. After examining the culture as a whole, one should be convinced that the Fubin culture was a regional Bronze Age culture in Guangdong. It centred around Raoping. As the cultural characteristics are also regional therefore it should not be identified as Shang. Its dates should be contemporaneous with that of the "Double-F" culture. This accounts for the overlapping of the two cultures at some sites. This is also supported by the large amount of protoporcellaneous greenware and the glazed ware discovered at sites of both cultures.

III. Characteristics of Bronzes:

Over eight hundred pieces of bronzes were excavated from Guangdong and nine tenth were from burials. These bronzes can be classified into two periods according to their sizes and characteristic features.

The first period spans from Western Zhou to early Warring-States period corresponding to the "Double-F" pottery cultural period. This period can be further sub-divided into two phases. The early phase continues into the middle Spring and Autumn period and the late phase ranges from late Spring and Autumn to early Warring-States.

Early Phase: Only slightly more than thirty pieces of bronzes have been found. With an exception of a bronze halberd collected from a burial at Fubin, Raoping, all were excavated from dwelling sites or hoards. The majority, some sixteen pieces, were from the upper layer of Shixia, Maba.

Ewer with dragon handle: It was unearthed in October, 1974 from Songxiangchang, Xinyi county. Of Western Zhou period, this is the earliest, the most elaborate and important bronze vessel ever found in Guangdong. The overall height is 26.2, the diameter is 14.2 cm. It is with an innovative shape, heavy body, delicate decoration and fine casting. The body is *li*-shaped, with flared mouthrim, long spout and three separated legs. The neck is decorated with a band of *kuei* pattern, the shoulder with a band of oblique spiral pattern. The body is divided into three zones, each of which is with a *tao-tie* pattern formed by spirals and separated by *kuei*-dragons. The cover and spout are topped by dragons in the round. This vessel is similar in shape and decoration to another bronze ewer in the Shanghai Museum. The only difference is that the Shanghai piece has a semi-circular handle, while the Xingyi handle is much more complicated. Its construction is ingenious with two *kuei*-dragons in openwork carving and joined by small tubes. The upper tube links up with a small dragon cast on the side of the body of the ewer (Supplementary illustration 5).

Bell with triangular pattern: It was excavated in July, 1979 from Huahu commune, Huilai county. The length of handle: 10, body length: 25, mouth width: 20, body thickness: 5 cm. The body is thick and heavy and with 18 short nipples on each side. Decorations consist of zig-zag bands, spirals and stylised "*wang*" spirals. The short verticle handle is with a looped ring for suspension. The decoration has a rather strong local Southern Yue characteristic. Its date should not be later than the Spring and Autumn period (Fig. 2).

Bell from Tiechang: Three bells were excavated from Meicun, Tiechang commune, Boluo county. The bodies are thick and heavy and decorated with interlocking spirals at the upper part. The casting was crudely done leaving numerous air holes on the surface. One of the three is 40 cm. long; the handle 13 cm. long and the mouth 22.8 cm. wide.

Zhongxin bell: Excavated from Penshan, Zhongxin commune, Lianping county, handle length: 13.5 cm., body length: 36 cm., mouth width: 25.5 cm. On the lower part of the handle is a protrusion for securing a ring. The back side of the body is undecorated but with eighteen nipples. On the front side there are also eighteen nipples arranged in bands enclosed by raised double lines and lattices. At the middle of the lower part of the body are three slightly raised studs arranged in a triangular configuration (Exhibit 59).

Drum from Zhongxin: It was unearthed together with the above bell. It is 52.3 cm. high, tapering towards the bottom and with an ovoid cross-section. The original tiger-shaped knob was lost. The knob platform is decorated with rhomboid spirals, the shoulder with a band of interlocking spirals above a band of triangular pattern. Each of the two sides are decorated with a medallion of intertwine *hui*-dragon in very realistic forms. The mouth part is decorated with bands of triangles, interlocking spirals and plaits (Exhibit 60).

Tripod with C-spiral pattern: Excavated from Huiyang county it is with a flared mouth, contracted neck, squat circular body, and cabriole legs. The body is decorated with c-spirals and triangular patterns, the legs with *tao-tie* patterns.

Minor bronzes such as weapons and tools are found in a large quantity, mainly from the upper layer of Shixia.

Spearhead: Leaf shaped. The point is of flat section and solid, the tubular socket is crested on the sides. There is one perforation but no loops for hafting. Length: 11.3 cm.

Dagger: Thin and simple, the shape is similar to those excavated in Hong Kong. The middle part of the thin blade edge slightly raised. The guard is not obvious and the handle is perforated.

Halberd: Found in the areas of Raoping and Haifeng. Halberds from Haifeng are similar in shape to those of the Shang and Zhou, with a slender and slightly curved blade terminating into small projections. The butt end is perforated and decorated with a human figure or interlocking spirals (Exhibit 53).

Broad axe: With fan-shaped blade, slanted shoulder, rectangular socket, a ridge round the top part. Traces of rottened wood may be found inside the socket of some of the pieces. At the middle parts of the lateral sides are seams of moulds. Length: 8.5 cm.

Scraper: "Willow-leaf" shaped, with thin and curved body. The point is triangular, the back end is flat, crested in the centre. Length: 8.5 cm.

Awl: With square section, one end tapers to a fine point. Length: 7.3 cm.

Arrowheads: With rhomboid sections, narrow flanges, and sharp points. The tang may be round or flattened. There is a particular type with crested front parts and grooved tangs. Remaining length: 6 cm.

Late Phase: Six tombs with bronze objects were found. Among the bronzes, over one hundred pieces were from Tomb No. 1 at Luoding, twenty-five pieces from Tomb No. 1, Qingyuan and thirty-nine pieces from another Tomb No. 2 at Qingyuan. Altogether 266 bronzes were unearthed from these six tombs. Other burial objects such as polishing stones and pottery ware are very few and amount to only sixteen pieces. In terms of shape and usage, these bronzes can be classified into six categories, i.e. cooking vessels, containers, musical instruments, weapons, tools and miscellaneous objects. Weapons and tools outnumber the rest. The characteristics of the different categories are as follows.

Cooking vessels: Tripod is the main form. There are two types. One type is with an ovoid body, broader at bottom, thin wall and often undecorated. The three solid splayed legs are long, semi-circular in cross-sections. The other type has a contracted mouth, deep body, round bottom, three cabriole legs, handles and finished with a cover. They are elaborately decorated. One of them is decorated with two bands of cloud pattern separated by a plait band on its cover and body, the legs are decorated with intricated *chi*-dragons. Height: 20.6, diameter: 23 cm.

Containers: Water, wine and storage vessels. Shapes include large jars, cauldrons, ewers and basins.

Large jars: Excavated from Tomb No. 1 and 2 at Qingyuan. One is with out-rolled mouth, round body, loop-handles and small footring. The body is decorated with fine "hook and volute" pattern with plaited panels. Height: 33.6, diameter at mouth: 22.8, at belly: 37.6, at bottom: 17.6 cm. The other is with a flattened mouthrim, short neck, globular body, low footring, a pair of semi-circular loop-handles on shoulder. The body is decorated with intricated *hui*-dragon pattern, triangular pattern, and on its upper part four roundels filled with "hook and volute" pattern. Height: 28.2, diameters at mouth: 18.8, at belly: 35.6, at bottom: 20 cm. (Supplementary illustration 6).

Cauldrons: With straight mouth, round body, four loop-handles, and footring. There is a ridge below mouthrim, the body is undecorated. Height: 45, diameter at mouth: 19.2, at belly: 38, at bottom: 22 cm.

Ewers: The most remarkable piece is from Tomb No. 1 at Luoding. It is with straight mouth, round shoulder, ovoid body, round bottom, flat ear, semi-circular loop-handle, and three cabriole legs. The body is decorated with delicate "S", plait and triangular patterns. The flat cover is also with "S" scrolls and with a chain connecting its central knob to the loop-handle, which is in the shape of a *chi*-dragon with two horns, double spine and a curled tail. The spout is in the shape of an animal mask with opened mouth and erected ears. Delicate spiral pattern is cast round the mouth. The handle is decorated with S-shaped cloud pattern. The ear is in the shape of intertwine snakes in openwork. The upper parts of the three legs are decorated with intricated *chi*-dragons. Height: 29, diameter: 12, length: 29.8 cm.

Basin: With straight mouth, flat mouthrim and flat bottom. The three legs are lost, leaving three nipple-shaped joint marks. The ovoid body is decorated with fine *hui*-dragons. Diameter at mouth: 36.6, at bottom: 21, height: 14.2 cm.

Musical instrument: Mainly chime bells with handles, small bells (*Zheng* and *duo*) are few.

Serial bells: Five bells were found from Tomb No. 1 and seven bells from Tomb No. 2 at Qingyuan. At Luoding, six serial bells with identical shape and decoration were unearthed. With their heights of 37.5, 32.5, 27.5, 25.9, 23.1, 19.5 cm. respectively, they were graduated in accordance with the musical scale. But the bells from Qingyuan tombs are without any common decorations, sizes or shapes and seemed to be grouped together in random order. Bells from Luoding are with slender bodies, long nipples, and decorated with interlocking spirals, very similar to the set of chime bells from the tomb of Zenghou Yi in Hubei. As to the bells from Qingyuan, those from Tomb No. 2 are similar to the Luoding ones but those from Tomb No. 1 are different from the former two. They are with wider and heavier bodies, and their nipples are shorter (Fig. 9:2).

Small bells — Zheng: The one from Qingyuan is slender and tall while that from Luoding is short and broad. Both are heavy and probably for practical use. Length: 35.7, 27.2, diameter: 13.3, 14.8 cm.

Small bells — Duo: With short handle of rectangular shape and compressed ovoid body, on which is decorated with spirals and plait pattern.

Weapons: There are swords, spearheads, daggers, halberds, arrowheads, axes and filials.

Swords: There are long and short types. First type: with short and thin blade, prominent median crest on which is decorated with a shield-shape design. There is a perforation at the end of the grip for attachment to an elliptical jade pommel. Second type: with round pommel, flanges round the grip, rhomboid guard, high raised median crest and sharp point (Fig. 10:1).

Spearheads: Both shapes and sizes vary a great deal. Spearheads from Qingyuan are with sharp points, midribs and tubular sockets. Six types of spearheads were found at Tomb No. 1 at Luoding. Type I spearhead is large in size. It is with long body, broad blades, prominent median crest, square loop, tubular socket, and cast with oblique spirals on two sides of the median crest. The patina is bluish green with some bluish mottles. Length: 24.6, width of flange: 5.1 cm. Type IV and V spearheads from the same tomb are cast with symbols (Fig. 10:3,4).

Daggers: Some are similar to those unearthed from Hong Kong and Qujiang, others are awl or chisel like. They are usually with rounded or flattened blades and handles topped with square perforated rings. On one dagger is an elephant on its ring, on another is a human figurine (Fig. 13:4).

Halberds: Only a few pieces have been found. The one excavated from Xiangang, Guangzhou is with a straight and short horizontal blade, a broad verticle blade with four perforations, a ridge between the butt end and the blades, and decorated with triangular and square spirals.

Slender axes: With long flattened body, elliptical socket, and decorated with animal mask on the front. Length: 11.5, width: 6.8 cm.

Arrowheads: Four-bladed, with thin flanges, raised median crest and a tapering small tang. Length: 7, width: 1.1 cm.

Filials: With tubular body and solid base.

Tools include axes, broad axes and scrapers.

Axes: Usually with a slender body, narrow rounded blade with lateral sides outcurved, and rectangular sockets. Axe from Tomb No. 2 at Qingyuan: Length: 8.8, width of blade: 3.1 cm. An axe from a tomb at Sihui is with the "*Wang*" mark.

Broad axes: The shape is similar to that of the early phase. Some are decorated with interlocking spirals on the sockets. Length of the bigger ones: 9.4, length of smaller ones: 8.3 cm. (Fig. 9.1)

Scrapers: Similar to that of the early phase. Some unearthed from Tomb No. 1 at Luoding are with "*Wang*" marks.

Miscellaneous objects: Human-headed shafts constitute this group. These have been found from Tomb No. 1 at Qingyuan and Tomb No. 1 at Luoding. Four pieces were found from each tomb. The Qingyuan shaft is a hollow rectangular rod which tapers towards the bottom. Lower end is with a horizontal perforation for the insertion of a cross-bar. The upper end is topped with a human bust. The human face is round, with horizontal eyes, closed mouth and broad flattened nose. The forehead is incised with grass pattern. The round protruding head is with a ridge-shaped bun. The round ears are perforated. Height: 42.5, width: 3.6, thickness: 3.2 cm. Originally these hollow shafts were probably inserted into wooden rods and fixed in position with cross-bars. The shafts from Luoding are also of rectangular section but solid. The body tapers towards a cuneiform perforation with a cross-bar at the lower end. The upper end is topped with a human head, without bust or neck. The head is with square face, protruding nose, indented eyes and mouth, but without ears. Length: 24, width of head: 3.2, width of shaft: 2.2 cm. Shafts of this type differ from the above and were probably mounted with wooden rods for use (Figs. 13:3,5, Exhibits 81, 82).

The second period ranged from middle to late Warring-States Period and coincided with the dates of the basket pottery culture. Bronzes were found in burials rather than dwelling sites. More than five hundred pieces of bronzes were found from over forty tombs. Amongst these tombs, the biggest was at Songshan, Zhaoqing, which yielded 108 bronzes, 21 potteries and 10 other objects of gold, jade, stone or glass. The basic bronze shapes are similar to those of the late phase of the first period. However there are new shapes as well as technical innovations.

Cooking vessels: In addition to tripods, pots made their appearance in the big tomb at Zhaoqing. It is with a straight body, out turned mouthrim, and a pair of plaited loop-handles. Diameter: 48, height: 30 cm. The pot is covered with smoke soot, indicating that it was for practical use. In comparison with the first period, small tripods increase in number and the bodies are thinner, with either cabriole or slender legs of triangular sections. Decorations on the covers are very complicated and include plait pattern and intricate *hui-* dragon scrolls. One piece is 6.9 cm. in height, 14.5 cm. in diameter (Fig. 3).

Containers: New shapes include large jar with silver inlaid, bottle with chain-handle, tripod basin, large bucket, etc.

Jar with silver inlaid: With broad mouthrim, high neck, slightly slanted shoulder, globular body, and flat bottom surmounted on a footring. A pair of free ring handles with owl-masks are set on the shoulder. The cover is with a ringed knob. The silver inlaid pattern composes of intertwine stylised birds and cloud scrolls in a free style. The thin lines of the pattern are silver inlaid, while the thick lines are red lacquered. The colour was still bright red during the excavation. Height: 22, diameter of mouth: 14.9, diameter of belly: 24, diameter of bottom: 14.8 cm. (Fig. 5, Supplementary illustration 7).

Bottle: The shoulder is applied with two monster masks which link up with a chain and a loop-handle that run through a pair of rings on cover. The cover is decorated with impoverished curves, the handle with feather pattern, the shoulder with a band of cicada triangles, the body with six bands of intricate *hui*-dragon pattern, and the footring with a plait band. Height: 30, diameter of mouth: 7, diameter of belly: 19, diameter of base: 11 cm. (Fig. 6, Exhibit 84).

Tripod basin: With straight walls, a pair of animal-masks holding free rings, and three cabriole legs. The delicate decoration on body is composed of "hook and volute" units, within which are tiny S-shaped and triangular spirals. Diameter of mouth: 57, height: 10 cm. (Fig. 7, Exhibit 85).

Bucket: Cylindrical in shape, the mouth slightly inturned, and the body tapers towards the base. The upper part is applied with two opposite semi-circular handles attached with cross-bars to the body. There are three bands of decorations. The upper and middle bands are interlocking spirals, S-shaped meanders and vertical striations. The lower band consists of two rows of vertical striations. On the handle are S-shaped spirals and feather patterns. Diameter: 42, height: 46 cm. (Fig. 8, Exhibit 86).

Musical instruments: Bells and small bells — *duo*. The bells are identical in shape to the ones from Luoding of the late phase in the first period. Six serial bells were unearthed from the big tomb at Zhaoqing. The largest 56.5 cm. in height and 25 cm. in length across the mouth (Fig. 11, 12).

Weapons: including swords, daggers, spearheads and arrow-heads. The sword unearthed from the big tomb at Zhaoqing is most remarkable. It is with a round pommel, round grip with two flanges and a guard. The midrib is brown coloured, the sharp blades are black coloured. Overall length: 71, length of blade: 59.5 cm. The guard is with carved decoration and inlaid with jade and semi-precious stones. The ridges on the grip are also decorated with delicate spirals. Arrowheads from the big tomb of Zhaoqing are also of unique shape. During excavation, they were tied together with silk or hemp strings, some of them were attached to lacquer fragments flaked off from the arrow container. The arrowheads are large in size, double-bladed with median crest and sharp points. The blades are with sharp edges and triangular or striated grooves. Remaining length: 14, largest width: 2.8 cm. The shape of the spears is regular and is similar to that of the Warring-States period in northern China. A lot of them are with "*Wang*" marks, and some are with shield-shaped patterns (Fig. 10:3).

Tools: New shapes like hoe, spade, boot-shaped axe, and pickaxe appeared. The shapes of the previous period such as axe, *yue*-axe, scraper, chisel, knife were still in use. Hoes and spades were only found from tombs of Guangning. The hoe is with a "tile-shaped" body while the spade is "U" shaped. They were probably farming tools. Boot-shaped axes were found from Deqing and Guangning and are with sockets. Scrapers are plentiful. Most of them are with triangular front points, flat ends, and of "V-shaped" sections. Average length: 5 to 10 cm. Some of the scrapers unearthed from the tombs at Guangning have a tilted front point and traces of string tied round the tang probably for hafting to a wood or bamboo handle. Some are with "*Wang*" marks on their tangs. A total of twelve pickaxes were found. They were all from Zhaoqing and have rounded front side, flat back side, curved body tapering towards the lower end which forms a point. The socket is semi-circular. Length: 7.8, width: 3.4 cm. Double-shouldered adzes are rectangular in shape and with flattened shoulders.

The broad blades are with straight or curved edges. The curved ones are used as adzes only, whereas the straight ones can be used both as adzes and axes.

Miscellaneous objects: Apart from the human-headed shafts, there are some round or square seal shaped objects which are difficult to give a label. They were unearthed from tombs at Gaodiyuan in Sihui, tombs in Guangning and the big tomb at Zhaoqing. The round objects are topped with free-ring knobs. The square ones are of cubical shape surmounted by a pyramid on the top with free-ring knobs. These objects were probably used as weights as they are filled with lead inside to make them heavy. The side length of the cubical type is 6 cm.

Based on the shapes and decorations of the specimens discussed above, there are four significant aspects in the bronzes unearthed in Guangdong:

(1) Some of them are identical in shape to similar bronzes of central China, e.g. two bronze large jars from the tomb of Qingyuan and the bronze ewer from the tomb of Luoding, etc.

(2) Some of them are similar in shape to bronzes unearthed from the Changjiang region. For example, tripod shapes include straight mouth with flattened rim, dish-mouth with semi-circular handles, or in-turned mouth with applied handles, etc. The three legs are usually solid, slender and splayed, the handles are decorated with triangulr and spiral pattern, plait pattern or cord pattern. The bodies are thin. Similar type of tripods are also found in Jiangsu, Jiangxi and Hunan. The various types of swords are also similar to those pupular in Lingbei.

The intimate relationship between Guangdong and Chu bronzes is also noteworthy. Examples can be found in the silver inlaid bronze jar; bottle with chain-handle; tripod basin from Zhaoqing; the ewer from Sihui; the basin, tripod and cauldron from Zhaoqing; and the drum from Lianping, etc. Their shape, decoration and casting technique are identical to the Chu bronzes. The large inlaid bronze jar from Zhaoqing with fluent pattern of intertwine birds and clouds is a standard Chu masterpiece. The large tripod and sword from the same tomb are identical to those from Chu tombs in Changsha. Bells were popular in Guangdong and were found in both large or medium sized tombs. Bells from the tombs of Luoding and Zhaoqing are exactly the same both in form and decoration as the well-known set of serial bells unearthed from the Zenghou Yi tomb at Sui county, Hubei, and yet different from bells of other regions. It seems that most of them were local made after Chu prototypes.

(3) There are still some other bronzes which are related to those found in Guangxi, Yunnan and Guizhou in southwestern China. Boot-shaped axes and slender axes, seldom found in the Chu area, were very common in Yunnan, Guangxi and Guizhou. Moreover the bronze bucket with vertical handles from Zhaoqing is also in typical Guangxi style. The decoration resembles those found on bronze drums of the same period and from the same area.

(4) A lot of the bronzes exhibit a strong local feature. Outstanding ones include human-headed shafts, double shouldered adzes, daggers with human shaped grip, fanshaped broad axes, round and cubical objects, as well as tripod basin, scrapers, large spearheads, large arrowheads, etc.

The "*Wang*" mark is a hallmark of Guangdong bronzes. It is mainly found on spearheads, scrapers and axes. The spearheads are similar in shape to those commonly used in the Warring-States period in central China, but an outlined "*Wang*" mark is usually cast on the round socket. The scrapers are with tilted points, double blades, crested back sides, flat tang also crested, and of "V-shaped" sections. Some scrapers unearthed from Guangning are with remains of string, indicating that they were hafted with bamboo or wooden handles and were used as weaving tools. Often outlined "*Wang*" marks are found on slender axes, but the fan-shaped broad axes are decorated with stylised triangular spirals. Bronzes with this "*Wang*" mark have been found not only in Deqing, Zhaoqing, Sihui, Guangning and Luoding in Guangdong, but also in Guangxi, Hunan, Jiangxi and Jiangsu.

A few of the bronze spearheads found in association with "*Wang*" marked ones are occasionally cast with a "H" mark which seems to be a simplified version of the more standard "*Wang*" mark.

As can be seen from the "*Yue-Wang*" inscribed bronze spearhead from Changsha, Hunan and a "*Wang*" marked spearhead from Shaoyang, this "*Wang*" emblem seemed to have first originated in the State of Yue and evolved from the *niaozhuan* (bird-seal) script of the "*Wang*" character. After the annexation of Yue by Chu, this emblem was still popular in Guangdong.

IV. Bronze Casting Technology:

In order to have a fuller understanding of the Bronze Age culture in Guangdong and to investigate the characteristics of the alloy composition and the treatment processes of the bronze of the Pre-Qin period, a joint project was carried out under the collaboration of the Guangdong Provincial Museum, Hua Jueming of the Institute of History of Natural Sciences, and Huang Weiqing and Wang Xiulan of the Harbin University of Technology. 38 bronzes of the Spring and Autumn and the Warring-States periods were selected for this study. Among these samples there are one metallic ingot, 14 tools, 14 weapons, 4 vessels, 3 musical instruments and 2 human-headed shafts. Apart from the bronze bell from Boluo county, which belongs to the Spring and Autumn period, the rest are of the Warring-States period. The various analytic and examination results indicate that the bronze technology in Guangdong had reached a comparatively high level.

(A) Bronze casting techniques

Within the Guangdong region no bronze foundry site of the Bronze Age has been found. But early stone and pottery moulds for fish hooks and axes have been excavated in Haifeng and Hong Kong. According to the typology and casting marks of the objects and a comparison of them with similar objects and moulds excavated at other areas, it is possible to reconstruct the casting techniques of the various types of bronzes. Basically they may be classified into the following types:

1. Single-mound casting (with core)
Example: A filial excavated at Niaodanshan, Sihui.

The thickness of the socket is about 1.6 mm. The cavity was formed by a central clay core. The casting mould was made from a real object or a clay positive model. After having been air dried and baked, the mould was covered with a layer of straw-tempered clay. When dried it was ready for pouring in. A clay core could be duplicated from the casting mould. After finishing by scraping and adding a sprue, the core could be made to match the mould. One side of the mould was flat and the other was with a cavity to form the shape and decorations of the object. There were tenons and mortices along the join of the castings to facilitate close fitting of the moulds.

2. Double-face mould (without core)
Example: mould for arrowhead.

The bronze arrowhead was excavated at Tongguagang, Guangning. Along the middle line of the lateral face of the tang there is a mould-join mark indicating that the object was made from a double-face mould. Many pieces of bronze arrowheads were excavated at Luoding. Their shape was similar and this indicates that the technique of casting several arrowheads with a single mould was employed.

Another example: mould for a sword.

The pouring sprue is located at the side of the sword grip. Its cross-section is oval in shape with a length of 1 cm. and a width of 0.6 cm. The mould seam is very obvious at the joins. There is an air vent at the tip of the sword pommel from which the air inside the mould cavity escapes during the pouring of the metal. This arrangement is to ensure the completeness of the sword edge in the casting.

3. Double-face mould (without core, uneven sections)
Example: scraper knife

The shape of the scraper knife is peculiar. It resembles the leaf of the willow. The front section is triangular with sharp edges, the rear part is flat while the mid-section has a median crest. Thus the mould should follow the contour of the knife and should be of uneven-section.

4. Double-face mould (with core)
Example: *Yue*-axe

There is a cavity in each of the castings and an obvious seam along the joins of the moulds on the object. The seams at the two sides of the bronze *yue*-axe excavated at Luoding have not been ground off and are clearly visible. The decorations were cast simultaneously. In order to ensure the smooth flow of the molten bronze and raising the pressure, this type of casting moulds had additional moulds which serve the purpose of a pouring basin and a sprue during the filling for casting. Similar type of casting was also adopted for socketed implements such as axes, hoes and spearheads, etc.

5. Multi-section mould (casting in one piece)
Example: Bell of the Spring and Autumn period excavated at Boluo
(cf. Fig. 4 for the different parts of the bell)

Overall height: 39 cm. *Yong* length: 128 cm. *Xin* length: 26.8 cm. The distance between *xin* is 22.6 cm., between *gu* 17.2 cm. Wall thickness: about 0.7-1.1 cm. Arrays of lattices design demarcate the *Zheng*. The slender nipples are rather pointed. There are interlocking spirals at the *Wu*. The *yong* is short and hollow inside connecting the main bell cavity and thus showing some primitive features.

There are continuous casting seams along the middle line on the lateral side of the *yong* indicating that the object was made from a mould in two sections with two clay cores. (The body of clay core extended through the extremity of the *yong*; the other core was for the suspension loop.) The *mei*-nipples and the lattice design were also fashioned in the mould. This was the general practice in the manufacture of early bells in central China. At the *gu* of the bell and the edge of the base there are air holes. Obviously molten bronze was poured in through the edge of the base (inverted pouring). Again this was the practice in central China for the casting of early bells. The ratio of the major dimensions of the bell are as follows: the ratio between width of *xian* to length of *xian* is 0.84, width of *gu* to length of *gu* :0.64. In comparison to the standards of bells as mentioned in the *Kaogongji*, "Dividing the *xian* into ten units, substracting two units the remaining eight units is the length for *zheng*, which is also the width for *xian*; substracting two units again, the remaining is the width of *gu*" (That is the two ratios are 0.8 and 0.6 respectively), the two sets of ratios are basically consistent. However the curvature of the *yu* is flatten and resembles the serial bells excavated at the Chu tombs of the late Spring and Autumn period in Xiasi, Xichuan, Henan.

The serial bells of the early Warring-States period excavated at Luoding are six in number. Among them Nos. 1, 2 and 4 has 36 *mei*-nipples each and Nos. 3, 5 and 6, 24 *mei*-nipples each. Thus they do not seem to be the same set. But the change in dimensional gradient is more or less in accordance with the paradigm. The overall heights in descending order are 37.5, 32.5, 27.5, 25.9, 23.1 and 19.5 cm. Hence the ratios between each neighbouring bells are 1.15, 1.18, 1.06, 1.12 and 1.18. On one face of the bell there are bands marking the *zheng* and the *gu* with interlocking spirals, on the other face there are *mei*-nipples only without any demarcating bands or decorations. Both the *wu* and *yong* are undecorated. At the top edge of the *zheng* and the *wu* there are narrow slits.

There are recesses at the corresponding positions in the inside wall. The body of the bells is narrow and slender. For example, Bell No. 1: *xian* length: 25.8, *xian* width: 15.8; *gu* width: 11 cm. This gives values of 0.6 and 0.4 as the ratios between *xian* width and *xian* length and *gu* width and *xian* length respectively. These figures deviate considerably from the standards as mentioned in *Kaogongji*. The wall of the lower edge of the bell is even and about 0.4 cm. thick. There is no sound groove structure. Clay cores still remain inside some of the bells, indicating that they were produced as funerary objects and were not for practical use. The casting is comparatively crude. To facilitate the insertion of the clay core, clay "chaplets" were used. As a result, after casting, there are narrow slits at the *zheng* and *wu* (They are not tuning holes as was suggested before). Generally such technical device was used for bells with loop-handles. They are the first known specimans in which such device was applied to bells with tubular handles and this has become a regional characteristic.

The set of six serial bells of the Warring-States period excavated at Zhaoqing bear narrow slits at the *wu* and *zheng*. Coarse and crude patterns are found on one side of the *gu* only. The wall of the bottom edge of the bells is thick and even (4 mm). Sound-groove structure is absent. The *yong* is hollow and joining with the main cavity of the bell body. However, the clay cores had been broken during the casting and molten bronze ran into the cracks. This is why not all clay cores were removed. This feature resembles those found in the serial bells from Luoding. It seems that they were also made for burial use.

6. Multi-section mould (separate casting and fusion welding)
Example: Bronze tripod of the Late Warring-States period excavated at Guangning (Ml3:1)

It has an in-turned mouth, bulging body and three solid slender feet splayed outwards. There are two mould seams on the body. One of the seams runs straight from the mouth-rim down to the tip of the foot; the other one runs down in between the other two feet and meets the circular seam at the bottom of the tripod. The wall of the body is about 2 mm. thick. The applied handle is only 1 mm. thick and with a clay core inside. Thus it is obvious that the tripod was cast from an assembly of two sections for the body, one section for the top, a clay core for the body and one section for the bottom. The applied handles were pre-cast and placed in the body mould after part of the clay core had been removed. During the casting the handles were fused onto the body. Consequently there are marks of excessive bronze enveloping around the handle and they are somewhat shaky.

Another example: bronze tripod of the Early Warring-States period excavated at Luoding (Ml:1).

It has a cover, an in-turned mouth, a deep body and cabriole feet. Decorations consist of the cloud, plait and inter-laced dragon patterns. It had been broken when unearthed. At the middle of the bottom of the vessel there is a circular mould seam within which is the remain of a sprue of 75 mm × 2 mm. The body has three equidistant seams. Clay cores were found inside the feet. There are two seams diametrically opposite to each other on the exterior. At the joining place of the feet and the body marks of fusion welding are visible. The body, the lugs and the feet were cast separately. The body was cast from an assemly of three sections for the body proper, a section with pouring sprue for the top, a clay core and a section for the base. The feet and the lugs were pre-cast and joined by fusion during the casting of the body.

The bronze ewer unearthed at Luoding (Ml:7) is a superb piece among the bronzes of the Warring-States period. Its body and the animal-shape spout, the dragon-shape handle, the lugs and the cover were elaborately decorated with patterns of triangles, clouds, plaits and interlaced dragon. The body is cast in one piece, while the feet, spout, handles, lugs and cover were cast separately and fused together. The handle including the tail of the dragon motif are hollow. The cavity was shaped by a clay core. From the seams at the horn of the dragon it can be known that the ewer was cast from an assembly of three pieces of section moulds. The pattern on the spout is extremely refined and signs of secondary carving are obvious, showing that it has been meticulously retouched after casting. The flat handle was also fusion welded. At the corresponding part on the inner wall of the ewer there is a thickened ridge to ensure a thicker wall at the place for a more secure join by fusion welding. The chain on the cover has a lighter weight indicating that it was probably made from an alloy of lead and tin. One end of the chain stretches into the handle and joins to it. At the base of the feet are round holes where "chaplets" for clay cores were positioned during the casting. Marks of fusion welding can be seen at the join of the feet and the body. The front surface of the upper part of the legs is decorated with interlaced dragon pattern, while casting seams flank the two sides. Thus is it obvious that the decoration was cast from a separate piece of mould.

7. Multi-section mould (separate casting and solder welding)
Example: Bronze basin unearthed at Luoding.

The diameter of the mouth is about 35 cm., the height from the mouth-rim to the base is 13 cm. The body has two mould-join seams diametrically opposite to each other. In the middle portion of the mould-join there are two longitudinal tenons. At the base of the basin there are also three tenons. From this, it is obvious that the body was cast from two identical section moulds. The two applied handles and three feet were cast separately. Then they were welded together individually to the pre-cast tenons. Owing to ageing, the soldering alloy became corroded by oxidation and the handles and feet fell apart (Exhibit 88).

(B) The Composition of the Bronzes

According to the condition of the bronzes, different analytic methods including qualitative chemical analysis, spectroscopic analysis, atomic absorption spectroscopy and low energy electron diffraction etc. were used for the determination of the chemical composition of the 34 bronzes. Metallic phase examination has been applied to all the samples, while tests of hardness or microhardness to 32 pieces.

1. Classification of alloys

The results of the analytic examinations indicate that the alloys contain many impurities. The main constituents are copper, tin and lead. Phosphorus and arsenic have also been found in a number of bronzes. Accordingly the alloys are grouped into three categories:

Tin bronze: The alloy contains only small amount of lead. Swords which require high quality belong to this category.

Tenary alloy of copper, tin and lead: In addition to copper and tin as the major constituents, the alloy contains a big amount of lead. For example, the small basins contain as much as 19% of lead. In the alloy the presence of lead is in the form of streaks, laminae or lattice.

Tenary alloy containing special elements: Some bronzes contain a fixed quantity of phosphorus. Large quantities of bismith and arsenic are also found in some of the bronzes.

2. Composition of alloys

According to the function of each type of bronzes, particular proportions in composition were used. Bells, tripods, weapons, utensils and tools etc. fall into five categories with respect to composition. The general features are:

In the categories of bells and tripods, there is more tin and lead. Usually tin is in the range of 13 to 16%. Such proportions in composition enhance the colour of the bells and the sharpness of the cast design.

The category of weapons includes swords, arrowheads, *yue*-axes and spearheads, etc. Sharpness and toughness are their requirement. For this purpose, they usually contain 12 to 22% of tin, and very little lead — basically within 2%. Thus it is easily seen that appropriate proportions of tin and lead were adopted to meet the requirements and their property display certain regularities. Hardness increases with the addition of lead. Some bronzes with similar compositions vary considerably in their degree of hardness. From their phase examination and other tests, it is found that some of the bronzes contain higher percentage of tin. The fact that bronzes being harder than they should be in terms of composition is due to the difference in their phase structure and casting condition. Or perhaps it is because they contain phosphorus and arsenic which are absent in ordinary bronzes.

(C) Post Casting Treatment and Hot Deformation Processing

Phase examinations indicate that thirty-eight pieces of bronzes were cast. Besides possessing the crystalline structure from casting, the bronzes also have other structural features showing that additional treatments have been made after casting to meet the requirement of shaping and function. For example, the *yue*-axe has undergone hardening processes; the axe has been annealed, surface processed and quenched etc.

1. Hardening

The bronze *yue*-axe excavated at Tomb No. 1 of Taiping commune at Luoding contains 13.9% of tin, 5.2% of lead and 0.1% of zinc. However, it is much harder than other weapons containing the same quantity of tin. Chemical analysis shows no existence of other peculiar elements. Its microscopic phase structure shows a directional sense. The needle-shape crystals are small, being distorted, deformed and broken. They are thus different from the usual crystals in the casting state. This indicates that the black and blue colours on the surface of the *yue*-axe are marks of the hot deformation process which was applied to the object to harden it after casting.

2. Hot deformation process and annealing

The tin component of the axe (tin 14.4%) is similar to that of the tripod (15.2%). But phase examinations show differences in their structure. The superficial appearance of the sample bears evidence of the hot deformation treatment. It can be inferred that the axe had undergone repeated hot deformation treatments and annealing. This results in the formation of single phase structure.

3. Surface treatment

The surfaces of the swords, *yue*-axes, spearheads and arrowheads of the Warring-States period are covered by a shiny dark green protective layer which prevents corrosion from the outside. Examinations reveal that the hardness of the superficial layer is greater than that of the inner layer. The identification of phase structure, energy dispersion spectroscopy and hardness tests have been applied to the bronze arrow-head excavated at Taiping commune, Luoding. From the phase diagram a boundary phase can be seen between the surface and the inner part. The energy dispersion spectrum shows that the surface envelopes a layer containing high chromium but the inner part contains none.

4. Quenching of a knife for splintting

The knife for splintting contains 19.5% of tin. But its structure is totally different from that of the arrow-head which has a similar elemental composition (18% of tin). The knife has distinct needle-shape formations which are characteristics resulting from quenching.

From the above analysis of the techniques of bronzes of the Spring and Autumn and the Warring-States periods, it can be inferred that single moulds or double-face moulds were usually used for casting simple tools, implements and weapons. For vessels and musical instruments of complicated shapes mutli-section moulds were used. With the exception of casting by lose-wax methods, almost all other methods prevailing at that time such as casting in one-piece, separate casting with fusion welding or soldering were used. Although some bronzes had forms and decorations bearing regional characteristics, the techniques were consistent with that of central China. For water containers such as basins which were generally not required to endure very high temperature, the feet were soldered on. On the other hand, cooking vessels such as tripods had to undergo elevated temperature. If soldering was used for joining the feet, the low-melting point alloy might melt when heated and the feet would fall apart. Therefore, for this type of vessels fusion welding or solid feet were adopted. As mentioned above, the tripod excavated at Luoding and Guangning are with fusion welded feet. The tripod from Tomb No. 16 at Guangning on the other hand is with solid feet, smoke soot is found at the base and it is therefore for practical use. Its base is only 1 mm. thick, mouth-rim only 2 mm. thick, indicating that the casting technique had already reached a comparatively advanced standard.

N. Barnard has done phase identification of small bronzes excavatged at Layer C at Lamma Island

and has found twin crystals of pure copper in the structure in the cast-state. The same phenonemon has also been found in the bronzes at Anyang. This shows that although the early bronzes excavated at this region is comparatively later than those of Shang Yin, there are similarities in casting techniques and they have certain primitive features.

The composition of the alloy is also the same as that in central China. The casters had good knowledge of the relation between the functional properties of the bronzes and their composition of tin and lead. This is illustrated in the manufacture of bronze swords. The use of multi-section mould deserves mentioning. The spine and the edge blade of a sword from Zhaoqing were cast separately using bronzes containing different proportion of tin. The spine was cast first and then fusion welded to the blades. The spine containing low percentage of tin is yellow in colour whereas the edge with higher tin content is whitish. Making use of alloys of different compositions the desired mechanical properties could be achieved. Thus the blade is made sharp and hard and can be sharpened easily; the spine is made supple and tough and can endure in beating and striking. This meets the functional requirement of being hard and tough at the same time. This is what was said in *Xunzi*, "The white is hard; the yellow tough. A combination of the white and the yellow makes a good sword which is both hard and tough". In the past this type of swords were mostly found in central China (for example the famous *Shaoyu* sword) and Jiangxi. It is for the first time that such type of swords was discovered in the Lingnan region.

The use of large qunatity of the tenary alloy of copper, tin and lead is also an important milestone in the development of bronze technology. In the Xiaotun period at Anyang the tenary alloy had already appeared though in small quatity. During the Spring and Autumn and Warring-States periods, it became the main alloy for bronzes. From the elemental composition of the bronzes of the Warring-States period excavated in Guangdong, it is known that seven pieces were made of tenary alloy, representing 25% of the total bronzes examined. It is obvious that the technique in the preparation of alloy had long passed the primitive stage and followed closely the development of central China.

With respect to processing after casting it is of great significance to establish the identification and recognition of forging and hot deformation processes in the manufacture of bronze cutlery. It has been suggested that only casting was known in China in the Pre-Qin times and that forging techniques had hardly developed.

Some even reckon that annealing only began as late as in Han. In fact although the manufacture of bronzes in Pre-Qin times was mainly by casting; however, for tools, weapons and cutlery, very often it was necessary to apply cold deformation treatment to increase their hardness. Repeated using made the edge blunt, forging treatment was required to restore the original sharpness. In the process, the previous hardening state had to be annulified by annealing before treatment. Messrs. Tang Lan and Guo Baojun quoted from the *Book of Poetry* which says, "Forging the halberds and spears, ... polishing and beating." The two verses clearly point out the age-old existence of deformation processes. However, in the past, scientific examination of objects was seldom carried out. Only superficial observation was occasionally done and hence without adequate scientific evidence to support the theory. But in the present examination of the bronzes excavated in Guangdong, it was found that many pieces of cutlery had undergone beating, annealing and quenching treatment. This proves, without doubt, that the application of various types of deformation process treatment for cutlery after casting prevaded in the Pre-Qin times, for the improvement of their function. In particular, for the bronze scraper knife which was mainly used for scraping bamboo splints, high tin-content bronze was used for casting to meet the requirement of hardness and sharpness. However, owing to the high tin content, the sharp edge was susceptible to breakage easily. The quenching treatment increases the degree of toughness and improves its function. Until now it is the first time that such treatment has been found on Pre-Qin bronzes and hence deserving our special attention. Concerning chromium treatment on the surface of bronze culteries, Mr. Tian Changhu of the Chengdu University of Technology and the Beijing Institute for Steel has discovered the presence of chromium on the surface layer of arrow-heads on several occasions. The discovery of another example from the Gaungdong bronzes this time rules out the possibility of a chance appearance of such objects. They were treated on purpose although the mechanism for the formation of the chromed layer and its functional purpose still necessitate further investigation.

Guangdong Province has good natural resources for the development of bronze metallurgy and foundry. In the west, north and east of Guangdong there are rich deposits of copper and tin ores. At Gangmei commune in Yangchun county, an ingot were found in association with an axe of the Warring-States period. It is about 20.6 cm. long and 6.2 cm. wide in the form of a deformed rectangle with slightly rounded ends. There are many gas pores on the surface of the flatten face. The other face is slightly arched. The thickest section is about 15 mm. There is no sign of a pouring sprue. This indicates that it was formed from the molten metal directly from the furnace, and solidified on the sand bed.

The Spring and Autumn period already saw the appearance of human-headed bronze shafts. From this it may be inferred that before that period a local bronze casting industry was already flourishing in Guangdong. The location where the bronze ingot was excavated is not far from the malachite mine which is still operative. Hence it may be established that the ingot was produced locally and belong to the same period as the bronze axe. If this assumption is correct, then Guangdong was able to extract and refine copper ore on its own in the Warring-States period at the latest. Bronze technology was closely associated with pottery making. In the Guangdong area geometric pottery flourished in the Neolithic period. The hard pottery with impressed pattern made in the Shang and Zhou times has a high degree of hardness which can only be achieved by a firing temperature of 1000°C or over. This provides the means to obtain the high temperature, material and techniques necessary for mould-making which are the requisites for the development of bronze technology. Moreover early stone and pottery moulds have been found both in Hong Kong and Haifeng. The production of dish-mouth tripods discussed above shows that complex pottery moulds were in use. Thus except for a few imports from the north, most bronzes were cast locally.

Since ancient times, there has been traffic between Lingnan area and central China. From the above analytic study of bronze typology and technology, it is evident a bronze industry was set up under the direct influence of central China especially that of Chu culture. At the same time communication with the minority groups in southwest China certainly existed also. Although the typology, decorations and artistic treatment of the bronzes bear regional characteristics, the development trend of the techniques and artistic expression of the area are consistent with that of central China and Chu culture. Being a sub-branch of the main Shang and Zhou bronze civilization, its regional characteristics, are overshadowed by national identities.

V. Social Aspects of Bronze Age Guangdong:

We know very little of the society of Guangdong in Bronze Age. With the help of archaeological materials and a few literary records, we have only restored a very small fraction of the social aspects in Guangdong.

(A) Physical features and customs of Guangdong people
1. Physical features

Society is made up of human beings. It has been a most interesting issue to find out what the Guangdong people looked like in the Bronze Age. As can be seen from available finds, there are four variants:

(a) Haifeng man

The Haifeng man is illustrated in a bronze halberd published on p. 95 of *Archaeological Discoveries of Eastern Guangdong*. The halberd is with slightly curved blade and straight butt end which has a perforation on its lower part and a human figure on the upper part. The human figure is with a round head, slim body, hands and legs out stretched. The most characteristic feature is the two long feathers arising from the head and spreading towards the two sides (Fig. 13:1).

(b) Hong Kong and Qujiang men

Two identical human heads are found on bronze daggers from Shibi, Hong Kong and Shixia, Qujiang. The head is with round face, big eyes, small nose, opened mouth, and two spiral buns on left and right sides of the top. These spiral buns are evolved from the long feathers seen on the halberd from Haifeng (Fig. 13:2, Exhibit 61).

(c) Qingyuan man:

One is from a human-headed shaft, and the other from a bronze dagger. The head on shaft has round face, deep eyes, broad nose, closed mouth, big perforated ears, incised grass pattern on forehead, and a ridge on top to represent the hair bun or for perforation (Fig. 13:3). The one on the dagger is a naked figure with round face, two hands resting on the waist and two separate legs. The breast and belly indicate that it is probably a female (Fig. 13:4).

(d) Luoding, Sihui and Guangning men

All are represented by human-headed shafts. The Luoding man has a squarish head, flattened round face, broad eyes and mouth, verticle nose, no hair style. The Sihui and Guangning men are with round head, monkey like face, triangular mouth, deep eyes and flat nose (Fig. 13:5). Among these human figure representations, the Haifeng man is the earliest, as the halberd is dated to W. Zhou. Then come the Hong Kong and Qujiang men, the sites of which can be dated to the Spring and Autumn period. The latest are the Luoding, Sihui and Guangning men who were of the Warring-States period. It was recorded in the geographic chapters, *Hanshu* that "Within an area of seven to eight thousand *li*, from Jiaozhi to Guiqi, the Bai Yue (Hundred Ye) people dwelt and intermixed. There were different clans and names". Thus the native people of Guangdong before the Qin and Han periods must have been one branch of the 'Hundred Ye'. They are also better known as Nan Yue (Southern Yue).

2. Life customs:

As can be seen from archaeological remains and literary records, the Nan Yue people in Guangdong had the following customs and habits:

(a) Hair-cut and tattoo

The custom of hair-cut and tattoo of the Yue people was recorded in ancient writings like *Mozi, Hanfeizi* and *Zhanguo ce* of the Warring-States period as well as in *Shiji* of the Han. According to *Huainanzi*, our main source on Guangdong, and its commentary by Gao You of the Han, there were more activities in water than on land in the south of Jiuyi. The people there cut their hair short and tattooed their bodies to resemble sea serpents, hoping that they would not be harmed by these creatures when they were in water. Jiuyi has been identified to be in Hunan province, near the Southern Ranges. It is therefore quite sure that Guangdong falls within the region mentioned in *Huainanzi*. Tattoo serves the additional purpose of tribal ancestor worship, with different patterns for different tribes. The tribes of Hainan Island also has the custom of tattooing, so that the dead would be recognised by the ancestors in order to facilitate reunion with the ancestors.

(b) Bleeding of arms

As recorded in *Huainanzi* and the commentary by Gao You, the Yue people had the custom of bleeding their arms to confirm a pledge or oath.

(c) Eating of fish, snake, and shellfish

The earliest record for the unusual diet of snake and shellfish was found in *Yi Zhoushu*, the others included *Huainanzi* and *Yantie lun*. Its history in the Lingnan region can be traced to the Neolithic period as indicated by the discovery of many shell mounds piled up by fishbones together with shells of clams, mussels, tortoises and turtles. Such a partiality for seafood continues until today and people in Guangdong still consider various kinds of shellfish as delicacies. The northern Chinese were amazed to find the people in Guangdong eating such exotic food as snakes and shellfish and therefore took note of this custom in writing, whereas the greater predilection for fish of the Guangdong people was hardly recorded.

(d) Dwellings of "pile-structure" type

As recorded in *Bowu zhi* by Zhang Hua and *Nanyue zhi* by Shen Huaiyuan, the houses in which the Southern Yue people dwelt were built upon trees or pillars. The kind of house belongs to the elevated "pile-structure" type, which has the upper part as living quarters and the lower part a shed for keeping domestic animals. This type of house was still popular in the Han dynasty, as indicated by many examples found among the pottery models of houses excavated from Han tombs.

However, archaeological evidence shows that not all houses were built on "pile-structure". In the mountainous sites in northern Guangdong there were houses built directly on the ground and in shell mound sites in Zhujiang delta there were houses built on burnt earth. At Maogang of Gaoyao county, remains of houses of "pile-structure" built upon thick wooden pillars in water were found. These pillars were connected by horizontal beams by means of mortises. These houses, about 4,000 years old, were dated to the late Neolithic period or later.

(e) Belief in ghosts and divination by chicken

Both *Shiji* and *Hanshu* recorded that the Southern Yue people believed in ghosts and used chickens for divination. These ceremonies were conducted by shamans who enjoyed high social status. Divination by means of chicken was in practice for a long time. The Li tribe preserved its rituals in entirely until the liberation in 1949.

(f) Peacock-shaped handles on doors

The use of peacock-shaped handles on doors as decoration, mentioned only in *Yantie lun*, was apparently a special characteristic of Southern Yue custom.

3. Mysterious rock carvings:

Rock carvings in relief, which fall into the category of art, stand apart from the usual Bronze Age artifacts of Guangdong such as bronzes, pottery and jade carvings. They were found mainly in Hong Kong, though it has been said that similar discoveries have been made on the islands of Zhuhai.

The earliest record for these rock carvings was found in "*Gazetter of Xin'an County*" of 1819. The first discovery was made by Mr. Chen Gongzhe at Shibi, on Dayushan, to be followed by many more. Just based on *Rock Carvings in Hong Kong* by William Meacham, the list includes Shibi, Putai (Po Toi), Donglong (Tung Lung), Dalangwan (Tai Long Wan), Changzhou (Cheung Chau), Damiaowan (Tai Miu Wan), Jiaoxizhou (Kau Sai Chau), etc.

The appearance of these mysterious rock carvings was quite puzzling. Years of investigation and research conducted by Hong Kong scholars were able to put forth the following answers:

(a) The rock carvings are dated to the Bronze Age.

(b) The designs on these rock carvings are identical to those found on pottery and bronzes of Bronze Age Guangdong.

(c) The origin and formation of these rock carvings are obviously related to the customs and beliefs of Bronze Age man, embodying meaning and significance incomprehensible to us in the modern age.

Based on available materials, all the rock carvings are done in relief with motifs identical to those on pottery and bronzes. These are stylized patterns and are not at all realistic. There are three types of designs. The first type is zoomorphic, which is comparatively few in number. Examples include the design of birds at Donglong and snakes at Putai and Changzhou. The second type is geometric, of which larger quantities are found. The various designs can all be identified with the decorations on bronzes, for example, typical spiral patterns can be seen at lower Shibi and the standard basket patern at upper Shibi. The motifs found at Putai are the same as those on bronze spearheads and bells, while those from Jiaoxizhou can be identified with some of the patterns on bronze spearheads. The third type is the combination of zoomorphic and geometric patterns. For instance, the rock carving at Dalangwan has designs resembling snake heads alongside spiral patterns. In some places the patterns are not identifiable. As far as I can see, with the exception of the bird pattern at Donglong, all these three types of designs can be found on bronzes and pottery unearthed in Guangdong. The snake head from Dalangwan is similar to the spiral and the "*Wang*"-mark on bronze bells excavated at Huilai county, and is essentially closely related to the spiral pattern. The appearance of the bird pattern at Donglong is not at all coincidental. From the feather headgear of the human figure on the bronze halberd of Haifeng, and the spiral-shaped feathers on the human heads on bronze daggers from Hong Kong and Qujiang, it is possible to surmise that the origin of the spiral pattern could have been inspired by bird feathers. It must have been fashionable at that time to put feathers on the head. As for the reasons for the use of feather headgear, it can be explained by the worship of birds as a visible form of totemism. Another possibility would be a sign of attaining adulthood. There exists a profound relationship between bird, snake and spiral patterns as well as the feather pattern, and further explorations are needed.

(B) Social classes in Guangdong

Following the introduction of bronzes of Shang and Zhou periods to Guangdong, the technique of bronze casting was also introduced. Bronzes were being produced in the Lingnan region the latest by the Spring and Autumn period. The manufacture and use of bronzes improved vastly the level of productivity and thus motivated developments in the Southern Yue society. A slave system resulted. The earliest evidence for the existence of slave system in Guangdong was found from two tombs of the late Spring and Autumn to early Warring-States periods at Matougang, Qingyuan county. The two tombs, quite large in size, were unfortunately so damaged that their construction is no longer discernible. Burial objects include 64 bronzes, featuring jars, chime bells, *zheng* bells, spearheads, axes, broad axes, daggers, arrowheads, chisels, human-headed shafts, scrapers, etc. Alongside are pottery jars decorated with *kui*-dragons, net and combed patterns, as well as whetstones. The presence of beautifully cast bronze jars, serial bells and the large quantity of weapons indicates that the buried dead were no ordinary people but slave owners and noble men. The existence of slave system is further proven by the bronze human-headed shafts found in the tombs. Apparently a slave is depicted, showing perforated ears and tattooed '↓' pattern on the forehead. Perforation of ears and tattooing of forehead were corporal punishments in practice during the Warring-States period, as recorded in *Zuozhuan* and *Shiji*. By using a penal code and system to control slaves and criminals, the slave system of Southern Yue has developed one step beyond the patriarchal slave system. It is doubtful that these human-head shafts were used for chariot fittings, as mention was made in *Huainanzi* about the more common use of boats as means of transport by the Yue people. They also served a different purpose from the staff head decorations seen in Shizhaishan of Yunnan. To be able to use the slave image in the human-headed shafts presupposes a privilege enjoyed by high-powered slave owners, thus the buried dead could only be aristocratic slave owners. Similar objects excavated from other tombs may not show perforated ears and tattooed foreheads, yet they are so ugly that they could possibly intend to be slave images.

The main source of slaves came from waging battles and the Yue people were known to have a lot of in-fighting among themselves, according to *Hanshu*. Since the Spring and Autumn period, the Chu state engaged in several battles with the Southern Yue, in an attempt to suppress the uprising there. The Southern Yue tombs of the Warring-States period contained many bronze weapons. Usually we find two bronze swords, a large one in Chu-Yue style and a short one, alongside sets of spearheads and arrowheads. At Guangning a small group of tombs with bronze swords was discovered. The fact that these were built closely together and that the combination of weapons was quite systematic, could mean that this was the burial ground for a garrison. Bronze tools were found in quite a few tombs, indicating that the army also took part in production activities.

Southern Yue people of the Warring-States period were valiant and bold. They were often armed with swords which were buried with them after death. Even though textual evidence shows that the Yue people were not adept at the use of bow and arrow, archaeological discoveries prove otherwise. Ever since the Neolithic period large quantities of stone arrowheads were produced and used, and in the Spring and Autumn and Warring-States periods, all tombs buried with bronze weapons were inevitably accompanied by bronze arrowheads.

Shiji recorded that after Yue was conquered by Chu, the Yue princes were scattered to the southern coastal area where they established themselves as regional rulers, paying tribute to the state of Chu. However, this does not mean that there was no inhabitants in the southern coastal region before the arrival of these Yue princes. Actually the indigenious Minyue, Nanyue, Xiou, Luoyue had already initiated developments which provided the foundation for the rule of the Yue princes. By the Warring-States period many small states ruled by princes and generals were established in the Southern Yue area. Therefore, the large tombs excavated at Qingyuan, Zhaoqing and Luoding, in which a sizable amount of bronze objects were found, could possibly be tombs of princes or generals of Southern Yue.

(C) Economic condition in Guangdong

1. Major advancements in handicrafts

(a) Bronze casting as the main industry of metallurgy in Southern Yue

The technique of bronze casting has been discussed in detail previously and there is no need to repeat here. I may add that the Guangdong people had not only mastered the technique of casting bronze with copper and tin, they also knew about the nature of lead. In a large tomb at Zhaoqing, it was found that a piece of lead was cast inside a square vessel, apparently to make use of the heavier weight of lead to increase gravity. To be able to differentiate and make use of the properties of lead and tin certainly can be considered an advancement in metallurgy. From the same tomb was unearthed a jade ring with a gold mount. Similar objects have not been found elsewhere and therefore it provides valuable information for the study of gold wares of Guangdong.

(b) Flourish of the pottery industry

The manufacture of impressed geometric pottery was an important industry in Guangdong, because of the large demand and extensive use in the daily lives of the people. Significant developments in the manufacture of pottery in Guangdong took place in the Spring and Autumn to the Warring-States periods in the following aspects:

(i) The manufacture of impressed geometric pottery reached its zenith in the Spring and Autumn period. The decorations, refined and elegant, consist of mainly motifs in relief, supplemented by incised designs. Both the designs and shapes take bronzes as prototypes. The hardness of the bodies shows that they were fired at a high temperature.

(ii) The impressed geometric pottery, made by the padding-and-modelling technique, declined in the Warring-States period because of the common use of the potter's wheel. The increased demand for pottery eventually replaced the padding-and-modelling technique by wheel-turning, which is capable of mass production. Consequently the new decorative technique of incising evolved and became popular in late technique of incising evolved and became popular in late Warring-States to early Western Han periods. By this time the only impressed decorations in use were the net and basket patterns. The adoption of wheel-turning means a great leap forward for the pottery industry for it is a more professional and commercial method. While the modelling method may be suitable for family production, the wheel is more appropriate in specialized workshops. As commercial products, many of the wheel-turned pottery carry on them incised marks or characters. The design of kilns also changed from the vertical to horizontal, enabling higher firing temperature and more space for the ware. The kiln excavated at Xigualing, Zengcheng, of the Warring-States period, measuring 9.8 m. long and 2 m. wide, can be considered a prototype for the later dragon kiln.

(iii) A number of proto-porcellaneous and glazed pottery was found from sites of the Spring and Autumn period. From the "double-F" pottery cultural layer at Shixia site, Qujiang, proto-porcellaneous wares with greyish white bodies and green or yellowish green glaze were unearthed. The shapes include bowls, stem-cups and jars. Glazed proto-porcellaneous pottery make up about 1.53% of all pottery finds. They are more commonly found in eastern Guangdong, while in northern and western Guangdong discoveries have also been made. These new products initiated a new direction in ceramic technology and became the dominant production of the pottery industry after Han.

(c) Further developments in other handicrafts

Building on the foundation of polished stone implements of lat Neolithic period, finely carved and highly polished stone and jade weapons of knives, swords, halberds and spearheads were made, using the bronze ones as prototype.

The lacquer wares from the Warring-States tombs at Zhaoqing were so damaged that only small fragments in black or red remained. Yet traces of gold leaf on some of the fragments can still be seen.

The existence of textiles can only be discerned from traces of hemp and silk left on pottery and bronzes. Yet there was textual evidence of the cultivation of hemp by men and production of silk by women in Hainan Island, as recorded in *Hanshu*. Therefore, silk and hemp weaving should have been quite advanced in Guangdong before Han, especially since a kind of hemp cloth used to be an important tribute to the court from Han times. After all, this kind of hemp cloth could well be one of the significant discoveries of Guangdong people.

The scraper is the most popular of bronze tools. Generally they are pointed and have double blades, yet some have a hooked-point which is ideal for scraping bamboo sticks or weaving bamboo. Impressions of bamboo weaving were found on the bottom of a bronze basin excavated at Guangning, demonstrating the popularity of this handicraft.

2. Advancements in agriculture

Until the late phase of primitive society, the prevalence of shell mound sites in the Zhujiang delta indicates that the people there relied on hunting and fishing for livelihood. Agricultural production was quite backward. In the Zhou period, some farmers with sheep as their totem arrived in Panyu of Zhujiang delta, bringing with them a fine species of rice which would grow "one stem with six ears". They also introduced the techniques of rice cultivation, changing the main productive activity for Guangdong people from hunting and fishing to agricultural cultivation. People could lead a stable living and Guangdong prospered. Rice cultivation spread from the mountainous region of northern Guangdong to Zhujiang delta and southern coastal area, exerting tremendous influence on social and economic developments in Guangdong. Well before early Han, rice was not cultivated in the south, the correct amount of water was also under control. In addition, Guangdong was also well-known for its tropical and sub-tropical fruits.

During the Spring and Autumn to the Warring-States periods, agriculture in Guangdong was still in the slash-and-burn phase. Bronze tools were much more efficient than polished stone ones for cutting down trees for burning. Therefore, a lot of bronze axes, broad axes, chisels and adzes were unearthed from dwelling as well as burial sites. In addition, bronze hoes and spades were frounded from a Warring-States tomb in Guangning, demonstrating the improvement of tools for cultivation. The excavation of iron axes and spades from a dwelling site at Baishiping proves that iron was in use by the late Warring-States period. Equipped with efficient and cheap farming implements, the agricultural production of Guangdong entered a new stage.

3. Emergence of cities with development in commerce and transportation

Panyu was the earliest city to appear in Guangdong. It was the municipal of Nanhai prefecture in Qin and Han periods, and its name was changed to Guangzhou in the Three Kingdoms period. However, there has long been arguments about the origin of Panyu as a city. One version based on *Guangzhou ji* by Pei Yuan of the Jin dynasty, relates Panyu to Chuting. The place was mentioned again in a legend recorded in *Yangcheng guchao*, that five immortals arrive at Chuting from Nanhai in the Zhou period. They left behind the rice which they brought along and when they disappeared in the sky the sheep that they rode on turned into stone. Thereafter, Guangzhou has been given names like "city of five sheep", "city of sheep", "city of immortals", and "city of grain" accordingly. Considering that the appearance of cities is the result of developments in politics, economics, and transportation, Guangdong in the Western Zhou period did not have the conditions for building a city, as it had barely entered Bronze Age and its productive power was still quite low. Qu Dajun suggested in *Guangdong xinyu* that Chuting was build later in the Spring and Autumn period after Nanhai was subjugated by the Chu. It seems that Qu's point was well taken. Another version that is quite persuasive relates Panyu to Nanwu city built by Gongshi Yu, a Yue prime minister. His story was recorded in the old version of *Zhushu jinian* and therefore was not a legendary figure. The building of Nanwu by Yu at the time of Nanwang of Zhou period was recorded in *Guangdong tongzhi*. Mr. Wu Tingjin, director of Guangdong Tongzhi Guan in Zhongshan University, noted that bricks from the Nanwu city and for the palace of the Yue Kingdom have been unearthed in Guangdong, thus Nanwu city could have come into existence by this time.

Even though the building of a Southern Yue city during the Warring-States period is debatable, textual evidence proves that Panyu was already a famous capital by this time. *Huainanzi* recorded that the army groups were sent along five routes by the First Emperor of Qin to conquer the Lingnan region, one route was to "the capital of Panyu". Thus it is quite clear that the capital of Panyu already existed before the Qin and was subsequently turned into Nanhai prefecture in the Qin period. Besides, *Shiji* and *Hanshu* both recorded that Panyu was a flourishing trading centre for pearls, ivory, rhinoceros skins, fruits, and cloth not only during Qin-Han periods, but even before.

Guangdong society went through major developments in the Spring and Autumn and Warring-States periods. With more frequent exchanges between the Central Plains and guangdong, their cultures grew closer and closer. Therefore, from late Spring and Autumn to Warring-States periods, quite a few Guangdong men distinguished themselves in the Central Plains. Those mentioned in ancient texts include Yong Huo, who became a general of Fu Chai, Prince of Wu; Gao Gu was prime minister to Weiwang of Chu and Gongshi Yu was prime minister of Yue. All three were natives of Nanhai. This kind of prominence would not be possible, if not for the social and economic developments in Guangdong.

The discussions in the foregoing pages are not necessarily conclusive. Comments are most welcome, particularly from scholars in Hong Kong. It is hoped that further cultural and academic exchanges between Guangdong and Hong Kong will bring about greater achievement in Bronze Age archaeology and research in the Guangdong region.

Bibliography:

1. Chen Gongzhe, "Arachaeological Excavations in Hong Kong", *Kaogu Xuebao*, 1957:4.

2. CPAM, Guangdong Province, "Bronze of Zhou Period Found at Qingyuan, Guangdong", *Kaogu*, 1963:2.

3. ----, "Tombs of Eastern Zhou at Qingyuan, Guangdong", *Kaogu*, 1964:3.

4. Guangdong Provincial Museum, "Tombs of Warring-States Period at Tonggugang, Guangning County, Guangdong", *Kaoguxue Jikan*, Vol. 1, 1981.

5. ----, "Tombs of Warring-States Period at Liaodanshan, Sihui, Guangdong", *Kaogu*, 1975:2.

6. ----, "Bronzes of Warring-States Period Unearthed from Luoding, Guangdong", *Kaogu*, 1983:1.

7. ----, "Preliminary Report on the Excavation of Ancient Tombs at Songshan, Beiling, Zhaoqing city, Guangdong", *Wenwu*, 1974:11.

8. He Jisheng, "A Discussion on the Bronze Age Culture of Eastern Zhou Period in Guangdong and Its Relationship to Impressed Geometric Pottery", *Wenwu jikan*, No. 3, Beijing, 1981.

9. Hua Jueming, Huang Weixin, Wang Xiulan and Xu Hengbin, "Studies on Casting Techniques of the Bronzes Unearthed from Guangdong Province", *Proceedings of the First National Academic Conference on the History of Ancient Technology*, 1983.

10. Jao Tsung-i, "Prehistoric Sites and their Culture in Hanjiang Region", Hong Kong, 1950.

11. Li Zhongda, Hua Jueming and Zhang Hongli, "Studies on the composition of Alloys in the Bronzes of Shang and Zhou Periods and Discussions on Compositions of Bells and Tripods", Papers read at the Second Annual Academic Conference on the History of Chemistry in 1982. in 1982.

12. Maglioni, Rafael, *Archaeological Discovery in Eastern Kwangtung*, Hong Kong, 1975.

13. Meacham, William, *Archaeology in Hong Kong*, Hong Kong, 1980.

14. ----, *Rock Carvings in Hong Kong*, Hong Kong, 1976.

15. ----, et al, *Sham Wan, Lamma Island — An Archaeological Site Study*, Hong Kong, 1978.

16. Schofield, Walter, *An Archaeological Site at Shek Pik*, Hong Kong, 1975.

17. Xu Hengbin, "A Discussion on the Singnificant Influences of Chu Culture on the Development of Guangdong History", *Proceedings of the Second Annual Meeting of the Chinese Archaeological Society*, Beijing, 1982.

18. ----, 'A Study on "Haircut and Tattoo"', *Minzu Yanjiu*, IV, 1982.

19. C.H. Yip, "Fifty Years of Hong Kong Archaeology", *Journal of the Hong Kong Archaeological Society*, Vol. VI, 1975.

20. Zhou Shirong, "Studies on Ancient Characters Unearthed from Chu Tombs in Hunan", *Hunan Kaogu Jikan*, Vol. 1, 1982.

廣東東周時期靑銅器墓葬制芻議

邱立誠
廣東省博物館

廣東境內自1962年在淸遠縣馬頭崗發現第一座以靑銅器為主要隨葬品的東周墓葬以來，這類墓目前已發現有三十七座。本文謹就墓葬制度的有關問題作初步探討。

一、墓地的選擇及墓坑形制

三十七座墓葬分佈在西江、北江和東江兩岸地區，其中大部份位於西江兩岸山地區，包括有廣寧①、肇慶②、羅定③、德慶④、懷集⑤等地的二十九座；北江、西江下游的粵中低地孤山區也有一些，包括有淸遠⑥、四會⑦兩地的五座；其餘的分佈在粵北的佛崗⑧、粵東的龍門⑨、揭陽⑩等地。

從地理情況看，這些墓葬均位於距離河流不遠、高度在距地面60米以下的低矮山崗上，如廣寧縣銅鼓崗墓地，墓葬分佈在高60米、長200米的橢圓形山崗，背臨北江支流的綏江；四會縣鳥旦山墓位於綏江與北江合流的三角洲地帶中的小高地，距北江、綏江、西江都在14公里以內；淸遠縣馬頭崗墓位於北江西岸10公里處；肇慶松山墓、德慶縣落雁山墓都靠近西江，羅定縣的四座墓則在西江南面支流的太平河、沙蒳河附近。由此看來，這些靑銅器墓均位於當時比較發達的交通要道。

這些靑銅器墓均係土坑豎穴墓，大致分作大、中、小三類（表一）。

大型墓只有肇慶松山墓一座。墓坑較大，長8米，寬約4.7米。有棺椁，可惜已腐爛，僅存數條枕木。隨葬品較多，達139件，其中靑銅器佔28%。這是廣東目前發現的東周墓葬中形制規模最大，隨葬品最多的一座。

中型墓八座。墓坑一般長3—4米，寬2米左右。隨葬品有數十件到一百多件不等。其中四會縣鳥旦山墓原報告認為前室沒有隨葬器物，在西壁則有木椁痕跡，但據羅定縣背夫山墓的情況來分析，這兩座墓的形制、規模大致相同，隨葬品的數量、組合和放置形式都非常接近，依此，鳥旦山墓的"前室"看來不是墓室範圍，"後室"才是墓室；淸遠馬頭崗的兩座墓，墓坑已被破壞，按其隨葬品的數量及組合情況，應屬中型墓；揭陽雲路一號墓，隨葬品被擾亂而收集不全，按其墓坑大小，亦列入此類。這類墓目前看不見有使用木椁的痕跡。

小型墓共二十八座。這類墓葬的墓坑，除個別長達4.75米外，一般長2.6—3.4米，寬0.6—1.5米，隨葬品多在20件以下，也有的在30—40件左右。

一個顯著的特點是，中、小型墓中有的在墓底設腰坑放置一件大陶器，這種腰坑僅比放置的陶器略大一點，其中有的是方形的，如四會鳥旦山墓、廣寧銅鼓崗墓及德慶落雁山墓等；也有的是圓形的，如羅定背夫山墓。設腰坑的做法，當是受中原商至西周時期墓葬的影響，不過已不像中原地區那樣用來埋一隻狗或殉人，而是埋一件陶器。這種形式，成為東周時期南越族較為流行的葬俗之一，至西漢初期還可見。

此外，淸遠馬頭崗春秋墓及廣寧銅鼓崗戰國墓中有的在墓底舖河卵石，這種做法也延至西漢早期。墓底舖石，起着散水的作用，看來也是學自中原地區。

二、隨葬品的組合及其放置形式

廣東東周時期的墓葬隨葬品，靑銅器可分成五類：1.食器。如鍋、鼎、壺、盉；2.容器。如罍、盤、筩、鑑；3.樂器。如鐘、鉦、鐸；4.兵器（圖二）。如劍、矛、戈、鏃、鉞；5.工具。如斧、鑿、削、篾刀、鋸、鐮。陶器則有數量不多的罐甕，有的還有瓿、盒等。此外，大中型墓還常見一種人首柱形靑銅器，上端為人首，下端為方柱，方柱下方有楔形插梢，人首為圓眼高鼻，有的貫耳（圖一：3）。這類器有大有小，大者高達40厘米，小者高20多厘米，每墓各出四件（兩對）。這類人首柱形器目前僅見於廣東境內北江及西江流域地區，很可能是當地越人特有的一種器具。有的人首柱形器的柱體上還鑄有"王"字形標記⑪，這種"王"字形圖案在西江流域地區的靑銅器墓中的矛、鉞、斧、篾刀的器身上是常見的。因此，將"王"字形圖案看作是南越郡國鑄造靑銅器的標記⑫，並不是沒有道理的。在江蘇、江西、湖南等地發現鑄有"王"字形標記的靑銅器⑬，亦應是南越郡國所製造。

隨葬品中，常見有兩種鼎，一種為直腹鼎（圖一：2），雙耳立於口沿上，耳為方形；另一種為盤口鼎（圖一：1），雙耳為繩索形環耳，立於口沿內側；三條外撇的實足斷面為扁圓形，鼎體外佈滿烟炱，爲實用器當無疑問。這些鼎一般通稱爲越式鼎，主要見於南方地區。事實上，廣東這時期青銅器墓中的隨葬品，青銅器大部份都是實用器，其中有的是經過使用損壞再修補投入使用，如肇慶松山墓的一件鼎，經過多次鉗補；有的是因使用而有些殘缺，如羅定背夫山墓出的一件叉，中柱已斷去一截。就陶器而言，全部都是實物器。

隨葬品的組合情況，在不同類型的墓中，各墓的器物組合無論是種類或是數量都有一些差異。組合的形式主要有以下幾種：

(1) 大型墓　青銅器鍋、鼎、罍、盤、壺、筒、鐘、人首柱形器、劍、矛、鏃、削；陶器甕、罐、瓿、盒。（肇松墓）

(2) 中型墓　青銅器鼎、罍、缶、盂、鑑、鐘、鉦、人首柱形器、劍、短劍、矛、戈、鉞、鏃、斧、鑿；陶器缶、罐。（羅太南M1、清馬M1）

(3) 中型墓　青銅器鼎、盂、鑑、鐸、人首柱形器、劍、短劍、戈、矛、鉞、鏃、斧、鑿、削、篾刀；陶器罐、甕。（四鳥墓、羅背墓）

(4) 小型墓　青銅器鼎、盤、鐸、劍、短劍、矛、鉞、鏃、斧、鑿、削、篾刀；陶器甕。（德落墓、廣銅M16）

(5) 小型墓　青銅器劍、矛、鏃、斧、鑿、削、篾刀；陶器瓿。（廣銅M10、M19）

在五種組合類型中，組合(2)的出現年代最早，流行於春秋中晚期到戰國初期，突出的特徵是，常見短劍（圖二：9），陶器花紋多是春秋時期流行的花紋；組合(3)的年代在戰國早期，器物特徵與組合(2)較爲接近，個別器物如劍、戈（圖二：5，10）爲戰國時流行的形制；組合(1)是個別例子，年代不會早於戰國中期，不出短劍，器物多流行於整個戰國時期，其中有的器物如銅筒、陶瓿、盒、罐等，更接近於晚期風格；組合(4)(5)的年代已在戰國中晚期，短劍已很少見到，青銅器也是戰國流行的形制，但陶器風格顯然晚於組合(2)(3)。

隨葬器物的組合情況還表明，各類組合的主要區別在於飲食器種類的多寡，而在兵器、工具的種類上是大同小異的，只是在數量上有較大的差異。組合(1)(2)(3)都隨葬有人首柱形器，這是它們與組合(4)(5)的一個顯著的區別，這類人首柱形器的放置形式以及其可以插於木柄上的作用說明，其用途應是一類儀仗用具，大概是一種象徵或顯示權威的標誌。此外，無論那一類組合，劍、矛、鏃這類兵器都是不缺的，說明南越人對兵器的重視，從中也反映出越人的征伐戰事是較頻繁的。

隨葬品放置的一般規律是，人首柱形器置於墓室前後兩端，呈兩對站立。墓室前端主要放置編鐘、鐸、鑑、盂等；中部大都置劍、矛、戈一類兵器；後端多置鼎、罍、盤一類器物及工具，青銅工具的旁邊多並排放置磨石；裝飾品多置於墓室中部，看來是與劍類放在死者身旁（或死者身上），但也有放在墓室的前後端，如羅定背夫山墓，墓室前後端兩對人首柱形器前均有一塊不大的石頭，石頭旁邊置一件玉器，前端的是一件玉玦，後端的一件因破碎器形不辨，這兩件玉器應是用作葬儀的。陶器的放置，除大陶器（甕或罐）置於腰坑外，大都放在墓室後端。就隨葬品的放置形式來分析，在埋葬墓主人時，曾舉行過一定規模的喪葬儀式。

三、關於墓主人身份及墓葬等級

由於葬具基本腐朽無存，無法從使用葬具的情況來進行探討。這裡僅從墓坑的規模結合隨葬器物的組合情況作粗略的分析。

廣東地處嶺南，東周時期爲百越之地。《漢書·地理志》載："自交趾至會稽七、八千里，百粵雜處，各有種姓"。兩廣地區，當時有南越，西甌（又稱駱越），其中南越族主要在今廣東省境，北界抵湖南、江西，繼而發展到廣西及以南地區，至秦末時立南越國。在秦以前，南越處於部落的分散狀態，沒有統一的政治組織。但從考古發現的資料看，南越族在東周時期應有分散的小邦國，史料記載戰國楚滅越後，"越以此散，諸族子爭立，或爲王，或爲君，濱於江南海上"[14]，再參照西甌人有君譯吁宋，有將桀駿[15]的情況來分析，廣東發現的東周時期的青銅器大墓，其墓主人當屬擁有相當財富的奴隸主貴族，其中有的可能就是"君王"、"將"一類的上層人物。

墓坑情況表明，大型墓不僅墓坑規模大，同時也是唯一可見使用木槨的大墓，隨葬器物的種類和數量都較之中小型墓要多，器物組合最爲完整。出土的青銅器如錯銀銅罍、提梁壺、三足盤等都是來自楚地的精品，金柄玉環（圖一：4）、玉帶鉤、琉璃珠等都是十分貴重的飾物，且墓中出有五鼎，依周制，已是"上大夫"的身份，可見該墓主人有很高的地位，很可能是屬於"君王"一級的南越郡國上層統治者。

中型墓的規模較之大型墓要小，雖然有的墓隨葬品數量也達一百多件，但在器物種類上顯然比不上大型墓。組合(2)是中型墓中較完整的，器物雖不似肇慶松山墓所出的精美，但在兵器、工具的種類上卻超過組合(1)；組合(3)的飲食器略少一些，而在兵器、工具類方面亦與組合(2)相同。這類墓一般都出有二鼎或三鼎，依周制亦在"大夫"一級，再從青銅兵器及工具較多的情況來分析，墓主人亦是有一定財富和權勢的，同樣享有"鐘鳴鼎食"的社會地位，大概屬"將"一級的南越族上層貴族。

小型墓中的隨葬器物組合(4)，鼎只出一件，多見一至二件劍及少量其他兵器、工具，這類墓的等級較低，大致相當於周制的"士"一級，墓主人應是擁有少量財富的小奴隸主；組合(5)不出鼎，隨葬品較少，其墓主人當是平時參加生產，戰時則持矛執弓佩劍參加征伐械鬥的平民。

四、結語

通過上述對廣東東周青銅器墓葬制度的分析，可以得到如下幾點認識：

1. 廣東東周時期的青銅器墓，是研究南越國以前南越族上中層社會狀況的重要資料。從中可以窺見南越地區秦以前的軍事、經濟、交通、手工業等方面的發展情況。代表各個等級的各類墓葬，說明廣東確實存在過青銅器時代，並產生了等級森嚴的奴隸制形態。

2. 廣東東周青銅器墓的隨葬器物組合有濃厚的地方特點。（1）隨葬品絕大部份是實用器；（2）大中型墓以兩對四件的青銅人首柱形器立放於墓室兩端；（3）越式青銅鼎體外佈滿烟炱，器壁極薄，三條實足則厚重；（4）兵器、工具普遍存在，多見劍、矛、鉞、斧、篾刀，少見戈，器身多見"王"字形圖案（圖二：7）；（5）陶器花紋為廣東地區常見的幾何印紋。

3. 大中型墓的隨葬品帶有楚文化影響的色彩。如蹄狀足大銅鼎、錯銀銅壘、三足盤、提梁壺等，造型風格與楚墓出土的完全相同，所飾的羽狀紋、鳥狀紋、飛鳥雲氣紋等，均係楚器流行的紋樣，尤其是成套編鐘的隨葬，不能不說是受楚國禮制的影响。這種情況顯然反映了南越族上層人物與楚國文化的接觸，同時也是嶺南地區與楚國有相當密切關係的物證。而小型墓則很少看到有楚器的風格。

4. 廣東各地青銅文化的發展是不平衡的，目前發現的東周青銅器墓主要集中在西江流域地區，雖然這與考古工作的不平衡有關，但至少亦反映了該地區在東周時期青銅器文化較為發達的事實。此外，還應注意到，廣東東周時期青銅器墓反映出來的楚器及受楚器風格影响的器物逐漸增多的事實，顯然是楚文化對廣東地區的影響逐步深入的結果。

5. 廣東東周時期的青銅器墓，其形制以墓底設腰坑為顯著特點，腰坑中置一件大陶器，與中原商周墓腰坑的用途相異，這顯然是地方葬俗的反映。廣西、湖南也發現有這類墓，如廣西平樂銀嶺山戰國墓（其中有的應晚至西漢初期）[16]，有不少都設腰坑，出土器物，其中許多與廣東東周青銅器墓所見的相同，這至少說明當時有南越族在廣西平樂一帶活動；湖南長沙、湘鄉也發現有數量不多的這類墓[17]，年代為春秋初期，形制及隨葬品與楚墓迥然不同，很可能是南越人墓葬，表明南越族的活動範圍在春秋時確曾抵達湖南，這與楚國南界逐漸南移的歷史事實是吻合的。

廣州西漢早期墓亦有少量設有腰坑[18]，這種墓除從墓葬形制及一些陶器還可看到與上述東周青銅器墓有相近之處以外，其他隨葬物的風格有較大的差異。這類西漢墓可看作是南越族葬俗延續性的反映。至西漢中期，這種墓就再也沒有出現。反映了漢文化與南越族文化逐步融合的一個側面。

註 釋

[1] 廣寧縣共二十二座。見廣東省博物館，《廣東廣寧縣銅鼓崗戰國墓》，《考古學集刊》第一集，北京，1981。

[2] 廣東省博物館，《廣東肇慶市北嶺松山古墓發掘簡報》，《文物》1974.11。

[3] 羅定縣太平南門洞共發現三座，見廣東省博物館，《廣東羅定出土一批戰國青銅器》，《考古》1983.1。羅平背夫山發現一座，發掘簡報未發表。

[4] 徐恒彬等，《廣東德慶發現戰國墓》，《文物》1973.9。

[5][8][9] 懷集、佛崗、龍門分別發現一座。參閱何紀生，《略論廣東東周時期的青銅文化及其與幾何印紋陶的關係》，《文物集刊》第三集，北京，1981。

[6] 廣東省文管會，《廣東清遠發現周代青銅器》，《考古》1963.2。《廣東清遠的東周墓葬》，《考古》1964.3。

[7] 四會縣烏旦山發現一座，見廣東省博物館，《廣東四會烏旦山戰國墓》，《考古》1975.2。龍江高地園發現二座，參見注[5]。

[10] 揭陽縣雲路中夏一號墓，見汕頭地區文管站等，《揭陽東周墓發掘報告》，《汕頭文物》第九期，汕頭，1982。此外，高州、廉江、始興、博羅、龍川等地也發現有東周時期的青銅器墓，本文沒有列入統計。

[11] 羅定縣羅平背夫山墓出土，發掘簡報未發表。

[12] 徐恒彬，《南越先秦史初探》，《百越民族史論集》，北京，1982。

[13] 吳山菁，《江蘇六合縣和仁東周墓》，《考古》1977.5；江西省博物館，《南昌東郊西漢墓》，《考古學報》1976.2；湖南省博物館，《長沙瀏城橋一號墓》，《考古學報》1972.1。

[14] 《史記·越王勾踐世家》。

[15] 《淮南子·人間訓》。

[16] 廣西壯族自治區文物工作隊，《平樂銀山嶺戰國墓》，《考古學報》1978.2。

[17] 高至喜，《湖南古代墓葬概況》，《文物》1960.3。湖南省博物館，《湖南韶山灌區湘鄉東周墓清理簡報》，《文物》1977.3。

[18] 廣州市文管會等，《廣州漢墓》，中國田野考古報告集考古學專刊丁種第21號，北京，1981。

廣東東周時期青銅器（部份）登記表

類別	墓號	墓室 長（米）	墓室 寬（米）	形制	隨葬品 青銅器	隨葬品 金、玉、琉璃器	隨葬品 石器	隨葬品 陶器	總計	備註
大型墓	肇慶松山墓	8	4.7	土坑木槨	108	9	1	21	139	
中型墓	羅定南門垌M1	4	2	土坑	136			1	137	
	羅定背夫山墓	4	2	土坑	98	3	8	7	116	
	四會鳥旦山墓	3.5	1 ?	土坑	59		3	1	63	
	清遠馬頭崗M1			土坑	25		2	2	29	擾亂，器物收集不全
	清遠馬頭崗M2	2.8 ?	1.1 ?	土坑	39		13	1	53	部份擾亂
小型墓	德慶落雁山墓	4.75	1.5	土坑	15		3	1	19	
	廣寧銅鼓崗M10	(殘)0.8	0.6	土坑	8			1	9	部份擾亂
	廣寧銅鼓崗M13	3.2	0.75	土坑	8			6	14	
	廣寧銅鼓崗M14	2.6	0.75	土坑	31		2	2	35	
	廣寧銅鼓崗M16	3.4	0.9	土坑	35		5		40	
	廣寧銅鼓崗M19	3.4	0.78	土坑	18		3	1	22	
	廣寧銅鼓崗M21	(殘)3	0.75	土坑	28		4		32	部份擾亂

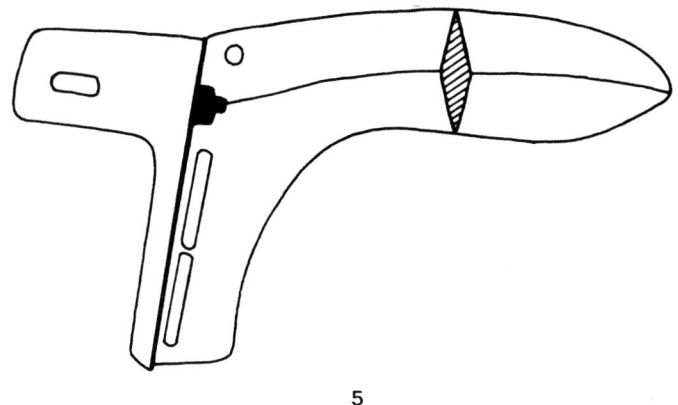
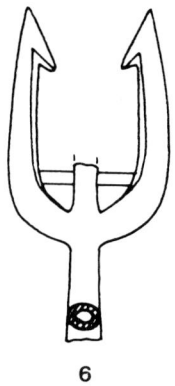

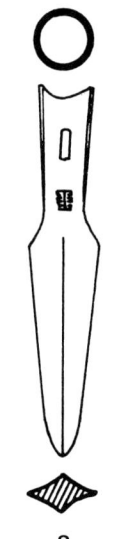
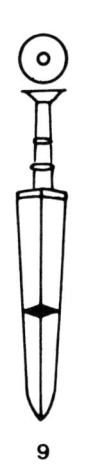
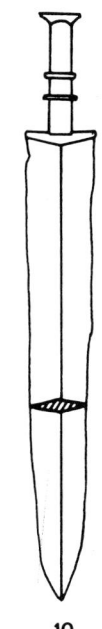

5. 銅戈
6. 銅叉（羅定背夫山墓）
7. 銅篾刀
8. 銅矛
9. 銅短劍（廣寧銅鼓崗墓）
10. 銅劍（四會鳥旦山墓）

5. bronze halberd
6. bronze fork (tomb at Beifushan, Luoding)
7. bronze scraper
8. bronze spearhead
9. bronze dagger (tomb at Tonggugang, Guangning)
10. bronze sword (tomb at Liaodanshan, Sihui)

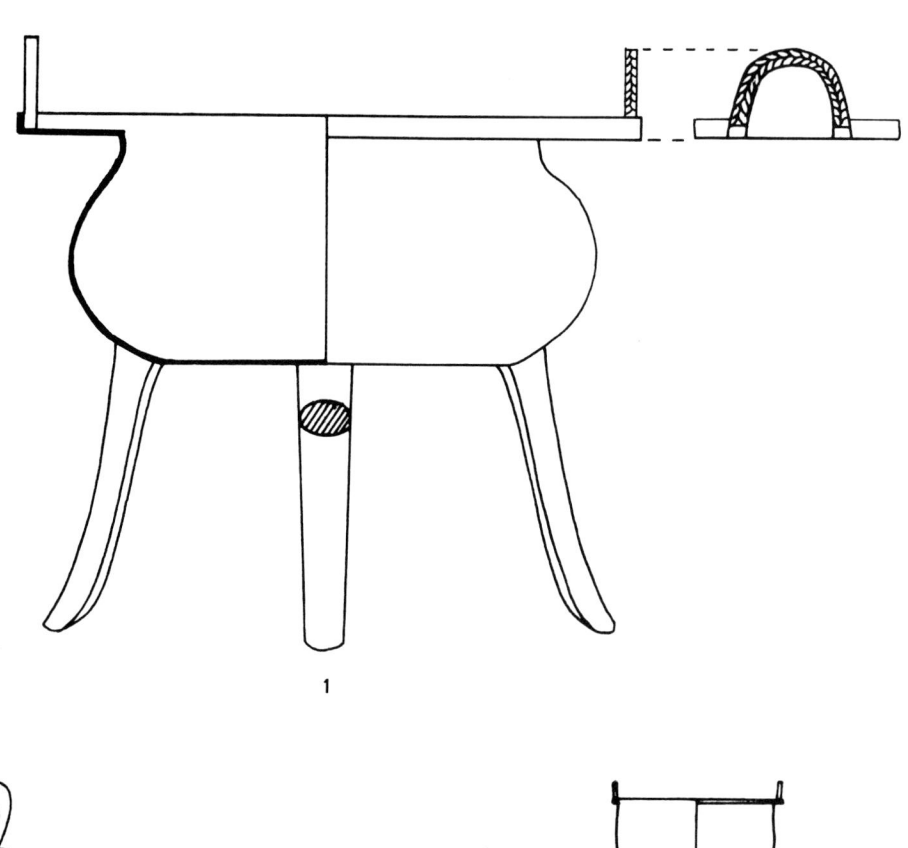
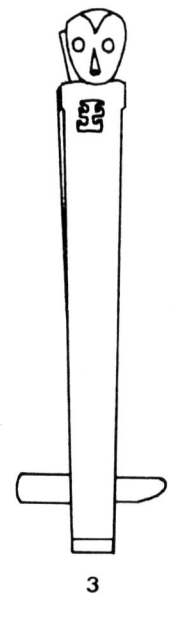
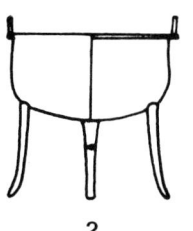
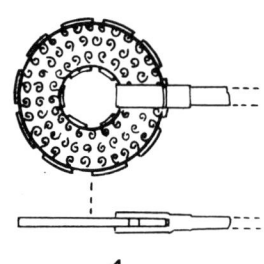

1. 銅鼎（羅定背夫山墓）
2. 銅鼎（四會鳥旦山墓）
3. 銅人首柱形器（羅定背夫山墓）
4. 金柄玉環（肇慶松山墓）

1. bronze tripod (tomb at Beifushan, Luoding)
2. bronze tripod (tomb at Liaodanshan, Sihui)
3. bronze human head topped vessel (tomb at Beifushan, Luoding)
4. Jade ring with gold mount (tomb at Songshan, Zhaoqing)

A Preliminary Discussion on the Bronze Burial System in Eastern Zhou Guangdong

Qiu Licheng

In Guangdong the first discovery of a tomb with bronze vessels as its main burial accessories was made in 1962 at Matougang, Qingyuan county. Subsequently a total of thirty-seven tombs of this type have been found. This essay will give a preliminary study on the burial system and some related aspects.

(I) Choice of the burial site and shapes of tomb pits:

These thirty-seven tombs are found along the riverbanks of Xijiang, Beijiang and Dongjiang. Most of them are concentrated on the hilly area at the Xijiang. These include the twenty-nine tombs at Guangning[1], Zhaoqing[2], Luoding[3], Deqing[4] and Huaiji[5]. There are also five tombs at Qingyuan[6] and Sihui[7] in Gushan in the downstream lowland region of Xijiang and Beijiang at central Guangdong. The rest are distributed at Fogang[8], northern Guangdong, Longmeng[9] and Jieyang[10] of eastern Guangdong.

From the geographical point of view, these tombs are usually constructed at low hills of not more than 60 metres in height and not far away from rivers. For example, the tombs at Tonggugang, Guangning county are found on an oval-shaped hill of 60 metres high and 200 metres long with their backs facing the Suijiang, a tributary of the Beijiang. The Niaodanshan tombs in Sihui county are located on the highland of the delta of Suijiang and Beijiang. This highland is within 14 miles from Beijiang, Suijiang and Xijiang. The Matougang tomb at Qingyuan is located 10 miles away from the western bank of Beijiang. The Songshan tomb at Zhaoqing and the Luoyanshan tomb at Deqing county are both situated near Xijiang. The four tombs at Luoding county are located near the Taiping He and Shaliang He which are the southern tributaries of Xijiang. From the above examples, it is evident that these bronze tombs are all located along vital communication lines of the time.

All of these tombs are of vertical shaft earth pit type and can be divided into three groups according to the size of the tomb chamber (Table 1).

There is only one large tomb at Songshan in Zhaoqing. The tomb chamber is quite large, 8 metres long and 4.7 metres wide. The inner and outer coffins are all disintegrated and only a few basal planks survive. Seventy-eight percent of the one hundred and thirty-nine burial objects are bronze vessels. This is the largest tomb with the greatest number of burial objects found at Guangdong so far.

There are eight medium scale tombs. Normally, the tomb chamber is 3-4 metres long and 2 metres wide. The number of burial objects vary from several dozens to more than one hundred. The original report of the Niaodanshan tomb at Sihui county pointed out that there was no burial objects in the front chamber of the tomb, with only traces of a wooden outer coffin at the western wall. However if one compares this tomb with the Beifushan tomb at Luoding county, it is evident that both tombs are very similar in shape, scale, and in the number, combination and arrangement of burial objects. Thus the "coffin chamber" of the Niaodanshan tomb should not be in the "front chamber" but should be in the "rear chamber" instead. The tomb chambers of the two tombs at Matougang, Qingyuan have been damaged, but according to the number and combination of burial objects, they might have been medium scale tombs of similar type as the above ones. The burial objects in the Jieyang Yunlu No. 1 tomb have been disturbed and incomplete, but the size of the tomb pit shows that it is also a medium scale tomb. Up to the present there is no sign of an outer coffin being used in any one of the tombs of this group.

There are twenty-eight small scale tombs. The usual size of the tomb pit is 2.6-3.4 metres long, and 0.6-1.5 metres wide, although some of them may reach 4.75 metres in length. The number of burial objects in most tombs are less than twenty, but some of them have 30 to 40 pieces.

In medium and small scale tombs, it is not unusual to have a "waist-pit" at the bottom of the tombs which is barely enough for a large piece of pottery. Some of these pits are square in shape, like the Niaodanshan tomb at Sihui, the Tonggugang tomb at Guangning and the Luoyanshan tomb at Deqing. Others are circular in shape, like the Beifushan tomb at Luoding. The custom of building a "waist-pit" was certainly under the influence of the burial practice of central China in the Shang to Western Zhou periods, except that there was some minor modifications. In the Central Plain, "waist-pits" were used to bury dogs or human sacrifice but in Gangdong the pits were built to bury pottery. This became a very common burial custom of the Southern Yue tribe in the Eastern Zhou period and continued well into the early Western Han.

Some of the Spring and Autumn period tombs at Matougang, Qingyuan, and the Warring-States tombs at Tonggugang, Guangning are paved with pebbles at the floor. This practice continued also into the early Western Han. Pebble paving at the bottom of tombs has the effect of dispersing water and seems to have been used initially in central China.

(II) Combination and arrangement of burial objects:

The bronzes and other burial objects found in Eastern Han tombs at Guangdong can be classified into five groups: (1) Food containers: pots, tripods, vases and ewers; (2) Liquid containers: bottles, dishes, buckets and basins; (3) Musical instruments: all types of bells; (4) Weapons (Fig. 2): swords, spearheads, halberds, arrowheads and axes; (5) Tools: axes, chisels, scrapers, knives, saws and sickles. Only a very limited types of pottery are found; they are jars, urns, vases and boxes. Apart from all these a peculiar type of bronze human-headed shafts were also found both in large and medium size tombs. These shafts are all topped with a human head with round eyes, high nose and occasionally with round ears. The lower part is of rectangular cross-section with a cuneiform shaped bolt below it (Fig. 1:3). Their heights vary and range from 40 cm. to 20 cm. Normally four pieces (two pairs) are excavated in each tomb. As these human-headed shafts were only discovered at the Beijiang and Xijiang district in Guangdong, they might well be a specific burial or sacrificial object of the local Yue tribe. Some of these shafts are decorated with "*Wang*" marks on the body[11]. This mark can also be found on spearheads, axes and knives excavated at the Xijiang area. Thus it seems logical to take this to be the hallmark of the bronze foundry of the Southern Yue State[12] as suggested by some authors. Bronzes with this mark found at Jiangsu, Jiangxi and Hunan[13] could have been made in the Southern Yue State as well.

There are two kinds of tripods among the burial objects. One type is with a straight body and two vertical handles set on the mouth rim (Fig. 1:2). Then there is another type with a bowl-shaped body, two braided handles set at the inner side of the mouth rim and three solid splayed legs of ovoid cross-section (Fig. 1:1). They are called '*Yue Style Tripods*' and mainly found in the southern region. Remains of smoke soot on the outside of these tripods show that they must have been produced for practical use. In fact almost all bronze vessels found in Guangdong tombs of the same period were for practical use. Some vessels had been damaged and were repaired and used again. A tripod excavated at the Songshan tomb in Zhaoqing for example had been restored several times. Some vessels were damaged after being used for a long period of time. A fork discovered at Beifushan in Luoding for instance was very much worn off and its middle section was broken off before the burial. All pottery burial objects were also made for practical use.

As to the combination of burial objects, there are variations both in quantity in different kinds of tombs. The major combinations are as follows:

(1) Large tomb: Bronze pots, tripods, large jars, pans, bottles, buckets, bells, human-headed shafts, swords, spearheads, arrow-heads, scrapers; pottery urns, jars, vases and boxes (Zhao-Song tomb)

(2) Medium tomb: Bronze tripods, large jars, pots, ewers, basins, large and small bells, human-headed shafts, swords, daggers, spearheads, halberds, broad axes, arrow-heads, axes, chisels, pottery pots and jars (Luo-Tai-South Ml, Qing-Ma Ml)

(3) Medium tomb: Bronze tripods, ewers, basins, small bells, human-headed shafts, swords, daggers, halberds, spearheads, broad axes, arrow-heads, axes, chisels, scrapers, knives; pottery jars and urns (Si-Niao tomb, Luo-Bei tomb)

(4) Small tomb: Bronze tripods, pans, small bells, swords, daggers, spearheads, broad axes, arrow-heads, axes, chisels, scrapers, knives and pottery urns (De-Luo tomb, Guang-Tong M16)

(5) Small tomb: Bronze swords, spearheads, arrow-heads, axes, chisels, scrapers, knives and pottery vases (Guang-Tong M10, M9)

Of the five combinations mentioned above (2) is the earliest. This combination was popular from the middle-late of the Spring and Autumn period to the early Warring-States period and characterised by bronze daggers (Fig. 2:9). The decorative patterns found on the pottery wares of this group are typical of the Spring and Autumn period. The date of combination (3) is early Warring-States period, as the shapes of burial objects, like swords and halberds (Fig. 2:5, 10) are typical of the period. The characteristics of burial objects are also similar to that of combination (2). Combination (1) is an exceptional case, its date being no earlier than the middle Warring-States period. There is no daggers found in this combination and the burial objects were popular wares throughout the Warring-States period. Moreover, bronze buckets, pottery vases, boxes and jars are very closed to the style of late Warring-States period. The dates of the combination (4) and (5) are of the late Warring-States period. Daggers are rarely found in these two combinations and the burial objects are typical Warring-States period but the pottery wares are obviously later than those of combinations (2) and (3).

The main difference amongst each combination is the variety of the types of food and wine vessels. The types of weapons and tools on the other hand are quite similar only differ in quantity. Combinations (1), (2) and (3) are clearly different from combinations (4) and (5) in having human-headed bronze shafts as burial objects. These shafts probably served some kind of ceremonial purpose as indicated by the way they were placed in the tomb. Some of them could also be hafted on a piece of wooden rod. They were thus symbols of power and dignity. Weapons, like swords, spearheads and broad axes are found in all combinations. This reflects that the Southern Yue people must have attached a special importance to weapons as a result of frequent wars within the state.

Burial objects were normally arranged with two pairs of human-headed bronze shafts placed vertically at the four corners of the tomb chamber. Gradually bells, small bells, basins and ewers were usually placed at the front chamber while weapons, like swords, spearheads and halberds were placed in the middle chamber. At the rear chamber, tripods, large jars, pans and tools were found. Polishing stones were placed next to bronze tools. Personal ornaments, together with swords were usually placed by the side of the deceased (or on the body) in the middle chamber, but in some tombs, like the Beifushan tomb at Luoding, they were placed at the front or rear chamber. In this tomb in front of each pair of the human-headed shafts, a piece of stone and a piece of jade were placed. The piece of jade at the front was a split-ring while the one at the back was crushed and impossible to reconstruct the original shape. Both pieces of jade must have been used in some sort of burial ceremony. Pottery burial objects were usually placed at the rear chamber except in the case of large pieces (such as urns or jars) which were put inside the "waist-pit". The above arrangement of burial objects indicates that burial ceremonies of some scale must have been carried out.

(III) The status of the deceased and grades of burials:

As the coffins are usually entirely disintegrated, observations and conclusions can only be made from the sizes of the tomb pits and combination of burial objects.

Guangdong is located at the Lingnan region and was inhabited by Bai Yue (the Hundred Yue) tribe in the Eastern Zhou Dynasty. In the geographic chapters, *Hanshu*, it was recorded that "From Jiaozhi to Guiqi, within an area of seven to eight thousand *li* the Bai Yue people dwelt and intermixed. There were different clans and names." The Southern Yue and the Xi Ou (also known as Luoyue) were the two major clans living in Guangdong and Guangxi during the period. The Southern Yue clan lived mainly in modern Guangdong where the northern boundary was first at Hunan and Jiangxi and later expanded to Guangxi and the southern area. It wasn't until the late Qin dynasty that the Southern Yue State was founded. Before that the Southern Yue tribes were dispersed without any unified political organization. However archaeological evidence shows that isolated small states might have already been formed in the Eastern Zhou dynasty. After the annexation of the Yue state by the Chu, the historical records say, "Since the Yue state was dispersed, their descendants struggled for the throne. In the end some of them became kings, princes or lords and settled along the coast of Jiangnan[14]." Moreover it was recorded that within the Xi Ou clan there were a "*Lord Yi Xusong*" and a "*General Jie Jin*"[15]. Thus the owners of the Eastern Zhou tombs found at Guangdong, especially those of the large tombs were from the upper classes. They were certainly wealthy slave owners and some of them could well be "*Kings*", "*Lords*" or "*Generals*". The size of a tomb pit would indicate the status of the owner, for example, not only would a member of the upper classes tomb cover a large area it would also contain a wooden outer coffin. Comparing with small to medium sized tombs, large tombs contained more varieties of the finest combination of burial objects. Bronze vessels, like jars with silver inlaid, bottle with chained-handle and tripod pans, were most exquisite bronzes from the Chu state. Ornaments in large tombs, like jade rings with gold fitting, jade garment hook and glass beads were extremely valuable items. Moreover, in a large tomb as many as five tripods have been found. This according to the ritual institutions of the Zhou dynasty respresented the status of "*upper rank official*". Thus the owners of the large tombs must have high status probably a "*King/Prince*" or a member of the ruling class of the Southern Yue state.

In medium sized tombs although there are over one hundred pieces of burial objects in some tombs, the types of vessels are obviously less than those of large tombs. Combination (2) is much more complete between the two. The quality of the vessels is poorer than in large tombs as exemplified by those found from the Songshan tomb at Zhaoqing, but there are more varieties of weapons and tools than combination (1). There are less food and wine vessels in combination (3), but the types of weapons and tools are similar to combination (2). Normally two or three tripods are excavated in these medium sized tombs. This indicates that the tomb owners were "*officials*" according to the ritual institutions of the Zhou. The large amount of bronze weapons and tools found in these tombs also shows that the tomb owners were rich, powerful and enjoyed a high social status. They probably were "*Generals*" of the Southern Yue state.

In combination (4) usually only one tripod was found. The main burial objects are one or two swords, a few weapons and tools. According to the ritual institutions of the Zhou, the owners of these tombs might have been of the "*Shi*-gentleman" class with a small amount of wealth and slaves. In combination (5) no tripod is found and the burial objects are few. The owners of these tombs were ordinary people who participated in production work in peace times and took up bows and arrows and swords to take part in military expeditions during war times.

(IV) Conclusion:

From the above analysis on the bronze burial systems of Eastern Zhou at Guangdong, the following conclusions can be made:

(1) These bronze burials in Eastern Zhou Guangdong provide valuable sources for the study of the social situations of the upper and middle classes of the Southern Yue clan before the establishment of the Southern Yue kingdom as well as the development of military, economy, transportation and handicraft in this region during the pre-Qin period. The different grades of the tombs testify that there is a Bronze Age in Guangdong, during which a rigidly stratified slavery system also appeared.

(2) The combinations of burial objects found in Eastern Zhou tombs at Guangdong have a strong regional characteristic. (i) Almost all burial objects were for practical use. (ii) There are two pairs of human-headed bronze shafts placed at the corners of the large and medium sized tombs. (iii) Remains of smoke soot are all over the outside of the "Yue style" tripods. The walls are very thin and the feet are solid and heavy. (iv) Weapons and tools are very common. The usual types are swords, spearheads, broad axes, axes and knives. Halberds are seldom found. The bodies are often cast with a "*Wang*" mark (Fig. 2:7). (v) The decorative motives of the pottery are geometric patterns commonly seen in Guangdong.

(3) The burial objects found in large and medium tombs show a strong influence from the Chu culture. Some of the finds such as bronze tripod with cabriole legs, silver inlaid bronze jar, tripod pans and bottle with chained-handle are almost identical to those unearthed from Chu tombs. The "hook and volute" pattern, bird design and bird-and-cloud pattern on these bronzes are also very popular among Chu bronzes. Burials with a set of serial bells are undoubtedly under the influence of the ceremonial system of the Chu. This indicates that there was a close relationship between the Lingnan region and the Chu state and the upper classes of the Southern Yue state must have the chance to get in direct contact with the Chu culture. However Chu style objects are hardly found in small tombs.

(4) The developmet of Bronze Age culture in Guangdong as a whole seems to be somewhat unbalanced. Most of the Eastern Zhou bronze burials are concentrated around the Xijiang region. This may well be due to an unbalanced archaeological work, but it also shows that the Bronze Age culture was better developed in this region. One should also note that the increased use of Chu style bronzes in tombs at Guangdong reflected the corresponding intensity of the gradual influence from Chu.

(5) A characteristic feature of the Eastern Zhou tombs at Guangdong is the "waist-pit" at the bottom of the tombs. A large pottery vessel was put inside this pit. This usage of the pit was totally different from central China and to a certain extent reflected the local burial custom. Similar tombs were discovered in Guangxi and Hunan.

For example, the Warring-States tombs at Yinglingshan, Pingle, Guangxi (some of them are of early Western Han period)[16] have also "waist-pits" and similar burial objects. This shows that the Southern Yue clan were also active in the Pingle area of Guangxi. A few tombs of this type were also found at Changsha and Xiangxiang of Hunan[17]. The dates of these tombs are of the early Spring and Autumn period. The shape of these tombs and the burial objects are different from the Chu tombs. It is highly possible that these were tombs of the Southern Yue people. This indicates that the extent of the activity of Southern Yue clan reached Hunan in the Spring and Autumn period. This also coincides with the historical fact of the gradual expansion of the Chu state towards the south.

"Waist-pits" have also been discovered in a few early Western Han tombs at Guangzhou[18]. While the shape of the tombs and some pottery finds are similar to those of the tombs mentioned above, the styles of most burial objects are very different. These Western Han tombs at Guangzhou can be seen as the survival of the burial custom of the Southern Yue kingdom and they disappeared after the mid. Western Han. This also reflects at the same time the gradual harmonization and intermixing between the Han and the Southern Yue cultures.

Footnotes:

1. There were altogether twenty-two tombs at Guangning county, see Guangdong Provincial Museum, "Warring-States Tombs at Tonggugang, Guangning county, Guangdong", *Papers on Chinese Archaeology*, No. 1, Beijing, 1981.

2. Guangdong Provincial Museum, "Brief Excavation Report of Ancient Burials at Songshan, Beiling, Zhaoqing City, Guangdong", *Wenwu*, 1974:11.

3. Three tombs were discovered at Nanmendong, Taiping, Luoding county, see Guangdong Provincial Museum, "Bronzes of the Warring-States Period Unearthed at Luoding, Guangdong", *Kaogu*, 1983:1. Another tomb was at Beifushan in Luoping, the excavation report of which has not yet been published.

4. Xu Hengbin, et al, "A Warring-States Tomb Found at Deqing, Guangdong", *Wenwu*, 1973:9.

5. 8, 9. Three tombs were found, one each at Huaiji, Fogang and Longmen, see He Jisheng, "A Brief Discussion on the Bronze Culture of Eastern Zhou Guangdong and its Relationship with Geometric Impressed Pottery", *Wenwu Jikan*, No. 3, Beijing, 1981.

6. CPAM, Guangdong Province, "Zhou Dynasty Bronzes Unearthed at Qingyuan, Guangdong", *Kaogu*, 1963:2 and also "Eastern Zhou Burials at Qingyuan, Guangdong", *Kaogu*, 1964:3.

7. One tomb was excavated at Niaodanshan, Sihui county, see Guangdong Provincial Museum, "A Warring-States Tomb at Niaodanshan, Sihui County, Guangdong", *Kaogu*, 1975:2. Two tombs were discovered at Gaodiyuan, Longjiang. cf. Note 5 above.

10. For the No. 1 tomb at Yunlu Zhongxia, Jieyang, see CPAM, Shantou Region, et al, "Report on the Excavation of the Estern Zhou Tombs at Jieyang", *Shantou Wenwu*, No. 9, Shantou, 1982. Moreover, Eastern Zhou bronze burials were also discovered at Gaozhou, Lianjiang, Shixing, Boluo and Longchuan, but they are not included in this paper.

11. Excavated from a tomb at Beifushan, Luoping, Luoding county, report of excavation hasn't been published.

12. Xu Hengbin, "A Preliminary Investigation of the History of the Southern Yue before the Qin Dynasty", *Collected historical papers on the Bai Yue people*, Beijing, 1982.

13. Wu Shanqing, "The Eastern Zhou Tomb at Heren, Luhe County, Jiangsu", *Kaogu,* 1977:5;
Jiangxi Provincial Museum, "Western Han Tombs in the Eastern Suburbs of Nanchang", *Kaogu Xuebao*, 1976:2; Hunan Provincial Museum, "The No. 1 Tomb at Liuchengqiao, Changsha", *Kaogu Xuebao*, 1972:1.

14. "Biography of Gou Jian, Prince of Yue", *Shiji*.

15. "Human World Admonitions", *Huainanzi*.

16. The Archaeological Team of Guangxi Zang Autonomous Region, "Excavation of Warring-States Tombs at Yinshanling, Pingle", *Kaogu Xuebao*, 1978:2.

17. Gao Zhixi, "An Introduction to Ancient Burials in Hunan", *Wenwu*, 1960:3; Hunan Provincial Museum, "Excavation of the Eastern Zhou Tombs at Xiangxiang in the Irrigation Area of Shaoshan, Hunan", *Wenwu*, 1977:3.

18. CPAM, Guangzhou, *Excavation of the Han Tombs at Guangzhou*, Beijing, 1981.

Table of Major Bronze Burials in E. Zhou Guangdong

Type	Site	Coffin Chamber length (m)	Coffin Chamber width (m)	Shapes	Burial Objects Bronze vessels	Burial Objects Gold, jade and glasses	Burial Objects Stone	Burial Objects Pottery	Total	Remarks
Large	Songshan tomb at Zhaoqing	8	4.7	vertical shaft earth pit with wooden coffin	108	9	1	21	139	
Medium	Luoding Nanmendong M1	4	2	vertical shaft earth pit	136	3		1	137	
	Luoding Beifushan tomb	4	2	"	98		8	7	116	disturbed
	Sihui Niaodanshan tomb	3.5	1?	"	59		3	1	63	partially disturbed
	Qingyuan Matougang M1			"	25		2	2	29	
	Qingyuan Matougang M2	2.8?	1.1?	"	39		13	1	53	
Small	Deqing Luoyanshan tomb	4.75	1.5	"	15		3	1	19	partially disturbed
	Guangning Tonggugang M10	(destroyed) 0.8	0.6	"	8			1	9	disturbed
	Guangning Tonggugang M13	3.2	0.75	"	8			6	14	
	Guangning Tonggugang M14	2.6	0.75	"	31		2	2	35	
	Guangning Tonggugang M16	3.4	0.9	"	35		5		40	
	Guangning Tonggugang M19	3.4	0.78	"	18		3	1	22	partially disturbed
	Guangning Tonggugang M21	(destroyed) 3	0.75	"	28		4		32	

廣東新石器時代文化年表

時代＼分區	粵北區	珠江三角洲地區	粵東區	雷州半島和海南島	粵西區	公元前
青銅時代			普寧池尾後山			1000
晚期	始興新村曲江鳥石床板嶺石峽文化	石峽中層，龍歸葡勺山，始興澄陂，韶關走馬崗	普寧虎頭埔		封開杏花塘角咀、佛子崗	1500
		曲江鮎魚轉，馬蹄坪	瀾石河宕、南海灶崗、增城金蘭寺中層、西樵山晚期遺存	揭陽埔田寶山嶺		2000
				揭陽南隴螺蛳山		
	石峽下層早期	深圳赤灣、鶴地山台山廣海筲箕山墩	潮陽左宣恭山、赤牛山	遂溪江洪鯉魚地		3000
中期		新會羅山咀、西樵山中期遺存、增城金蘭寺下層、東莞萬福庵下層、深圳小梅沙	海豐沙坑	夾砂粗紅陶與磨光石器共存之遺址（海南島）		4000
			潮安陳橋村、石尾山			5000
早期	翁源青塘、始興玲瓏岩			封開黃岩洞、陽春獨石仔		8000

Chronological Table of Neolithic Guangdong

Period＼Region	Northern Guangdong	Zhujiang Delta	Eastern Guangdong	Leizhou Peninsula and Hainan Island	Western Guangdong	Years B.C.
			Houshan in Chiwei, Puning			1000
Late Phase	Xicun in Shixing; Chuang-banling at Wushi; Qujiang Shixia Culture	Middle layer of Shixia; Pushaoshan in Longgui; Chengbo in Shixing; Zoumagang in Shaoguan	Futoupu in Puning		Xinghuatongjiaozui and Fozigang in Fengkai	1500
			Baoshandong in Putian, Jieyang			2000
		Hedang in Lanshi; Zaogang and Tongxingang in Nanhai; Middle layer of Jinlansi in Zengcheng; late sites in Xiqiaoshan.	Wugongshan in Nanlong, Jieyang			
		Nianyuzhuan and Matiping in Qujiang	Zuoxuangongshan and Chiniushan in Chaoyang			
	Early phase of lower layer of Shixia	Hedishan in Chiwan, Shenzhen; Pucaoshantong in Guanghai, Taishan		Liyudi in Jianghong, Suiqi		3000
Middle Phase		Luoshanzui in Xinhui; Middle phase sites of Xiqiaoshan; Lower layer of Jinlansi in Zengcheng; Lower layer of Wanfu'an in Dongguan; Xiaomeisha in Shenzhen.	Shakeng in Haifeng	Sites with red coarse tempered pottery and polished stone implements (Hainan Island)		4000
			Chenqiaocun and Shiweisha in Chao'an			5000
Early Phase	Qingtang in Wenyuan; Linglongyan in Shixing			Huangyandong in Fongkai; Dushizai in Yangchun		8000

廣東靑銅時代年表

時代	主要遺址與墓葬			公元前
	粵西	粵中、粵北	粵東	
戰國	德慶落雁山墓 肇慶松山墓 四會鳥旦山墓 羅定太平南門垌墓	始興白石坪遺址 增城西瓜嶺遺址	揭陽雲路中夏墓	211年 475年
春秋		清遠馬頭崗墓 廣州東郊暹崗遺址 曲江馬壩石硤遺址上文化層		770年
西周			平遠石正陶窰 饒平浮濱、聯饒墓葬	1122年
商				1766年

Chronological Table of Bronze Age Guangdong

Period	Major Dwelling and Burial Sites			Years B.C.
	Western Guangdong	Middle & Northern Guangdong	Eastern Guangdong	
Warring-States	Burial at Loyanshan, Deqing Burial at Songshan, Zhaoqing Burial at Niaodanshan, Sihui Burial at Nanmentong, Luoding	Baishiping site at Shixing Xigualing site at Zengcheng	Burial at Yunluzhongxia, Jieyang	221 475
Spring and Autumn		Burial at Mataogang, Qingyuan Xiangang site, eastern suburb, Guangzhou Upper layer at Shixia, Maba, Qujiang		770
W. Zhou			Pottery kiln at Shizheng, Pingyuan Burials at Lianrao and Fubin, Raoping	1112
Shang				1766

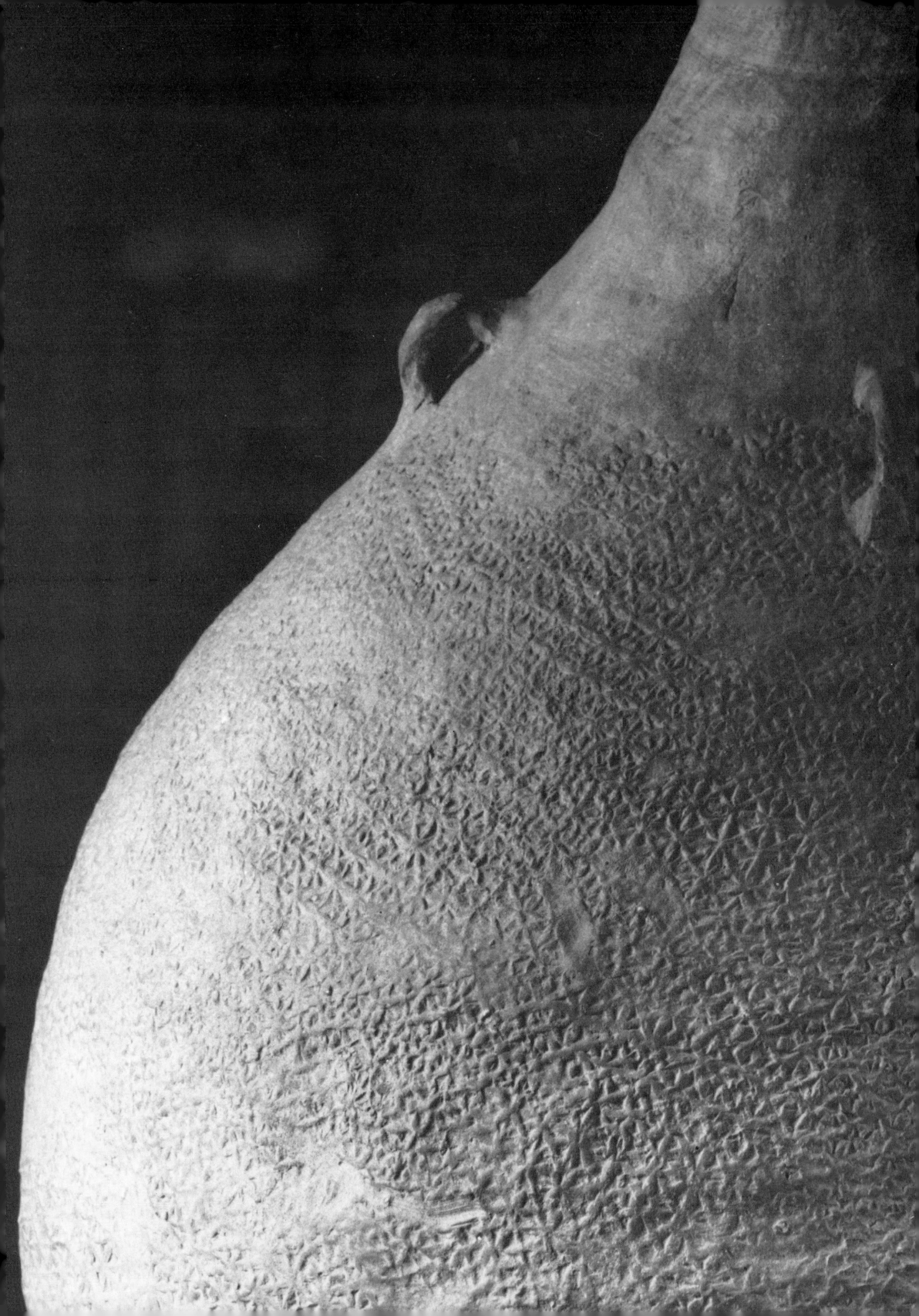

展品目次

1. 砍砸器，新石器時代早期
2. 穿孔器，新石器時代早期
3. 斧形器，新石器時代早期
4. 細石器，新石器時代中期
5. 細石器，新石器時代中期
6. 刮削器，新石器時代中期
7. 尖狀器，新石器時代中期
8. 石錘，新石器時代中期
9. 斧形器，新石器時代中期
10. 石刀，新石器時代中期
11. 石砑，新石器時代中期
12. 有肩石砑，新石器時代中期
13. 骨錐，新石器時代中期
14. 骨鑿，新石器時代中期
15. 骨鏟，新石器時代中期
16. 陶釜，新石器時代中期
17. 圈足陶杯，新石器時代中期
18. 彩繪陶盤，新石器時代中期
19. 有段石砑，新石器時代晚期
20. 長身石砑，新石器時代晚期
21. 有肩有段石砑，新石器時代晚期
22. 有肩石砑，新石器時代晚期
23. 石钁，新石器時代晚期
24. 石鏟，新石器時代晚期
25. 石鉞，新石器時代晚期
26. 石鏃，新石器時代晚期
27. 石琮，新石器時代晚期
28. 石臂環，新石器時代晚期
29. 石笄，新石器時代晚期
30. 象牙筒形器，新石器時代晚期
31. 骨梭，新石器時代晚期
32. 骨錐，新石器時代晚期
33. 陶鬹，新石器時代晚期
34. 白陶鼎，新石器時代晚期
35. 盤形鼎，新石器時代晚期
36. 圈足盤，新石器時代晚期
37. 三足盤，新石器時代晚期
38. 陶豆，新石器時代晚期
39. 陶壺，新石器時代晚期
40. 陶釜，新石器時代晚期
41. 陶罐，新石器時代晚期
42. 圈足罐，新石器時代晚期
43. 陶罐，新石器時代晚期
44. 夾砂粗陶缶，新石器時代中晚期
45. 幾何印紋陶片，新石器時代晚期
46. 銅戈，西周
47. 石戈，商周
48. 石矛，商周
49. 釉陶大口尊，商周
50. 釉陶把壺，商周
51. 釉陶豆，商周
52. 釉陶罐，商周
53. 青銅戈，商周
54. 石戈，商周
55. 硬陶大尊，商周
56. 陶罐，西周
57. 陶罐，西周
58. 陶附耳罐，西周
59. 銅甬鐘，春秋
60. 銅錞于，春秋
61. 人面紋匕首，春秋
62. 青銅人面紋短劍，春秋至戰國
63. 銅劍石膏模型，春秋
64. 殘銅戈，春秋
65. 銅鉞，春秋至戰國
66. 銅斧，春秋至戰國
67. 原始瓷鉢，春秋
68. 陶罐，春秋至戰國
69. 釉陶罐，春秋
70. 陶罐，春秋
71. 陶罐，春秋至戰國
72. 夔紋硬陶片，春秋至戰國
73. 幾何印紋硬陶片，春秋至戰國
74. 石環，春秋至戰國
75. 石英環及圓心等，春秋至戰國
76. 網墜，春秋至戰國
77. 陶紡輪，春秋至戰國
78. 陶牛，春秋至戰國
79. 陶牛首，春秋至戰國
80. 玉帶鈎，戰國
81. 人首柱形器，戰國
82. 人首柱形器，戰國
83. 銅甬鐘，戰國
84. 銅提梁壺，戰國
85. 銅三足盤，戰國
86. 銅附耳匜，戰國
87. 銅鼎，戰國
88. 銅鑒，戰國
89. 銅劍，戰國
90. 銅矛，戰國
91. 銅斧、銅鈴、陶範，春秋至戰國
92. 銅鉞，戰國

93. 銅靴形鉞，戰國
94. 銅箭鏃，戰國
95. 銅斧，戰國
96. 銅鑿，戰國
97. 銅篾刀，戰國
98. 原始瓷盉，戰國
99. 米字紋陶罐，戰國
100. 陶匏壺，戰國

（展品除特別註明外，均由廣東省博物館借出）

List of Exhibits

1. Stone chopper, Early Neolithic period
2. Stone tool, Early Neolithic period
3. Stone axe-shaped tool, Early Neolithic period
4. Microlith, Mid Neolithic period
5. Microlith, Mid Neolithnic period
6. Stone scraper, Mid Neolithic period
7. Stone point, Mid Neolithic period
8. Stone hammer, Mid Neolithic period
9. Stone axe-shaped tool, Mid Neolithic period
10. Stone knife, Mid Neolithic period
11. Stone adze, Mid Neolithic period
12. Stone shouldered adze, Mid Neolithic period
13. Bone awl, Mid Neolithic period
14. Bone chisel, Mid Neolithic period
15. Bone shovel, Mid Neolithic period
16. Pottery cauldron, Mid Neolithic period
17. Pottery cup with pierced ring foot, Mid Neolithic period
18. Pottery dish with pierced foot, Mid Neolithic period
19. Stone stepped adze, Late Neolithic period
20. Stone long adze, Late Neolithic period
21. Stone stepped and shouldered adze, Late Neolithic period
22. Stone shouldered adze, Late Neolithic period
23. Stone pickaxe, Late Neolithic period
24. Stone shovel, Late Neolithic period
25. Stone yue-axe, Late Neolithic period
26. Stone arrowheads, Late Neolithic period
27. Stone zong, Late Neolithic period
28. Stone bracelet, Late Neolithic period
29. Stone hairpin, Late Neolithic period
30. Ivory cylindrical object, Late Neolithic period
31. Bone shuttle, Late Neolithic period
32. Bone awl, Late Neolithic period
33. Pottery pitcher, Late Neolithic period
34. White pottery tripod, Late Neolithic period
35. Pottery tripod-dish, Late Neolithic period
36. Pottery dish with footring, Late Neolithic period
37. Tripod dish, Late Neolithic period
38. Pottery dou, Late Neolithic period
39. Pottery vase, Late Neolithic period
40. Pottery pot, Late Neolithic period
41. Pottery jar, Late Neolithic period
42. Pottery jar with footring, Late Neolithic period
43. Pottery jar, Late Neolithic period
44. Coarse pottery pot, Mid to late Neolithic period

45. Geometric pottery fragments, Late Neolithic period
46. Bronze halberd, Shang to Zhou
47. Stone halberd, Shang to Zhou
48. Stone spearhead, Shang to Zhou
49. Glazed pottery vase, Shang to Zhou
50. Glazed pottery ewer, Shang to Zhou
51. Glazed pottery stem-cup, Shang to Zhou
52. Glazed jar, Shang to Zhou
53. Bronze halberd, Shang to Zhou
54. Stone halberd, Shang to Zhou
55. Hard pottery vase, Shang to Zhou
56. Pottery jar, W. Zhou
57. Pottery jar, W. Zhou
58. Pottery jar, W. Zhou
59. Bronze bell, Spring and Autumn period
60. Bronze drum, Spring and Autumn period
61. Bronze dagger with human mask design, Spring and Autumn period
62. Bronze dagger, Spring and Autumn to Warring-States periods
63. Plaster cast of a bronze sword, Spring and Autumn period
64. Fragment of a bronze halberd, Spring and Autumn period
65. Bronze *Yue*-axe, Spring and Autumn to Warring-States periods
66. Bronze axe, Spring and Autumn to Warring-States periods
67. Proto-porcelain dish, Spring and Autumn period
68. Pottery jar, Spring and Autumn to Warring-States periods
69. Glazed pottery pot, Spring and Autumn period
70. Pottery jar, Spring and Autumn period
71. Pottery jar, Spring and Autumn to Warring-States periods
72. Potsherds with "double-F" design, Spring and Autumn to early Warring-States periods
73. Potsherds with geometric design, Spring and Autumn to Warring-States periods
74. Stone flanged ring, Spring and Autumn to Warring-States periods
75. Quartz rings and core, Spring and Autumn to Warring-States periods
76. Net weights, Spring and Autumn to Warring-States periods
77. Pottery spindle whorls, Spring and Autumn to Warring-States periods
78. Pottery figurine of an ox, Spring and Autumn to Warring-States periods
79. Pottery ox head, Spring and Autumn to Warring-States periods
80. Jade garment hook, Warring-States period
81. Bronze shaft with human head, Warring-States period
82. Bronze shaft with human head, Warring-States period
83. Bronze bell, Warring-States period
84. Bronze bottle, Warring-States period
85. Bronze tripod-basin, Warring-States period
86. Bronze bucket, Warring-States period
87. Bronze tripod, Warring-States period
88. Bronze basin, Warring-States period
89. Bronze sword, Warring-States period
90. Bronze spearhead, Warring-States period
91. Pottery moulds for bronze axe and bell, Spring and Autumn to Warring-States periods
92. Bronze axe, Warring-States period
93. Bronze axe of boot-shape, Warring-States period
94. Bronze arrowheads, Warring-States period
95. Bronze axe, Warring-States period
96. Bronze chisel, Warring-States period
97. Bronze knife, Warring-States period
98. Proto-porcelain jar, Warring-States period
99. Pottery jar, Warring-States period
100. Pottery gourd shaped bottle, Warring-States period

Note: Unless otherwise mentioned exhibits are from the Collection of the Guangdong Provincial Museum.

S3

S2   27

106

33

49

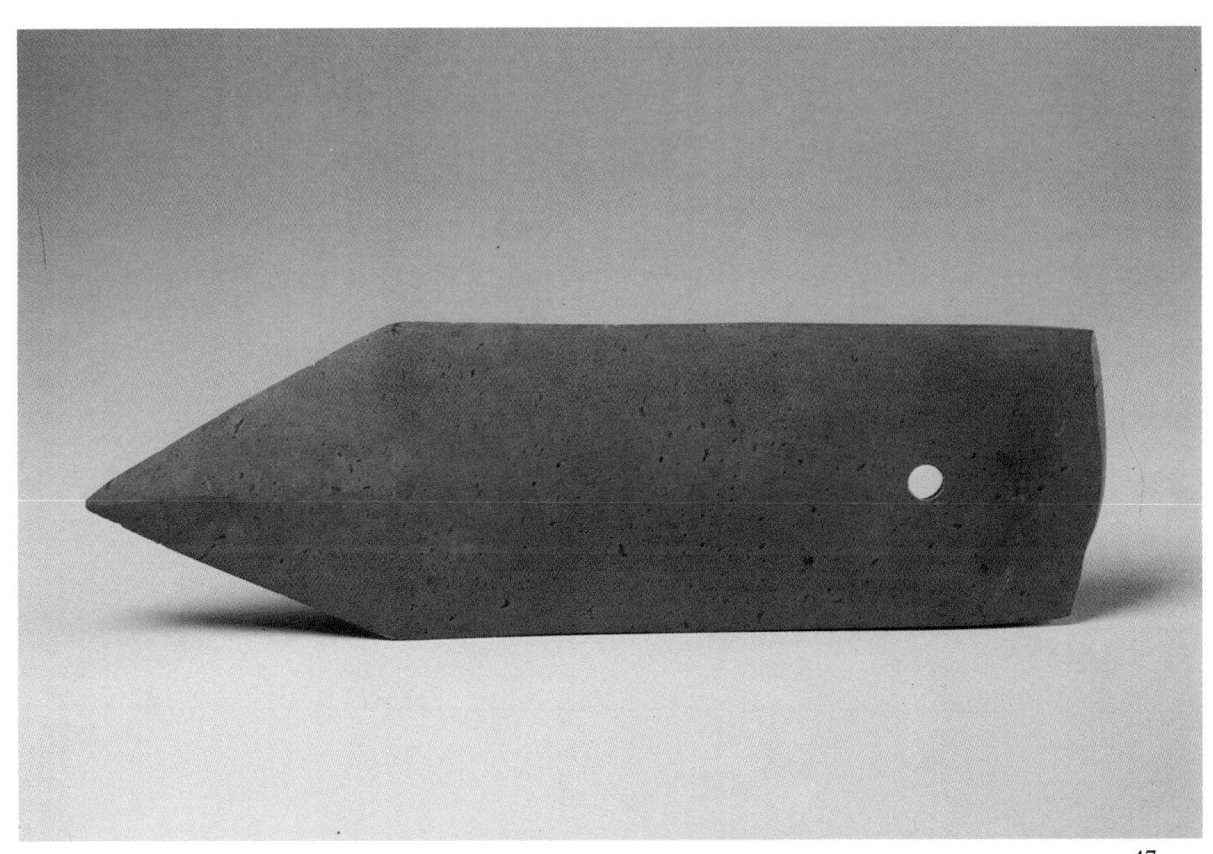

47

53

109

66, 95, 65

62

110

83

88

85

86

陽春縣獨石仔洞穴遺址

新石器時代早期
洞長40、寬2-8、高6-10米

獨石仔遺址發現於1960年。其後先後三次進行發掘，共得遺物400多件，動物化石千餘件。遺址地層有三個文化層。出土遺物有打製石器、穿孔石器、局部磨製石器以及骨器、蚌器等。文化特徵是：石器原料均係河礫石，石核石器多，石片石器少；打製石器均單面打製，多是簡單加工；器形種類不多。但上文化層的打製石器和穿孔石器較之下文化層的要規整一些；上文化層出現了刃部磨製的切割器，而下文化層不見。這表明上下文化層之間有着承襲和發展的文化關係。

圖一：獨石仔洞穴遺址平面圖。

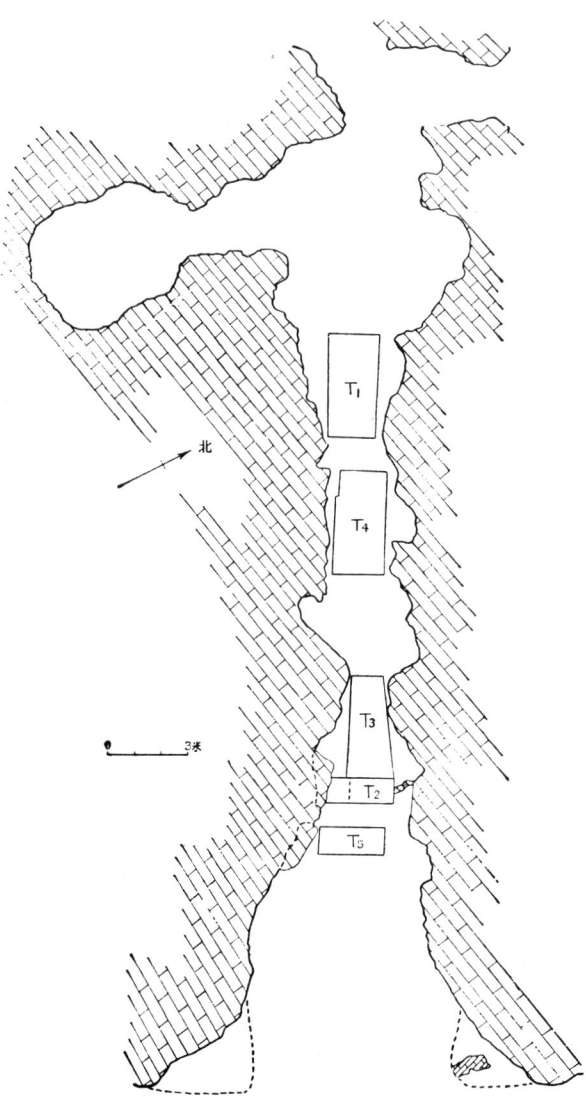

Cave site at Dushizai, Yangchun county

Early Neolithic period
Length of cave 40, width 2-8, height 6-10 m.

The Dushizai site was discovered in 1960. In the years following three excavations were conducted and the finds include 400 archaeological relics and more than a thousand animal fossils. The site, consisting of three cultural layers, yields stone tools, both chipped, perforated or partly polished, and also bone and shell specimens. All the stone tools are made from river gravel. The majority of them are cores with only a few flakes. The chipped stone tools are unifacially worked, roughly retouched and of limited shapes. However, chipped and perforated stone tools from the upper layer are more regular in shape than those from the lower layer; and scrapers with polished blades are only found in the upper layer. This indicates that there is a culutral continuity within the layers.

Fig. 1: Plan of cave site at Dushizai.

1. 砍砸器

新石器時代早期（公元前8000－前5000年）
身長9.5、刃寬10cm
1978年陽春縣獨石仔洞穴遺址出土

砍伐工具。石英砂岩礫石製作，器身略作三角形，單面單向打擊刃部，梯級加工出一個凸刃，刃緣有凹凸不平的砍砸疤痕。這類石器是華南地區新石器時代早期洞穴遺存中常見的打製石器。遺址出土的螺蚌殼標本經碳十四測定年代為距今14900±300年。

1. Stone chopper

Early Neolithic period (8000-5000 B.C.)
Length 9.5, width of blade 10 cm.
Excavated in 1978 from cave site at Dushizai, Yangchun county

Made from quartzose sandstone gravel, this chopper is triangular in shape with its blade unifacially chipped in one direction and retouched to form a protruding blade. The working edge is irregular. This type of chipped stone implements are commonly found from early Neolithic cave sites in south China. Shell specimens from the site have been carbon dated to 14900±300 B.P.

2. 穿孔器

新石器時代早期（公元前8000－前5000年）
身高5.5、最大徑11cm.
1973年陽春縣獨石仔洞穴遺址出土

礫石製作。器體為橢圓形。雙面鑿打加磨穿孔。兩面孔徑不一致。這類穿孔器在廣東、廣西的洞穴遺存中較為常見，常與打製石器和局部磨製石器共存。估計是用作製造石器的石錘或在孔中插木棒作挖掘塊莖植物時用具。後一種用途可見於現代南非布須曼人。

圖二：挖掘棒，採集食物工具，現代南非布須曼人用以挖掘塊莖植物。

2. Stone tool

Early Neolithic period (8000-5000 B.C.)
Height 5.5, largest diameter 11 cm.
Excavated in 1978 from cave site at Dushizai, Yangchun county

Made from gravel. This stone tool is elliptical shaped, bifacially chipped and polished with a conical perforation. Similar tools are often found from cave sites in Guangdong and Guangxi provinces and they are associated with chipped and partly polished stone tools. This piece is possibly a stone hammer for producing stone artefacts or being hafted as a digging-stick for excavating tubers. The use of the later kind can be seen in the modern Bushmen in South Africa.

Fig. 2: Digging-stick tool for gatnering food.
Used for digging plant with stem tuber by the Bushmen of south Africa.

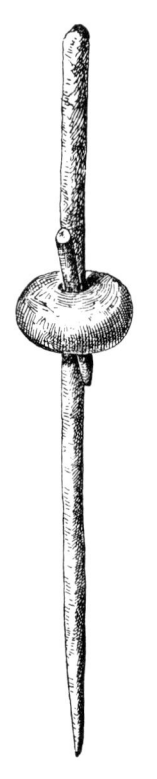

3. 斧形器

新石器時代早期（公元前8000－前5000年）
身長8.3、刃寬6.5 cm.
1978年陽春縣獨石仔洞穴遺址出土

刀斧類工具。器身扁寬，雙面圓刃。器體大部份加磨。上部殘缺。正面尚有打擊石片疤。獨石仔遺址出土的局部磨製石器是廣東發現年代較早的磨製石器。

3. **Stone axe-shaped tool**

Early Neolithic period (8000-5000 B.C.)
Length 8.3, width of blade 6.5 cm.
Excavated in 1978 from cave site at Dushizai, Yangchun county

Used as a knife or axe, this specimen is broad and flat with a bifacial round blade. It is mostly polished but with its upper part broken and with chipped marks on its front side. Partially polished stone tools unearthed from Dushizai site are of a comparatively early date.

西樵山 XIQIAOSHAN

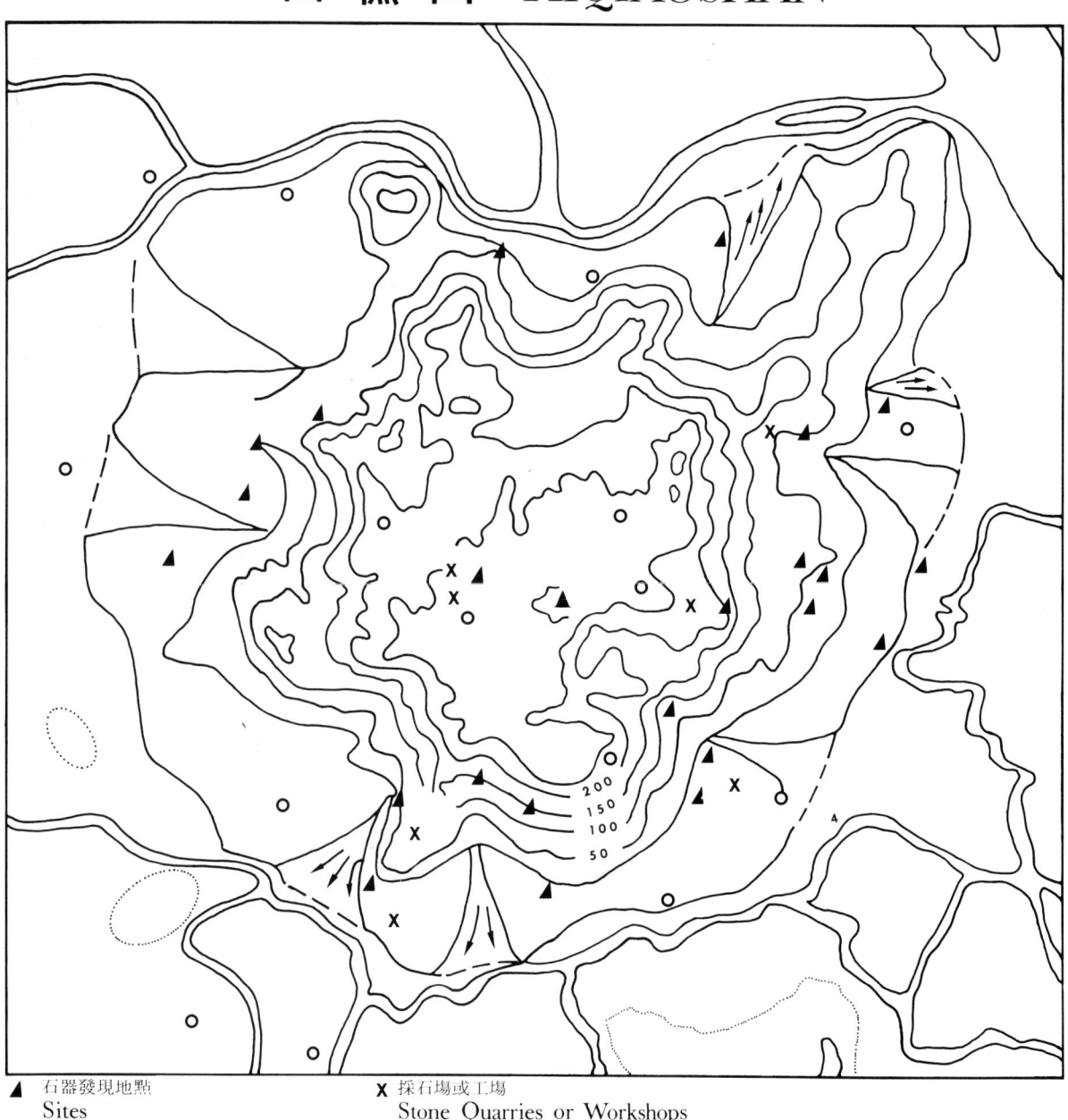

▲ 石器發現地點
  Sites

X 採石場或工場
  Stone Quarries or Workshops

南海西樵山遺址

新石器時代——青銅時代
南海縣官山

著名的南海西樵山，原是形成於白堊紀的一座古火山。山頂有廣闊的谷地和緩丘陵起伏的地面，遺址範圍大，遺物豐富，自1958年起，先後發現有文化層堆積和遺物的地點共二十處。出土大量的打製石器，有石核、各種石片及砍砸器、尖狀器、刮削器、石錘和有肩石錛、梯形石錛的半成品、殘次品。石料均取用此山盛產的霏細岩、燧石和瑪瑙石。其文化遺存可分三類。第一類爲細石器遺存，在東部山麓旋風崗出土，用燧石、半透明瑪瑙石和極少數霏細岩製作，不見磨光石器和陶片。第二類爲打製石器和繩紋、划紋夾砂陶、泥質陶共存。第三類爲打製石器和曲尺紋、葉脉紋等幾何印紋陶共存。後兩類遺存中出土少量磨光石器，如有肩石斧、錛和礪石。上述三類遺存未發現地層叠壓關係。

關於西樵山遺址的年代，一般認爲上限爲新石器時代中期，延續到廣東青銅時代（春秋時期）。另一種看法是，上限爲新石器時代初期，延續到晚期。

西樵山遺址是我國華南地區重要的石器製造場所。

Xiqiaoshan sites in Nanhai county

Neolithic to Bronze Age
Guanshan, Nanhai county

The famous Xiqiaoshan in Nanhai county is an old volcano formed during the cretaceous period. From 1958 onwards, twenty sites with rich cultural layers and abundant remains are found over a large area at its ridges where there are vast valleys and undulating hills. The wide varieties of chipped stone implements unearthed consist of cores, flakes, choppers, points, scrapers, hammers, shouldered adzes, trapezoid adzes, half-worked tools and wasters. The rock material, including felsite, chert and agate, are all from local sources. The cultural remains of this site may be classified into three types. The first type is represented by microlithes made from chert and semi-illuminative agate, and a few from felsite. These were unearthed from Xuanfenggang, in the eastern slope, where polished stone implements and pottery are absent. The second type is represented by chipped stone implements in association with incised or corded sandy and fine pottery. The third is characterised by chipped stone implements co-existing with pottery with geometric impressed design of angular or herring-bone patterns. In the last two types, small amount of polished stone implements of shouldered axes, adzes and polishing stones are also found. However no successive stratification for these three types is available.

The general view for the dates of Xiqiaoshan sites is from middle Neolithic to Bronze Age of Guangdong (corresponding to the Spring and Autumn period). Another view puts it entirely within the Neolithic period extending from early to late phases.

The Xiqiaoshan sites are important workshops for stone implements in south China.

4. 細石器

新石器時代中期（公元前5000－前3000年）
高 3.1 cm.
1977年南海縣西樵山出土

燧石小石核。器呈錐體。器身有許多小石片疤。西樵山細石器與華北地區細石器遺存有十分密切的關係，並具有地方特色。

5. 細石器

新石器時代中期（公元前5000－前3000年）
長 3 cm.
1977年南海縣西樵山出土

小型刮削器。燧石石片製作。有一個不大規整的刃緣。這類細石器是在複合工具上使用的。

6. 刮削器

新石器時代中期（公元前5000－前3000年）
刃寬 5 cm.
1959年南海縣西樵山出土

靠細岩石片製作。器體薄。打製後加磨出鋒利的刃緣。刃面略呈扇狀，這是一件小型工具。

4. Microlith

Mid Neolithic period (5000-3000 B.C.)
Height 3.1 cm.
Excavated in 1977 from Xiqiaoshan, Nanhai county

Made from tiny chert core. This specimen is conical in shape with traces of small flakes. The microlithes from Xiqiaoshan seem to be closely related to those of Northern China and at the same time exhibiting distinct local characteristics.

5. Microlith

Mid Neolithic period (5000-3000 B.C.)
Length 3 cm.
Excavated in 1977 from Xiqiaoshan, Nanhai county

Tiny scraper made from chert flake with a somewhat irregular blade. Probably part of a composite tool.

6. Stone scraper

Mid Neolithic period (5000-3000 B.C.)
Width of blade 5 cm.
Excavated in 1959 from Xiqiaoshan, Nanhai county

Made from felsite flake. It was chipped and polished to form a fan-shaped blade. A micro stone implement.

4

5

6

7. 尖狀器

新石器時代中期（公元前5000－前3000年）
長6.6 cm.
1959年南海縣西樵山出土

霏細岩小石核製作。通體打擊，在一端加工出一個銳鋒。此器製作方法尚留舊石器時代打製石器的特點。

8. 石錘

新石器時代中前（公元前5000－前3000年）
最大徑10cm.
1959年南海縣西樵山出土

器身近扁圓體。多見經敲砸而留下的疤痕。這是製造石器的一種工具。這類石錘常見於中國舊石器時代中晚期遺址。在華南地區新石器早期遺址中也較多見。

7. Stone point

Mid Neolithic period (5000-3000 B.C.)
Length 6.6 cm.
Excavated in 1959 from Xiqiaoshan, Nanhai county

Made from small felsite core. This point is chipped all over and retouched to form a sharp point at one end. It still preserves the characteristic workmanship of the palaeolithic period.

8. Stone hammer

Mid Neolithic period (5000-3000 B.C.)
Largest diameter 10 cm.
Excavated in 1959 from Xiqiaoshan, Nanhai county

Of compressed globular shape with signs of being used. This seems to have been a tool for manufacturing stone artefacts. Stone hammers are found from middle to late Palaeolithic sites all over China and in south China they are also found from early Neolithic sites.

9. 斧形器

新石器時代中期（公元前5000－前3000年）
長10、刄寬5.2 cm.
1959年南海縣西樵山出土

霏細岩石片製作。器體大部份打製加工，下部加磨出雙面圓刄。器身上部一側打製一個單肩。此器形不規整，是一件原始型石斧。

9. **Stone axe-shaped tool**

Mid Neolithic period (5000-3000 B.C.)
Length 10, width of blade 5.2 cm.
Excavated in 1959 from Xiqiaoshan,
Nanhai county

Made from felsite flake. Its body was mostly chipped with a polished bifacial round blade. One lateral side at the top is chipped with a single-shoulder. The irregular shape indicates its primitiveness.

10. 石刀

新石器時代中期（公元前5000－前3000年）
刃寬4.6 cm. （殘）
1963年增城縣金蘭寺遺址出土

扁條形。器中棱起。兩個長邊作刃。一為薄刃，一作鋸齒狀刃緣。

10. Stone knife

Mid Neolithic period (5000-3000 B.C.)
Width of blade (fragmentary) 4.6 cm.
Excavated in 1963 from Jinlansi,
Zengcheng county

A slender flat knife with a median crest and double blade edges, one bevelled and one notched.

11. 石錛

新石器時代中期（公元前5000－前3000年）
長9.2、刃寬4.8 cm.
1963年增城縣金蘭寺遺址出土

磨製石器。工具。長身，略作梯形。刃端較寬，單面直刃。器身兩側及頂端尚留有打製痕跡。廣東新石器時代中期的磨製石器，器身常常留有打擊疤痕，說明通體磨製技術還未完善。

11. Stone adze

Mid Neolithic period (5000-3000 B.C.)
Length 9.2, width of blade 4.8 cm.
Excavated in 1963 from Jinlansi,
Zengcheng county

A polished stone tool of slender trapezoid shape. The blade is broad, straight and unifacial. Chipped marks are left on the top and the lateral sides. This is a common feature found on polished stone tools of middle Neolithic period in Guangdong indicating that the technique of polishing the surface was still imperfect.

12. 有肩石錛

新石器時代中期（公元前5000－前3000年）
長7.5、刃寬6.5 cm.
1963年增城縣金蘭寺遺址出土

器身較寬。上部有不大對稱的雙肩。單面刃，刃緣微凸。此器形不規整，器身尚見打製疤痕。這是廣東地區年代較早的雙肩石器。

12. Stone shouldered adze

Mid Neolithic period (5000-3000 B.C.)
Length 7.5, width of blade 6.5 cm.
Excavated in 1963 from Jinlansi,
Zengcheng county

A broad adze with asymmetrical shoulders. Its blade is unifacial with a slightly convex edge. The shape is irregular and chipped marks are over the body, indicating an early date.

13. 骨錐

新石器時代中期（公元前5000－前3000年）
長5.4 cm.（殘）
1960年潮安縣陳橋村遺址出土

通體磨製。器為瘦長錐體，下端有經使用留下的鈍鋒。廣東地區這時期的貝坵遺址中常見有骨器，但器形多是不大規整。

14. 骨鑿

新石器時代中期（公元前5000－前3000年）
長7.3（殘）、刃寬1.8 cm.
1960年潮安縣陳橋村遺址出土

骨片製作。刃面略窄，兩面加磨。下端有一個薄薄的刃緣。

15. 骨鏟

新石器時代中期（公元前5000－前3000年）
長15.2、肩寬7.2 cm.
1960年潮安縣陳橋村遺址出土

柄端較長，刃面較寬。雙肩略對稱，刃緣作斜弧狀。背面僅刃口加磨，正面全部加磨。

13. Bone awl

Mid Neolithic period (5000-3000 B.C.)
Length (remaining) 5.4 cm.
Excavated in 1960 from Chenqiaocun, Chaoan county

This awl in stylus shape is polished all over. The sharp point has now worn off due to use. Bone tools, mostly of irregular shapes, are often found from shell mounds of middle Neolithic period in Guangdong.

14. Bone chisel

Mid Neolithic period (5000-3000 B.C.)
Length (remaining) 7.3, width of blade 1.8 cm.
Excavated in 1960 from Chenqiaocun, Chaoan county

Made of bone, this chisel tapers towards the blade which is bifacially polished.

15. Bone shovel

Mid Neolithic period (5000-3000 B.C)
Length 15.2, width of shoulder 7.2 cm.
Excavated in 1960 from Chenqiaocun, Chaoan county

This shovel is with a long handle, a broad blade, symmetrical shoulders and asymmetrical arc shaped blade. The front side is entirely polished whereas the reverse side is only polished around the blade.

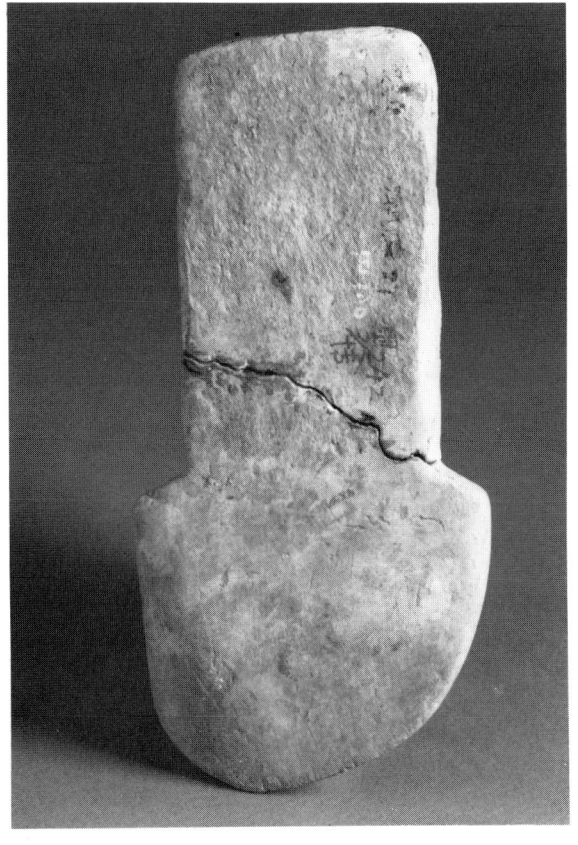 

16. 陶釜

新石器時代中期（公元前5000—前3000年）
高8、口徑11cm.
1960年增城縣金蘭寺遺址出土

夾砂陶。手製，火候低。敞口圓唇，頸微束，深腹圜底。上腹拍印繩紋，紋飾粗獷。繩紋陶出現於新石器時代早期，至中期仍較多見。這時期出土的陶器製作還較粗糙，形多不規整，反映出這時製陶技術水平還較低下。

16. Pottery cauldron

Mid Neolithic period (5000-3000 B.C.)
Height 8, diameter of mouth 11 cm.
Excavated in 1960 from Jinlansi, Zengcheng county

Coarse tempered pottery. This cauldron is hand built and low fired, with a wide mouth, everted round rim, contracted neck, deep body and round bottom. The upper body is crudely impressed with cord pattern. Pottery with impressed cord pattern made its appearance in early Neolithic period and continued into the middle Neolithic period, however early pieces as represented by this specimen are mostly crudely made and irregularly shaped testifying the low standard of pottery technique.

17. 圈足陶杯

新石器時代中期（公元前5000－前3000年）
高10.3、口徑8.4cm.
1970年香港春磡灣出土
香港博物館藏品

春磡灣遺址位於港島南部，六十年代早期發現，其後經多次調查及發掘，出土遺物甚多；尤以泥質紅陶及彩繪陶器（見展品18號）最具特色。此杯為泥質細紅陶，上有白陶衣，高圈足穿孔，杯身飾刻劃曲尺紋，剛健有力。遺址的碳十四測定數據有二個
（ⅰ）370cm木炭（I.8827）：4570±130B.P.
（ⅱ）455cm木塊（I.8830）：5455±105B.P.
（半衰期5568，未經校正）

圖三：陶杯剖面圖。

17. Pottery cup with pierced ring foot

Mid. Neolithic period (5000-3000 B.C.)
Height 10.3, diameter of mouth 8.4 cm.
Excavated in 1970 from Zhongkanwan,
Hong Kong
Collection of the Hong Kong Museum of History

Zhongkanwan (Chung Hom Wan) is a small bay facing west on the southern part of Hong Kong Island. A series of investigations and excavations were carried out on the site after its first discovery in the early sixties. Pottery finds were abundant and the most characteristic and significant is painted ware (see No. 18). This cup though not painted is of the same pinkish chalky paste covered with a white slip. The high footring is pierced and the upper part of the exterior is incised with bands of vertical wavy lines. Two radiocarbon dates are available: (i) charcoal sample (370 cm. I-8827): 4570±130 B.P.: (ii) log of wood (455 cm. I-8830): 5455±105 B.P. (Half life 5568, not calibrated).

Fig. 3: Cross-section of the cup.

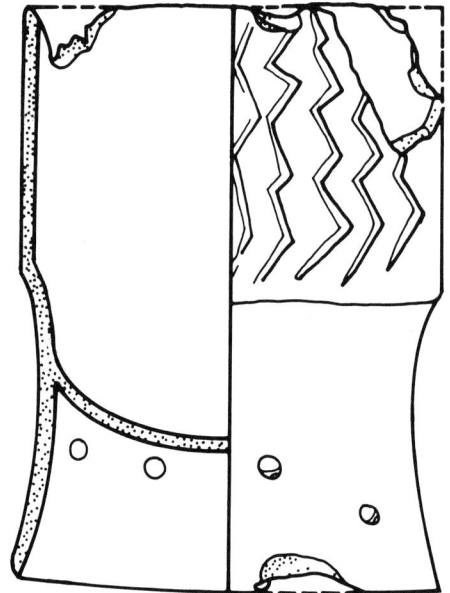

18. 彩繪陶盤

新石器時代中期（公元前5000－前3000年）
口徑15.4、殘高6 cm.
1970年香港春坎灣出土
香港博物館藏品

細泥紅陶，直口，圜底，高圈足下端已殘缺，尚有鏤孔痕跡。器表塗牙白陶衣，部份剝落，上繪赭紅彩的圓圈波浪紋。香港出土的彩陶也有加飾刻划花紋的。

圖四：香港出土的彩陶盤剖面圖。

18. Pottery dish with pierced foot

Mid. Neolithic period (5000-3000 B.C.)
Diameter at mouth: 15.4, remaining height 6 cm.
Excavated in 1970 from Zhongkanwan,
Hong Kong
Collection of the Hong Kong Museum of History

Earthenware made of a fine polished red clay coated with a creamy slip; with a straight mouth, round bottom and a high footring, the lower part of which is now missing, but there are signs that the footring was pierced with small round holes. The outside is painted in ochre with a highly stylised band of wavy pattern. On other painted pottery found in Hong Kong the painted design is sometimes combined with simple incised or carved patterns.

Fig. 4: Painted pottery dishes found in Hong Kong.

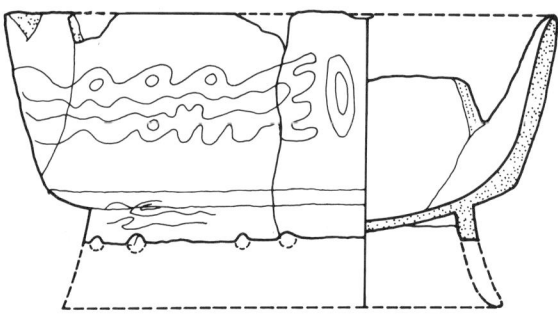

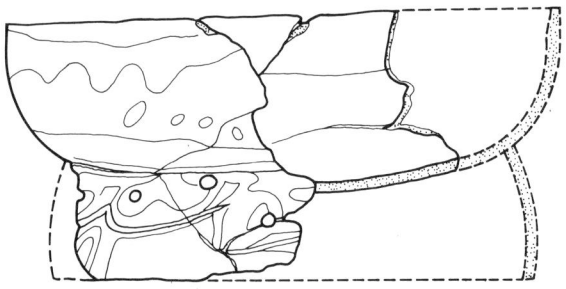

輔助照片1. 彩陶盤

新石器時代中期（公元前5000－前3000）
高8.6、口徑23.6cm.
1980年深圳市小梅沙出土

細泥沙黃陶。直口，圜底，大圈足。器表塗暗紅色陶衣後加赭紅色彩繪，彩繪為浪花紋，凝重淳樸。此器是廣東早期彩繪陶器的精品。

Supplementary illustration 1
Painted pottery basin

Mid Neolithic period (5000-3000 B.C.)
Height 8.6, diameter of mouth 23.6 cm.
Excavated in 1980 from Xiaomeisha, Shenzhen city

Buff earthenware made from fine sandy clay with a straight mouth, round bottom and large footring. The body covered with a deep red slip is painted in ochre with stylised wave pattern. This is a rare piece of painted pottery of an early date from the Guangdong area.

曲江馬壩石峽遺址

新石器時代——春秋
曲江縣馬壩獅子岩

石峽遺址發現於1972年，位於馬壩鎮西南2.5公里的獅子山麓，是一處山崗遺址，面積約三萬多平方米。1975年至1978年先後三次發掘，揭露遺址面積三千六百多平方米。清理墓葬一百三十二座。發現了三個文化交疊層，上層是廣東青銅時代，相當於西周晚期至春秋時期；中層是以曲尺紋、長方格紋、雙線方格紋等幾何印紋軟陶爲特徵的遺存，年代相當於夏商之際或更晚些；下層是石峽文化，是這次考古發掘的重要發現。石峽文化區別於廣東以往發現的新石器時代晚期文化，它有獨特的埋葬習俗，墓坑用火燒烤，流行單人二次遷葬。陶器以素面爲主，流行子口帶蓋，三足器和圈足鏤孔。磨製精緻，種類繁多的石器是石峽文化的另一特點。從出土大型石器和炭化稻谷、稻米，說明了原始農業是古代石峽居民主要從事的生產活動。墓葬中出土的木炭經炭十四測定年代爲公元前2380—前2070年（樹輪校正：公元前2865—前2480年）。

Shixia site in Maba, Qujiang

Neolithic to Spring and Autumn periods
Shiziyan, Maba, Qujiang

The Shixia site situated at Shiziyan, 2.5 kilometres southwest of Maba was first discovered in 1972. It is a hillock site occupying an area of about 30 thousand square metres. From 1975 to 1978, three trial excavations were conducted over an area of 3,600 square metres and 132 tombs were found. There are three cultural layers. The upper layer is dated to the Bronze Age of Guangdong region, corresponding to late W. Zhou to Spring and Autumn periods of the central China; the middle layer characterised by geometric impressed wares with angular meander, rectangular and double-lined square pattern, is dated to the Xia to Shang Dynasties or later; the lowest layer is of Shixia culture, the most significant discovery of these excavations. The Shixia culture stands out from other cultures of late Neolithic Guangdong in its peculiar burial custom. The grave pits were usually burnt and the practice of secondary burial was very popular (i.e. the dead was burried twice). The pottery is mostly plain, and characterised by stepped mouth with cover, tripods and footrings with perforations. Stone implements are finely polished and of a great variety of shapes. The large stone implements and carbonized grains and rice unearthed from the site show that primitive agriculture was obviously the main productive activity of the ancient Shixia people. A charcoal sample from a Shixia tomb has been carbon dated to 2380-2070 B.C. (dendrochronologic calibrated: 2865-2480 B.C.)

19. 有段石錛

新石器時代晚期（公元前3000－前1500年）
長11.5、刃寬5、厚2.2 cm.
1977年曲江縣馬壩石峽遺址61號墓出土

灰色泥質板岩製成。長方形，平頂，正面平直，背面上部有梯級狀的橫脊，把石錛分為兩段，錛的刃口，一面斜削，一面平直，因此稱作"有段石錛"。安柄後，可用來鋤地、砍伐樹木。這是富有南方特點的石製生產工具。

圖五：石錛裝置使用圖。

19. Stone stepped adze

Late Neolithic period (3000-1500 B.C.)
Length 11.5, width of blade 5, thickness 2.2 cm.
Excavated in 1977 from Tomb No. 61 at Shixia, Maba, Qujiang county

Made from grey clayish slate, this adze is of rectangular shape with straight edges and sides. A horizontal step on the upper part of the front side divides the adze into two sections. The blade is unifacially bevelled. When hafted it was used for digging or chopping trees. A very characteristic piece of stone productive tool commonly use in southern China.

Fig. 5: Stone adze hafted in wooden handle.

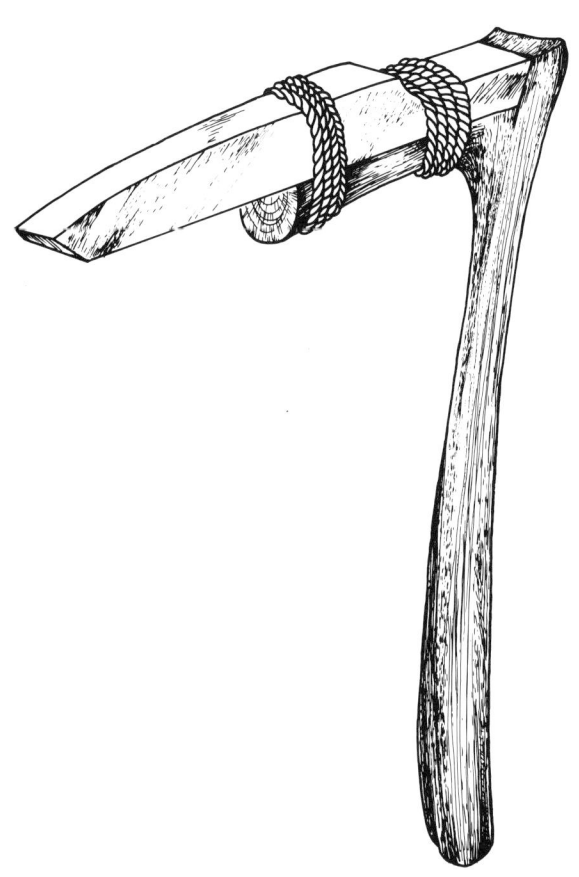

20. 長身石錛

新石器時代晚期（公元前3000－前1500年）
長17.5、刃寬6.4、厚2.5 cm.
1977年曲江縣馬壩石峽遺址99號墓出土

淺灰色砂質板岩製成。長身、平頂、正、背面拱起，斷面橢圓形，單面刃，磨製十分精緻。這種大型長身石錛裝上短柄後，可用於掘土、砍伐樹木，挖掘墓坑。

20. Stone long adze

Late Neolithic period (3000-1500 B.C.)
Length 17.5, width of blade 6.4, thickness 2.5 cm.
Excavated in 1977 from Tomb No. 99 at Shixia, Maba, Qujiang county

Made from pale grey sandy slate. The body is rectangular with a straight top edge. Both the front and back sides are convex forming an elliptical cross section. The blade is unifacially and finely polished. When hafted with a short handle, this type of long adze is used for digging and wood chopping.

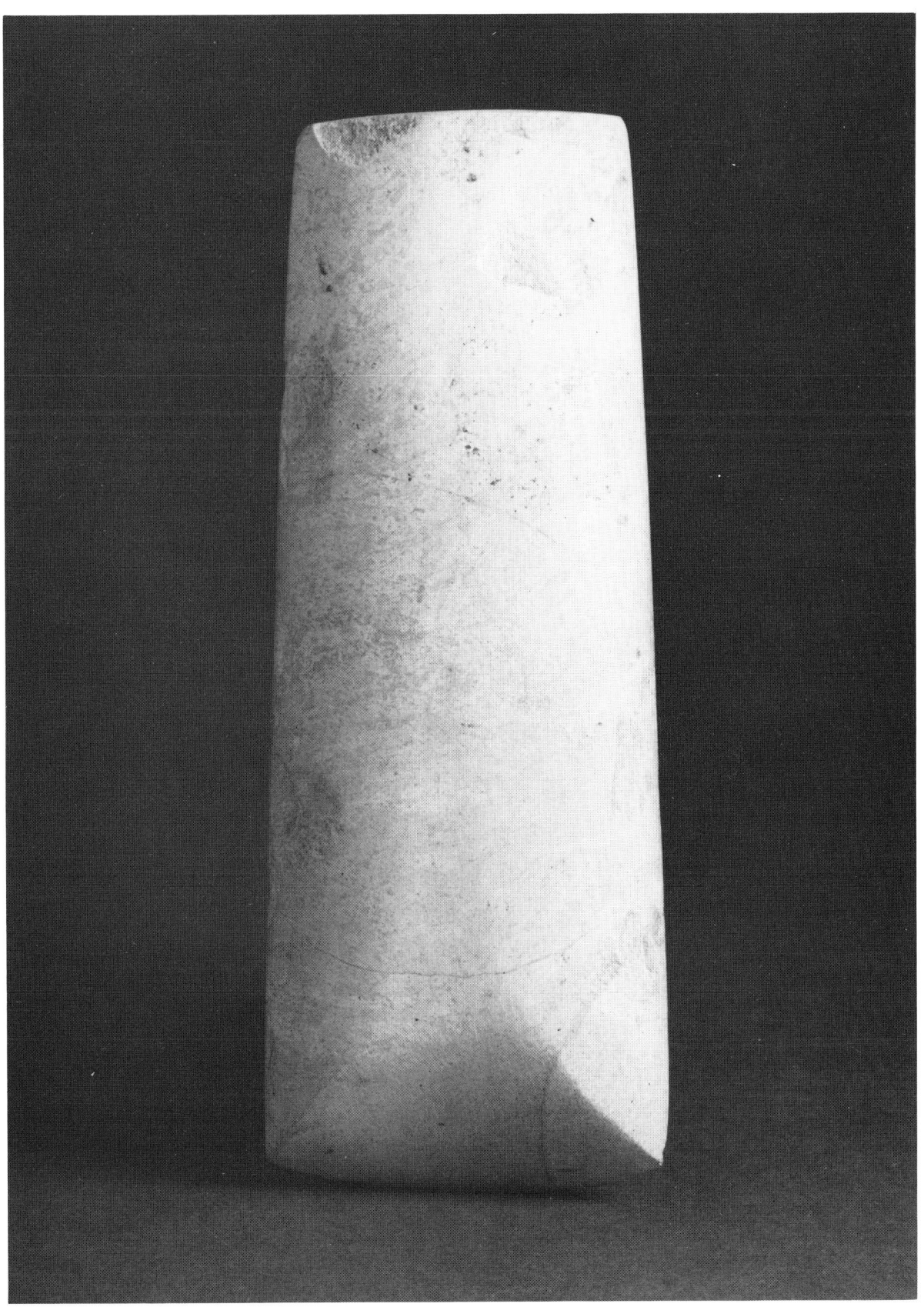

21. 有肩有段石錛

新石器時代晚期（公元前3000－前1500年）
長7.8、刃寬4.2 cm.
1978年佛山市瀾石河宕遺址出土

灰色細砂岩製成。頂窄，刃寬，呈梯形，單面斜刃，柄部有肩和段。珠江三角洲貝坵遺址出土的石器，以中、小型居多，有肩有段石錛則是該地區富有特色的石器。安上木柄後，用作砍木、掘土。

21. Stone stepped and shouldered adze

Late Noelithic period (3000-1500 B.C.)
Length 7.8, width of blade 4.2 cm.
Excavated in 1978 from Hedang, Lanshi, Foshan city

Made from fine greyish sandstone. This adze is of trapezoidal shape with a narrow butt and a broad blade. The blade edge is unifacially bevelled and the butt is supported by a step and double shoulders. The sizes of stone implements unearthed from shell mounds in Zhujiang Delta area range from small to medium. Amongst them the stepped and shouldered adzes show strong local characteristics. When hafted, they are used for chopping and digging.

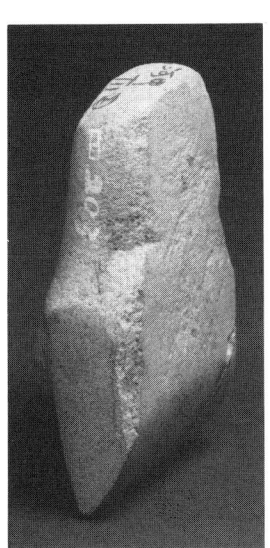

151

22. 有肩石錛

新石器時代晚期（公元前3000－前1500年）
長10、柄寬4、刃寬6.8 cm.
1978年南海縣大同灶崗遺址出土

灰色細砂岩製成。雙肩明顯對稱，單面斜刃。有肩石錛在珠江三角洲地區新石器時代遺址中較多見。

22. Stone shouldered adze

Late Neolithic period (3000-1500 B.C.)
Length 10, width of butt 4, width of blade 6.8 cm.
Excavated in 1978 from Zaogang, Datong, Nanhai county

Made from fine greyish sandstone. The two shoulders are very symmetric and the blade edge is unifacially bevelled. Shouldered adzes are commonly found in Neolithic sites in Zhujiang Delta area.

23. 石钁

新石器時代晚期（公元前3000－前1500年）
長18、上刃寬2.2、下刃寬4.4、厚2.3 cm.
1977年曲江縣馬壩石峽遺址105號墓出土

灰色泥質板岩製成。厚體狹長條形，上刃窄，下刃寬，單面斜刃，正面內凹，背面拱起，側視呈弓形，又稱"弓背錛"。主要用於深挖土。是石峽文化富有地方特色的生產工具之一。

23. Stone pickaxe

Late Neolithic period (3000-1500 B.C.)
Length 18, width of upper blade 2.2, width of lower blade 4.4, thickness 2.3 cm.
Excavated in 1977 from Tomb No. 105 at Shixia, Maba, Qujiang county

Made from grey clayish slate. Slender in shape, this axe has a narrow upper blade and a broad lower blade. Both blade edges are unifacially bevelled. Laterally the axe is curved into a bow shape. Thus it is also called a "bow-back" adze. Used for deep digging, this is one of the characteristic productive tools of Shixia culture in Guangdong.

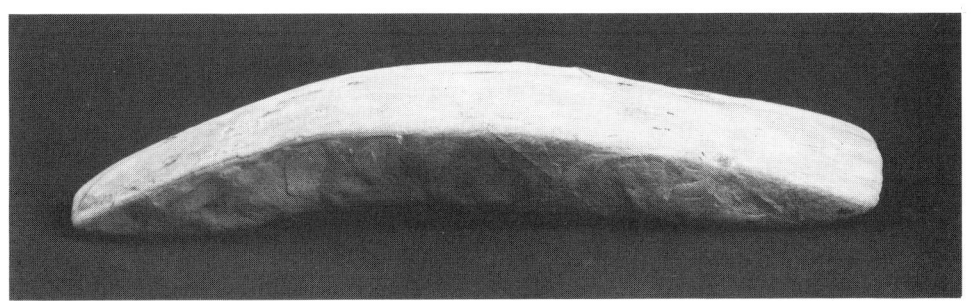

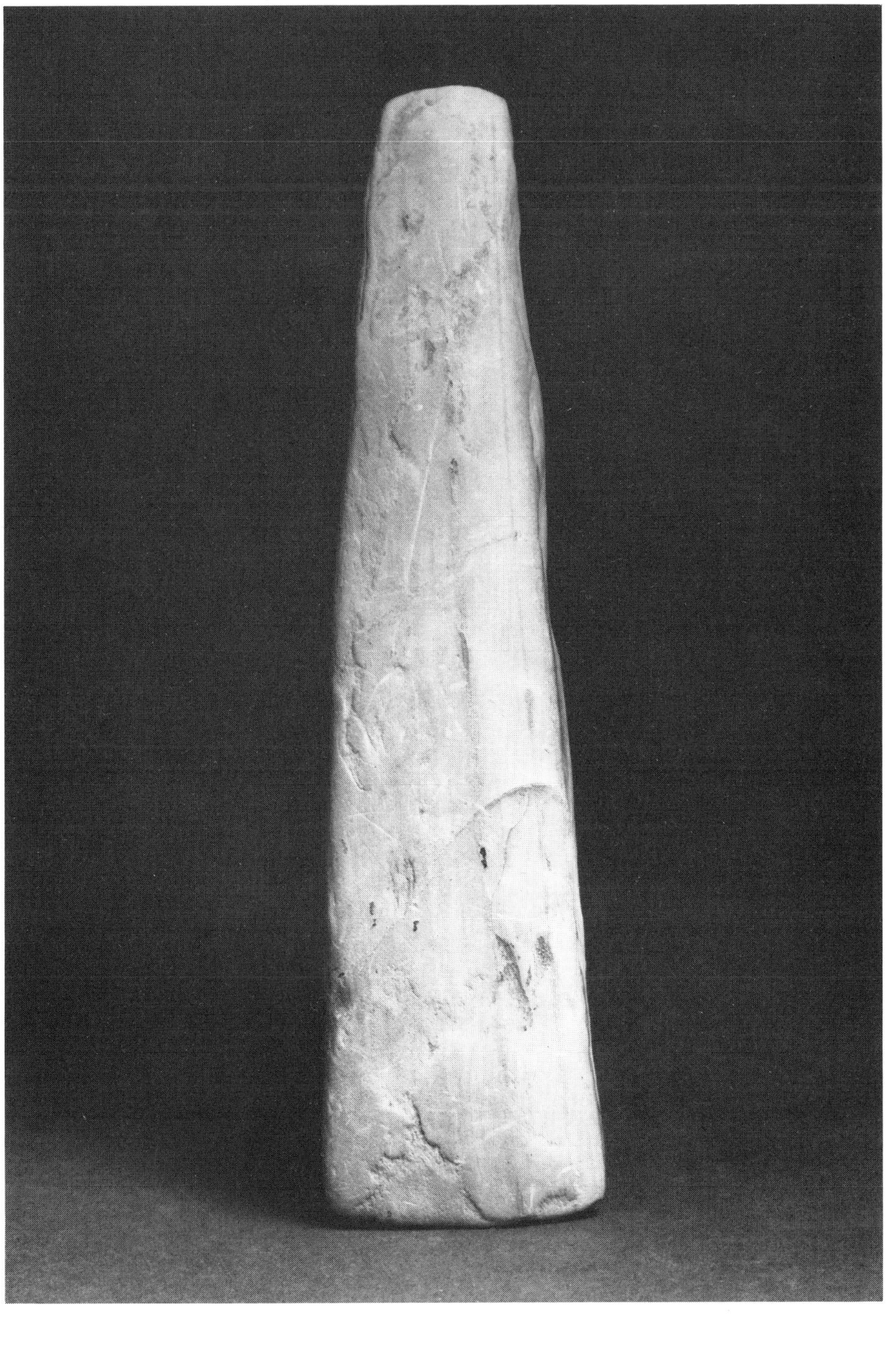

24. 石鏟

新石器時代晚期（公元前3000－前1500年）
長15、刃寬9.3、厚1 cm.
1977年曲江縣馬壩石峽遺址44號墓出土

灰色泥質板岩製成。扁平長梯形，斜首，亞腰，雙面斜刃，刃端弧，上部穿孔。這種石鏟在我國東南沿海地區新石器時代晚期文化中發現較多。

24. Stone shovel

Late Neolithic period (3000-5000 B.C.)
Length 15, width of blade 9.3, thickness 1 cm.
Excavated in 1977 from Tomb No. 44 at Shixia, Maba, Qujiang county

Made from grey clayish slate, this shovel is of flat trapezoidal shape with a slant top edge, contracted waist, and a perforation on its upper part. The blade edge is curved and bifacially bevelled. Shovels like this are commonly found from late Neolithic sites in southeastern coastal region of China.

25. 石鉞

新石器時代晚期（公元前3000－前1500年）
長17.7、刃寬8.5、厚0.8 cm.
1977年曲江縣馬壩石峽遺址47號墓出土

器呈扁平長身薄體，斜首，亞腰，刃端呈斜弧狀，上穿一孔。石峽遺址墓葬中出土的石鉞，絕大多數用高嶺岩製成，呈牙白色，石質硬度低，無實用價值。可能是一種專用於陪葬的明器。47號墓同時出土了大小石鉞共六件。

25. Stone *yue*-axe

Late Neolithic period (3000-1500 B.C.)
Length 17.7, width of blade 8.5, thickness 0.8 cm.
Excavated in 1977 from Tomb No. 47 at Shixia, Maba, Qujiang county

This axe is of long and flat shape with slant top edge, contracted waist, asymmetrically curved blade edge, and on its upper part a perforation. Stone *yue*-axes unearthed from Shixia tombs are mostly made from *kaolin* stone, which is ivory white in colour and very soft. Such axes were probably not for practical use and were produced as burial objects. There are six stone *yue*-axes of different sizes unearthed from the same tomb.

26. 石鏃

新石器時代晚期（公元前3000－前1500年）
長7.7－10.6cm.
1977年曲江縣馬壩石峽遺址20、43、67、80、108號墓出土

灰色泥質板岩製成，柳葉形，窄葉尖鋒，挺身兩面有凸脊。是新石器時代人們常用的狩獵工具，亦是男性成員常備的武器。

圖六：石峽遺址108號墓隨葬器物。

26. Stone arrowheads

Late Neolithic period (3000-1500 B.C.)
Length 7.7-10.6 cm.
Excavated in 1977 from Tombs 20, 43, 67, 80, 108 at Shixia, Maba, Qujiang county

Made from grey clayish slate. All arrowheads found are of "willow-leaf" shape with tapering twin-blades, sharp points and well polished midribs on both sides. Bows and arrows were basic hunting tools for the Neolithic people, as well as weapons which the males usually carried.

Fig. 6: Tomb 108 at Shixia with finds in situ.

27. 石琮

新石器時代晚期（公元前3000－前1500年）
高4.4、邊長6.7、內徑5.6 cm.
1975年曲江縣馬壩石峽遺址17號墓出土

灰色矽卡岩製成。內圓外方，內圓邊兩端凸出。每方角用淺雕凸弦紋和圓圈紋構成一組獸面紋。外緣四邊稜角和內圓孔周邊因使用過，留下磨損痕迹。

圖七：石峽17號墓隨葬器物。

27. Stone *cong*

Late Neolithic period (3000-1500 B.C.)
Height 4.4, side length 6.7, internal diameter 5.6 cm.
Excavated in 1975 from Tomb No. 17 at Shixia, Maba, Qujiang county

Made from greyish siliceous stone. *Congs* are usually of square prismatic shape with tubular projections at either end. This *cong* has its four corners each decorated with a monster mask design under two bands of raised horizontal lines. Its original sharp cut corners are now much worn off due to use.

Fig. 7: Tomb 17 at Shixia with finds in situ.

163

輔助照片2. 大石琮

新石器時代晚期（公元前3000－前1500年）
高13.8、邊長6.6－7、孔徑4.8－5.2cm.
1977年曲江縣馬壩石峽遺址105號墓出土

灰色矽卡岩製成。內圓外方，四邊平直，呈直角，上大下小，從上到下淺雕五組距離相等的凸弦紋。內圓孔用兩頭管鑽，孔內遺留有殘斷石芯。

圖八：孔內兩頭管鑽痕跡。

Supplementary illustration 2
Large stone *cong*

Late Neolithic period (3000-1500 B.C.)
Height 13.8, side length 6.6-7, internal diameter 4.8-5.2 cm.
Excavated in 1977 from Tomb No. 105 at Shixia, Maba, Qujiang county

Made from grey siliceous stone. This *cong* is of slightly tapering, square prismatic shape with thick-walled tubular projections at either end. The decoration is divided into five equal bands, each of which consists of two raised bands over stylised monster masks at the corners. The perforation was drilled from both ends resulting in an overlap at the middle.

Fig. 8: Interior view of perforation showing the overlap.

輔助照片3. 石琮

新石器時代晚期（公元前3000－前1500年）
高3.3、邊長7.5、內徑5.6 cm.
1977年曲江縣馬壩石峽遺址69號墓出土

白色高嶺岩製成。內圓外方，外緣呈弧形、鈍角。每方角用淺雕橫紋構成一組花紋。因使用過，琮的內外稜角磨損變圓。佩戴位置與石臂環相同，應是實用裝飾品。

Supplementary illustration 3
Stone *cong*

Late Neolithic period (3000-1500 B.C.)
Height 3.3, side length 7.5, internal diameter 5.6 cm.
Excavated in 1977 from Tomb No. 69 at Shixia site, Maba, Qujiang county

Made from pale buff *kaolin* stone, this *cong* is of square prismatic shape with tubular projections at either end. On each corner is a stylised monster mask pattern formed by incised and carved lines in relief. All sharp cut angles are now much worn off due to use. Probably worn as an ornament like that of a stone bracelet.

28. 石臂環

新石器時代晚期（公元前3000－前1500年）
高3.9、徑6.3 cm.
1977年曲江縣馬壩石峽遺址51號墓出土

此器用帶褐色斑點石紋的長英角岩製成。肉窄而厚，環形，呈寬帶狀，是佩戴在手臂上的裝飾品。黃河下游大汶口文化和長江下游良渚文化的墓葬中都有出土。

29. 石笄

新石器時代晚期（公元前3000－前1500年）
長14.7cm.
1977年曲江縣馬壩石峽遺址21號墓出土

牙白色高嶺岩製成。扁圓柱體，笄頭磨成短柄，上穿一小孔，下端漸細成鈍尖，是古人用來盤頭髮的簪子。這件笄是隨葬石笄中最長的一件。

28. Stone bracelet

Late Neolithic period (3000-1500 B.C.)
Height 3.9, diameter 6.3 cm.
Excavated in 1977 from Tomb No. 51 at Shixia site, Maba, Qujiang county

Made from brown spotted quartzose breccia. This thin-walled cylindrical ring is an arm ornament. Bracelets are also found in tombs of the Dawenkou culture and the Liangzhu culture in the eastern coastal area.

29. Stone hairpin

Late Neolithic period (3000-1500 B.C.)
Length 14.7 cm.
Excavated in 1977 from Tomb No. 21 at Shixia site, Maba, Qujiang county

Made of ivory *kaolin* stone. This hairpin is of a rod shape with an oval cross-section. Its upper end was polished to form a short perforated handle and its lower end tapering to a blunt point. Hairpins were used by ancient people for fixing hair buns. This is the longest stone hairpin so far unearthed in Guangdong.

佛山河宕遺址

新石器時代晚期
佛山市瀾石

河宕遺址是珠江三角洲冲積平原上的一處土墩類型貝坵遺址。1977年冬在佛山市郊瀾石河宕舊墟發現。遺址面積約一萬平方米，發掘面積750平方米。出土了豐富的遺物、遺跡和墓葬。是廣東近年來較重要的發現。

河宕遺址陶器較典型特徵是85％以上的器表拍印幾何印紋，紋樣多達二十多種。拍印技術嫻熟，印痕清晰，排列規整。清理了七十七座墓葬，人骨架保存得較好，均為淺穴墓，流行單人仰身直肢葬，成年男性頭部向西，女性均向東，並發現十九個成年男女，生前有人工拔牙的習俗，拔除上頜側門齒。

河宕遺址是珠江三角洲新石器時代晚期的典型遺址，相同的文化遺存在南海灶崗、螺崗、通心崗、船埋崗等地都有發現。經炭十四測定年代，(3)層為公元前3070－前2955年（樹輪校正：公元前3680－前3550年）；(2)層為公元前2150－前1655年（樹輪校正：公元前2580－前1960年）。

Hedang Site at Foshan

Late Neolithic period
Lanshi, Foshan city

Hedang is a shell mound site situated at the alluvial plain of the Zhujiang Delta. It was first discovered in the winter of 1977 in the old market area at Hedang, Lanshi in the suburb of Foshan city and the total area is estimated to occupy more than 10,000 square metres. Only 750 square metres have been excavated yielding fruitful archaeological specimens. It is a most significant discovery in Guangdong in the recent years.

The pottery from Hedang site is characterised by impressed geometric patterns. Eighty percent of them are impressed with over 20 varieties of patterns. The sharp and well layout of the impressed units indicate a relatively advanced pottery technique. Seventy-seven tombs were excavated and many of which contain well preserved skeletons. All these tombs are shallow earth pits for single, upfaced and extended burials, with the males facing west and the females facing east. Furthermore nineteen males and females adults were found with their side incisors of maxilla pulled off when alive.

The Hedang site is a representative site of late Neolithic period in the Zhujiang Delta. Similar cultural sites have also been found at Zaogang, Luogang, Tongxingang, Quanmaigang in Nanhai county.

Two radiocarbon dates are available: third layer 3070-2955 B.C. (dendrochronologic calibrated: 3680-3550 B.C.), second layer 2150-1655 B.C. (dendrochronologic calibrated: 2580-1960 B.C.).

30. 象牙筒形器

新石器時代晚期（公元前3000－前1500年）
高7.8、厚0.1－0.2 cm.
1978年佛山市瀾石河宕遺址甲區65號墓出土

這件用象牙製作的筒形器，磨製極精，器表光澤潤滑，器壁薄如蛋殼，實是一件罕見的珍品。甲區65號墓主人，是一位25歲左右的男性，出土時一對束腰象牙筒形器放置在墓主人的頭頂。

30. Ivory cylindrical object

Late Neolithic period (3000-1500 B.C.)
Height 7.8, thickness 0.1-0.2 cm.
Excavated in 1978 from Tomb No. 65, Area A, Hedang, Lanshi, Foshan city

With finely polished smooth surface and wall of "egg-shell" thickness, this is a rare and exquisite ivory object. During excavation, a pair of these ivory objects were found above the head of the buried dead, a male in his mid twenties.

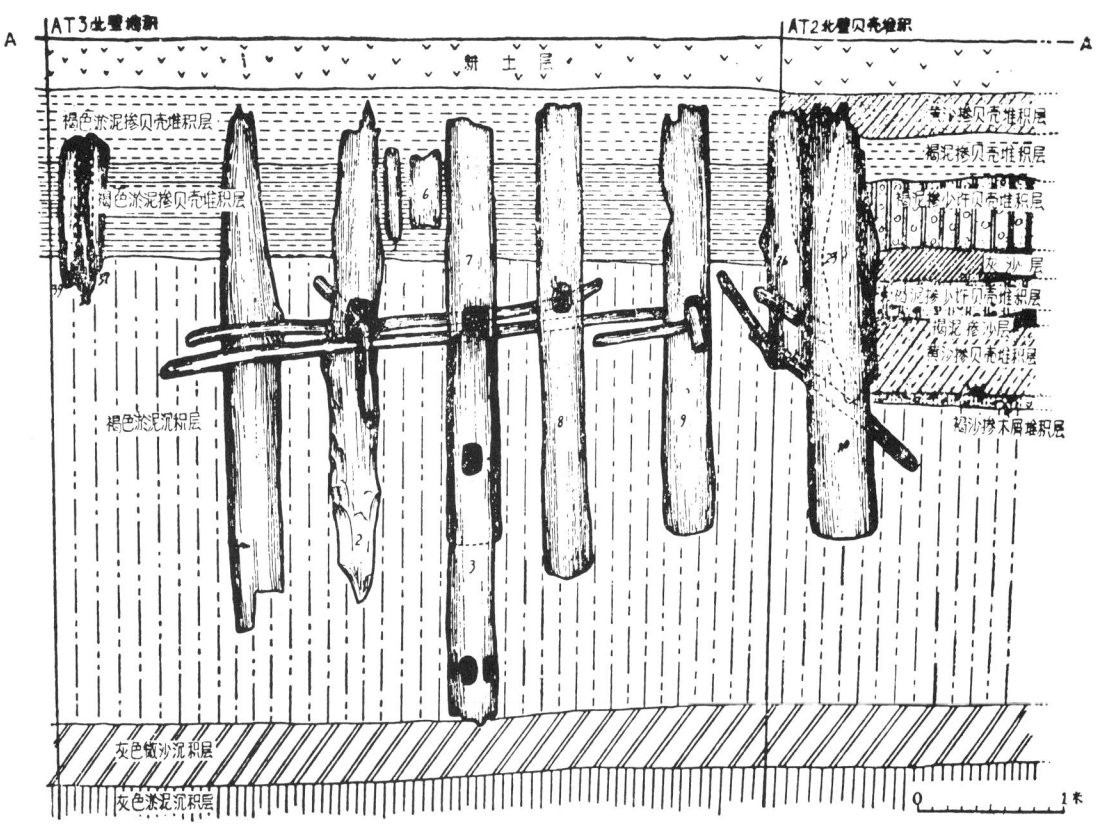
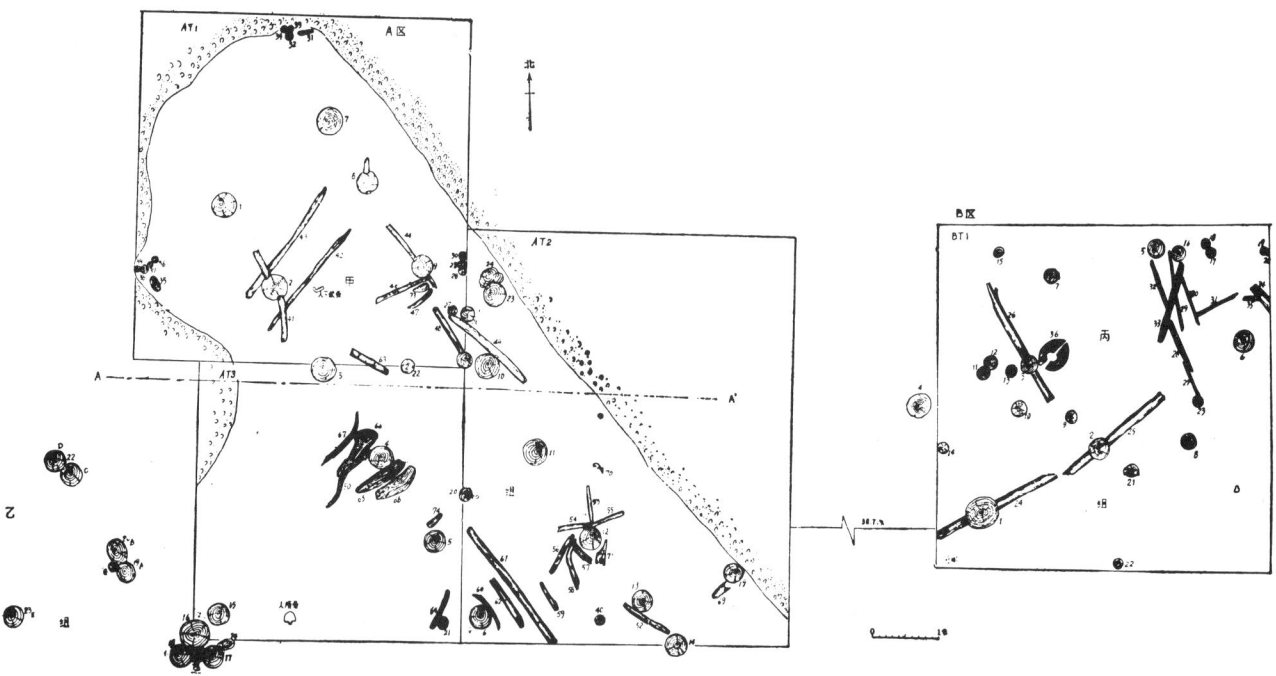

茅岗水上木构建筑遗址A、B区发掘平面图

A区: 1—18.木柱 19—40、75.木桩 40—60.擡木支架条 61—64.树皮板 65—74.垫木块 A、B、C、D、E、F.填土时露出的木柱（未发掘）

B区: 1—6.木柱 7—23.木桩 24—35.木条 36.烧灼过的圆木板

高要茅崗遺址

新石器時代晚期
高要縣金利

遺址於1978年10月在金利區茅崗鄉石角村前的魚塘中發現，是一處水上木構建築遺址。遺址面積約十萬平方米，已發掘112平方米。木構建築的支架如木樁、木柱、圓形木條和舖墊在支架上的樹皮板等都在堆積層中發現。清理了三組建築遺迹，平面佈局爲長方形，每組總長14.7、寬1.7米。文化層堆積厚達5米以上，爲褐色淤泥摻貝殼沉積層，文化特徵與珠江三角洲新石器時代晚期遺存相類似。出土遺物較豐富，有陶器殘片近萬件，絕大部份陶器表面拍印幾何紋，陶色以灰陶、黑陶居多。生產工具有石斧、石錛、石鑿和骨錐、骨梭、骨鏃。同時出土了哺乳動物、水生動物的遺骨，蚧殼和炭化果核。炭化木頭經炭十四測定年代爲公元前2340－前2120年（樹輪校正：公元前2815－前2540年）。

茅崗遺址的水上木構建築，是廣東境內的首次發現。

Maogang site at Gaoyao

Late Neolithic period
Jinli, Gaoyao county

This site with remains of wooden structure buildings above water was discovered in October 1978 in a fish pond in front of Shijiao village at Maogang, Jinli. The site occupies an area of 100 thousand square metres and 112 square metres were excavated, yielding planks supported by piles, pillars, and beans. Three groups of building remains were found and each group (14.7 m. long and 1.7 m. wide) was of rectangular shape. The cultural layers, more than 5 m. in depth were a mixture of brownish soil and shell. Cultural characteristics resemble those of other late Neolithic sites in the Zhujiang Delta.

The cultural relics unearthed are abundant. There are nearly ten thousand pieces of pottery sherds which are mostly grey or black in colour and impressed with geometric design. There are also productive tools including stone axes, adzes and chisels, bone awls, shuttles, and arrowheads, alongside bones of marine or mammalian animals, shells and carbonized fruit stones.

A carbonized piece of wood from the site has been carbon dated to 2340-2120 B.C. (Dendrochronologic calibrated: 2815-2540 B.C.). This is the first ever discovered site with remains of wooden structure buildings above water in Guangdong.

31. 骨梭

新石器時代晚期（公元前3000－前1500年）
長13.5cm.
1978年高要縣茅崗遺址出土

用動物肢骨製成。長形扁體，兩端磨成錐狀，一端有穿孔，繫繩用，是織網工具。

31. Bone shuttle

Late Neolithic period (3000-1500 B.C.)
Length 13.5 cm.
Excavated in 1978 from Maogang, Gaoyao county

Made from animal limb bone, this shuttle is of rod shape with oval cross-section and with tapering ends. One end is perforated for attachment to a thread. Probably a tool for weaving nets.

32. 骨錐

新石器時代晚期（公元前3000－前1500年）
長11.3cm.
1978年高要縣金利茅崗遺址出土

形為扁體。一端磨成錐叉，鋒部有一凹槽，形成倒鈎。

32. Bone awl

Late Neolithic period (3000-1500 B.C.)
Length 11.3 cm.
Excavated in 1978 from Maogang, Gaoyao

This awl is flat in cross-section with one end polished to a sharp point. Near the point there is a backhook and a groove.

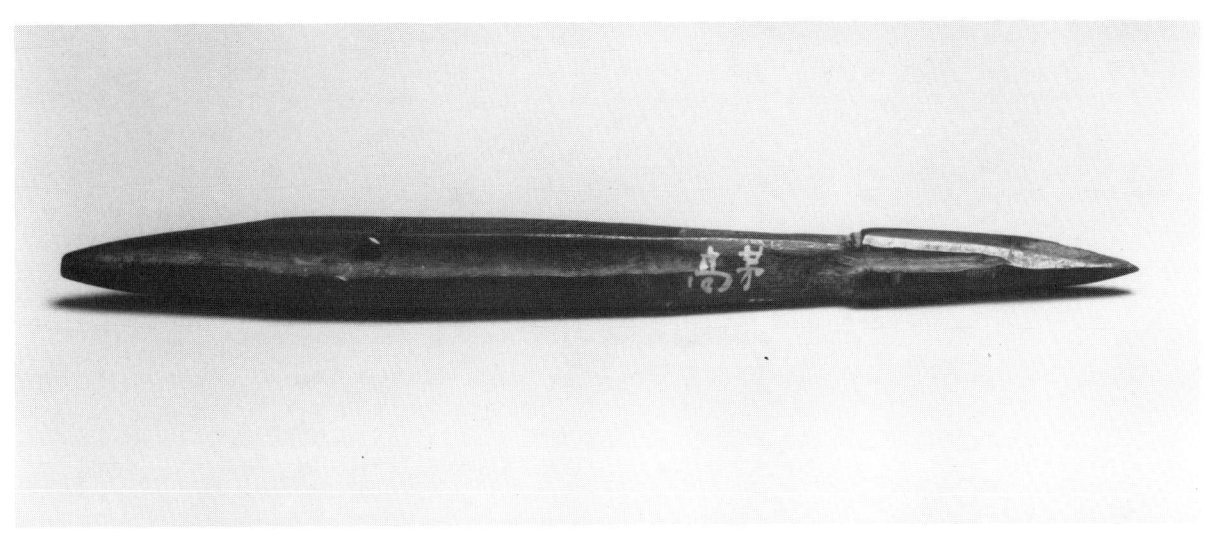
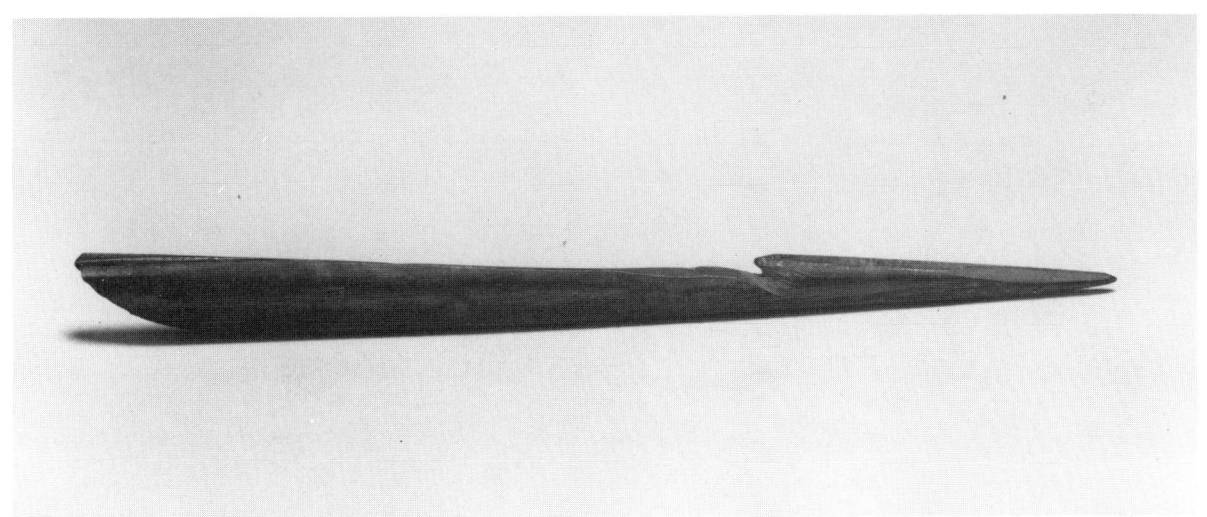

33. 陶𬊤

新石器時代晚期（公元前3000－前1500年）
高28、口徑3.3－4.5cm.
1977年曲江縣馬壩石峽遺址54號墓出土

灰色夾細砂陶。盛水或煮食物用。鳥喙形流口，長頸昂起，圓肩，繩狀鋬跨在肩腹之間，羊乳狀袋足，分襠鼎立。陶𬊤爲中國黃河、長江流域中、下游新石器時代晚期文化遺址中常見。石峽墓葬所出的陶𬊤。可能是在與諸考古學文化的交流中，傳播或吸收所致，所以數量很少。

圖九：山東大汶口遺址出土的陶𬊤。

33. Pottery pitcher

Late Neolithic period (3000-1500 B.C.)
Height 28, diameter of mouth 3.3-4.5 cm.
Excavated in 1977 from Tomb No. 54 at Shixia, Maba, Qujiang county

Finely tempered greyish pottery. This pitcher was probably used as a water container or cooking vessel. It has a sharp spout, a long trumpet neck, a cord-shaped handle supported by three bulging hollow legs. Pottery pitchers are commonly found in late Neolithic sites in the middle to lower regions of Yellow and Yangzi Rivers, but few are unearthed from Shixia tombs. However their occurence in Shixia sites indicates a possibility of cultural interchange and cross-influence from other Neolithic cultures.

Fig. 9: Pottery pitchers from Dawenkou sites in Shandong.

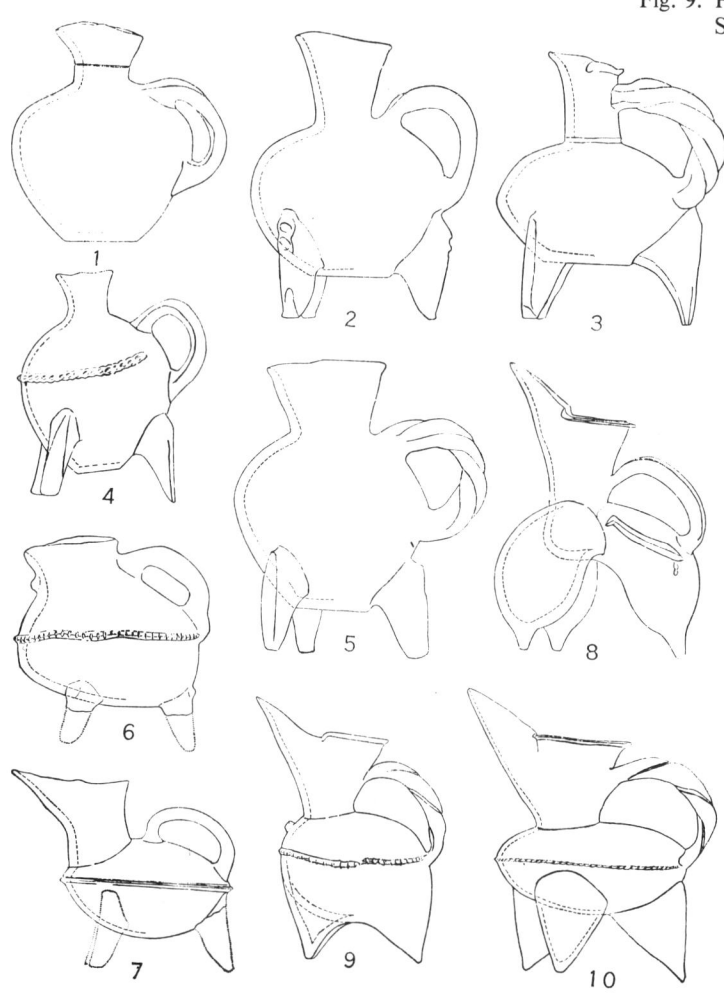

34. 白陶鼎

新石器時代晚期（公元前3000－前1500年）
通高21.9、口徑8.4 cm.
1975年曲江縣馬壩石峽遺址10號墓出土

細泥質陶，器表白色泛黃。盛食物用。子口微歛，束頸，削肩，扁圓腹，圜底，連襠梯形足，足各穿三孔。蓋作覆豆式，喇叭形蓋鈕穿三孔。是一件少見的珍品。

圖十：陶鼎剖面圖。

34. White pottery tripod

Late Neolithic period (3000-1500 B.C.)
Overall height 21.9, diameter of mouth 8.4 cm.
Excavated in 1975 from Tomb No. 10 at Shixia, Maba, Qujiang county

Finely gained earthenware food container of yellowish white colour. It is with a stepped mouth, contracted neck, sloping shoulder, squat body, round bottom and three trapezoid legs, each of which has three small perforations. The cover is an overturned *dou*-stemcup with a splayed grip which has also three small perforations. A unique specimen.

Fig. 10: Cross-section of the tripod.

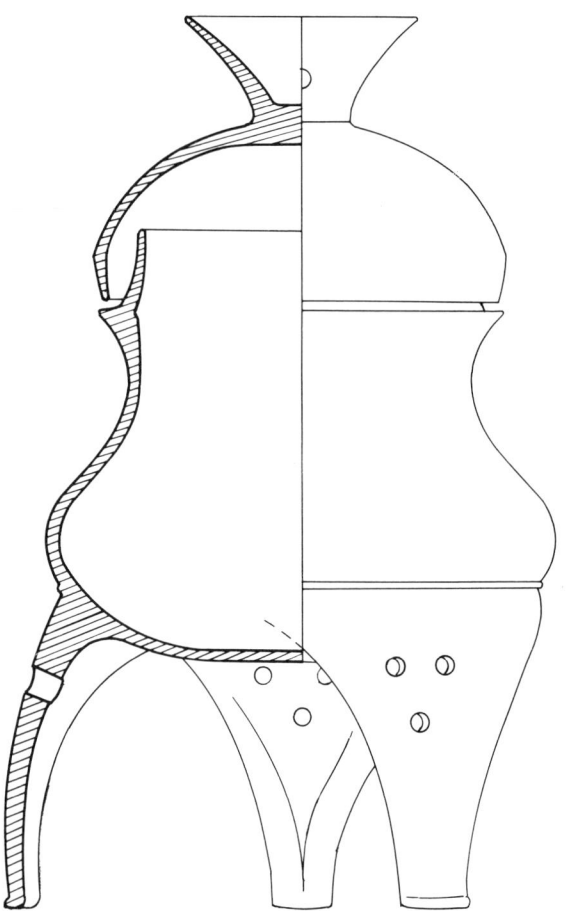

35. 盤形鼎

新石器時代晚期（公元前3000－前1500年）
高17、口徑22.5cm.
1975年曲江縣馬壩石峽遺址5號墓出土

灰褐色夾砂陶。子口，淺盤，平底，下加三條扁體鑿形足。鼎蓋用夾砂陶豆，應是炊煮器。這是石峽文化陶器中的典型器之一。

36. 圈足盤

新石器時代晚期（公元前3000－前1500年）
高9.3、口徑16.6cm.
1975年曲江縣馬壩石峽遺址17號墓出土

橙紅色細泥質陶。子口，淺盤，圓底，束腰形大圈足，足上飾一對橢圓形大鏤孔。出土時有陶豆覆置盤上作蓋。盛食物用，是石峽文化陶器中的典型器之一。

35. Pottery tripod-dish

Late Neolithic period (3000-1500 B.C.)
Height 17, diameter 22.5 cm.
Excavated in 1975 from Tomb No. 5 at Shixia, Maba, Qujiang county

Greyish brown tempered earthenware, with a stepped mouth, shallow dish body, flat bottom supported by three flat chisel-shaped feet. The original cover should also be *dou*-stemcup shaped as in the previous example (see No. 34). This is a cooking vessel and is one of the representative shapes of Shixia pottery.

36. Pottery dish with footring

Late Neolithic period (3000-1500 B.C.)
Height 9.3, diameter 16.6 cm.
Excavated in 1975 from Tomb No. 17 at Shixia, Maba, Qujiang county

Finely grained orange red earthenware with stepped mouth, shallow body and flat bottom, mounted on a high splaying footring with a pair of large elliptical perforations. During excavation an overturned *dou* was found on the top of it and probably served as a cover. This is a food container, one of the representative pottery shapes in Shixia culture.

37. 三足盤

新石器時代晚期（公元前3000－前1500年）
高9、口徑16.2cm.
1973年曲江縣馬壩石峽遺址3號墓出土

橙黃色泥質陶。子口，淺盤，圜底，連襠三角形足，足上飾小鏤孔。三足盤是石峽文化常見的陶器，盛食物用。根據盤足的不同形制。還有瓦形足和梯形足三足盤。

圖十一：石峽遺址出土的陶盤。

37. Tripod-dish

Late Neolithic period (3000-1500 B.C.)
Height 9, diameter 16.2 cm.
Excavated in 1973 from Tomb No. 3 at Shixia, Maba, Qujiang county

Orange yellow earthenware, with stepped mouth, shallow body, round bottom, and three connected triangular feet with perforations. Tripod-dishes served as food containers are usually found in Shixia culture sites. There are also dishes with arch-shaped or trapezoid feet.

Fig. 11: Pottery dishes unearthed at Shixia.

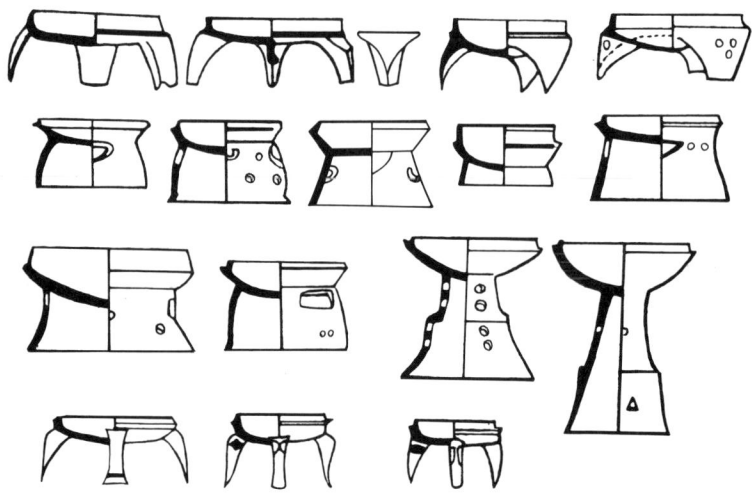

38. 陶豆

新石器時代晚期（公元前3000－前1500年）
高12.5、口徑18.4cm.
1973年曲江縣馬壩石峽遺址3號墓出土

灰褐色泥質陶。直口，弧壁，深盤，半實心細把凸棱喇叭形足。可盛食物又可作盤蓋的兩用器皿。是石峽文化陶器中的典型器之一。此器與陶三足盤（見前展品37號）共出，出土時陶豆覆蓋於盤上。

38. Pottery *dou*

Late Neolithic period (3000-1500 B.C.)
Height 12.5, diameter of mouth 18.4 cm.
Excavated in 1973 from Tomb No. 3 at Shixia, Maba, Qujiang county

Greyish brown earthenware with straight mouth, deep dish body and concave sides. The splayed foot stem is half solid with two horizontal flanges near the base. *Dou*, a food container is a representative shape of Shixia pottery. This piece was found together with the previous specimen (No. 37). During excavation the *dou* was overturned and probably meant to be the cover of the tripod-dish.

39. 陶壺

新石器時代晚期（公元前3000－前1500年）
高19、口徑8、腹徑16.5cm.
1976年曲江縣馬壩石峽遺址25號墓出土

橙紅色泥質陶。盛水的器具。子口，直長頸，廣肩，扁圓腹，圈足。子口和圈足是石峽文化陶器中流行的造型，富有特色。

圖十二：石峽25號墓陶壺出土情況。

39. Pottery vase

Late Neolithic period (3000-1500 B.C.)
Height 19, diameter of mouth 8, diameter of body 16.5 cm.
Excavated in 1976 from Tomb No. 25 at Shixia, Maba, Qujiang county

Water container, orange red earthenware with stepped mouth, straight long neck, squat body, and footring. Stepped mouths and footrings are characteristic features of Shixia pottery.

Fig. 12: Tomb No. 25 at Shixia with the vase in situ.

40. 陶釜

新石器時代晚期（公元前3000－前1500年）
高12.5、口徑17cm.
1977年曲江縣馬壩石峽遺址42號墓出土

灰褐色夾砂陶。敞口，寬沿外折，削肩，扁圓腹，圜底，器表拍印籃紋。石峽文化的炊煮器，除各類三足鼎之外，釜最常見。

圖十三：石峽42號墓隨葬遺物。

40. Pottery pot

Late Neolithic period (3000-1500 B.C.)
Height 12.5, diameter 17 cm.
Excavated in 1977 from Tomb No. 42 at Shixia, Maba, Qujiang county

Greyish brown tempered earthenware with wide mouth, out-turned rim and a round body. The outside is impressed with basket pattern. Alongside tripods, pots are the most common cooking vessels in Shixia.

Fig. 13: Tomb No. 42 at Shixia during excavation.

41. 陶罐

新石器時代晚期（公元前3000－前1500年）
高22.6、口徑7.6 cm、腹徑22.3 cm.
1977年曲江縣馬壩石峽遺址42號墓出土

土黃色泥質陶。素面。直口，斜肩，鼓腹，圜底，矮圈足。盛水用。

41. Pottery jar

Late Neolithic period (3000-1500 B.C.)
Height 22.6, diameter of mouth 7.6, diameter of body 22.3 cm.
Excavated in 1977 from Tomb No. 42, Shixia, Maba, Qujiang county

This yellowish earthenware is a water container. The outside is undecorated with a straight upright mouth, slant shoulder, bulging body and round bottom supported by a low footring.

42. 圈足罐

新石器時代晚期（公元前3000－前1500年）
高11.6、口徑9 cm.
1978年佛山市瀾石河宕遺址24號墓出土

橙紅色泥質陶，器表素面磨光，平沿，侈口，短頸，廣肩，扁圓腹，高喇叭形圈足，可盛水或盛食物用。24號墓主人是一位成年男性，生前施行過拔除上頜側門齒。

42. Pottery jar with footring

Late Neolithic period (3000-1500 B.C.)
Height 11.6, diameter 9 cm.
Excavated in 1978 from Tomb No. 24 at Hedang, Lanshi, Foshan

Orange red earthenware with plain but polished surface. It has a flared mouth, flat rim, short neck, broad shoulder, squat body, and high splayed footring, and was probably used as a container for water or food. The buried dead of this tomb was a male adult with his side incisors pulled off in his life time.

43. 陶罐

新石器時代晚期（公元前3000－前1500年）
高17.5、口徑8.3 cm.
1978年增城縣出土

灰色泥質陶。侈口，直頸，削肩，圈足。肩部拍印籃紋。盛水或盛食物用。

43. Pottery jar

Late Neolithic period (3000-1500 B.C.)
Height 17.5, diameter 8.3 cm.
Excavated in 1978 from Zengcheng county

Greyish earthenware with flared mouth, collar neck, slant shoulder and footring. The outside is impressed with basket pattern. Probably used as a water or food container.

44. 夾砂粗陶缶

新石器時代中晚期（公元前3500－前2000年）
口徑18、高12cm.
約1975年香港南丫島深灣"F"層出土
香港博物館藏品

香港南丫島深灣遺址在三十年代已發現，但有規模的科學發掘在七十年代才展開，經先後數期的清理，確定了文化層位的發展次序和年代。此器為夾砂粗陶，侈口，束頸，圓底，下半部拍印繩紋，上半部有篦划波浪紋。器表呈灰白及淺紅色，色澤不均，應與燒窰氣氛不穩定有關。此器出深灣遺址較低的"F"層，同出的木碳標本（R4585/1）經碳十四測定年代為4000±300B.P.（半衰期5570，未校正），又同層的陶片熱釋光測定數據為ca2900B.C.

44. Coarse pottery pot

Mid to late Neolithic period (3500-2000 B.C.)
Diameter at mouth 18, height 12 cm.
Excavated in mid seventies from Shenwan, Nanyadao, Hong Kong
Collection of the Hong Kong Museum of History

The Shenwan (Sham Wan) site in Hong Kong had already been known to pre-war archaeologists but it was not until the seventies that extensive and systematic excavations were undertaken, yielding abundant finds and a clear cut cultural sequence and stratigraphy. This coarse corded and tempered pot was found from "Assemblage F" of the site and seems to be of an early date. The surface colour, greyish white mixed with pinkish buff, certainly a primitive feature, is probably due to a miscontrol in the firing or atmosphere. The outside was combed with a wavy band on a corded background. A charcoal sample from the same assemblage has been carbon dated to 4000±300 B.P. (R4585/1, half life 5570, not calibrated). This date is also confirmed by a T-L date of ca. 2900 B.C. on pottery samples from the same stratum.

45. 幾何印紋陶片

新石器時代晚期（公元前3000－前1500年）
1973年至1978年佛山瀾石河宕貝坵遺址、高要金利茅崗遺址、曲江馬壩石峽遺址中文化層和普寧廣太虎頭埔等地出土

幾何印紋是我國江南地區陶器表面的花紋裝飾之一，富有地方特色，花紋主要流行規整的幾何形圖案，故冠以"幾何"兩字。幾何印紋陶產生於新石器時代晚期，鼎盛於商周至春秋，到戰國至秦漢便趨向衰落。廣東境內新石器時代晚期文化遺存中幾何印紋陶不僅數量多，且紋樣繁縟，主要有方格紋、曲尺紋、編織紋、雲雷紋等二十多種。

45. Geometric pottery fragments

Late Neolithic period (3000-1500 B.C.)
Excavated from 1973 to 1978 from Hedang, Foshan; Maogang, Gaoyao; Shixia, Qujiang and Futoupu, Puning, etc.

Impressed geometric pattern is one of the most distinct local characteristics of early pottery in the Jiangnan region. Geometric pottery was first produced during the late Neolithic period, flourished from the the Shang to Spring and Autumn periods, and gradually declined through the Warring-States to the Qin Han periods. Geometric pottery from late Neolithic Guangdong sites is not only large in quantity but there is also a great variety of designs. There are more than 20 different types including square, angular, basket and spiral patterns.

201

饒平塔仔金山一號墓

商周
長 4.2、寬 2.9 cm.
饒平縣浮濱

1974年在饒平縣浮濱塔仔金山和聯鐃頂大埔山兩處墓地，共清理了二十一座墓葬。形制均爲土坑豎穴墓。其中兩座還有二層台。一號墓位於塔仔金山的頂部中央。墓坑最大，隨葬品亦最多。墓地中出土器物除一件青銅戈外，其餘爲石器和陶器。石器有戈、矛、錛、鑿等；陶器有尊、壺、豆、鉢、杯、缶、罐等。其中以石戈和陶大口尊，深腹豆最具特色。這類器物目前僅見於粵東地區和閩西南，很可能在這個區域範圍內存在一個有別於幾何印紋陶文化系統的另一文化類型。

圖十四：一號墓平面圖。

Tomb No. 1 at Tazaijinshan, Raoping

Shang to Zhou
Length 4.2, width 2.9 m.
Fubin, Raoping county

A total of twenty-one tombs were unearthed in 1974 from two burial sites in Tazaijinshan, Fubin and Dingdapushan, Lianrao. All tombs were of vertical earth pit type and two of them with double-stepped platforms. Tomb No. 1 at the middle of the peak of Tazaijinshan was the largest of these burials. The funerary objects from this tomb were very rich and include stone halberds, spearheads, adzes and chisels, and pottery vases, bottles, stem-cups, bowls, cups, pots, urns and a unique piece of bronze halberd. Amongst them, stone halberds, pottery vase with wide mouth and stem-cups with deep sides are the most characteristic shapes and are found exclusively in eastern Guangdong and southwestern Fujian, where a distinct local culture might have co-existed with the more widely spreaded geometric pottery cultural complex.

Fig. 14: Plan of the tomb.

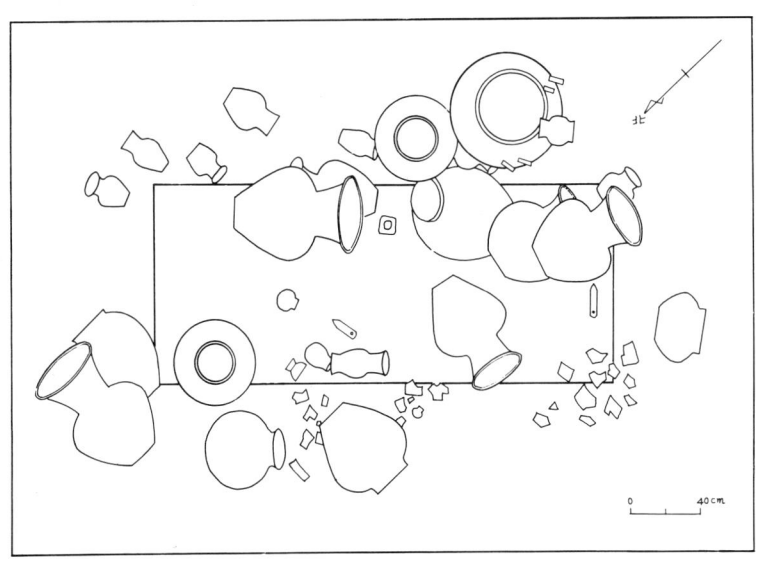

46. 銅戈

商周
長17.5、援長13.3cm.
1974年饒平縣頂大埔山出土

兵器。平內長援。援狹窄，隆脊有棱，兩側有刃，無胡。援與內之間有一道不大明顯的欄，內有一圓穿，援部欄側亦有一圓穿。此器是一件原始型銅戈，與中原地區的青銅戈有明顯區別。這是廣東發現年代較早的青銅器。

47. 石戈

商周
長25cm.
1974年饒平縣塔仔金山6號墓出土

兵器。平內有一圓穿。援較內略寬。前出收殺三角形銳鋒。援部近鋒一段隆脊。饒平出土的石戈，其中反映了從無欄戈到有欄戈的發展過程，這是中原地區所不曾見到的。

圖十五：銅戈裝置使用圖。

46. Bronze halberd

Shang to Zhou
Overall length 17.5, length of blade 13.3 cm.
Excavated in 1974 from Dingdapushan, Raoping county

Weapon. This halberd has a square tang and a slender blade with sharp edges and a median crest. There is no vertical extension of the blade (*hu*), but a slightly raised ridge (*lan*) between the blade and the tang. The tang has one circular perforation, and the blade has another next to the ridge. This halberd is in primitive style and differs considerably from those of the Middle Plains. Probably one of the earliest bronze specimen found in Guangdong.

47. Stone halberd

Shang to Zhou
Length 25 cm.
Excavated in 1974 from Tomb No. 6 at Tazaijinshan, Raoping county

Weapon, with a flat tang and a circular perforation. The blade slightly wider than the tang terminates into a triangular, crested, sharp point. Stone halberds unearthed from Raoping show the development of ridges which separate the blade from the tang. This is not seen in the Middle Plains.

Fig. 15: Bronze halberd in wooden haft.

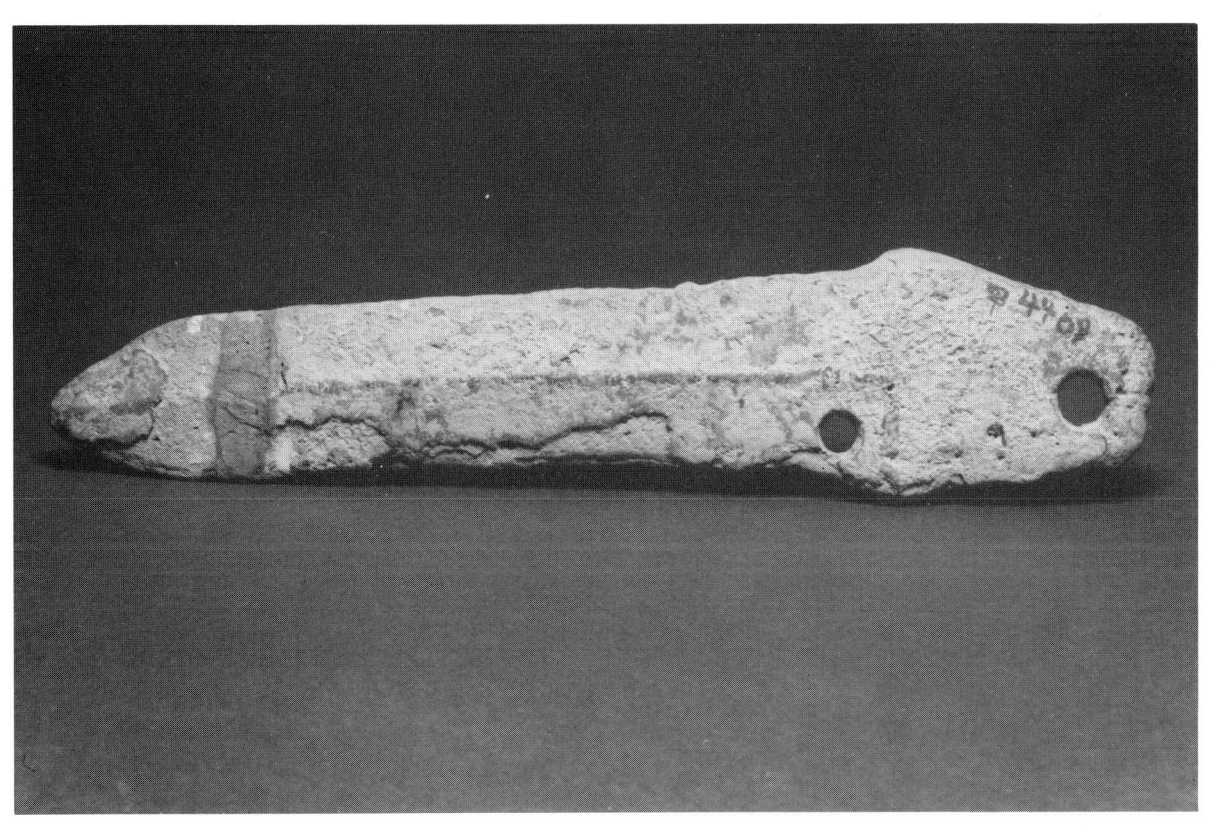

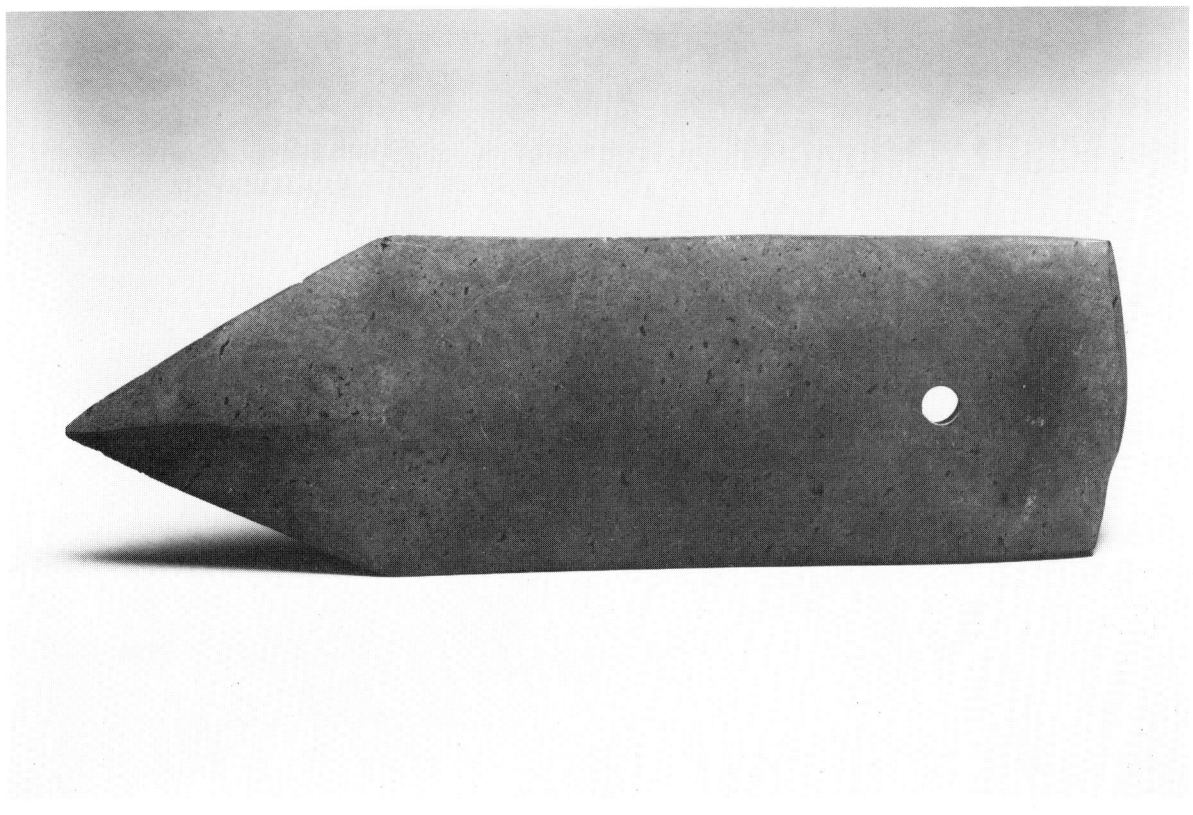

205

輔助照片4. 石戈四項

商周
長16.5－22cm.
1974年饒平塔仔金山出土

兵器。均直援直內無胡，有一穿。其中也有不同的特點：有的援部向前呈斜弧線內收成鋒；有的援部束腰，前出收殺三角形瘦長銳鋒；有的微出雙肩；有的略見凸出的欄部。

**Supplementary illustration 4
Stone halberds**

Shang to Zhou
Length 16.5-22 cm.
Excavated in 1974 from Tazaijinshan, Raoping county

Weapons. While all of them have square tangs, straight perforated blades, there are also variations among them. The blade may be curved, slanted or contracted into triangular points. In the last specimen two ridges appear at the end of the blade and probably represent the final stage in the development of stone halberd in Guangdong.

207

48. 石矛

商周
長14.2cm.
1974年饒平塔仔金山出土

武器。器身較薄。桂葉形，葉較長，前段脊略棱起，兩側有刃，前出收鋒，後有短而平的柄。

圖十六：石矛裝置使用圖。

48. Stone spearhead

Shang to Zhou
Length 14.2 cm.
Excavated in 1974 from Tazaijinshan, Raoping county

Weapon, of thin "laurel-leaf" shape. The slender blade has sharp edges and a median crest at its front part. The rear part terminates into a small rectangular butt end.

Fig. 16: The stone spearhead hafted to a wooden rod.

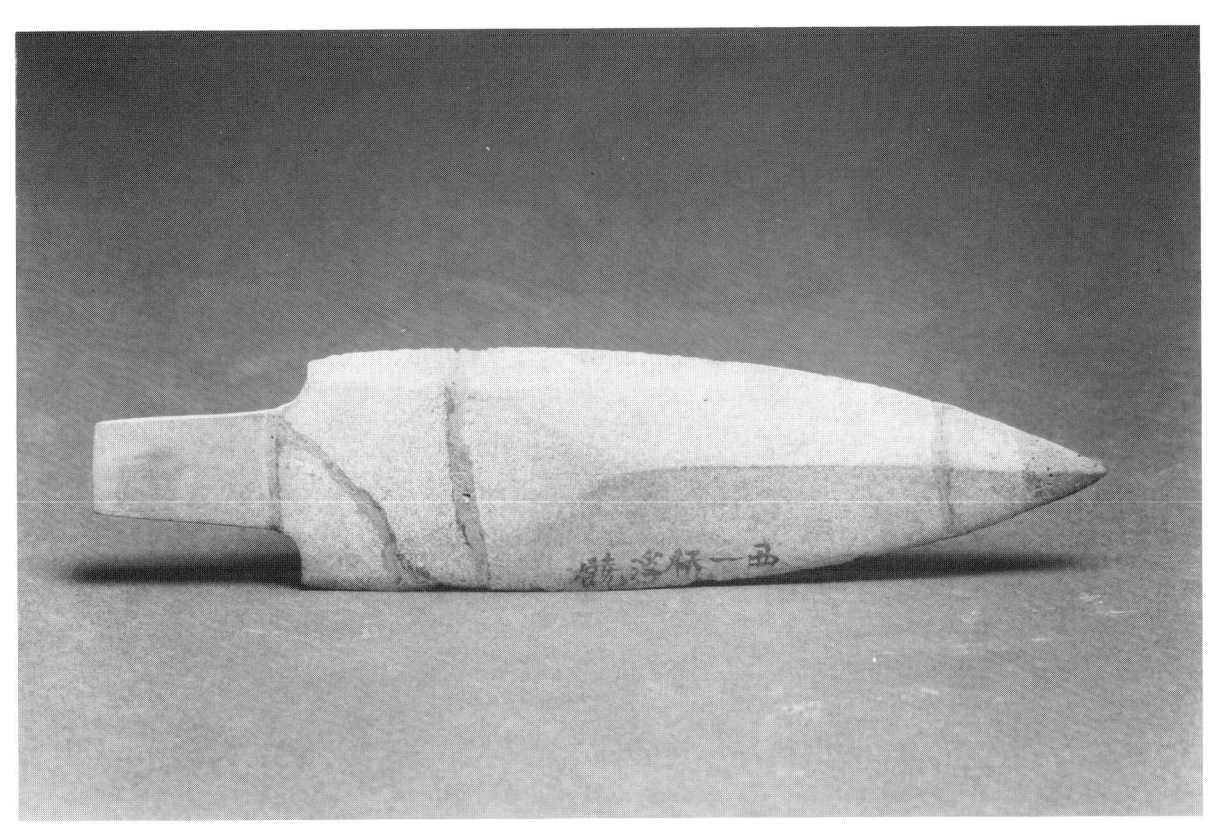

49. 釉陶大口尊

商周
高39.5、口徑23.7cm.
1974年饒平縣塔仔金山1號墓出土

硬陶。水器。大敞口，寬沿，長頸，斜肩折腹。小平底。肩有三枚鋦釘。肩與腹拍印直條紋。器表施厚薄不均的醬黑色釉，部份有脫落。此器造型獨特，是廣東發現的早期釉陶器。

49. Glazed pottery vase

Shang to Zhou
Height 39.5, diameter 23.7 cm.
Excavated in 1974 from Tomb No. 1, Tazai-jinshan, Raoping county

This hard earthenware water container has a trumpet mouth, broad mouth rim, long neck, angular shoulder, and a small flat bottom. There are three round lugs on the shoulder. Both the shoulder and body are impressed with striated pattern under an uneven dark brown glaze which is now partly flaked off. An unusual and early piece of glazed pottery found in Guangdong.

211

50. 釉陶把壺

商周
高20,腹徑17cm.
1974年饒平縣塔仔金山11號墓出土

硬陶。水器或酒器。敞口有流,圓腹圜底。與流口相對的另一側附一個把耳。肩部有三枚鉚釘。腹部拍印直條紋。腹部刻划一個"丫"記號。器內外均施醬黑色釉,部份脫落。

圖十七:刻划記號拓本。

50. Glazed pottery ewer

Shang to Zhou
Height 20, diameter of belly 17 cm.
Excavated in 1974 from Tomb No. 11 at Tazaijinshan, Raoping county

Earthenware water or wine container with flared mouth, small spout, round body and bottom, a handle and three round lugs on the shoulder. The exterior is impressed with striated pattern and incised with a '丫' mark all under a dark brown glaze, which is now partly flaked off.

Fig. 17: Rubbing of the incised mark.

51. 釉陶豆

商周
高15.5、口徑15.4cm.
1974年饒平縣塔仔金山15號墓出土

硬陶。盛食器，口微斂，口沿兩邊對稱有鏤孔。深腹，喇叭形圈足。器表裡施醬褐色釉。這類器物目前僅見於粵東普寧縣以東地區至閩西南，頗具地方特色。

51. Glazed pottery stem-cup

Shang to Zhou
Height 15.5, diameter of mouth 15.4 cm.
Excavated in 1974 from Tomb No. 15 at Tazai-jinshan, Raoping county

Fine earthenware food container with wide mouth, deep body and high spreaded footring. Two sets of small perforations around the mouth rim in opposite positions and both interior and exterior are applied with brown glaze. Stem-cups of this regional shape are found only in the area east of Puning, in eastern Guangdong and in southwestern Fjuian.

52. 釉陶罐

商周
高23.5、口徑10cm.
1974年饒平縣塔仔金山出土

硬陶。口微敞，大斜肩，折腹，小平底。腹部拍印直條紋。器表裡施醬黑色釉，下腹多已脫落。釉質不均勻。

52. Glazed jar

Shang to Zhou
Height 23.5, diameter of mouth 10 cm.
Excavated in 1974 from Tazaijinshan, Raoping county

Fine earthenware with slightly flared mouth, slanted shoulder, angular body, and small flat base. The body is impressed with striated pattern under a dark brown glaze, which is uneven and mostly flaked off at the lower part.

53. 青銅戈

商周
通長23、通高6.2cm.
麥兆良神父藏品
現存香港博物館

微胡，有欄，直身稍彎，援部有中脊，長方形內，後緣圓角轉，下角有刺，裏段有一穿，一面飾人像紋，另一面光素無紋，有安柲的朽木痕跡。

53. Bronze halberd

Shang to Zhou
Overall length 23, height 6.2 cm.
Collection of Fr. Raphael Maglioni, The Hong Kong Museum of History

The butt end is of rectangular shape with rounded off ends and a triangular projection at the lower end. The assymetrical blade has a median crest and separated from the butt end by two vertical flanges. The perforated tang is decorated on one side with a cast human figure in intaglio. Remains of wooden haft found on both sides of the tang.

54. 石戈

商周
殘長30.4、通高7cm.
1968年香港沙洲出土
香港博物館藏品

沙洲位於香港之西端，是珠江河口衆多的"啞鈴形"小島之一，遺物出土於島上的狹部沙丘。此戈援首銳鋒已殘，有中脊，平內有一圓穿，援內交界突出不太明顯的欄，型制與饒平塔仔金山出土的很接近（見輔助照片4）。

圖十八：內部人像紋拓片。

54. Stone halberd

Shang to Zhou
Remaining length 30.4, overall height 7 cm.
Excavated in 1968 from Shazhou, Hong Kong
Collection of the Hong Kong Museum of History

Shazhou (Sha Chau) located on the western limit of Hong Kong territory is one of the many "Dumb-bell islands" at the Zhujiang estuary. The site is on the "tombolo" linking two low hills on the island. This stone halberd of pale yellow slate was broken at the tip of the blade. The perforated butt end is of rectangular shape and the blade has a median crest and sharpened edges. The overall shape is identical to the ones found at Tazaijinshan, Raoping (see Supplementary illustration 4).

Fig. 18: Rubbing of the human figure on the tang.

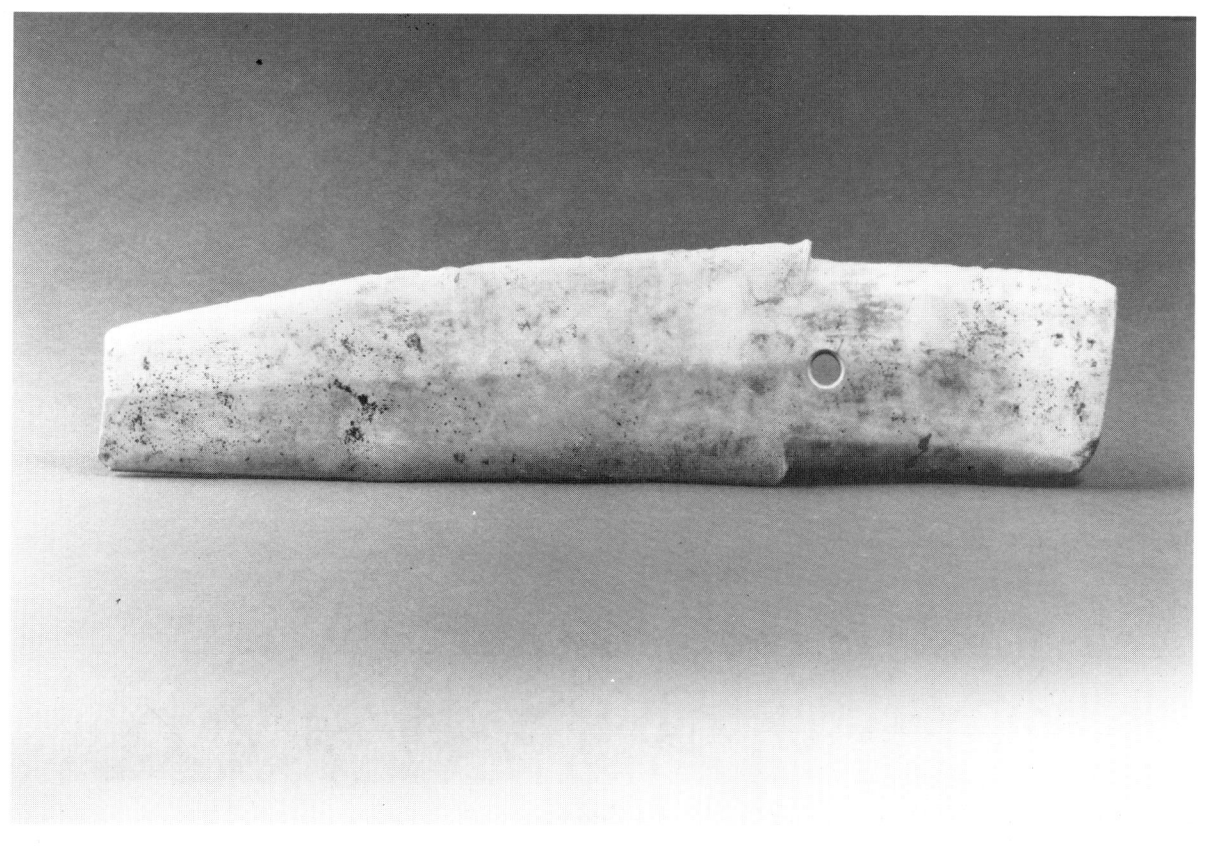

219

55. 硬陶大尊

商周
高66、口徑50cm.
約1940年廣東蕉嶺出土
麥兆良神父藏品
現存香港博物館

泥質灰硬陶。器形雄偉，大敞口，寬沿，鼓腹，圜底，肩部有三直耳，俱已殘缺。器身拍印籃紋，並飾弦紋數道，口沿刻划幾何紋。器形與中原商代的大口尊很相似，但也有一定的地方特色。（參見展品49）

55. Hard pottery vase

Shang to Zhou
Height 66, diameter at mouth 50 cm.
Excavated in late thirties from Jiaoling, Guangdong
Collection of Fr. Raphael Maglioni, The Hong Kong Museum of History

Hard geometric ware of monumental size. The globular body is topped by a trumpet mouth with a flattened rim on which is incised with geometric designs. The shoulder is set with three loop-handles, all of which are now broken. The outside of the body is impressed with "basket" pattern and with two combed horizontal bands. Similar shapes are also found in Shang sites in central China but this specimen has distinct provincial features which differentiate it from the northern parallels (cf. exhibit 49).

平遠水口三號陶窰

西周
平遠縣石正

水口陶窰發現於1974年。共清理四座。水口窰是一種圓穴式升焰窰，結構分上下兩層，上層為窰室，下層是火膛，中間是窰算，火膛一側有火門。算孔徑上小下大。窰室平面為圓形或橢圓形，窰壁略作弧形狀，窰算和窰壁用泥拌草塗抹和夯築，經高溫焙燒而堅硬，窰算面較平。

三號窰窰床壁殘高110 cm，中部橫寬183 cm，壁厚5-10cm，底寬166×154 cm；算中心厚20cm，周邊厚54cm。有九個算孔。火膛寬162 cm，高88cm，深180cm。

圖十九：陶窰平、剖面圖。

Kiln No. 3 at Shuikou, Pingyuan

W. Zhou
Shizheng, Pingyuan county

Four kiln structures were discovered in Shuikou in 1974. All of them are updraught kilns of round pit shape, each of which has a kiln chamber above a firing chamber. The chambers are separated by a grate with flat surfaces and conical openings as smoke vents. The lower part of the firing chambers opens to one side. The plans of the Shuikou kilns are either of round or elliptical shape with the walls slightly in-curved. Both the walls and the grates were built from a mixture of clay and grass, tempered and hardened by the firing.

The dimensions of kiln no. 3 are: for the remaining height of wall: 110 cm.; width at the middle: 183 cm.; thickness of wall: 5 to 10 cm.; kiln floor: 166×154 cm.; thickness at the middle of the grate: 20 cm.; thickness round the sides of the grate: 54 cm.; no of smoke vents: 9; firing chamber: width: 162 cm.; height: 88 cm.; depth: 180 cm.

Fig. 19: Plan and cross-section of the kiln.

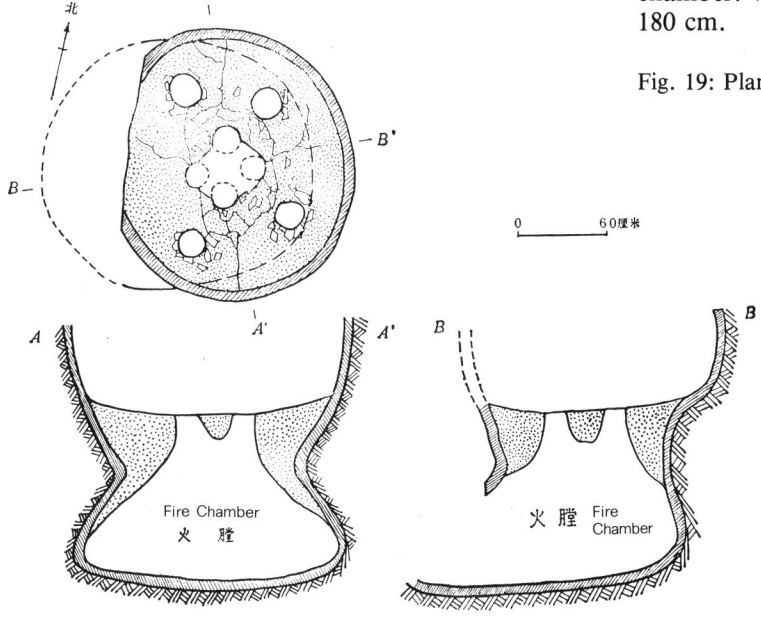

56.陶罐

西周（公元前1122－前770年）
高26.5、口徑28.5cm.
1974年平遠縣水口陶窰出土

淺紅色軟陶。口外侈，束頸，鼓腹，圜凹底。腹部至底拍印方格紋。腹部周圍有四組三圓點的赭色彩。器物加彩繪是水口陶窰的顯著特點。

56. Pottery jar

W. Zhou (1122-770 B.C.)
Height 26.5, diameter of mouth 28.5 cm.
Excavated in 1974 from Shuikou, Pingyuan

Soft pinkish pottery with flared mouth, contracted neck, globular body and indented bottom. The outside is impressed with net pattern and painted in ochre with four groups of three round dots. Painted decoration is a very characteristic feature of Shuikou ware.

57. 陶罐

西周（公元前1122－前770年）
高10、口徑10cm.
1974年平遠縣水口陶窰出土

硬陶。敞口，弧腹，圜底。頸部以下拍印不大規整的方格與雲雷紋組合，腹部見有黑色的"＋"字形劃彩。水口陶窰的雲雷紋陶器（片）佔全部陶器（片）的7.2％。

57. Pottery jar

W. Zhou (1122-770 B.C.)
Height 10, diameter of mouth 10 cm.
Excavated in 1974 from Shuikou kiln, Pingyuan county

Hard pottery with flared mouth, globular body and round bottom. The area below the neck is impressed with a rather irregular design of net and spiral pattern. A 'cruciform' mark is painted in black on one side of the body. Only 7.2% of Shuikou ware is decorated with spiral design.

58. 陶附耳罐

西周（公元前1122－前770年）
高11.2cm，口徑9cm.
1974年平遠縣水口陶窰出土

灰色硬陶。敞口，束頸，弧腹，圜凹底。肩部一對鼻狀穿孔貫耳。腹至底拍印方格紋。水口陶窰的器物紋飾以方格佔絕大多數，器形流行鼓腹圜底或圜凹底，這也是很顯著的另一個特點。

58. Pottery jar

W. Zhou (1122-770 B.C.)
Height 11.2 cm., diameter of mouth 9 cm.
Excavated in 1974 from Shuikou Kiln, Pingyuan county

Greyish hard pottery with flared mouth, contracted neck, globular body, indented bottom, and a pair of vertical loop-handles on the shoulders. The outside is impressed with net pattern. Most of Shuikou pottery is decorated with net pattern and with a globular body resting on a round or indented bottom.

輔助照片5.　銅盉

西周（公元前1122－前770年）
通高26.2cm.
1972年信宜縣出土

酒器。此器造型新穎，形體厚重，花紋繁縟，刻鏤精細。器身為"鬲"體，龍頭形的壺嘴昂起，三足分立，鋬手由兩個鏤空的夔龍相合而成，蓋鈕亦為凸起的主體式龍頭裝飾。通身飾有夔紋、雷紋、饕餮紋，其形制與紋樣均係中原文化的風格。

Supplementary illustration 5
Bronze ewer

Western Zhou (1122-770 B.C.)
Height 26.2 cm.
Excavated in 1972 from Xinyi county

This wine vessel, *He*-ewer of unusual and voluminous shape is elaborately decorated. The body is in the shape of a *li*-tripod with a dragon-head spout, three hollow legs and a handle formed by two *kui*-dragons in openwork. The knob on cover is also in dragon form in high relief. The whole body is filled with *kui*-dragon, spirals and *tao-tie* patterns. Both the shape and decoration are in the bronze style of central China.

輔助照片6　　銅罍

春秋（公元前770－前476年）
高35.5、口徑23cm.
1962年清遠縣馬頭崗1號墓出土

容器。直口，平沿外翻，高頸，圓腹，圈足底，腹部一對鈕耳。鈕耳各有活動環耳。器身及足部飾雙繩索紋，成三行二十四格，每格內均飾以二行四組浮凸的羽狀雲紋。羽狀雲紋是楚器最為盛行的紋飾之一。說明這件青銅器與楚國的關係比較密切。

Supplementary illustration 6
Bronze *lei*-jar

Spring and Autumn period (770-476 B.C.)
Height 35.5, diameter of mouth 23 cm.
Excavated in 1962 from Tomb No. 1 at Matougang, Qingyuan county

This container has a straight mouth, with flattened rim, long neck, globular body and footring. A pair of loop handles with free rings are set on the shoulder. The exterior is divided into 24 panels in three rows by double-plaits. Each panel is filled with raised "hook and volute" pattern arranged in four units on two rows. The "hook and volute" pattern is one of the most popular decoration on Chu bronzes of the Spring and Autumn to Warring-States periods. This indicates that there is a close relationship between this bronze vessel and Chu culture.

59. 銅甬鐘

春秋（公元前770－前476年）
通高49.5cm.
1964年連平縣忠信壩上彭山出土

甬部中空，干旋齊備，用於懸掛。一面無紋，另一面鉦篆之間用雙線和尖狀小乳釘作界線。鼓面附三枚扁平乳釘，排成品字形，兩面各有十八個長而細的枚。出土時與銅錞于並排放置。

59. Bronze bell

Spring and Autumn period (770-476 B.C.)
Overall height 49.5 cm.
Excavated in 1964 from Pengsha, Bashang, Zhongxin, Lianping county

A bronze bell with a hollow tubular handle on which is a loop for suspension. The upper part on one side is divided up into rectangular panels with double raised lines and small bosses in relief, all above a group of three larger bosses near the curved base. On both sides are eighteen protruding nipples. During excavation, this bell was found lying next to a bronze *chunyu*-drum (see No. 60 below).

60. 銅錞于

春秋（公元前770－前476年）
高51.5、口徑27.2×21.3cm.
1964年連平縣忠信壩上彭山出土

形狀上大下小，橫斷面為橢圓形。肩寬，肩以下內收，口部稍外撇，頂部鈕座飾斜格雷紋，肩部有一周繩紋和鈎連雷紋及二十六組三角形紋，口部花紋與肩部相同，兩側鼓面飾虺紋，由八條大小不同的蛇，盤繞而成。蛇頭有雙眼，身披鱗片，十分逼真。其他部份為素面。頂上原有虎形鈕，可懸掛。
《國語吳語》："吳既陳，去晉軍一里，昧明，王乃秉枹，親就鳴鐘、鼓、丁寧、錞于、振鐸，勇怯盡應。"說明單個的鐘和錞于，應是軍隊行進或戰鬥時用的軍樂器。

60. Bronze drum

Spring and Autumn period (770-476 B.C.)
Height 51.5, diameter of mouth 27.2 × 21.3 cm.
Excavated in 1964 from Pengshan, Bashang, Zhongxin, Lianping county

This bronze *chunyu*-drum has a broad shoulder, a contracted waist, and a slightly flared mouth. The cross section is elliptical and tapers towards the mouth. The top platform is decorated with rhomboid spirals, the shoulder and mouth with plait bands, angular meanders and 26 groups of triangular patterns. One two sides near the mouth are two groups of interwoven snakes. Originally, it was with a suspension ring in the form of a crouching tiger. As recorded in *Wuyu* in *Guoyu*, single bells and *chunyu*-drums were used as musical instruments in military marches or in battles.

61. 人面紋匕首

春秋（公元前770－前476年）
（殘）長16.5cm.
1977年曲江縣馬壩石峽遺址上文化層出土

扁體。實心，器身兩面有脊，近格部鑄人面紋。圓眼，大口，扇耳，一面無冠，一面人頭上鑄雷紋似冠。與夔紋陶共存。

62. 青銅人面紋短劍

春秋至戰國（公元前770－前221年）
通長27.4、寬5.1cm.
1962年香港大嶼山石壁出土
香港博物館藏品

劍身為寬葉形，較薄，中部扁平，鑄人面紋及卷雲紋，兩側呈突棱，至前端滙聚，直達銳鋒。狹臘，扁圓形莖，中空，飾細線回紋內填圓圈紋。同類型的短劍在廣州㘵崗也有出土。

圖二十：廣州㘵崗出土銅劍拓本。

61. Bronze dagger with human mask design

Spring and Autumn period (770-476 B.C.)
Remaining length 16.5 cm.
Excavated in 1977 from upper cultural layer at Shixia, Maba, Qujiang county

This dagger is of tapering shape with a median crest and sharp blades on both edges. Near the handle on each side is cast with a human mask with round eyes, big mouth and fan shaped ears. One of the masks is crowned with spirals. This specimen was found in association with pottery with *kui* ("Double-F") design.

62. Bronze dagger

Spring and Autumn to Warring-States periods (770-221 B.C.)
Overall length 27.4, width 5.1 cm.
Excavated in 1962 at Shibi (Shek Pik), Dayushan (Lantau Island), Hong Kong
Collection of the Hong Kong Museum of History

The thin blade of this dagger is of "willow-leaf" shape, tapering toward the front sharp tip. The centre is flat and cast on both sides with an "almond shape" human head surrounded by spiral scrolls. The short guard is tilted at both ends and joins with the hollow tubular grip on which is finely cast with angular meanders and small spirals. A very similar dagger has been found in Xiangang, Guangzhou.

Fig. 20: Rubbing of a dagger found in Xiangang, Guangzhou.

63. 銅劍石膏模型

春秋（公元前770－前476年）
殘長24.6cm、原器殘長32.3cm.
約1925年香港南丫島大灣出土
石膏模型爲芬戴禮神父藏品
現存香港博物館

此銅劍原件現藏英國倫敦大英博物館，原爲蕭思雅教授（1885－1958）於二十年代在南丫島大灣採集。劍體扁長，有中脊，銳鋒已殘，莖部扁平，有一穿，（石膏模此部份已佚），劍葉飾三組變形饕餮紋。

64. 殘銅戈

春秋（公元前770－前476年）
殘長11.8、高12cm.
約1932年香港南丫島大灣出土
芬戴禮神父藏品
現存香港博物館

直援已殘缺，寬胡，欄側四穿，上一下三，長方形內有長穿，胡刄稍殘，有使用痕跡。戈爲中國特有的勾殺兵器，其形制的演變，集中於胡、穿部份。（參見展品46，53）此戈胡部已出現，且有四穿，是較爲晚出的標本，穿孔的增加，使戈頭緊縛於木柲上，不易脫裂。

圖二十一：廣州淹崗出土的銅戈及銅刀拓本。

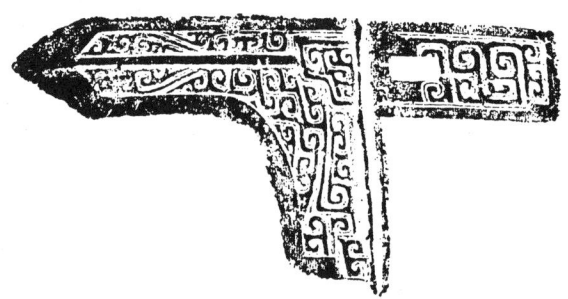

63. Plaster cast of a bronze sword

Spring and Autumn period (770-476 B.C.)
Remaining length 24.6, length of actual specimen 32.3 cm.
Original collected in the twenties at Dawan (Tai Wan), Nanyadao, Hong Kong
Collection of Fr. Daniel J. Finn, Hong Kong Museum of History

The original sword was found by Prof. J. Shellshear (1885-1958) in Dawan, Lamma Island and is now in the British Museum, London. The present cast made before the War had been in the study collection of Fr. Finn since 1936. The tip of the tapering and assymmetrical blade is now missing. The square shoulders are attached to a flat rectangular tang in which is a small hole (This part of the cast is now missing as well). The decoration consists of three *taotie* marks arranged in three pairs of panels symmetrically placed along the central crest.

64. Fragment of a bronze halberd

Spring and Autumn period (770-476 B.C.)
Remaining length 11.8, height 12 cm.
Excavated in early twenties in Dawan, Nanyadao, Hong Kong
Collection of Fr. Daniel J. Finn, Hong Kong Museum of History

The tip of the blade has been broken off. The lower edge is elongated and runs down the whole incurving line to add to the efficiency in ripping and chopping. Four holes are found on the ridge separating the blade and the butt end which is of flat rectangular shape with a long perforation. This specimen represents a more advanced form of the Chinese halberd (cf. exhibits 46, 53). The extension of the blade and the increased numbers of perforations provide additional joints for making the hafting more secure.

Fig. 21: Bronze halberd and knife found at Xiangang, Guangzhou.

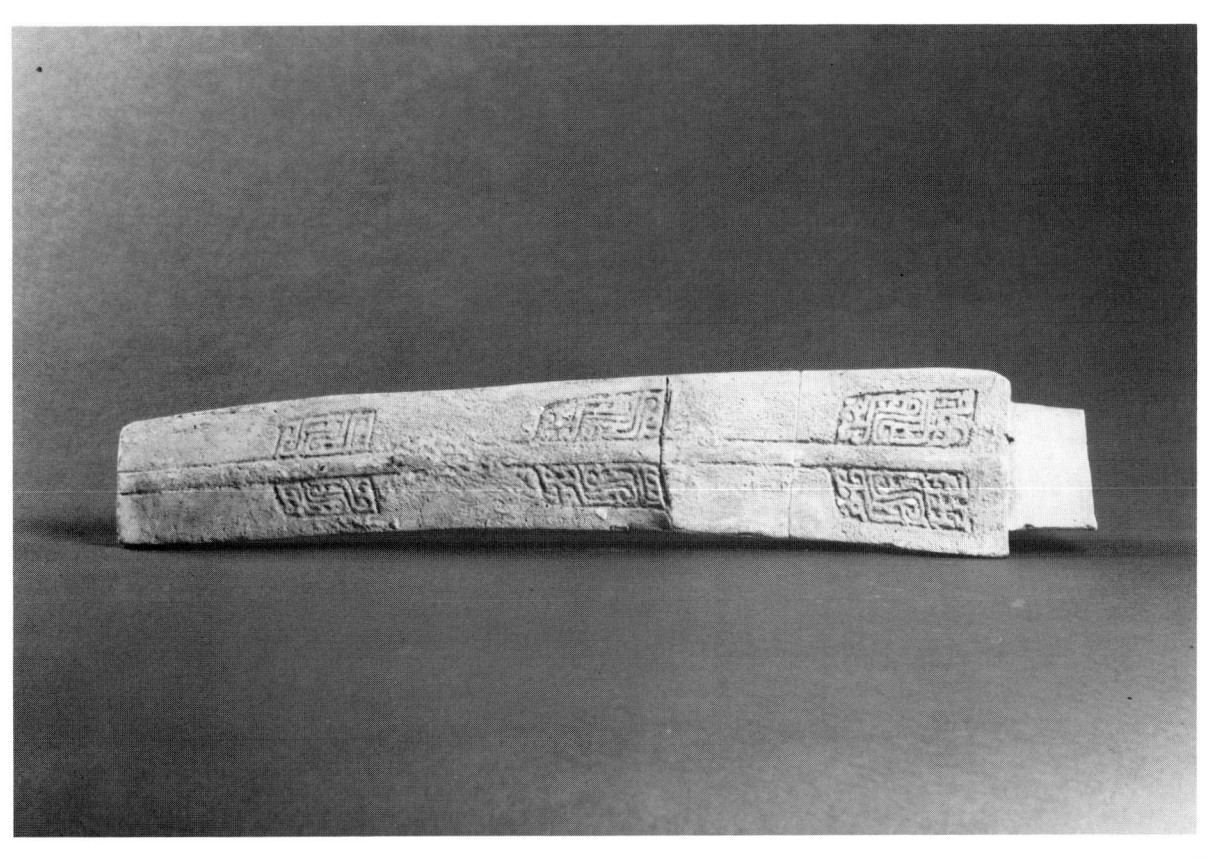

237

65. 銅鉞

春秋戰國（公元前770－前221年）
長9.4、刃寬7.6 cm.
1963年清遠縣馬頭崗2號墓出土

兵器。長方銎。刃面呈扇形，銎身飾勾連雷紋，外圍飾一周細繩索紋，刃部飾一行鋸齒紋。扇形鉞是兩廣春秋戰國時期流行的器形。

65. Bronze *Yue*-axe

Spring and Autumn to Warring-States periods (770-221 B.C.)
Length 9.4, width of blade 7.6 cm.
Excavated in 1963 from Tomb No. 2 at Matougang, Qingyuan county

Weapon. This axe is with a rectangular socket and a fan shaped blade. The socket is decorated with interlocking spirals enclosed by a narrow plait band and the blade with a triangular band. *Yue*-axes with fan-shaped blades are very popular during the Spring and Autumn and Warring-States periods in Guangdong and Guangxi.

66. 銅斧

春秋戰國（公元前770－前221年）
長12.1、刃寬5.8 cm.
1963年青遠縣馬頭崗2號墓出土

工具。長身楔形。長方銎，銎口向下收成弧形。雙面圓刃，刃面略向外弧出。上部飾勾連雷紋。

66. Bronze axe

Spring and Autumn to Warring-States periods (770-221 B.C.)
Length 12.1, width of blade 5.8 cm.
Excavated in 1963 from Tomb No. 2 at Matougang, Qingyuan county

Tool. This axe is of elongated cuneiform shape with a rectangular socket which narrows toward the blade. The blade is round, bifacial, and slightly outcurved. The upper part of the axe is decorated with interlocking spirals.

67. 原始瓷鉢

春秋（公元前770－前476年）
高4、口徑13.5cm.
1977年曲江縣馬壩石峽遺址上文化層出土

胎質細膩，白中帶黃，燒成溫度相當高。器形規整，器壁厚薄均勻。鉢內底心有螺旋紋，內外施黃綠色青釉。是用來盛食物的器具。

67. Proto-porcelain dish

Spring and Autumn period (770-476 B.C.)
Height 4, diameter of mouth 13.5 cm.
Excavated in 1977 from upper layer at Shixia, Maba, Qujiang county

This food container is with a compact high fired, yellowish white body. Its shape is well thrown with body walls of very even thickness. A spiral pattern is on the interior. The whole is covered with a yellowish green glaze.

65

66

67

68. 陶罐

春秋戰國（公元前770－前221年）
高19、口徑11.4cm.
1963年清遠縣馬頭崗2號墓出土

硬陶。口小腹大，直口深腹，平底。肩部有三個橫耳。肩飾弦紋與篦紋相間，腹飾方格紋。春秋時，罐類最大腹徑往往在下部，戰國時，最大腹徑漸往上移。

68. Pottery jar

Spring and Autumn to Warring-States periods (770-221 B.C.)
Height 19, diameter of mouth 11.4 cm.
Excavated in 1963 from Tomb No. 2 at Matougang, Qingyuan county

Stoneware. This jar has a small mouth, big globular body, flat bottom, and three horizontal loop-handles on the shoulder. The shoulder is decorated with alternating bands of dotted combing, incised rings and the body impressed with net pattern. During the Spring and Autumn period, jars of this type have the widest diameter at the lower part of the body whereas in the later Warring-States period the widest diameter is found on the upper part of the jars (see No. 71 below).

69. 釉陶罐

春秋（公元前770－前476年）
腹徑25、高25、口徑17cm.
約1940年廣東五華出土
麥兆良神父藏品
現存香港博物館

小口，短頸，鼓腹，圜底，最大腹徑在下半部。肩飾篦點紋三行，下拍印夔紋五道，間有重叠，下半部印方格紋。胎質灰白堅實，上有薄而不均的褐黑釉，這是迄今已知最精美完整的夔紋陶罐標本。

圖廿二：拍印夔紋細部。

69. Glazed pottery pot

Spring and Autumn period (770-476 B.C.)
Greatest diameter 25, height 25, diameter at mouth 17 cm.
Excavated in early forties at Wuhua, Guangdong
Collection of Fr. Raphael Maglioni, Hong Kong Museum of History

The body is of very compact porcellaneous stoneware covered with a thin, crazed and uneven dark brown glaze. The greatest diameter is in the lower half of the body. The compressed ovoid body is topped by a short collared neck below which are three bands of combed dots. The main decoration is five bands of impressed "Double-F" designs in double line above net pattern. In some places the "double-Fs" are partially overprinted. This unique specimen is the finest and most complete "double-F" pot so far known to be extant.

Fig. 22: Detail of the impressed "double-F" design.

70. 陶罐

春秋（公元前770－前476年）
高32、口徑14.5cm.
1958年五華縣東山上嶺出土

頸部很短，口小腹大。肩部四個橫耳，圜凹底。近口沿處有一周箆點紋，肩與上腹有二組夔紋。中間有一組雙線斜格加乳釘雷紋，下腹至底部為方格紋。這是一件組合花紋陶器。西周春秋時期是廣東幾何印紋陶的鼎盛時期，陶器花紋多見組合紋。夔紋陶是這時期最為典型的花紋，紋飾整齊精細，多呈帶狀環繞器身。

圖二十三：陶罐花紋拓片。

70. Pottery jar

Spring and Autumn period (770-476 B.C.)
Height 32, diameter of mouth 14.5 cm.
Excavated in 1958 from Shangling, Dongshan, Wuhua county

This jar is with short neck, small mouth, globular body, indented bottom and four horizontal loop-handles on the shoulder. The mouthrim is decorated with a band of dotted combings and the shoulder and upper body with a band of double-line rhomboid lattices in between two bands of *kui*-dragon ("double-F") pattern. Further down on the body is impressed with net pattern. In Guangdong, the W. Zhou to Spring and Autumn periods were the time when geometric pottery production was at its great prosperity. The decoration is usually composed of a combination of different patterns arranged in bands, and the *kui*-dragon ("double-F") pattern is the most popular motif.

Fig. 23: Rubbing of the impressed design.

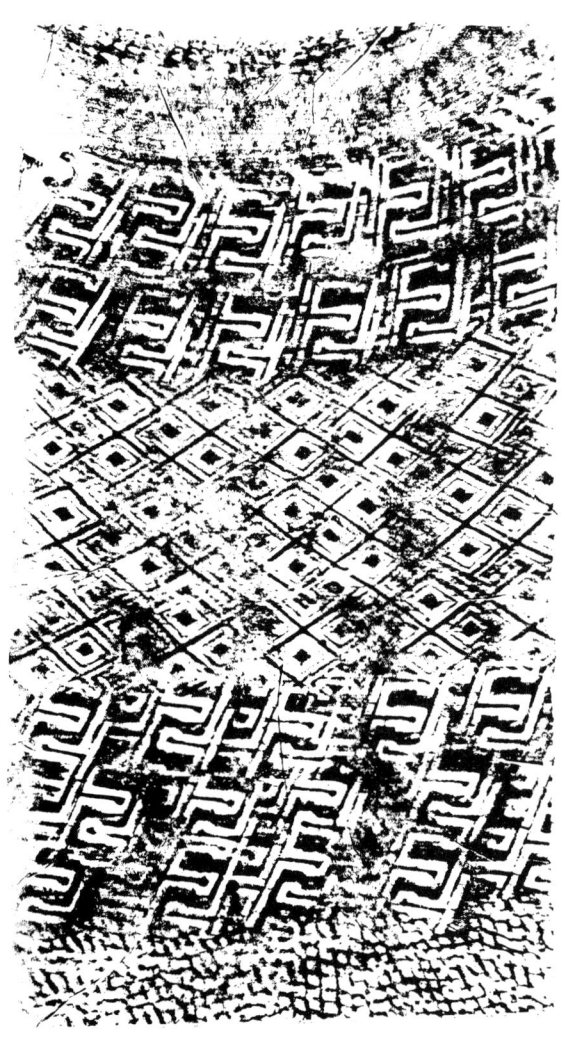

71. 陶罐

春秋至戰國（公元前770－前221年）
高25.1、腹徑35.2cm.
1977年香港南丫島榕樹灣出土
香港中文大學文物館藏品

泥質灰陶，小口微敞，矮頸，鼓腹，圜底，肩部近頸處飾篦點紋，下拍印棱形雷紋，底飾方格紋。此罐最大腹徑已向上移，年代亦較前數器（見展品68－70）爲晚。

圖二十四：腹部花紋拓片。

71. Pottery jar

Spring and Autumn to Warring-States periods (770-221 B.C.)
Height 25.1, greatest diameter 35.2 cm.
Excavated in 1977 at Yongshuwan (Yung Shu Wan), Nanyadao (Lamma Island), Hong Kong
Collection of the Art Gallery, the Chinese University of Hong Kong

Unglazed greyish earthenware, the small mouth is slightly flaring. The compressed ovoid body is decorated with two bands of combed dots near the collar-neck, impressed lozenge diapers round the shoulder up to midway of the body, below which is impressed with net pattern. The shape of this specimen, slightly different from the previous examples (Exhibits 68-70), with the greatest diameter moved upwards, represents a late examples of this type of hard geometric pots.

Fig. 24: Rubbing of the impressed diaper design.

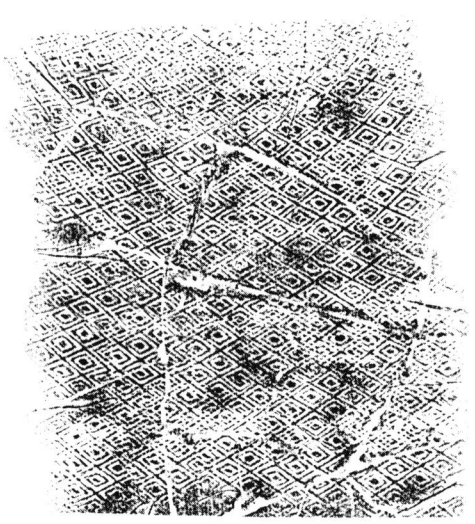

72. 夔紋硬陶片

春秋至戰國初期（公元前770－前221年）
殘長16.5－5 cm.
1958年香港大嶼山萬角咀出土
香港博物館藏品

萬角咀位於大嶼山東岸，於一九五八年由香港大學考古隊發掘，出土文物甚多，其中夔紋陶尤其精美。夔紋陶的出現，標誌着廣東幾何印紋陶的鼎盛期。多以泥質陶為主，夾砂陶較少，火候較高；粵東出土的夔紋陶也有掛釉的。（見展品70）拍印花紋一般都極清晰規整，富浮雕感覺。

圖二十四A.夔紋陶片花紋拓片。

72. Potsherds with "double-F" design

Spring and Autumn to early Warring-States periods (770-221 B.C.)
Length 16.5-5 cm.
Excavated in 1958 from Wanjiaozui (Man Kok Tsui), Lantau Island, Hong Kong
Hong Kong Museum of History

The site of Wanjiaozui is located at the eastern coast of Lantau Island and was excavated by the Hong Kong University Archaeological Team in 1958 when large quantities of geometric pottery was found. This site is noted for the abundance of "double-F" potsherds which represent the highest standard geometric pottery ever produced in Hong Kong and Guangdong. The body is fairly compact, hard and seldom tempered with coarse sand. The firing temperature is high and in some pieces there is a green or dark brown glaze. There are numerous variants of the design which is as a rule finely impressed in well organised bands intermixing with other simpler geometric designs.

Fig. 24A: Rubbings of the design on the potsherd.

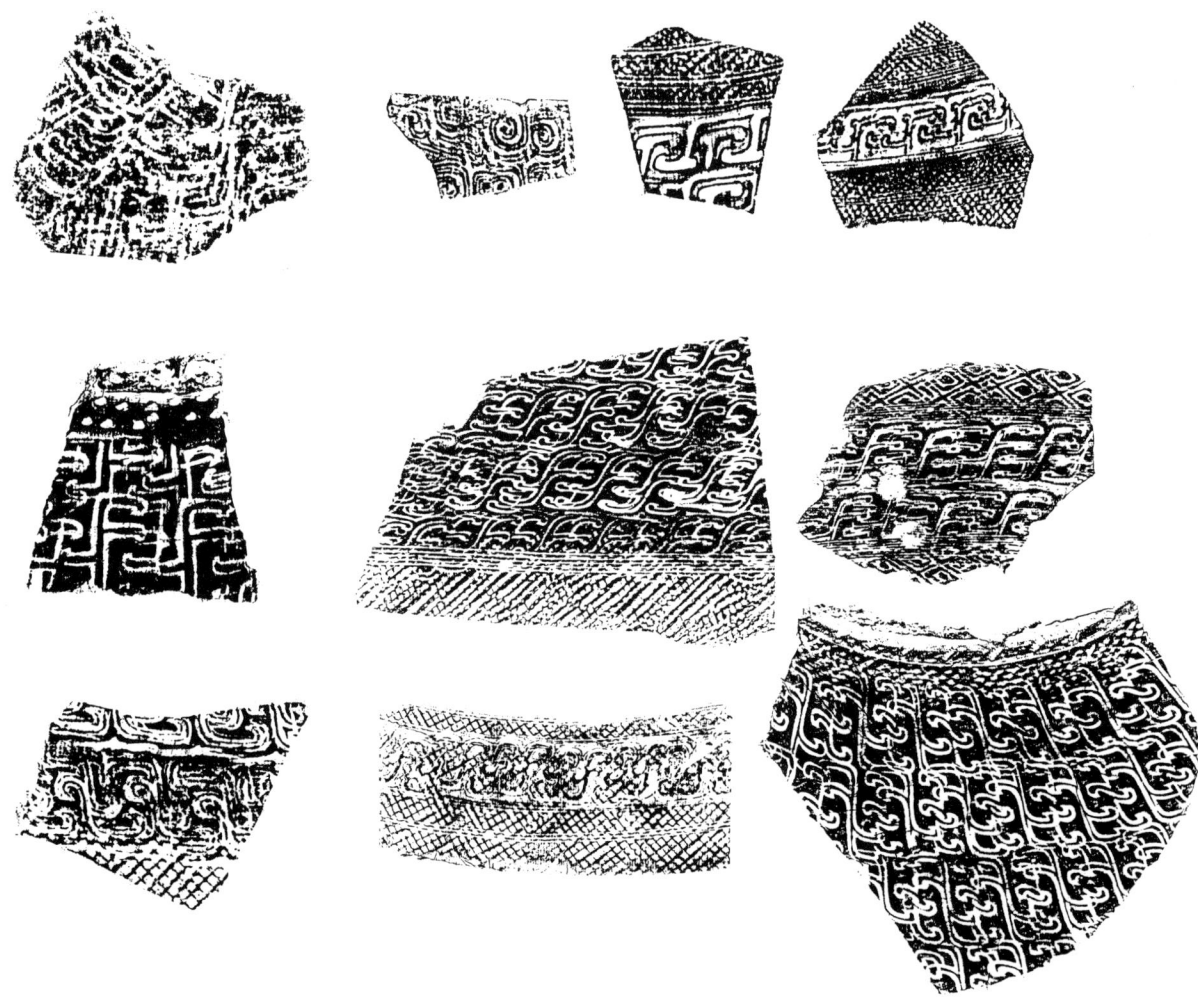

73. 幾何印紋硬陶片

春秋至戰國（公元前770－前221年）
殘長11.2－5 cm.
1958年香港大嶼山萬角咀出土
香港博物館藏品

與夔紋陶共出的幾何印紋硬陶花紋很多，較常見的有回紋，棱形雲雷紋，勾連雷紋，方格網紋，篦划紋，籃紋，弦紋，圓圈紋，繩紋等。在同一器物上，通常是二種以上花紋組合出現，單一花紋極為少見。

圖二十四B.幾何印紋硬陶花紋拓片

73. Potsherds with geometric design

Spring and Autumn to Warring-States periods (770-221 B.C.)
Length 11.2-5 cm.
Excavated in 1958 Wanjiaozui, Dayushan, Hong Kong
Hong Kong Museum of History

There is a wide range of other geometric patterns found in association with the characteristic "double-F" motif. The more common ones include square or rhomboid lozenge diapers, interlocking square spirals, square net pattern, combed dots, basket pattern, impressed circles, cord pattern and incised grooves. Usually two or more variations are found on the same piece and are arranged in horizontal bands.

Fig. 24B: Rubbings of the design on the sherds.

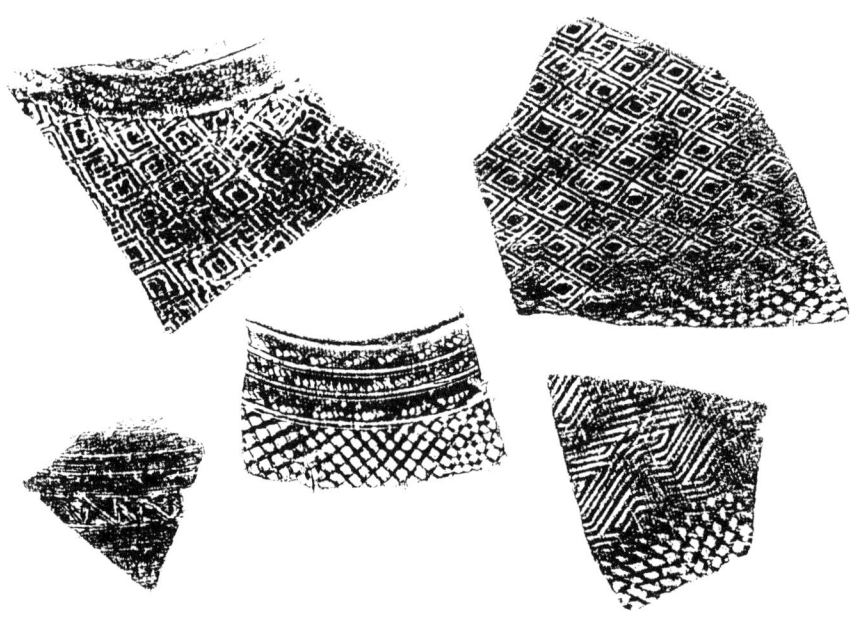

74. 石環

春秋至戰國（公元前770－前221年）
外徑10.8、高1.8cm.
1977年香港大嶼山蟹地灣出土
香港博物館藏品

蟹地灣位於大嶼山東岸，於一九五八年發現，一九七六至七九年間為配合愉景灣基建計劃先後進行了四期的清理發掘，出土器物多屬青銅器時代。
此石環直切面呈「T」字形，表面光滑有褐色土斑。同類器在中原商墓常有出土，但在南方一直延續使用至漢代。

74. Stone flanged ring

Spring and Autumn to Warring-States periods
(770-221 B.C.)
External diameter 10.8, height 1.8 cm.
Excavated in 1977 from Xiediwan (Hai Dei Wan),
Dayushan, Hong Kong
Hong Kong Museum of History

The Xiediwan site is situated on Lantau Island on a small peninsula jutting off the east coast. It was first discovered in 1958 and a series of four phases of excavation were carried out from 1976 to 1979 to coincide with the Discovery Bay development project. The finds are mainly of the Bronze Age. This T-sectioned ring has a flanged vertical projections on both sides of the inner edge. Similar discs are commonly found in Shang tombs of central China but the same form perpetuated well into the Han in the south. They all appear to have been fashioned as bracelets.

75A. 石英環一套八項

春秋至戰國（公元前770－前221年）
外徑5.4－1.7cm.
1979年香港大嶼山蟹地灣出土
香港博物館藏品

此套石英環出土於蟹地灣遺址探方第十一號，共出兩套，另外的一套只餘六件。全部石環都通體磨光，平背，正面近孔處較外緣處爲厚，中孔爲一面管鑽穿；製作極精，應是用作裝飾品。

75B. 殘石環及圓心

春秋至戰國（公元前770－前221年）
石環外徑4.8、厚0.4、圓心徑1.8、厚1.3cm.
1958年香港大嶼山萬角咀出土
香港博物館藏品

萬角咀遺址是香港地區青銅時代的石器作坊，發現了不少石環廢料。如圖所示，左方的殘石環有未完成的管鑽痕跡；右方是石環的圓心，雙面對鑽，所以在中央尚留有連接痕。

75 A. Set of quartz rings

Spring and Autumn to Warring-States periods (770-221 B.C.)
External diameters 5.4-1.7 cm.
Excavated in 1979 from Xiediwan, Dayushan, Hong Kong
Hong Kong Museum of History

This set of eight rings was found in Square 11 at the Xiediwan site together with another incomplete set of six, all of polished white quartz and of the same shape, one side flat and the other side bevelled. The central hole was bored from one side. Similar rings are also commonly found in other Hong Kong sites and are obviously ornamental in purpose.

75 B. Incomplete stone ring and quartz core

Spring and Autumn to Warring-States periods (770-221 B.C.)
Ring: external diameter 4.8, thickness 0.4 cm.
Core: diameter 1.8, thickness 1.3 cm.
Excavated in 1958 from Wanjiaozui, Dayushan, Hong Kong
Hong Kong Museum of History

The Wanjiaozui site, apart from yielding abundant hard geometric pottery is also noted for the large quantities of stone discs and cores, often of quartz. The specimen illustrated in the left is a partially bored fragmentary ring. It seems that the drilling was performed with a hollow instrument and an abrasive. The quartz core on the right is lopsided as the boring was done from both sides.

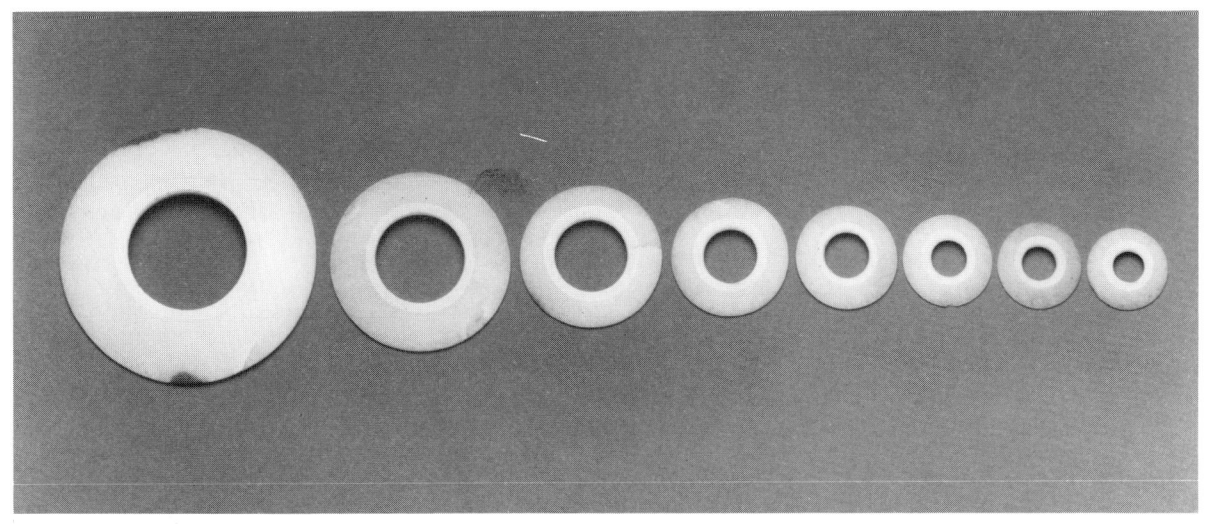

255

76. 網墜

春秋至戰國（公元前770－前221年）
徑3.8，3.3、厚1.6，1.4cm.
1958年香港大嶼山萬角咀出土
香港博物館藏品

有泥質和石製兩種，圓形中央穿孔；同遺址共出的還有銅質魚鈎，顯示當時的人濱海而居，捕魚為生。

76. Net weights

Spring and Autumn to Warring-States periods (770-221 B.C.)
Diameter 3.8, 3.3, thickness 1.6, 1.4 cm.
Excavated in 1958 from Wanjiaozui, Dayushan, Hong Kong
Hong Kong Museum of History

These were fishermen's net weights. Roughly made from either stone or pottery, they are usually circular with a central perforation. From the same site a bronze fish-hook was also found. This indicates that the early inhabitants of Bronze Age Hong Kong lived by the seashore and whose subsistence depended mainly on fishing.

77. 陶紡輪

春秋至戰國（公元前770－前221年）
徑3.3，3、厚2,0.9cm.
1958年香港大嶼山萬角咀出土
香港博物館藏品

泥質灰陶，圓形中空，一件斜面印圓圈紋。紡輪是紡紗工具，使用時加上木杆，利用紡輪和杆的自身重量和旋轉時的力，可以牽伸和加拈纖維成細紗線，比起原始的手搓進步和省力。

圖二十五：紡輪使用圖。

77. Pottery spindle whorls

Spring and Autumn to Warring-States period (770-221 B.C.)
Diameter 3.3, 3, thickness 2, 0.9 cm.
Excavated in 1958 from Wanjiaozui, Dayushan, Hong Kong
Hong Kong Museum of History

Made of pale grey pottery, these two spindle whorls are of circular shape with a central hole. One of them is impressed on the bevelled edge with six double circles. These whorls act as weights when attached to a spindle stick. A fine and even thread will be produced when the fibres are paid out while the spindle is rotated by hand, dropped and allowed to swing.

Fig. 25: Spindles in use.

257

78.陶牛

春秋至戰國（公元前770－前221年）
長13、殘高7.6cm.
1979年香港大嶼山蟹地灣出土
香港博物館藏品

泥質灰陶動物塑像，頭部戳印圓圈紋，雙目及四足俱殘缺。牲畜形像的出現，說明當時的農業已有一定的水平。

78. Pottery figurine of an ox

Spring and Autumn to Warring-States periods (770-221 B.C.)
Length 13, remaining height 7.6 cm.
Excavated in 1979 from Xiediwan, Dayushan, Hong Kong
Hong Kong Museum of History

Unglazed greyish buff earthenware. The horns are missing as well as the four limbs. The head has a number of punched holes to represent the eyes and holes for some sort of harness. The appearance of figurines of domesticated animals indicates that the inhabitants were practising a fairly advanced mixed economy and agriculture.

79.陶牛首

春秋至戰國（公元前770－前221年）
長4、寬4.8cm.
1958年香港大嶼山萬角咀出土
香港博物館藏品

泥質灰陶動物塑像，原身軀已佚失，雙眼由小圓泥塊堆成，鼻原有穿孔現已殘缺。

79. Pottery ox head

Spring and Autumn to Warring-States periods (770-221 B.C.)
Length 4, width 4.8 cm.
Excavated in 1958 from Wanjiaozui, Dayushan, Hong Kong
Hong Kong Museum of History

Greyish buff earthenware, the original trunk and four limbs are both missing. The eyes are formed by appliqué small lumps of clays. The through hole for a nose-ring at the tip of the head is now also broken off.

80.玉帶鈎

戰國（公元前476－前221年）
長4.4、寬1.1cm.
1972年在肇慶市松山墓葬出土

裝飾品。鈎端似鴨頭。這類器在廣東發現極少，屬較珍貴的飾物。

80. Jade garment hook

Warring-States period (476-221 B.C.)
Length 4.4, width 1.1 cm.
Excavated in 1972 from a tomb at Songshan, Zhaoqing city

Ornament. One end of this hook is carved into a duck-shaped head. Jade objects must have been rather precious as they are rarely found in Guangdong sites.

78

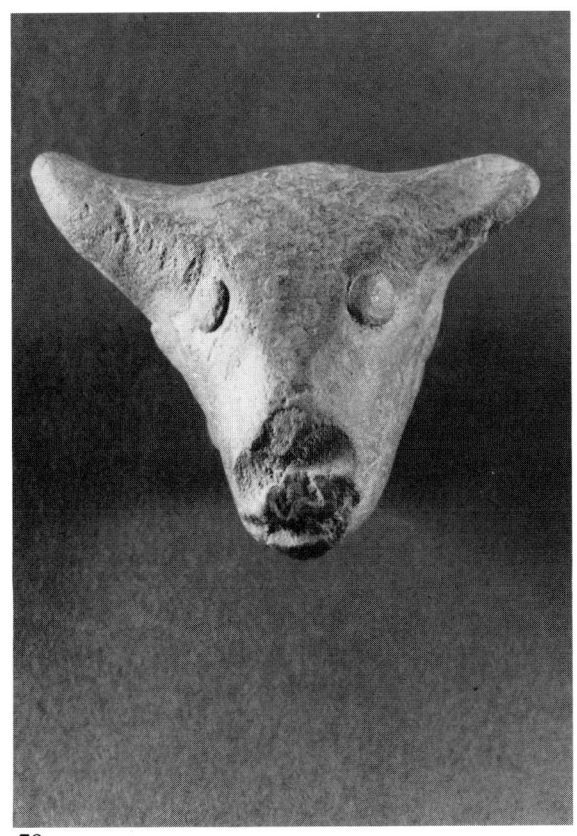

79

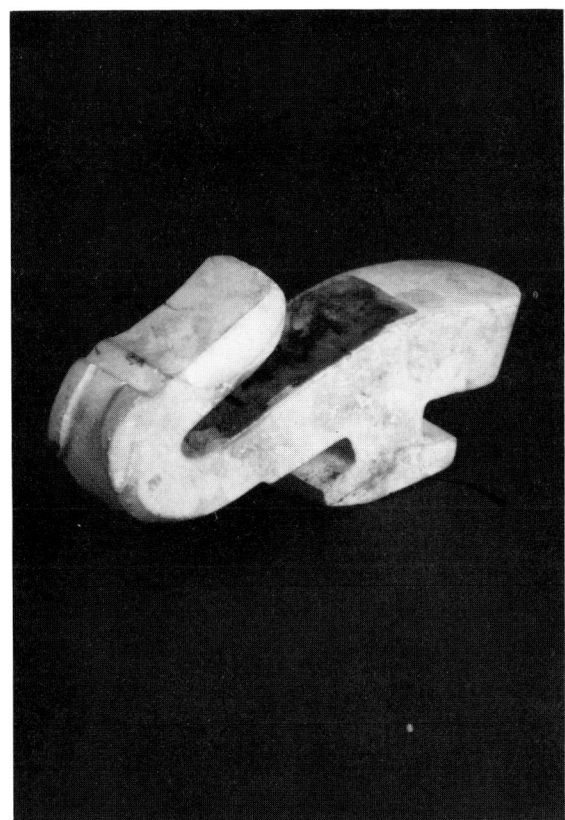

80

81. 人首柱形器

戰國（公元前476－前221年）
通高21.5cm.
1973年四會縣鳥旦山墓葬出土

分人首器體兩段。上段如人的胸以上部份，下段為長方形柱體。人頭顱頂較寬，兩圓耳，眼眶深陷。有睛、縮頸，吻部凸出，嘴較大。柱體下端有長條形插梢。這類器在廣東西江兩岸地區青銅器墓常有發現。均是兩對四件立放於墓室前後兩端，面朝墓外。是當地越人特有的隨葬器物和葬式。可能是一種儀仗器。

圖二十六：柱形器出土情形。

81. Bronze shaft with human head

Warring-States period (476-221 B.C.)
Height 21.5 cm.
Excavated in 1973 from a tomb at Niaodanshan, Sihui county

This shaft of rectangular rod shape is surmounted by a human bust at the top. The head has a broad scalp, two round ears, deep eyes with pupils, depressed cheeks and a big mouth with bulging lips. The bottom end of the rod is perforated and inserted with a cross bar. These shafts are often found from Bronze Age tombs in the Xijiang region of Guangdong. They were erected in two pairs at the four corners of the tomb chamber, always with the heads facing outward. This type of funerary object, as well as the burial practice were particular to the Yue people, and the shafts were probably ceremonial objects.

Fig. 26: The shaft in situ during excavation.

261

82. 人首柱形器

戰國（公元前476－前221年）
通高40cm.
1974年四會縣高地園墓葬出土

顱頂大，頷小，兩眼眶深陷，柱體中空。西江兩岸地區各青銅器墓所出的人首柱形器，其形象都有一些差異，尤以四會高地園出土的形制最大，獨具一格。

82. Bronze shaft with human head

Warring-States period (476-221 B.C.)
Height 40 cm.
Excavated in 1974 from a tomb at Gaodiyuan, Sihui county

The head is with broad scalp, narrow chin, and deep-set eyes supported by a hollow rectangular shaft. There are some slight differences amongst the shafts found from tombs bearing bronzes in the Xijiang region, however, those unearthed from Gaodiyuan are the largest.

肇慶松山戰國墓

長8、寬約4.7 m.
肇慶市北嶺

土坑木槨墓。於1972年發掘。棺槨已腐爛，尚存七條墊木。依據朽木測量，槨長7 m，寬4.5 m，高1.3 m。墓中隨葬器共139件，銅器佔108件，其他有金、玉、石、琉璃器、陶器等，漆器已腐朽。其中較珍貴的器物有錯銀銅罍、銅提梁壺、銅附耳筩、大小相遞的編鐘一組、以及金柄玉環、玉帶鈎等。這是廣東境內目前發現青銅時代墓葬中形制最大，隨葬品最多的一座。出土遺物除具有嶺南特色外，也有濃厚的楚器風格，說明此墓與楚文化的關係較爲密切。

圖二十七：隨葬器物平面圖

Tomb of Warring-States period

Songshan, Zhaoqing
Length 8, width c. 4.7 m.
Beiling, Zhaoqing city

Excavated in 1972, this is a large scale wooden chambered tomb built in an earth pit. The chamber is mostly decayed with only seven basal planks still barely recognizable. Judging from the remains of the wooden planks the chamber is estimated to be 7 m. in length, 4.5 m. in width and 1.3 m. in height. Among the 139 burial objects unearthed there are 108 bronzes, and the rest are gold, jade, stone, glass, pottery wares as well as disintegrated lacquerware. Rare and unique objects include a bronze *lei*-jar with silver inlay, a bronze vase with chain handle, a bronze bucket, serial bells, a jade ring with gold fitting and a jade garment hook. Among all the tombs of the Bronze Age so far found in Guangdong this one is the largest both in size and in quantity of burial accessories. The burial objects exhibit not only the local Guangdong characteristics but also a strong Chu influence.

Fig. 27: Plan of the burial.

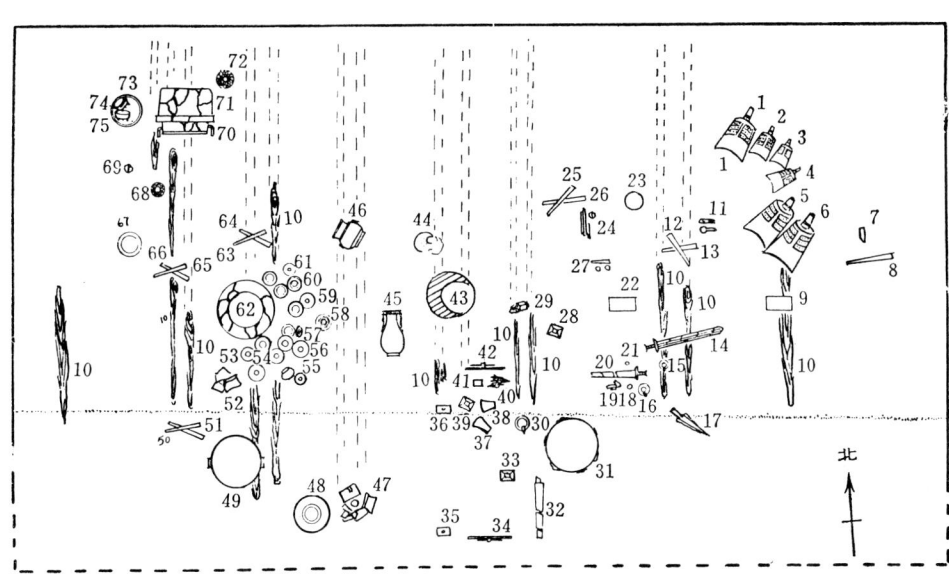

1－6.銅編鐘　7、8、12、13、25、26、50、51、63－66.銅鏃形器　9、22、34、42.鋪首　10.殘留木頭
11.殘銅器　14、20.銅劍　15、16.金柄玉環　17.銅矛　18.玉片　19.玉帶鈎　21.琉璃珠
23.殘銅器　24.刻刀、削刀及陶珠　27.玉棒、玉片　28、29、33、39.方形器　30.銅環　31.銅三足盤
32、35、36.銅柱　37.銅斧　38.銅錛　40.銅鐮　41.礪石　43.底坑　44、60、61、68、72.陶罐
45.銅提梁壺　46.錯銀銅罍　47.銅罍　48.陶蓋　49.附耳筩　52.米字紋陶片　53－59.陶盒
62、73.陶瓿　67.陶缽　69.陶珠　70、74、75.銅鼎　71.銅鍋

83. 銅甬鐘

戰國（公元前476－前221年）
通高45cm.
1972年肇慶市北嶺松山墓葬出土

樂器。甬作高筒形，上有繩索式的旋，口如月牙形，有十八個柱狀枚。正面鼓部由兩組勾連雷紋組成圖案。背面無紋。廣東地區多見甬鐘而少見鈕鐘。該墓出土六件銅鐘。大小相遞，鑄造精緻，花紋統一，風格具有嶺南特點。

圖二十八：甬鐘剖面圖。

83. Bronze bell

Warring-States period (476-221 B.C.)
Height 45 cm.
Excavated in 1972 from a tomb at Songshan, Beiling, Zhaoqing city

Musical instrument. On the long tubular handle is a plaited ring for suspension. There are 18 protruding nipples on both sides, but only the front side is decorated with two bands of interlocking spirals on the lower part. Bells found in Guangdong are mostly with tubular handles, bells with arched loops for supension are rare. There are six serial bells unearthed from this tomb, all are with the same elaborately cast pattern portraying a characteristic Lingnan style.

Fig. 28: Cross-section of the bell.

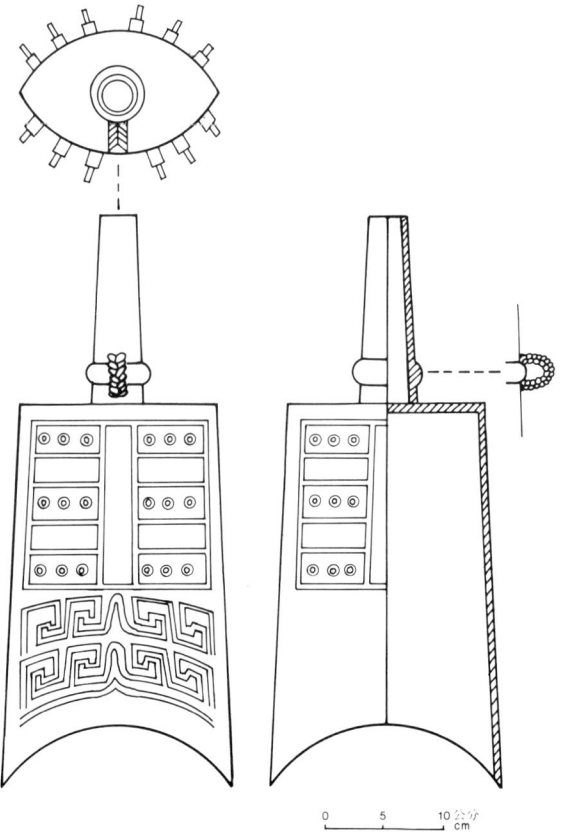

輔助照片7. 錯銀銅罍

戰國（公元前476－前221年）
高22、口徑14.9cm.
1972年肇慶市松山墓葬出土

容器。平口，沿寬厚，肩緩平，圓腹，平底加圈足。有蓋。蓋上有鈕，鈕上有環。器體飾錯銀花紋，由相勾連的飛鳥和雲氣紋組成。腹部雙耳舖首作鴞頭形，線條花紋亦作錯銀。飛鳥雲紋是楚器流行的花紋裝飾。此器紋飾輕快流暢，變化多樣；細線錯銀，粗線填朱漆，工藝巧妙，是富有典型性的楚國器物。

圖二十九：錯銀花紋摹本。

**Supplementary illustration 7
Bronze jar with silver inlay**

Warring-States period (476-221 B.C.)
Height 22, diameter 14.9 cm.
Excavated in 1972 from a tomb at Songshan, Zhaoqing city

This container is with everted flat mouth rim, sloping shoulder, ovoid body and flat bottom supported by a footring. The cover is topped by a central knob with a movable ring. The body is decorated with intricate bands of stylised flying birds and cloud pattern with silver and lacquer inlay. The two handles on the shoulder are in owl head shape, on which the linear decoration is also silver inlaid. The decorative motifs are very popular among bronzes of the Chu state.

Fig. 29: Drawing of the inlaid pattern.

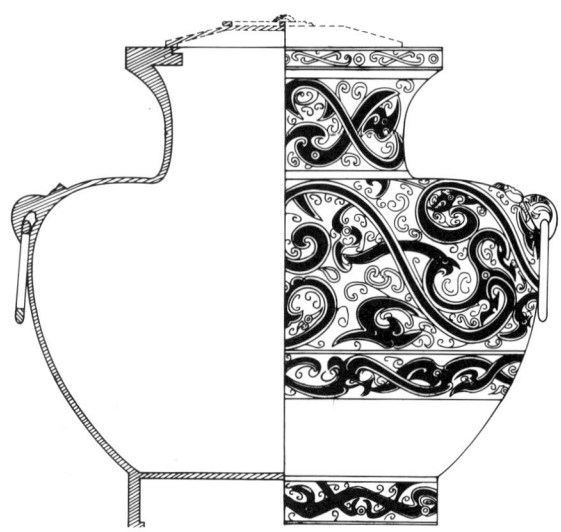

84. 銅提梁壺

戰國（公元前476－前221年）
通高30、口徑7 cm.
1972年肇慶市北嶺松山墓葬出土

酒器。肩部有四個獸頭鋪首耳，上銜鏈和提梁，蓋上有雙環。鏈從環中出，造型美觀，比例勻稱。蓋中飾竊曲紋，提梁上飾羽狀紋，肩上有一周蟬形紋，腹部飾六周蟠虺紋，圈足底上有一周絢紋。此器形制花紋與楚器十分接近，看來是來自楚地。

圖三十：提梁壺剖面圖。

84. Bronze bottle

Warring-States period (476-221 B.C.)
Height 30, diameter 7 cm.
Excavated in 1972 from a tomb at Songshan, Beiling, Zhaoqing city

On the shoulder of this wine vessel are two monster masks, from which arise two chains that pass through two rings at the covers and join with the loop handle at the top. The shape is well proportioned and elegant. The centre of the cover is decorated with impoverished curves, the handle with feather pattern, the shoulder with a band of cicada triangles, the body with six bands of intricated *hui*-dragons pattern, and the footring with a plait band near the base. Both the shape and decoration of this vessel are distinctively of Chu style.

Fig. 30: Cross-section of the bottle.

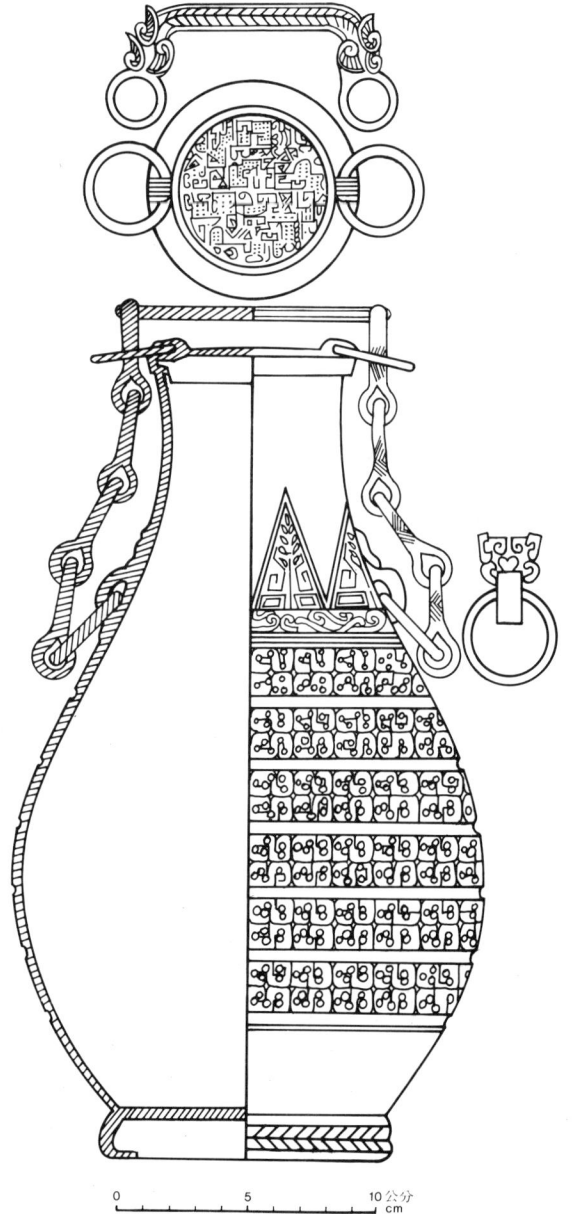

85. 銅三足盤

戰國（公元前476—前221年）
通高10、口徑37cm.
1972年肇慶市北嶺松山墓葬出土

盛器。直口直身，口與底大小相近，有一對鋪首作獸首銜環，三個獸頭蹄形足。器身花紋細緻，以上下相對的勾形羽狀紋爲主體組成圖案，羽狀紋內有纖細的S形圓渦紋和三角形渦紋，出土時塗有一層很厚的漆。此器形制與楚器相同。

85. Bronze tripod-basin

Warring-States period (476-221 B.C.)
Height 10, diameter 37 cm.
Excavated in 1972 from a tomb at Songshan, Beiling, Zhaoqing city

This container has straight walls so that its mouth and base are identical in diameter. The two handles at the sides are in the shape of monster masks holding movable rings. The three cabriole legs are topped by similar monster masks. The main decorative design is composed of "hook and volute" units, each of which is filled up with tiny S-shaped and triangular spirals. A rather thick layer of lacquer covered the whole surface when unearthed. The shape is identical to that of the Chu wares.

273

86. 銅附耳筩

戰國（公元前476－前221年）
高46、口徑42cm.
1972年肇慶市北嶺松山墓葬出土

容器。其形如圓柱桶狀。上部附對稱的兩個半圓形耳，圓耳中又貫耳。器身飾三組帶狀花紋，上中兩組由相連的勾連雷紋、S形圓渦紋和柵紋組成，下一組由兩條柵紋組成，圓耳上飾S形圓渦紋和羽狀紋。此器頗具地方特色。其風格與其他青銅器迥異，同類器形在廣州西漢墓還可見到。

圖三十一：銅筩剖面圖。

86. Bronze bucket

Warring-States period (476-221 B.C.)
Height 46, diameter 42 cm.
Excavated in 1972 from a tomb at Songshan, Beiling, Zhaoqing city

This container is of cylindrical shape with two vertical semi-circular handles applied diagonally near the mouth. The body is decorated with three bands of designs. The top and middle bands consist of interlocking spirals, S-shaped meanders and vertical striations. The band near the base is formed by two rows of vertical striations. On the handles are S-shaped spirals and feather pattern. The style of this vessel, differs considerably from the other bronzes from the same tomb and portrays a strong local characteristic. Buckets of similar shape are also found in W. Han tombs in Guangzhou.

Fig. 31: Cross-section of the bucket.

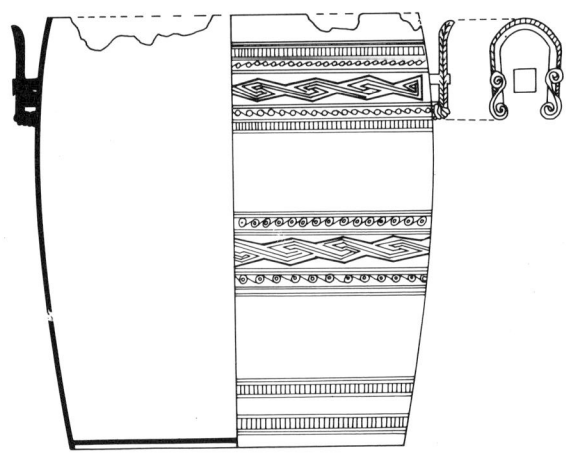

87. 銅鼎

戰國（公元前476－前221年）
高19.5、口徑18.6cm.
1977年廣寧縣銅鼓崗出土

炊煮器。直口折平沿，平底，最大徑在下腹。沿上一對長方直耳，內側飾繩紋，三條長細實足，足端外撇。這是越式鼎的其中一種，是廣東地區春秋戰國時期墓葬中常見的。鼎外多佈滿烟炱，說明是實用器。類似的鼎在江蘇、江西、湖南、廣西等地也有出土，中原地區很少見到。

87. Bronze tripod

Warring-States period (476-221 B.C.)
Height 19.5, diameter 18.6 cm.
Excavated in 1977 from Tonggugang, Guangning county

Cooking vessel. This tripod is with straight mouth, out-turned flat rim, and flat bottom. The largest diameter is at the lower part of the body. Two vertical rectangular handles set diagonally on the rim are decorated with cord pattern. The three legs are solid, slender and slightly flaring. This type of tripods of the local Yue style are usually found in Guangdong tombs from the Spring and Autumn to Warring-States periods. Smoke soot is normally found on the outside of these tripods indicating that they were for practical use. Similar tripods are also unearthed in Jiangsu, Jiangxi, Hunan, and Guangxi, but rarely found in Central China.

277

88. 銅鑒

戰國（公元前476－221年）
高14.2、口徑36.5cm.
1977年羅定縣南門峒1號墓出土

直口平沿，腹微鼓，平底加三個乳狀矮足。肩腹部飾細密的蟠螭紋，雙耳，耳上有當，當上飾蟠螭紋組成的獸面紋。在銅鏡使用以前，鑒是用來盛水以照影，盛行於春秋戰國。此器形制與長江以南各地所出的相似。說明南方各地之間有密切的文化關係。

88. Bronze basin

Warring-States period (476-221 B.C.)
Height 14.2, diameter 36.5 cm.
Excavated in 1977 from Tomb No. 1 at Nanmengdong, Luoding county

This basin with straight mouth, flattened rim, robust body, flat bottom and three low nipple-shaped feet. The outside is decorated with tiny intricate *chi*-dragon scrolls. The two handles on the sides are attached to monster masks composed of "hook and volute" scrolls. Basins of this type, most popular during the Spring and Autumn to Warring-States periods, when filled with water were used as mirrors or as washing bowls. The shape of this basin resembles those unearthed from Jiangnan sites, indicating a close cultural relationship among the different cultures of south China.

89. 銅劍

戰國（公元前476－前221年）
長47.6cm.
1973年四會縣鳥旦山墓葬出土

兵器。劍首喇叭形，莖圓柱形，上有兩道凸起的圓箍。臘寬有從，劍葉中間隆起成脊，兩鍔垂末小撇。劍是東周時期各地常見的器物。廣東出土的數量也很多。

90. 銅矛

戰國（公元前476－前221年）
長15.5cm.
1977年廣寧縣銅鼓崗16號墓出土

兵器。骹正面有一個直鈕，銎孔直透矛葉中脊，脊有凸起棱線。廣東出土東周時期的矛數量甚多，器形大體相同，但不見楚墓常見的骹部兩側半環鈕矛。這是地方特點的反映。

圖三十二：銅矛出土情形。

89. Bronze sword

Warring-States period (476-221 B.C.)
Length 47.6 cm.
Excavated in 1973 from a tomb at Niaodanshan, Sihui county

Weapon. This sword is with a concave pommel disk, a round handle with two flanges and a broad and crested guard. The blade has faceted edges, a median crest and of rhomboid cross-section. In the Eastern Zhou period, swords were very popular in many regions, and a large quantity has been found in Guangdong.

90. Bronze spearhead

Warring-States period (476-221 B.C.)
Length 15.5 cm.
Excavated in 1977 from Tomb No. 16 at Tonggugang, Guangning county

Weapon. The tubular socket has a loop on its front side, and the socket goes right down to the midrib of the blades. A large number of spearheads of the Eastern Zhou period are excavated from Guangdong. All of them are of a similar shape, never with two loops as those unearthed from Chu tombs. This reflects a strong local style.

Fig. 32: The spearhead in situ during excavation.

91A-C. 銅斧、銅鈴陶範

春秋至戰國（公元前770－前221年）
長（A） 8.6　闊9　　厚5　cm.
　（B） 10.8　　7.2　　　4 cm.
　（C） 8.8　　 6.9　　　3.6cm.
A. 約1932年香港南丫島大灣出土
B, C. 約1940年粵北採集
芬戴禮神父及麥兆良神父藏品
現存香港博物館

這些陶範都是雙面範的一面，另一半已失佚；鑄造時加上型芯，可鑄成空心的斧或鈴。陶範的發現說明廣東出土的青銅器，大部份應是本地鑄造的。

91 A-C. Pottery moulds for bronze axe and bell

Spring and Autumn to Warring-States periods (770-221 B.C.)
Length (A) 8.6　　width 9　　thickness 5 cm.
　　　(B) 10.8　　　　7.2　　　　　　4 cm.
　　　(C) 8.8　　　　 6.9　　　　　　3.6 cm.

(A) Excavated in early thirties from Dawan, Nanyadao, Hong Kong; (B), (C) Excavated in eastern Guangdong in early forties
Collections of Frs. Daniel J. Finn and Raphael Maglioni, Hong Kong Museum of History.

These are halves of a twin mould; their companion halves are now lost. With a central core, bronze axes with a hollow socket and bells with hollow interior can be cast from these moulds. The discovery of bronze moulds indicates that most of the bronzes found in Guangdong were locally cast.

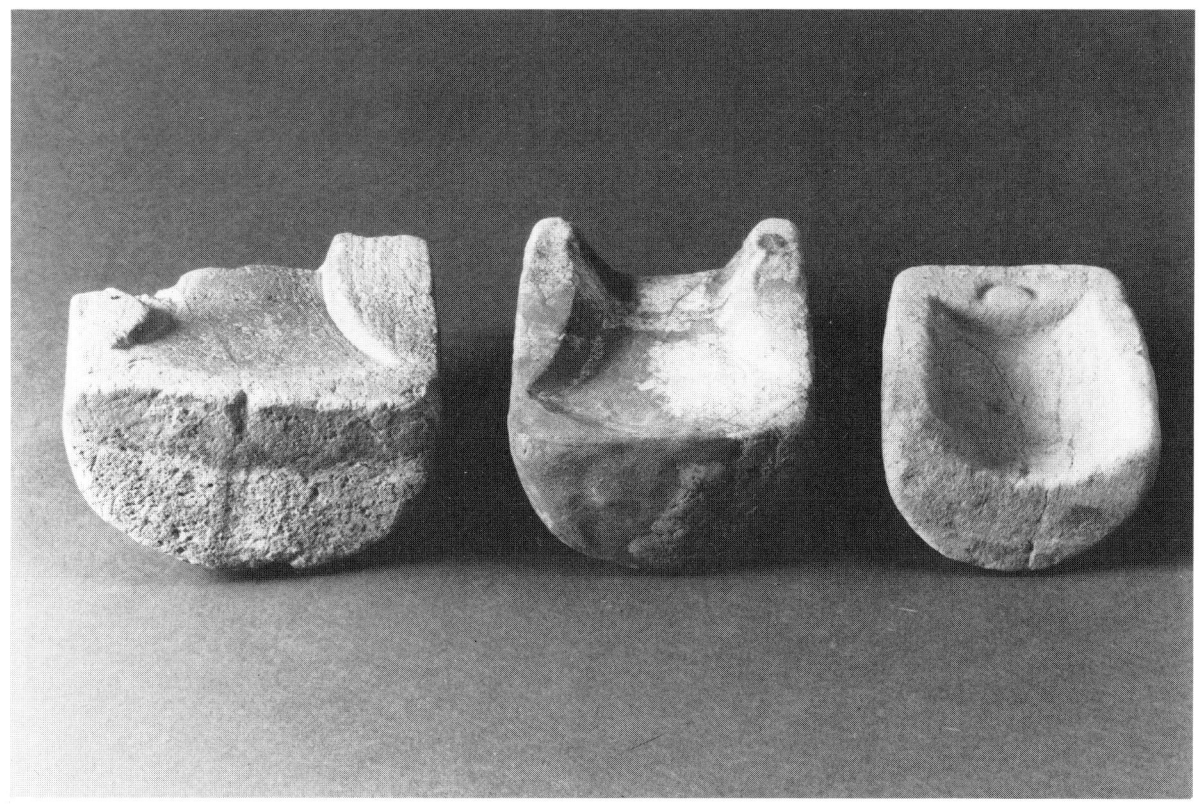

92. 銅鉞

戰國（公元前476－221年）
身長8.8、刃寬7 cm.
1976年陽春崗北出土

兵器。長方銎。刃面較寬，兩側弧出，雙面圓刃。此器與銅錠共存，為在粵西地區尋找這時期的冶銅遺址提供了實物標本。

92. Bronze axe

Warring-States period (476-221 B.C.)
Length 8.8, width of blade 7 cm.
Excavated in 1976 at Northern Yangchungang

This weapon is with a rectangular socket and a broad bifacial blade, the lateral sides of which curved outwards. This axe was found together with a bronze ingot and they are valuable clues for locating bronze foundries in the western Guangdong area.

93. 銅靴形鉞

戰國（公元前476－221年）
長 9、刃寬12cm.
1977年廣寧縣銅鼓崗墓葬出土

兵器或工具。器體靴形，刃作弧形，柄較長，橢圓銎口。這種器形目前僅見於廣東、廣西、雲南，且數量不多，與其他斧鉞有很大區別。

93. Bronze axe of boot-shape

Warring-States period (476-221 B.C.)
Length 9, width of blade 12 cm.
Excavated in 1977 from a tomb at Tonggugang, Guangning county

This weapon or tool is boot-shaped, with a curved blade, a long handle and a socket of ovoid cross-section. The shape differs considerably from other types of axes occurs only in Guangdong, Guangxi and Yunnan and very few pieces have so far been discovered.

94. 銅箭鏃

戰國（公元前476－前221年）
長 7.1 cm.
1977年羅定縣南門垌1號墓出土

兵器。雙翼。器身窄長而薄，脊較高，後鋒距離較小。鋌尾端尖細。

94. Bronze arrowheads

Warring-States period (476-221 B.C.)
Length 7.1 cm.
Excavated in 1977 from Tomb No. 1 at Nanmengdong, Luoding county

Weapon with slender and tapering body, pointed tang, high raised midribs, twin narrow blades which terminate into sharp bards.

95. 銅斧

戰國（公元前476－221年）
長15.3、刃寬5.2 cm.
1973年四會縣鳥旦山墓葬出土

工具。長身楔形。雙面圓刃。銎口兩面微凹入，下有一道微凸起的寬帶，帶下方有"王"字形圖案。這種"王"字形圖案在廣東西江流域地區的東周墓隨葬青銅器上常有發現。在湖南、江西、江蘇等地也有，可能是鑄造地的族屬標誌。

圖三十三："王"字形圖案拓片。

95. Bronze axe

Warring-States period (476-221 B.C.)
Length 15.3, width of blade 5.2 cm.
Excavated in 1973 from a tomb at Niaodanshan, Sihui county

Tool. This axe is of slender cuneiform shape with a round bifacial blade. A 'wang' character design is cast beneath a low band round the slightly depressed socket mouth. The same design is often found on burial bronzes from Eastern Zhou tombs in the Xijiang region of Guangdong, as well as in Hunan, Jiangxi, and Jiangsu. It probably represents a tribal symbol of the bronze foundry.

Fig. 33: Rubbing of the cast motif on the axe.

96. 銅鑿

戰國（公元前476－前221年）
長10.6、刃寬0.9 cm.
1977年廣寧縣銅鼓崗14號墓出土

工具。器身細長，方銎。雙面刃。刃口較小。銎口內尚存朽木。這種器物各地所見大體相同。

97. 銅篾刀

戰國（公元前476－前221年）
長9.2 cm.
1977年廣寧縣銅鼓崗墓葬出土

柳葉形。器身前寬後窄，尾端平，前有三角尖鋒，刃口在兩側。中脊隆起有棱線，斷面呈人字形。這種器物也有稱作銳、刮刀或刻刀，在廣東出土很多，遺址與墓葬均見，分析是加工竹木器的工具。

96. Bronze chisel

Warring-States period (476-221 B.C.)
Length 10.6, width of blade 0.9 cm.
Excavated in 1977 from Tomb No. 14 at Tonggugang, Guangning county

This tool is with a slender tapering body, a rectangular socket and a small bifacial blade. Inside the socket is a piece of much decayed wood. A very common shape and occurs in many regions.

97. Bronze knife

Warring-States period (476-221 B.C.)
Length 9.2 cm.
Excavated in 1977 from a tomb at Tonggugang, Guangning county

The knife is of "leaf" shape, with a triangular tip, double blades, and a median crest. The cross section is "V"-shaped. Knives in this shape are also called "assegai" tips, scrapers or engravers. Many such knives have been unearthed from both dwelling and burial sites in Guangdong and were probably carpentry or bamboo working tools.

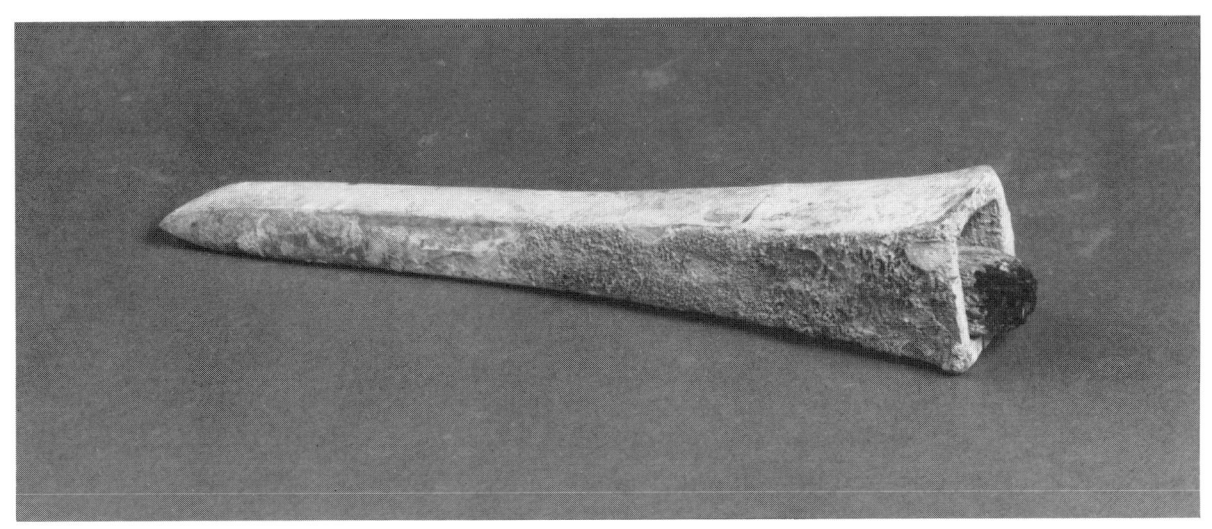

98. 原始瓷瓿

戰國（公元前476－前221年）
高19.5、口徑13.8cm。
1972年肇慶市北嶺松山墓葬出土

容器。器身大腹平底，雙耳，飾篦點紋、曲線紋、弦紋和柵紋。施較厚的醬黃色釉。此器是廣東出土原始瓷器中的精品。

98. Proto-porcelain jar

Warring-States period (476-221 B.C.)
Height 19.5, diameter 13.8 cm.
Excavated in 1972 from a tomb at Songshan, Beiling, Zhaoqing city

This container is with an ovoid body, flat bottom, and two handles. The decoration includes dotted combings and yellowish combed zig-zag and striated patterns under a thick yellowish brown glaze. A rare and exquisite piece of proto-porcelain excavated in Guangdong.

99. 米字紋陶罐

戰國（公元前476－前221年）
高45、口徑25cm.
1974年佛山市出土

硬陶。口沿外翻，上腹徑大，下腹漸收，平底。器身拍印米字紋。米字印紋是廣東戰國時期具有典型性的紋飾。

99. Pottery jar

Warring-States period (476-221 B.C.)
Height 45, diameter 25 cm.
Excavated in 1974 from Foshan city

The mouthrim of this stoneware jar is out-rolled and its body tapers towards the flat base. The body is impressed with basket pattern which is a classical motif of wares of the Warring-States period in Guangdong.

100. 陶匏壺

戰國（公元前476－前221年）
高51、口徑8cm.
1972年德慶縣落雁山墓出土

容器。硬陶。小口，圓腹，平底。口內有凸出的三粒蓋托，口外有四個綁蓋的豎形小耳。壺身拍印米字紋至底部。愈往下器壁愈厚，最厚處達4.5 cm。此器具有濃郁的地方特點。

100. Pottery gourd shaped bottle

Warring-States period (476-221 B.C.)
Height 51, diameter of mouth 8 cm.
Excavated in 1972 from a tomb at Luoyanshan, Deqing county

This stoneware container is with a small mouth, a round body and a flat base. Inside the mouthrim are three protruding studs for supporting the cover and on the shoulder are four vertical loop-handles for securing with string. The body is impressed with fine basket pattern. The body wall becomes thicker towards the base, reaching a maximum of 4.5 cm. This vase exhibits strong local characteristics.

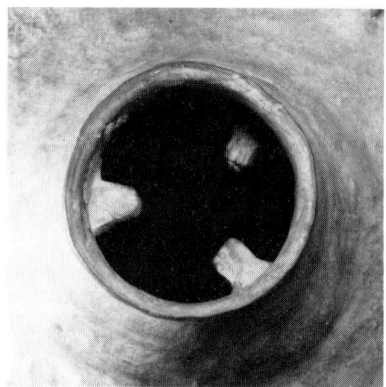

圖三十五：匏壺口內細部。

Fig. 35: Detail of the mouth showing protruding studs.

圖三十四：匏壺出土情形。

Fig. 34: The bottle in situ during excavation.

主要參攷書目

1. 安特生,《香港遺址地貌》,《遠東博物館館刊》,第二卷,1939
2. 饒宗頤,《韓江流域史前遺址及其文化》,香港,1950
3. 陳公哲,《香港考古發掘》,《考古學報》,1957.4
4. 芬戴禮,《舶遼洲考古發現》,(原刊於《香港自然雜誌》,1933-1936),1958年重印,香港
5. 廣東省博物館,《廣東南海西樵山出土的石器》,《考古學報》,1959.4
6. 戴維思等,《香港大嶼山萬角咀,考古遺址30號》,《亞洲雜誌》,第四卷,1960
7. 廣東省文管會,《廣東潮安的貝坵遺址》,《考古》,1961.11
8. 廣東省博物館,《廣東東部地區新石器時代遺存》,《考古》1961.12
9. 廣東省文管會,《廣東清遠發現周代青銅器》,《考古》,1963.2
10. 廣東省文管會,《廣東清遠的東周墓葬》,《考古》,1964.3
11. 香港考古學會,《香港考古學會會刊》,1968-
12. 戴維思,《香港考古史》,《亞洲雜誌》,卷十二,1969
13. 徐恆彬等,《廣東德慶發現戰國墓》,《文物》,1973.9
14. 廣東省博物館等,《廣東肇慶市北嶺松山古墓發掘簡報》,《文物》,1974.11
15. 施戈斐侶,《大嶼山石壁遺址考古勘察》,香港考古學會專刊第一本,香港,1975
16. 麥兆良,《粵東考古發現》,香港考古學會專刊第二本,香港,1975
17. 廣東省博物館,《廣東四會鳥旦山戰國墓》,《考古》,1975.2
18. 徐恆彬,《廣東信宜出土西周銅盉》,《文物》,1975.11
19. 秦維廉,《香港古石刻》,香港,1976
20. 秦維廉編,《南丫島深灣考古遺址調查報告》,香港考古學會專刊第三本,香港,1978
21. 蘇秉琦,《石峽文化初論》,《文物》,1978.7
22. 廣東省博物館等,《廣東曲江石峽墓葬發掘簡報》,《文物》,1978
23. 廣東省博物館,《廣東考古結碩果,嶺南歷史開新篇》,《文物考古工作三十年》,北京,1979
24. 秦維廉,《香港考古》,香港,1980
25. 廣東省博物館,《廣東廣寧縣銅鼓崗戰國墓》,《考古學集刊》,1,北京,1981
26. 楊式挺等,《談談佛山河宕遺址的重要發現》,《文物集刊》,3,北京,1981
27. 何紀生,《略論廣東周時期的青銅文化及其與幾何印紋陶的關係》,《文物集刊》,3,北京,1981
28. 朱非素等,《談談馬壩石峽遺址的幾何印紋陶》,《文物集刊》,3,北京,1981
29. 徐恆彬,《試論楚文化對廣東歷史發展的重要作用》,《中國考古學會第二次年會論文集》,北京,1982
30. 邱立誠等,《廣東陽春獨石仔新石器時代洞穴遺址發掘》,《考古》,1982.5
31. 莫稚,《深圳市考古重要發現》,《文物》,1982.6
32. 廣東省博物館,《廣東羅定出土戰國青銅器》,《考古》,1983.1
33. 楊式挺,《香港與廣東大陸的歷史關係》,《嶺南文史》,1983.2
34. 秦維廉,《沿海新石器時代越族的起源和發展》,《中國文明的起源》,伯克萊,1983
35. 廣東省博物館,《廣東平遠縣西周陶窰清理簡報》,《考古》,1983.7
36. 廣東省博物館,《廣東高要縣茅崗水上木構建築遺址》,《文物》,1983.12
37. 廣東省博物館,《廣東南海縣西樵山遺址》,《考古》,1983.12
38. 廣東省博物館,《廣東饒平古墓葬發掘簡報》,《文物資料叢刊》,8,北京,1984

Selected Bibliography

1. Andersson, J.G., "Topography of the Hong Kong Sites", *Bulletin of the Museum of Far Eastern Antiquities*, Vol. II, 1939.
2. Rao Zongyi, *Neolithic Sites and Cultures in Hanjiang Area*, Hong Kong, 1950.
3. Cheng Gongzhe, "Archaeological Excavations in Hong Kong", *Kaogu Xuebao*, 1957:4.
4. Finn, Daniel, J., *Archaeological Finds on Lamma Island*, (originally published in *The Hong Kong Nationalist*, 1933-1936), reprinted 1958, Hong Kong.
5. Guangdong Provincial Museum, "Stone Implements Unearthed at Xiqiaoshan, Nanhai County, Guangdong", *Kaogu Xuebao*, 1959:4.
6. Davis, S.G. and Tregear, Mary, "Man Kok Tsui, Archaeological Site 30, Lantau Island, Hong Kong", *Asian Perspective*, Vol. 4, 1960.
7. CPAM, Guangdong Province, "Shell Mound Sites at Qiao'an, Guangdong", *Kaogu*, 1961:11.
8. Guangdong Provincial Museum, "Neolithic Sites in Eastern Guangdong", *Kaogu*, 1961:12.
9. CPAM, Guangdong Province, "Zhou Dynasty Bronzes Unearthed at Qingyuan, Guangdong", *Kaogu*, 1963:2.
10. CPAM, Guangdong Province, "Eastern Zhou Burials at Qingyuan, Guangdong", *Kaogu*, 1964:3.
11. Hong Kong Archaeological Society, *Journal of the Hong Kong Archaeological Society*, 1968—
12. Davis, S.G., "History of Archaeology in Hong Kong", *Asian Perspective*, Vol. XII, 1969, pp. 19-26.
13. Xu Hengbin, "A Warring-States Tomb Found at Deqing County, Guangdong", *Wenwu*, 1973:9.
14. Guangdong Provincial Museum, et al, "Brief Excavation Report of Ancient Burials at Songshan, Beiling in Zhaoqing City, Guangdong", *Wenwu*, 1974:11.
15. Schofield, Walter, *An Archaeological Site at Shek Pik*, Journal Monograph I, Hong Kong Archaeological Society, Hong Kong, 1975.
16. Maglioni, Raphael, *Archaeological Discovery in Eastern Guangdong*, Journal Monograph II, Hong Kong Archaeological Society, Hong Kong, 1975.
17. Guangdong Provincial Museum, "A Warring-States Tomb at Niaodanshan, Sihui County, Guangdong", *Kaogu*, 1975:2.
18. Xu Hengbin, "A Western Zhou Bronze Ewer Unearthed at Xinyi, Guangdong", *Wenwu*, 1975:11.
19. Meacham, William, *Rock Carvings in Hong Kong*, Hong Kong, 1976.
20. Meacham, William (ed.), *Sham Wan, Lamma Island, An Archaeological Site Study*, Journal Monograph II, Hong Kong Archaeological Society, Hong Kong, 1978.
21. Su Bingqi, "Preliminary Discussion on Shixia Culture", *Wenwu*, 1978:7.
22. Guangdong Provincial Museum, et al, "Brief Excavation Report of Neolithic Burials at Shixia, Qujiang County, Guangdong", *Wenwu*, 1978:7.
23. Guangdong Provincial Museum, "Archaeological Finds in Guangdong", *Three Decades of Cultural and Archaeological Work*, Beijing, 1979.
24. Meacham, William, *Archaeology in Hong Kong*, Hong Kong, 1980.
25. Guangdong Provincial Museum, "A Warring-States Tomb at Tonggugang, Guangning County, Guangdong", *Kaoguxue Jikan*, Beijing, 1981, Vol. I.
26. Yang Shiting, et al, "On the Important Discoveries at Hedang Site, Foshan", *Wenwu Jikan*, 1981, Vol. III.

27. He Jisheng "A Brief Discussion on the Bronze Age Culture of Eastern Zhou Guangdong and its Relationship with Geometric Impressed Pottery", *Wenwu Jikan*, 1981, Vol. III.

28. Zhu Feisu, et al, "On Geometric Pottery from Shixia, Maba", *Wenwu Jikan*, 1981, Vol. III.

29. Xu Hengbin, "On the Importance of Chu Culture in Guangdong Historical Development", *Proceedings of the Second Annual Meeting of the Chinese Archaeology Society*, Beijing, 1982.

30. Qiu Licheng et al, "Excavation of the Neolithic Cave Site at Dushizai, Yangchun County, Guangdong", *Kaogu*, 1982:5.

31. Mo Zhi, "Important Archaeological Discoveries in Shenzhen City", *Wenwu*, 1982:6.

32. Guangdong Provincial Museum, "Bronzes of the Warring-States Period Unearthed at Luoding, Guangdong", *Kaogu*, 1983:1.

33. Yang Shiting, "Historical Relationship between Hong Kong and Guangdong Mainland", *Lingnan Wenshi*, 1983:2.

34. Meacham, William, "Origins and Developments of the Yueh Coastal Neolithic: A Microcosm of Culture Change on the Mainland of East Asia", *The Origins of Chinese Civilization*, Berkeley, 1983.

35. Guangdong Provincial Museum, "Brief Excavation Report of Western Zhou Kiln Sites at Pingyuan, Guangdong", *Kaogu*, 1983:7.

36. Guangdong Provincial Museum, "Remains of Wooden Structure above Water at Maogang, Gaoyao County, Guangdong", *Wenwu*, 1983:12.

37. Guangdong Provincial Museum, "The Xiqiaoshan Site at Nanhai County, Guangdong", *Kaogu*, 1983:12.

38. Guangdong Provincial Museum, "Brief Excavation Report of Ancient Burials at Raoping County, Guangdong", *Wenwu Zhiliao congkan*, 1984, Vol. VIII.

廣東出土先秦文物

出版：廣東省博物館
　　　香港中文大學文物館
國際統一書碼：962-7101-02-8
印刷：香港明愛印刷訓練中心
一九八四年九月初版

Archaeological Finds from Pre-Qin Sites in Guangdong

Copyright 1984 by the Guangdong Provincial Museum
and the Art Gallery, the Chinese University of Hong Kong.
All rights reserved.
ISBN 962—7101—02—8
Printed by Caritas Printing Training Centre, Hong Kong.